The Armstrong Nose

Selected Letters of Hamish Henderson

Best wishes

Hamish

30 Aug. '96

Other books by Hamish Henderson

Ballads of World War 2 (1947)

Elegies for the Dead in Cyrenaica (1948)

Translator, *Prison Letters of Antonio Gramsci* (1974)

Alias MacAlias: Collected Essays (1992)

Translator, *The Obscure Voice: Translations from Italian Poetry* (1994)

The Armstrong Nose

Selected Letters of Hamish Henderson

Edited by Alec Finlay

Polygon
EDINBURGH

Published by
Polygon
22 George Square
Edinburgh
EH8 9LF

Set in 11/13pt Perpetua by
Hewer Text Composition Services, Edinburgh
Printed and bound in Great Britain by
Cromwell Press, Melksham, Wiltshire

ISBN 0 7486 6191 3

A CIP record is available for this title

The Publisher acknowledges subsidy from the

THE SCOTTISH ARTS COUNCIL

towards the publication of this volume.

Contents

Contents

Contents

Contents

Contents

Contents

Contents

Contents

Editor's Preface

As Murdo MacDonald says in his Introduction, these letters draw you in; they draw you in to a life that has been an act of witness, an odyssey through some of the crucial historical and cultural events of the century. Take, for example, the many letters which trace a path back to the Thirties: to the emergence of the dark shadow of Fascism, and a generation preparing for war, to the strain of hope which emerges, whether in the innocence of childhood games in the burns under Ben Gulben, at the head of Glenshee, or, journeying into the adult world, in the anti-fascist struggles in Spain and Germany, the nascent buds of post-war renewal. Henderson has always encouraged others to see before them the possibility of 'a newly united country at the dawn of freedom'.[1]

During this eventful decade he left his home in the town of Blairgowrie to finish his schooling in England, lost his mother, began his study of Modern Languages at Cambridge, and aided Jewish refugees to escape from Germany. In 1937, aged 17, perched between childhood and adulthood, Henderson had two experiences which encapsulate the synchronicity of his life of witness. In April, visiting Germany on a school-boy exchange — his first encounter with this ancient homeland of the poets — he saw the insidious horror of Nazi Germany at first hand. Standing amongst the cheering crowds in the Tiergarten on Hitler's birthday he found himself within a few feet of the dictator. A few months later, he spent his summer holiday roving the Highlands, cycling the roads around Blair, travelling to Aberdeen, where he got permission to enter the strong room of the Old Library in the University, and here, for the first time, he looked through the original manuscript of the Greig-Duncan Folksong collection. Politics, poetry and folksong were already inextricably part of his life.

The Armstrong Nose tells much of the story that followed. In order to tell it as fully as possible, along with Henderson's own letters I have included a selection of letters from his most important correspondents. These help to broaden and illuminate his poetry, critical writings, and give a record of the progress of the Folksong Revival (as the Revival was largely an oral movement these letters represent one of the most complete documentations of it that we have). Letters from most of the prime movers in the Revival, from Norman Buchan, Ewan MacColl and Alan Lomax, and from traditional singers, such as Willie Mitchell, John MacDonald, and most important of all, Jeannie Robertson, are included (none of Hamish's letters to Jeannie have survived).

I have included all of the correspondence between Hugh MacDiarmid[2] and Hamish Henderson that is of literary or biographical significance. Along with their letters relating to the 'Honor'd Shade Flyting' (1959–60) and 'Folk Song Flyting' (1964), I have included the most important letters from the other contributors to these disputes.

The afterword presents a critical overview of Henderson's life and work, but is not intended to be comprehensive; a further commentary will appear in the forthcoming volume of *Selected Poems, Songs and Translations*, which is currently in preparation. This will be the final volume in what is, in effect, a *Collected works* published by Polygon.

Alec Finlay
Edinburgh

1 Carla Sassi, 'The Italian Song lines', published as an Afterword to Hamish Henderson's *The Obscure Voice: Translations from Italian Poetry*, (Morning Star Publications: Edinburgh, 1994).

2 For ease of reference I have used the name Hugh MacDiarmid for all references to MacDiarmid and/or C.M. Grieve.

Editor's Acknowledgements

I would like to thank Dr Hamish Henderson for his patience and encouragement throughout the preparation of this book, and in all the work we have shared in the ongoing gathering, editing and publication of his collected works.

Polygon, Dr Henderson, and I are indebted to the institutions and individuals who have helped to collate the letters, and given permission for their publication. I have made frequent reference to three particularly useful sources in the footnotes to the letters: W.R. Aitken's Bibliography of MacDiarmid, published in *Hugh MacDiarmid: Man and Poet* (ed. Gish, Edinburgh University Press, 1992); Alan Bold's *MacDiarmid: Christopher Murray Grieve, A Critical Biography* (John Murray: London, 1987), and his edition of *The Letters of Hugh MacDiarmid* (Hamish Hamilton: London, 1984). Readers are referred to Henderson's *Elegies for the Dead in Cyrenaica*, his collected essays, *Alias MacAlias*, both published by Polygon; and two magazines which have done feature issues on his life and work, *Chapman* magazine 42, Winter 1985, *Chapman* magazine 82, Winter 1996, and *Tocher*, no. 43, 1991.

With regard to the Afterword and the footnotes, I have been greatly aided by conversations with, and correspondence from, Murdo MacDonald, Alan Johnston, Roderick Watson, Duncan Glen, Timothy Neat, Edwin Morgan, Ian Stephen, Joy Hendry, Peter Cudmore, Ian Hamilton Finlay, Jean Redpath, Isobel MacLeod, Siobhan O'Casey, Angus Calder, Christopher Whyte, Carla Sassi, W.N. Herbert and Esther Hovey. Thanks also to the many correspondents who have willingly provided background information to their correspondence with Henderson.

Much of the initial reading and research for *The Armstrong Nose* was done during a stay in the warmth of late autumn Spoleto; I would like to thank Sol and Carol LeWitt for their generosity in making that possible. My research was aided by recourse to the collections of the National Library of Scotland, Edinburgh City Library, the Scottish Poetry Library, and the libraries of Hamish Henderson and Ian Hamilton Finlay. I would like to thank Marie Salton and Harry Gilonis for the careful attention they gave to the manuscript, and Sonia Senatore, for access to her complete collection of letters relating to the 'Folk Song Flyting' of 1964.

Particular thanks are due to two people, whose help and responsiveness was invaluable in the later stages of the making of this book: first, Margaret Bennett, one of our finest Gaelic singers, whose good-natured dedication to folk-culture is natural heir to Henderson's, and who gave me the benefit of her knowledge of the folksong revival. And second, as these Letters recall the life and work of Hugh MacDiarmid at every turn, the timely arrival of Alan Riach, overall editor of the *MacDiarmid 2000* project, was of enormous help. The longer that I have considered MacDiarmid and Henderson, their lives and their work, the more convinced I am that the polarized opposition between them, which has often been assumed by commentators in recent years, obscures the complementary character of their projects. In resolving this argument to the extent that I have been able, I owe a great debt to the perspicacity of Alan Riach's comments.

I would like to thank my father and mother, and many friends, for the support they have given me during the making of this book. I would also like to thank Kathryn MacLean, Jeanie Scott and Marion Sinclair at Polygon. Finally, just as he was essential to *Alias MacAlias*, so, once again, the hard work and diligent care of Hamish Henderson's assistant Paul Fernie in helping to gather together the material included here, was invaluable and much appreciated.

Alec Finlay

Introduction

There is a voice in these letters which we need to hear. In a letter from 1948 one finds it challenging literary preconceptions with a precise cultural understanding: 'The reason why the makars are so boisterously assailed by all and sundry is not primarily because they write in Lallans, but because they form an *avante-garde.*' Yet it is the same voice that comes through in a bleak description sent from Italy in 1943: 'The landscape is a mountain Paschendale – bogged-down mud and blood'. In these letters Hamish Henderson speaks with a voice of humanity and experience, and – perhaps above all – in a way which invites response. Such responses give this collection of letters a further dimension; for example when C. M. Grieve closes a letter to Henderson in Belfast in 1949: '. . . regards to Hewitt, Davie and all' the link between Ulster's great poet of the mid-century and the author of *The Democratic Intellect* is suddenly illuminated. A letter from Henderson to Grieve a year later casts the net wider, and in the same movement begins to pull it in: 'I am working hard on Gramsci's *Letters from Prison* . . .' This awareness of Gramsci (and the need to translate him), which Henderson gained during World War II from his Italian Partisan comrades, becomes a way of focusing the relationship between folk culture, politics and ideas which in due course is expressed in Henderson's fundamental contribution to the folksong revival and to the establishment of the School of Scottish Studies at Edinburgh University. That contribution is underlined here not only by correspondence with outstanding singers like Jeannie Robertson but also by the memorable flyting, on the subject of the folksong revival, between Henderson and Grieve (the latter writing as Hugh MacDiarmid) which took place in January 1960 in the pages of the *Scotsman*. This is just one example of how this book is a key to understanding the dynamics of Scottish culture today.

Issues surface and resurface in this book. For example, in a letter to his close friend Marian Sugden, dated 1951, Henderson mentions a talk he had given – on the invitation of Edwin Muir – at Newbattle Abbey College near Dalkeith. This college was and is the only residential educational institution in Scotland dedicated to extending higher-educational opportunity to unqualified, working-class students, and reference to it pulls the reader across almost forty years. For in 1989 one finds Henderson deploring, in the pages of the *Scotsman*, the closure of Newbattle: 'Why are we faced with this wretched situation? Because Scotland is ruled, against its wishes, by the rump of the native Tory Party (a philistine junta if ever there was one).' As of writing, Newbattle is about to re-open, and that is a matter for celebration, but this must be tempered by the fact that it is re-opening into a climate where education has become part of the kingdom of meaningless paperwork that is that junta's legacy. Hamish Henderson's letters link the present with the last fifty years in a way that enables us to grasp realities and distrust illusions.

Having charted a course through these letters I feel myself tugged back towards them, on the one hand to read a defence, from the mid-1980s, of Jake Harvey's memorial to Hugh MacDiarmid (a curious echo, here, of the defence of the work of Jacob Epstein written by MacDiarmid's friend William McCance in the 1930s), on the other hand to explore eye-witness accounts of the Fascism of Hitler in the Berlin of 1937 and that of John Cormack in the Edinburgh of 1955. Or again, to read correspondence with Ewan MacColl or Ian Hamilton Finlay. Or a letter to Sir Alexander Gray about his fine Scots translations of Scandinavian and German ballads. But enough of the Introduction. Let the book draw you in.

Murdo Macdonald
Edinburgh

A note on references

EUL (Edinburgh University Library Special Collection)

Grieve/MacDiarmid: File MS 2951.3.
Cruickshank (Helen B.): Gen. 1929/2.
Gray (Sir Alexander): Gen. 1731

NLS (National Library of Scotland)

Maurice Lindsay collection: Acc. 4791, fos. 227–230.
Robert Garioch (including a copy of Letter 177, the original of which is in the EUL Grieve file): MS 26563, fos. 83–90.

Northwestern University Library, Evanston, USA

Northwestern University Archives: Erich Heller Papers, Series 11/3/15/3, Box 5, Folder 23.

Selected Letters

1942

1 To the Armstrong family[1]

[*Draft from Henderson's wartime notebooks: airgraph letter*]

[Cairo, May 1942]

Hiya folks!

Fetch out the magnifying glass, 'cos I'm going to pack this page as tight as I can. – What's Cairo like? The oddest thing about it [is that it] so closely corresponds to one's romantic notions of it. I've always had rather a penchant for Mamelukes and seraglios, and it's all here – beggars and Bedouins, mosques and muezzins, fezzes and fellahin, an old Auntie Yashmak and all. And the Pyramids, like the Leaning Tower of Pisa, are just too like their picture to be true. And garrys (old-fashioned cabs, drawn by skin and bone horses, in which you feel like Queen Victoria driving through a foreign capital) – and importunate shoe-shine boys yelling 'Officer polish', and sticking to you like leeches, defying you to boot them away; bazaars stacked with bracelets made in Bagdad and Birmingham; garish night-clubs reminding one of pre-war Paris – all this and much more.

Love, Hamish

---

1 Henderson first met the Armstrong family soon after he returned from Germany in 1939, and lodged with them when he was in Cambridge. The Reverend Alan Armstrong, who was ordained in the Church of Ireland, served as Rector in the village of Dry Drayton near Cambridge. See also 'The Armstrong Nose', Letter 241.

1943

2 To Violet Armstrong[1]

[Draft from Henderson's wartime notebooks: airgraph letter]

[Tunisia, March 1943]

Dear Violet,

I'm writing you this letter from 'somewhere in Tunisia'. Our camp is a plantation of olive trees, and as there's a bit of a wind blowing; the loose sand is infiltrating into my forty-pounder tent with its usual crude but successful tactics. It's also quite hot, and the flies are beginning to be a blasted nuisance again. I'm now in my second African year, and Africa is still pretty bloody, but we're getting places at long last; and old Rommel is still at large but his days are numbered. Tripoli is not a bad town, but very 'provincial' compared to Cairo — the old Turkish citadel is the one building of note in it. Its harbour is fine, but not a patch on Alex. The local Iti [*sic*] civilians thought our Highland pipe bands were just the cat's pyjamas.

Love, Hamish

---

1 Violet Armstrong, daughter of the Reverend Alan Armstrong.

3 To Reverend Alan Armstrong

[Draft from Henderson's wartime notebooks]

[Italy, 25 October 1943]

The landscape is a mountain Paschendale — bogged-down mud and blood. Jerry artillery is very accurate. Troops shivering in water-logged fox-holes. A lot of sufferers from bad feet, including myself. (A septic toenail was wrenched from my left foot yesterday!)

I am local Partisan king[1] round these parts, and my recruiting efforts in Florence and Borgo San Lorenzo are paying dividends — saving British lives and taking Jerry ones, in brief — the root function of the job.

H.

---

1 Henderson was serving as a Captain in the Intelligence Corp, and was assigned to the Partisan brigades fighting in the Apennines.

1945

4 G.S. Fraser[1] to Hamish Henderson

[Cairo, 1 January 1945]

2879388, S.Q.M.S. G.S. Fraser,[1]
News Division, Ministry of Information,
6 Sharia Antikhana el Masria, Cairo.

Dear Hamish

I am a terribly bad correspondent. But with 1 January 1945, I have written on my desk diary, for each day of this first week of the year: letter to so-and-so. You come under 1 January. Often enough I've thought of that phrase in your last letter to me: 'Jerry has had it, but an army of one-eyed halfwits could hold you up in these hills of sorrow,' and thought of us in our comfort here in Cairo, our intrigues, petty quarrels, paper wars, and you out there in the night, in the cold, in the rain and the mud, and yet always (as Haig Gudenian wrote to me when he met you once and drank wine with you in some mountain village) 'like the laird of the surrounding hills'. God (or Time, or History, or what phrase you like from the new philosophies) keep you safe this year . . .

I met John Speirs[2] the other night at a Christmas party, and had a long talk about poetry and Scotland and you. It's the first time I've seen him, since he was a lanky student-teacher at the Grammar School, years ago, encouraging me to prefer Herrick's Daffodils to Wordsworth's . . . 'like to the pearls of morning dew', do you remember? never to be seen again. It was good to have somebody decent to talk to at a party where the other representatives of British Culture and Administration were looking around in a tight-lipped, narrow-eyed way that said as plain as words: 'Too many battle-dresses.' In fact, when we arrived at this party (to which we had been properly invited) one of their plump little bitches opened the door and screamed like a fishwife, 'No, this is not the sort of place you think it is!' However, I find that whatever else the barrack square has done for me: it has left me with a feeling of pleasant indifference to the rudeness of the middle classes.

I am writing to Tambimuttu[3] to recommend Ruth Speirs' translations, though they hardly need my recommendation; she too was one of the nice people at this party, attempting to jitterbug with some erks, and then relaxing with the remark, 'But I can't keep my legs apart . . .'

I lead an ambiguous life in this city, between battle dress and an old sports jacket, between the Sergeants' Mess and the Turf Club. I am always terribly short of money, but make ends meet so far somehow. There are interesting people at times. John Gawsworth, a friend of Hugh McDiarmid, an untidy RAF Sergeant, youngest Fellow of the Royal Society of Literature, such pretty old-fashioned Georgian lyrics, and such an agreeable sardonic pirate himself, weaved drunkenly through Cairo; dipping his pen in his brandy glass and conjuring money from the air; always nearly being arrested because when drunk he has Scottish Jacobite-Irish Republican-French Royalist synthesis (completely artificial, for I would say he was a typical London adventurer) that sets him marching against England; terribly bitter — against Lawrence Durrell,[4] particularly, whom he had helped in the old days in London, with hospitality and money, but who wanted nothing of him, would not answer his letters, or see him, in his present shabby estate — and terribly warm-hearted; especially to me, whom he is recommending as *the* coming poet to Masefield, Arthur Machen, Norman Douglas, Lord Alfred Douglas, and all the great stuffed owls of English literature, with all of whom he is apparently on genial terms. He has a really good and scholarly knowledge of bibliography (he used to make a living by picking up bargains in the second-hand sections of the big London bookshops, and then taking them upstairs to sell to the rare book departments), and of minor poetry of the nineties. He was the kind of person whom official Cairo culture regards as a calamity or a joke: I liked him very much.

I thought your latest 'Fragment of an Elegy'[5] strong and moving like the others; like Whitman, the whole thing will be even more impressive when you have it in bulk. It's like a broad river carrying a lot of gravel along with it.

My best love, Hamish; please write to me again. My book of poems[6] is out, by the way, and I am sending you a copy as soon as I can get back some I have lent to people.

George

---

1 G.S. Fraser (1915–80), poet and critic; Fraser and Henderson first met while they were serving in Egypt.

2 John Speirs, academic and literary critic; author of *The Scottish Literary Tradition* (Chatto & Windus: London, 1940; reprinted Faber & Faber: London, 1940). Henderson met Speirs in Cairo in 1942. He was teaching at the Fuad el Awal University. It was at one of these wartime gatherings that Henderson heard Ruth Speirs read from her translations of Rilke's *Duino Elegies*.

3 James Tambimuttu, editor of *Poetry London*, one of the leading poetry magazines of the 1940s.

4 Lawrence Durrell (1912–90), English novelist and poet, author of *The Alexandria Quartet*.

5 'Fragment of an Elegy' became the first of the *Elegies for the Dead in Cyrenaica*, published in *New Writing and Daylight*, edited by John Lehmann (Hogarth Press: London, Winter 1943/4).

6 *Home Town Elegy* (London, 1944).

5 **To John Lehmann**[1]

[*Draft from Henderson's wartime notebooks*]

[Italy, Winter 1944/5]

Dear John Lehmann,

These hills are a great breeding ground of blasphemy. The Partisans swear by Madonna the pig and Jesus the assassin, and in spite of Monty's old Orders of the Day his veterans in the Apennines are now much given to taking in vain the name of the God of Battles. Sitting round a fire in this mountain croft, the members of the 36th Garibaldi Brigade (Biaconcini) discuss the best ways of executing Fascists.

I'm getting in the habit [of blasphemy] myself. This morning our local river was in spate, and no jeeps could get across – no one has had the nerve to build a bridge yet, as the area concerned is under immediate enemy observation – who should come up but an RC padre in his jeep, and start raising hell about not being allowed to cross. 'You'll never make it, Sir,' says the CMP.[2] The padre insists. The CMP holds his ground . . . I comment (sotto voce): 'If he wants to cross this bloody Wadi he'll have to get out and walk on the waves.'

I notice by my notebook that I promised you a letter about Florence, but I'm so smemorizzato and generally cack-brained now I can't recollect if I did write it or not. When I can concentrate I'm writing a poem about Alexandria now,[3] which I'll let you have when it's finished. Luigi[4] has written and dedicated to me a poem called 'Linea Gotica'. It's in alcaics!

From G.S. Fraser I got a letter which gives me quite a nostalgia for Cairo. He describes John Gawsworth, who sounds an agreeable humbug, and has seen that soft-tongued satirical man John Speirs at a party . . . Christ I'm in limbo now, marooned on the mountains of the moon. I'll not read 'A Walk in the Sun' yet – the irony is too devilish.

Yours, H. Henderson

PS It's snowing again.

---

1 John Lehmann (1907–87), publisher, poet and editor; Lehmann published Henderson's *Elegies for the Dead in Cyrenaica* in 1948.
2 Military Policeman.
3 The third of the *Elegies*, 'Leaving the City'.
4 Luigi Castigliano, Lecturer at the University of Milan; Henderson first met him on the beachhead at Anzio after Castigliano had crossed over to join the Allies. The second of the *Elegies*, 'Halfaya', is dedicated to him.

1946

6 To Maurice Lindsay[1]
[*NLS*]

[Downing College, Cambridge, 27 April 1946]

Dear Maurice Lindsay,

I've just received your letter of 4 Apr., which was forwarded on to me from Portree. A lot of things are much clearer to me now than before. The first is why I never got your first letter, and likewise why this second letter was not given to me by the nice little bit of stuff in Portree Post Office when I called in there ten days ago.

I'll give you five guesses. Or would you prefer fifty? – The reason is that by a readily understandable piece of verbal association you have transformed the name Hamish Henderson into Hamish Hamilton – the latter being as you know a well-known publisher. So that's the reason why Mairi in Portree told me there was no letter for Henderson – 'but just the one for a Mr Hamilton'.

The only solution, I suppose, is to call myself in print what the north calls me – Seumas mac Eanruig.[2] It's not so alliterative, but on the other hand is the real MacKay, as one might say. On the other hand, again, it would floor my Italian public. So what have you? I'll probably fall back on my Army Personal Number eventually!

Am glad to hear that the Govoni poem is to appear in *PS 3*:[3] I had gathered it probably would be from MacLellan. As for the other two, you can certainly have 'Karnak' for *PS 4*, but I'm afraid 'Acroma' is no longer on the market. Still I shall send you some more shortly if you would like to see them.

Poetry Scotland is a great thing, and I'm sorry that owing to my isolation among Panzerschrecks and Partisans I remained unaware of its existence for so long. However as MacL. may have told you I showed a copy of *PS 1* to some of our more interesting prisoners, including some Wehrmacht I.O.s and SS high-ups – some of whom were quite cultured individuals – and they all without exception picked on Somhairle mac Gill-eain's[4] poem as the most interesting thing in it. One asked – how typically deutsch this is! – for a Gaelic primer; he wanted to tackle this question of Scottish culture *vor allen Dingen grundsätzlich*.[5] This in spite of the fact he was going to be shot and knew it.[6]

There is also a great interest for Scotland in Italy: one of my Milanese friends, Luigi Castigliano, has already a good grasp of the vernacular; he writes in a letter: 'There are 29,899 different words in *Ulysses*, and that should be muckle enough for a poor Eyetye; and now a flavouring with MacDiarmid!' In two months with the

8/Argylls he learnt all there is to know about the Clan Campbell and Inveraray, and developed an addiction to pipe-music.

And another has sent me a *Cartolina dall' Italia* which you might like to have. It might look quite effective, being short, if printed in original and translation.

All the best,

> Yours, Hamish Henderson

---

1 Maurice Lindsay (b. 1918), Scottish poet and critic; editor of magazines and a number of collections of Scottish poetry: *Modern Scottish Verse: An Anthology of the Scottish Renaissance* (Faber & Faber: London, 1945), was of particular importance as it was the first collection featuring the Renaissance to appear outside Scotland.

2 Henderson's name in Gaelic; he did in fact use this as an occasional pseudonym in the 1940s.

3 *Poetry Scotland*, anthologies edited by Maurice Lindsay. Corrado Govoni, Italian poet; Henderson's translation of his 'Dialogue of the Angel and the Dead Boy' was published in the third anthology (William MacLellan: Glasgow, 1946). 'Karnak', 'Acroma': the eighth and sixth of the *Elegies*. Henderson's poem 'Scottish Childhood' was published in *Poetry Scotland 4*.

4 Somhairle MacGill-Eain, the Gaelic poet Sorley MacLean (b. 1911). Henderson first met Sorley (and his brother Calum I. MacLean) in 1946. He wrote one of the first critical appreciations of MacLean's poetry, ' "There's a Fine Poet in Gaelic": Sorley MacLean', which appeared in the *Daily Worker*, 24 November 1949, reprinted in *Alias MacAlias*.

5 Trans. 'to get to the bottom of things' (H.H.).

6 This was SS Colonel Kappler, who commanded the squads who massacred 335 civilians in the Ardeatine caves, 24 March 1944. Kappler was convinced he would be executed, but in the event he was sentenced to life imprisonment by an Italian military court.

7 To Hugh MacDiarmid

[*EUL*]

[Isle of South Uist, 21 December 1946]

Dear Hugh MacDiarmid,[1]

A few weeks ago, when the Plastic Scots controversy was resounding in the *Glasgow Herald* I sent off a letter which probably arrived too late to be published. Either that, or the Editorial Diarist couldn't take it. In any case, I don't think it appeared, and so I'm sending you a copy now (reconstructed from the rough notes I kept after writing the original). You might be able to make use of it in some form or other.

Enclosed also is a poem[2] from the *Voice of Scotland*.[3]

> Yours, Hamish Henderson

1 This is Henderson's first letter to MacDiarmid.
2 'Here's to the Maiden', a poem in Scots, appeared in *Voice of Scotland*, III. 3, March 1947.
3 *Voice of Scotland: A quarterly magazine of Scottish arts and affairs*, edited by MacDiarmid, 1938–9 and 1945–58. Henderson contributed to six issues: III.3, March 1947; III.4, June 1947; IV.2, December 1947; IV.3, March 1948; IV.4, June 1948; V.1, September 1948.

8 To the *Glasgow Herald* on 'Plastic Scots' (unpublished)

[*EUL; draft sent to Hugh MacDiarmid*]

Sir,

The heavy-handed sarcasm of your Editorial Diarist at the expense of writers who experiment with Scots deserves an answer, despite its cheapness. For it is clear that the Diarist is unfamiliar with all the more important facts about the making of a poem, and about the nature of language. He is unaware, for example, that the linguistic problems which he parodies have existed for a good proportion of writers in every country and in every age.

Take, for example, the famous eighteenth-century Italian poet Alfieri.[1] He was a Piedmontese aristocrat who was brought up to speak the local dialect (basically Italian, with a strong French flavouring), and also French, which was the language of the Turin court and politically dominant in the little Kingdom, just as English is here today. His acquaintance with Tuscan, the traditional Italian literary dialect (in which he afterwards wrote excellent verse), was in his youth almost nil. He relates in his autobiography with engaging candour that until he was well into his twenties he displayed no inclination to write, and very little to read, so that until manhood the incomparable treasure of Italian poetry was literally a closed book to him.

It was no accident that Alfieri's return from linguistic exile to the language of his country coincided with a revulsion towards all things French, which expressed itself both politically and personally. Indeed, this Gallophobia became towards the end of his life something in the nature of an obsession, for he declares in his *Vita* that the ugliest women he had ever seen were to be found in Paris! However, the essential thing for lovers of literature (as against types with the mentality of your Editorial Diarist) is that he won through and wrote memorable verse from which his upbringing had almost totally estranged him.

In spite of the sneers of linguistic quislings, who find it convenient to side with the big battalions of London press lords and Glasgow Englishmen, Scottish poets will find more and more support now in erecting a dam against the 'mòr-shruth na

Beurla'.[2] Most of them realize this, and realize too that it is not enough merely to use the 'language of the outlaw'. Like their compeers of former ages, they must also re-create and reshape it.

Hamish Henderson (Seumas mac Eanruig)

---

1 Alfieri (1749–1803), Italian poet, born in Asti.
2 Trans. 'big flood of English' (H.H).

1947

9 To Hugh MacDiarmid

[*EUL*]

[Arisaig, 24 March 1947]

Dear Hugh MacDiarmid,

I was very sorry to come on you tonight in an awkward moment. Maybe on my next visit I'll have more luck.

You'll find enclosed an article on the 'National Assembly'[1] which I meant to show you. I was for sending it to the *New Scot*,[2] but perhaps you can make better use of it.

I'd appreciate a line telling me what you intend doing with it.

Yours sincerely, Hamish Henderson

[PS] The Marxist lectures[3] I'm giving to the B.A. boys in Fort William come to an end in three weeks' time, so I hope to be in Glasgow again about the middle of April. When I'm back, I'll look you up again.

---

1 Unpublished.
2 *New Scot*, political journal published by The Scottish Reconstruction Committee.
3 Henderson lectured on Marxism and Culture for the Workers Educational Association in Lochaber, from January to March 1947.

10 To the *Glasgow Herald* (unpublished)

[Undated 1947]

Sir,

Your Editorial on the second Scottish National Assembly[1] was well answered by Mr James A.A. Porteous.

There is, however, one passage in that Editorial which Mr Porteous passes over without comment. Perhaps he was wiser to do so. I refer to your ignoble jibe directed against certain unnamed Scottish Nationalists, making out that their activities are prompted merely by a sense of personal grievance.

It is clear that in this passage you are referring to Hugh MacDiarmid, and to others of his way of thinking.

Allow me to assure you, Sir, that — not only in my opinion but in that of many others — the passage referred to shows a quite exceptional meanness, even for your newspaper. I think that future generations of Scots will know better how to appraise the motives of those who for years have been working with single-minded devotion for the cause of the commons of Scotland.

I am etc., Hamish Henderson

1 The National Assembly, organized by John MacCormick's National Covenant Association.

11 **To Hugh MacDiarmid**

[*EUL: postcard of Buchaille Etive Mor, Glen Coe*]

[Arisaig, 25 [August?] 1947]

Dear Chris,[1]

Just arrived back in Arisaig in time for the games. Some passable piobearachd this morning! I looked in and saw Valda[2] on the way up — had a fine evening with F.G.[3] Kenneth[4] has started work on my ballads.[5] I fly to Germany[6] on the 31st.

Yours ever, Hamish

1 Henceforth Henderson refers to MacDiarmid by his Christian name rather than his literary pseudonym.
2 Valda Grieve (1906–89), MacDiarmid's wife.
3 Francis George Scott (1880–1958), composer and friend of MacDiarmid's.
4 Kenneth Campbell (alias MacKenzie), director of the Caledonian Press in Glasgow, along with his brother Calum. The Campbells were friends and patrons of MacDiarmid. They published *Voice of Scotland, The National Weekly* which appeared from September 1948–July 1953, and various other Nationalist publications.
5 *Ballads of World War II*, a collection of soldiers' songs; three were written by Henderson and the rest were popular soldier songs collected during the Desert and Italian campaigns. Published by the fictitious 'Lili Marlene Club' (Glasgow) in order to avoid the attentions of the censor, and printed at the Campbells' Caledonian Press, 1947.
6 Henderson taught at a summer school organized for Volkshochschullehrers (Adult Education teachers) in Bad Godesberg, August 1947.

12 **To Hugh MacDiarmid**

[*EUL*]

[Dry Drayton, Cambridgeshire, 7 November 1947]

Dear Chris,

I'll be on my way North in a day or two's time, so I hope to see you then. Meanwhile here's a translation of a German communist poet which might do for the *Voice*.[1]

In the November *Our Time* I've got a review of *A Kist of Whistles*.[2] The Editor limited me to 500 words, so it's more by way of being a boost than anything else . . . I also took the opportunity of asking delegates to a Caudwell[3] conference in London the other day why the devil they were so keen on sacking up Shelley to be the Revolution's standard-bearer, and yourself unobtainable on the Party's bookstalls!

But in Germany it's a different story; a young writer called Vogt[4] – both his parents were killed by the Nazis – is now engaged on translating you, and in the Soviet *Haus der Kultur* in Berlin your name is known . . . In the Summer School at Godesberg where I did some lecturing the Morgenfeier always included the reading of poems. It's true that they started off with many old stagers from the world's troop of laureates: Dante, Goethe, Pushkin, Blok, Marlowe

> (Vixere fortes ante MacDiarmida
>   multi . . . !)

but before the course was done they had got round to yourself, Somhairle[5] and George Campbell Hay.[6] Davvero!

All the best

Yours, Hamish

PS Are you using my Ballad of Sicily?[7]

---

1 'The Allies' by Rudolf Leonhard, translated by Hamish Henderson, appeared in *Voice of Scotland*, IV.2, December 1947.

2 Hugh MacDiarmid, *A Kist of Whistles: New Poems* (William MacLellan: Glasgow, 1947). *Our Time*, left-wing periodical published in the 1940s; both Henderson and MacDiarmid were contributors.

3 Christopher Caudwell, alias of Christopher St John Sprigg (1907–37); poet and author. Killed on his first day in action in the Spanish Civil War.

4 Heinz Vogt, German student; Henderson met him at the summer school and they struck up a strong friendship. Vogt is mentioned in Henderson's essay 'Germany in Defeat', reprinted in *Alias MacAlias*.

5 Sorley MacLean.

6 George Campbell Hay (1915–84), also known by his Gaelic name Deorsa mac Iain Deorsa, poet and translator. Hay was a gifted linguist and wrote poetry in Gaelic, Scots and English. His best-known collection is *Wind on Loch Fyne* (William MacLellan: Glasgow, 1948). He served in the North African Desert Campaign and the Middle East; some of his finest poems, such as 'Bizerta', recall these events.

7 'Ballad of the Simeto', published by Nicholas Moore in *New Poetry*, 1944, and reprinted in *Chapman* 42, VIII.5, Winter 1985; not to be confused with Henderson's song 'The 51st Highland Division's Farewell to Sicily'.

1948

13 **To Hugh MacDiarmid**
[*EUL*]

[Edinburgh, 3 February 1948]

Dear Chris,

The address is 31, not 38 Great King St, I find. But the number in this case doesn't matter so much, if you remember to put 'Clutterbuck'[1] on the envelope it just can't go wrong!

Ten minutes after I arrived yesterday we got down to serious drinking, and before the night was out had polished off several gins, a bottle of vino (Bordeaux) and a near-lethal dose of Hungarian Cseresnye. Glory O (as I sang before the night was out) to every ranting roving blade who can organize himself a bit of the real MacAoidh even in these degenerate days!

Ref. Hugh (Chester White)[2] Roberton. I enclose a quotation from the article of a Belgian music critic which I copied down when I was in Holland. It's clear that this Belgian has a far more correct line on Kennedy-Fraser than most of the damnfool local critics who yammered away about the Festival.

In case you can't read my scrawl, here's the 'fair copy':

Ce que nous avons regretté, c'est que plusieurs de ces chants ont été donnés dans des versions arrangées qui les dénaturent parfois, les échelles mélodiques si particulières de ces chants s'opposant par nature aux harmonies traditionnelles.[3]
La Dernière Heure

This morning I spent two happy hours being shown over Younger's brewery. I think I'll talk my way into a taster's post in this racket. It would be God's own job altogether!

I'll let you have the German article[4] in a day or two.

Love to Valda,

All the best,

Yours, Hamish

---

1 Michael Clutterbuck, employed as a manager in Younger's Brewery, Edinburgh. Henderson made his acquaintance in the Army.

2 Hugh Roberton, conductor of the Glasgow Orpheus Choir; the choir often performed Marjorie Kennedy-Fraser's settings of Gaelic songs. MacDiarmid wrote critically of Roberton's work in his essay 'Hugh Roberton and the Musical Festival Movement', published in *Scottish Studies* (Leonard Parsons Ltd: London, 1926).

3 Trans. 'What we have regretted is that several of these songs have been given in arranged versions which sometimes distort them; the melodic scales so characteristic of these songs are opposed in their very nature to traditional harmonies' (H.H.).

4 'Germany in Defeat' appeared in two parts in *Voice of Scotland*, IV.3, March 1948 and IV.4, June 1948, reprinted in *Alias MacAlias*.

14 To Hugh MacDiarmid

[*EUL*]

[Edinburgh, February 1948]

Dear Chris,

I've nearly finished my German article, and you'll have it by Friday. Hope it's still in time for the next issue. I'm returning to Glasgow myself within the next day or two.

Meanwhile here's a short poem in Lallans. Use it if you want.

I've drunk Youngers' dry – right down to the fermenting vats! God, it was good while it lasted.

You wanted to know what Daiches[1] is like. I enclose an extract from a letter of Geoffrey Wagner[2] (an English Lecturer at Rochester University N.Y.) to Neil McCallum[3] the Edinburgh writer. (Don't quote it in full, as Neil wants to use it himself in an article.)

Maybe Kenny[4] has told you that a woman rejoicing in the name of Gita de la Fuenté – she's a soprano in the Carl Rosa opera company and lives in a house called 'Little Chittagong' in a London suburb – has ordered a copy of my Ballads. I strongly suspect her real name's Maggy MacSporran, but I think I'll saunter round to the stage-door and find out!

Love to Valda,

   Yours ever, Hamish

---

1 David Daiches (b. 1912), distinguished Scottish literary critic; he contributed an Introduction to the 1953 edition of MacDiarmid's *A Drunk Man Looks at the Thistle* (Caledonian Press: Glasgow, 1953, xii-xx).

2 Geoffrey Wagner, American academic; see Letter 50.

3 Neil McCallum, Edinburgh critic and novelist; worked as an advertising agent; author of *Journey With a Pistol: A Diary of War* (London, 1961), a novel describing his experiences in the Libyan campaign of 1942–3, and *It's an Old Scottish Custom* (Denis Dobson: London, 1948).

4 Kenny Campbell of the Caledonian Press.

15 To Sir Alexander Gray[1]

[*EUL*]

[Edinburgh, 16 February 1948]

Dear Sir Alexander,

I've been reading your *Arrows*[2] with great interest – I find I know the originals in many cases. 'Ade zur guten Nacht' is a song which has long been among my favourites, and I sang it with German friends last Summer at Bonn and Godesberg. That wonderful second verse

> (Es trauert Berg und Tal
> Wo ich viel tausend mal
> Bin drüber gangen usw)[3]

has a passionate simplicity which leaves Troilus in the shade. All yesterday and today I've been admiring the felicity of your translation.

Among others that have impressed me are 'May Frost', 'Morning Hymn' and 'The Rain's Gone By'.

Have you ever made a version of that sixteenth-century ballad 'Und in dem Schneegebirge'?[4] I heard it last sung by a Bonn student[5] in the coal-cellar (under the ruins of his house) which is now his only habitation. He is the son of a Social Democratic deputy of the Reichstag who was murdered by the Nazis together with his wife.

When I found the ruins of the family (a grandmother, the student and his younger brother) in a corner of the basement of its shattered house I wondered what sort of spirit could thrust itself upwards out of this shambles. But before the evening was out the four of us were singing folksongs – and the one that has remained in my mind is that mountain song:

> Und in dem Schneegebirge,
>   da fliesst ein Brünnlein kalt;
> und wer des Brünnlein trinket (bis)
>   der jungt und wird nicht alt.

(ER)
> 'Ich hab' daraus getrunken,
>   gar manchen frischen Trunk.
> Ich bin nicht alt geworden
>   Ich bin noch allzeit jung.'

(SIE)
> 'Die Brünnlein, die da fliessen,
>   die soll man trinken;
> Wer eine Feinsherzliebste hat,
>   der soll ihr winken.'

(ER)   'Ich winkte mit den Augen,
                   ich trat dir auf den Fuss.'

(SIE)   'Ach, wie ein schweres Leiden,
                   Wenn einer scheiden muss.'

(ER)   'Ade mein Schatz ich scheide,
                   Ade mein Schätzelein!'

(SIE)   Wann kommst du aber wieder
                   Herzallerliebster mein?'

(ER)   'Wenn es wird schneien Rosen
                   und regnen Kühlen Wein
                Ade mein Schatz ich scheide
                Ade mein Schätzelein.'

(SIE)   'Es schneit ja keine Rosen
                   und regnen kühlen Wein
                So kommst du ach nicht wieder,
                Herzallerliebster mein!'

(BEIDE)   Und in dem Schneegebirge
                   Da fliesst ein Brünnlein kalt,
                Und wer des Brünnlein trinket,
                   der jungt und wird nicht alt.[6]

Your reference (page 25) to the murderer of Kotzebue reminds me of the spirited Italian ballad of 'Caserio', the anarchist who was guillotined at Lyons.

> 'Il sedici d'agosto
>   sul far' della mattina
> il boia priperava
>   la rea ghigliottina.'[7]

It's very kind of you to take an interest in my *Ballads of WW II*. I've asked Kenny[8] (the Secretary of the LM Club) to send you the first of the new batch – but you mustn't expect too much. These degenerate days hardly produce 'O Strassburg' or 'Lament of the Border Widow' – but (I'm afraid) they can still produce Rabelaisian ballads that would not shame the Middle Ages.

Once again, many thanks for the *Arrows*.

Yours sincerely, Hamish Henderson

1 Sir Alexander Gray (1882–1968) poet and translator; Professor of Political Economy at Aberdeen and later Edinburgh. Henderson was an admirer of Gray's translations of German and Scandinavian ballads and poetry.

2 *Arrows: A Book of German Ballads and Folksongs attempted in Scots* (Grant & Murray: Edinburgh, 1932).

3 Trans.   'Mountain and valley mourn,
              where I've crossed over
                 many thousand times.'
              (H.H.)

4 Trans. 'Up in the snowy mountains.' (H.H.)

5 Heinz Vogt.

6 Trans.   Up in the snowy mountains there flows
              a cold stream; and who drinks from it he stays
                 young and doesn't grow old.

              I have drunk from it, many a fresh dram;
              I haven't grown old, I've stayed
                 young.

              (*She*) The streams that flow there, you
              must drink of them; he who has a
                 darling, must make a sign to her.

              (*He*) I signalled to you with my eyes, I pressed
              my foot on yours.

              (*She*) O what a heavy sorrow. When
              we've got to part.

              (*He*) Adieu, my treasure. I'm leaving.
              Adieu my precious treasure.

              (*She*) When will you come back
              My darling?

              (*He*) When it snows roses
              and rains cool wine.
              Adieu my sweet, I'm leaving –
              Adieu my darling.

              (*She*) It'll never snow roses.
              Or rain cool wine.
              So your not coming back
              My heart's darling.

(*Both*) And in the snowy mountains
  there flows a cold stream
And who drinks of it
  Stays young and doesn't grow old.
(H.H.)
Folksong from the Glatz Mountains, also known as 'Der Jungbrunnen', originally of Silesian origin.

7 Trans. 'At dawn on 16th August the executioner was preparing the fatal guillotine.' (H.H.)
8 Kenny Campbell of the Caledonian Press; the Lili Marlene Club.

16 To Hugh MacDiarmid
[*EUL*]

[Cambridgeshire, 1 March 1948]

Dear Chris,

I've hitchhiked to England to tear the guts out of *Our Time* for failing to print your Lenin page and Mike's *Gyndagooster*.[1]

Here I find there's been a new Thermidor — Holbrook[2] and Manifold[3] have been liquidated, and a cadaverous school-marmy Czech called Jellinek[4] reigns in their stead!

Whether I've got to be a new Barras, and wield the sword of Vendémiaire is not quite clear yet. Anyway I got cracking on this cove Jellinek, and the result has been gratifying. He's agreed to do a complete Scottish number of *Our Time*[5] in the Spring or early Summer — containing a Lenin page twice as long, a full-length article by myself on the Scottish Renaissance, an article (? by MacDougall) on John Maclean, a study of Lewis Grassic Gibbon (? by yourself), plus stories, poems etc. *And* Gyndagooster! I also sold him a copy of the Ballads.

By Christ, if I'd added an article by Valda on you I swear by all things heroic he'd have accepted it!

Running in London now is *The Gorbals Story* (see enclosure), a *succès fou*. It's not all *that* good, which is eloquent of the depths to which the English stage has sunk.

I enclose a poem by Edward Thompson[6] (son of the Edward you knew), who's now living in Wester Ross. Write to him and make contact. (Maybe it would do for the *Voice*.) Anyway he's a worthwhile contact, for he'll be a power yet in the CP [Communist Party].

Yesterday I got a terrible letter from Heinz[7] describing Winter in Duisburg, and deaths from freezing in the cellars of that ruined shambles. A pity it didn't come earlier — it would have done very well as a supplement to my German article.

The *Voice* sells out in Cambridge and Collets London – I'm convinced the circulation could be increased tenfold.

Love to Valda,

Yours ever, Hamish

PS The *Swordsman*[8] is on here. I'm going along today for a laugh.

Edward's address:
13 Laide
by Achnasheen
Ross-shire

---

1 Probably an article by the young Michael Grieve (1932–95), son of Valda and Christopher Grieve, then only 16 years old. 'Gyndagooster'; Shetlandese for 'a strong, sudden gust of wind, a strong sweeping wind; a storm, esp. of short duration', *Dictionary of the Older Scottish Tongue*.
2 David Holbrook (b. 1923), poet and novelist; both he and Henderson studied at Downing College. Henderson's circle during his second period of study at Cambridge included Holbrook, the social and political thinker Raymond Williams, Marian Sugden, Matthew Hodgart, the Oxford economist Eprime Eshag, and E.P. Thompson, all of whom held left-wing sympathies or were members of the Communist Party.
3 John Streeter Manifold (1915–85), Australian left-wing poet, born in Melbourne; writer of ballads and collector of folksongs, editor of the *Penguin Australian Song Book* (Harmondsworth, 1965). His *Selected Verse* appeared in 1948.
4 Frank Jellinek, left-wing journalist and historian; editor of *Our Time*.
5 For a more detailed discussion of this special Scottish issue of *Our Time*, which was largely edited by Henderson, see pp. 307–9 Afterword.
6 E.P. Thompson (1924–94), Marxist historian, peace campaigner; author of *The Making of the English Working Classes* (Gollancz; London, 1963), editor of *The New Reasoner*. Henderson first met Thompson at Cambridge in 1946.
7 Heinz Vogt.
8 *The Swordsman* (1947); a film. *Halliwell's Film Guide* describes it thus: 'A young 18th-century Scot tries to end a family feud so that he can marry the girl of his choice. Amiable costume programmer, forgettable but enjoyable.'

17 To Hugh MacDiarmid
[*EUL; postcard, 'Comrie from the South'*]

[Comrie, 18 March 1948]

Dear Chris,

I'm giving the patter to a prize set of morose and bloody-minded Jerries[1] in the uplands of Comrie, and listening with delight to the fine speech of the locals.

See you at the Montale[2]-Feier on Saturday.
Love to Valda,

   Hamish

---

1 Henderson had a short-term job teaching German prisoners of war held in camps in Perthshire, Argyll, Inverness and Caithness.
2 Eugenio Montale (1896–1981), Italian poet. Montale visited Britain, along with Alberto Moravia and Elsa Morante, in a trip organized by the British Council in 1948. For the Scottish part of their trip Henderson acted as a guide, introducing them to MacDiarmid. He has since translated two poems of Montale's relating to this visit, 'Letting go of a Dove' and 'Wind on the Crescent', published in *The Obscure Voice*, Under the Moon Series 1/3 (Morning Star Publications: Edinburgh, 1994).

18 To Hugh MacDiarmid
[*EUL*]

[Edinburgh, 23 April 1948]

Dear Chris,

Here's the 'Twa Blads frae Africa'.[1] You'll get Amleto's[2] poem and the German article[3] just as soon as I can write them.

Moray House[4] has its point. I'm beginning to inject a little of the Lili Marlene Club spirit into the joint. You can be sure that at least one generation of students will get the John Maclean line with their religious instruction. *And* like it, by Christ!

Neil[5] seems to have enjoyed your company. His article will be out (*DV*)[6] next Friday (the 30th).

Love to Valda,

   Yours ever, Hamish

---

1 Poem which Henderson has since lost.
2 Amleto Micozzi, Italian poet and critic; Henderson first met him in Rome in 1944. Henderson's translation of Micozzi's poem 'Grido' appeared in *Voice of Scotland*, IV.4, June 1948.
3 The second part of Henderson's essay 'Germany in Defeat'.
4 Henderson attended a teacher training course at Moray House College in Edinburgh in the Spring term of 1948. He was training as a teacher in Modern Languages, but he left the course to take a job with the Workers Educational Association in Belfast.
5 Neil MacCallum; the article was on the Nationalist question, and specifically on the most recent meeting of the Scottish National Assembly in Glasgow. It appeared in the *New Statesman and Nation*, to which MacCallum was an occasional contributor. MacDiarmid's influence is mentioned:

A number of young poets, without being a school, are putting forth a coherent plea for a creative Scottish literature in which the three main languages of Scotland will each play its part. The poets are fathered and inspired by the indefatigable anti-Sassenach and battleship-of-letters Hugh MacDiarmid . . .

6 *DV*, *deo volente*: God willing.

19 To Hugh MacDiarmid

[*EUL*]

[Edinburgh, 29 April 1948]

Dear Chris,

I enclose an article from a fellow in Zürich about two post-war German novels.[1] It would go in very nicely along with the second instalment of my 'Germany in Defeat'.

Last night I spoke for Communism against Sir Will Y. Darling, that bloated go-by-the-wall. I tore strips off him in a debate in the Edinburgh Union, countering his gibes about the Communist record in the war by facts and figures about the Partisan struggle. I then took his fatuous ballocks about the Tory record and cracked hell out of them — referring to the Tory record in the Highlands, and finishing with a denunciation of the Clearances in the grand manner.

The voting was 54 (for us) and 159 against — not bad in this city of dopes and ditherers.

Tonight I'm going to the Shinty Club dance, which should be good. I'm taking a British Council secretary who's promised to type out my Mardel[2] book in exchange for a bit of houghmagandie!

Love to Valda,

Yours ever, Hamish

PS From Australia I've received a copy of *Rebel Songs*,[3] a fine collection of bawdy cum bolshie ballads ranging from 'Hallelujah I'm a Bum' to 'Botany Bay'. Also a bouquet for *Ballads of World War II*, which seems to have a grand future before it in Australia.

I think the enclosed article is the first mention in Scotland (and England!) of two books of great importance.

---

1 'Two German Novels of the Present Day', by Walter Glaettle, translated by Henderson. The novels are *Die Stadt hinter dem Strom* by Hermann Kasack, and *Nekyia* by Hans Erich Nossack. This article appeared in *Voice of Scotland*, IV.4, June 1948.

2 J. Mardel, publisher in Edinburgh; his imprint Serif Books published the first edition of Sydney Goodsir Smith's *Under the Eildon Tree* (1948) and Marian Angus's *Selected Poems* (1950). Henderson submitted a manuscript of light ballads and translations, including the 'Ballad of Corbara' and a translation of an episode from Heine's *Germany: A Winter's Tale*; however, this collection never appeared.

3 *Rebel Songs*, a collection of folksongs edited and collected by the Australian poet John Manifold.

20 From 'The Makars Club' to the *Scotsman*[1]

[Edinburgh, 30 April 1948]

Sir,

Mr James Bridie[2] is reported to have made at St Andrews University on 29 April a public speech in which he said that he objected to modern Scottish makars laying down the law about how Scottish writers are to express themselves. Mr Bridie went on to say that 'a really ambitious writer is better employed in enriching English than in discarding it'. Mentioning by name Hugh MacDiarmid, Sydney Goodsir Smith, and Douglas Young, he stated that they belonged to the middle classes and that English was their mother tongue.

As a group of individuals employing Lallans for poetical purposes, we protest against Mr Bridie laying down the law, and at the same time misleading and misinforming the public. We who are widely known as 'The Lallans Makars' have laid down no law except in so far as we have asserted that the Scots literary tradition in Lallans, whose highest exponents have been William Dunbar, Robert Burns, and Hugh MacDiarmid, ought to be continued and extended, and that it can be maintained in its integrity only if it be cultivated with a critical self-respect and an awareness of the native organic principles of Lallans (often called 'Braid Scots') as a separate literary language, not as a dialect of English or of any other Germanic language.

We have never attempted to lay down a law that all writers of Scots birth should write exclusively in Lallans, any more than that they should write exclusively in Gaelic, or in the language of the world's majority nation, Chinese. Concerned with quality rather than quantity, we are not concerned to deny the utility of current English for journalism, commerce, and many other purposes, including those undergraduate whimsies that audiences find so entertaining and Mr Bridie finds so lucrative.

Being individually and as a group primarily interested in poetry and verse, we point to the fact that truer and fuller expression has been attained by Scots poets in Lallans than in English, even during the most recent generations of the four centuries during which the higher income groups in Scotland have sought to employ English for poetry.

On some matters of fact, it may be worth mentioning that Mr Hugh MacDiarmid was born and remains a proletarian whose mother tongue was the dialect of Langholm; that Mr Sydney Goodsir Smith's infancy was passed in a Scottish household in the classless society of New Zealand; and that Mr Douglas Young's first language was Urdu and his second Lallans.

Assuming, however, that Mr Bridie's scale of literary values be a just one, and that the enrichment of English is more important than the maintenance and enrichment of Lallans, we would point out that if English (or any other language) is to be enriched from Lallans, then pedigree Lallans stock must be bred for the hybridization, or, to change the metaphor, the pure Scots spirit must continue to be distilled if Scotland is to contribute any potent element to a polyglot international medium. Since poetry is the most intense form of literary expression, that in which words receive their highest emotional charge, we believe that the integrity of Lallans poetry and its linguistic basis is worthy of more respect than our eminent compatriot has on this occasion shown.

> We are etc., Albert D. Mackie, Hamish Henderson, Maurice Lindsay, J. Ritchie, Alexander Scott, Sydney Goodsir Smith, Douglas Young

1 The letter was probably authored by Douglas Young.
2 James Bridie, pen name of O.V. Mavor (1888–1951); major Scottish dramatist of the twentieth century.

21 To the *Scotsman*

[Edinburgh, 15 May 1948]

Sir,

Few contributors to this unenlightening correspondence seem to have grasped the fundamental questions at issue. Allow me to give some direction to the debate by making one or two necessary points.

Firstly: the reason why the makars are so boisterously assailed by all and sundry is not primarily because they write in Lallans, but because they form an *avant-garde*. One need hardly point out that an *avant-garde* as such is traditionally suspect. Keats, for example, would consider the present correspondence merely as so much matey badinage: in his day he had to take infinitely worse slangings. In fact, Byron's celebrated line about Keats being killed off 'by one critique' (and an Edinburgh critique at that!) had a certain degree of truth in it.

Secondly: the language the makars use is looked upon as archaic, not because it has ceased to be spoken, but because it is no longer the 'done thing' to speak it. If some of the critics of Lallans writers had been conscripted into the R.S.F.[1] or the Cameronians they would pretty quickly have altered their ideas about the vitality of spoken Scots.

Thirdly: Lallans poems *have* been translated into English, and most, granted any sensibility on the part of the reader, can be immediately apprehended as poetry. The following is a prose version of Hugh MacDiarmid's famous poem 'The Eemis Stane': 'In the very dead of the cold harvest night the world, like a loose tombstone, sways in the sky; and my eerie memories fall like a down-drive of snow. Like a down-drive of snow so that I cannot read the words cut on the stone, even if the moss of fame and the lichen of history had not overgrown them.'

I submit that the above prose translation, although it cannot hope by its very nature to recapture the sonorous yet subtle beauty of the Scots, is nevertheless adequate proof that one is dealing here with a poem of the first order. Another thing about it which leaps to the eye is that it is in the 'modern' idiom, having far more in common with the poetry of Jouve and Montale than with that of, say, Walter de la Mare. Furthermore, it makes as bold and imaginative a use of Scots as Eliot has made of English.

After countless inroads the old Scots tongue now stands like a great ruined broch, with the rubble of centuries lying round it. Stones from that rubble have for too long gone to nothing higher than the building of dykes around lowly Kailyairds. In poems like 'The Eemis Stane' an attempt has at last been made to put stone on stone, to rebuild the tower. Is it strange that modern Scottish poets, the heirs of Dunbar and Henryson, should consider this task well worthy of their labours?

Of course, they may fail. Possibly they are not equal to the task. But history will at any rate give them credit for bringing the Scottish cultural predicament ruthlessly into the light of day.

> I am etc., Hamish Henderson

---

1 Royal Scots Fusiliers.

22 To Hugh MacDiarmid
[*EUL*]

[Edinburgh, 10 July 1948]

Dear Chris,

Here's Corbara,[1] in case you want it for the *Voice*.

I've thought of asking Kenny[2] to do an edition of it similar to the one he did of 'Setterday Nicht Symphony'[3]. Do you think that's a good idea?

All the best to Tito.[4]

> Yours, Hamish

---

1 Henderson's 'Ballad of Corbara' was published in *Voice of Scotland*, VI.1, September 1948. It celebrates the bravery of 'Corbara', a Partisan who fought in Emilia, and was captured and shot by the Germans in 1944.
2 Kenny Campbell of the Caledonian Press.
3 'Setterday Nicht Symphony' by John Kincaid, published in *Fowrsom Reel*; Kincaid was a member of the 'Clyde Group'.
4 'Probably a sardonic reference to the recent Stalin–Tito break' (H.H.).

23 To Hugh MacDiarmid
[*EUL*]

[Cambridgeshire, 19 August 1948]

Dear Chris,

I enclose two reviews from today's *Worker*[1] which may interest you. Fraser's *Vision of Scotland*[2] contains a number of quotes from articles etc by me.

Our Time is using Foggie's[3] portrait of you as an illustration . . . The poetry I've chosen for the Scottish number is all stuff meant to give background to my article:

your 'Common Riding'

Sydney's 'Ballad o' John Maclean'

Sorley's 'Clan Maclean' (translated)

Campbell Hay's 'Lomsgríos na Tíre' etc

My motorbike's on the road again: I'm leaving for Scotland on it tomorrow.

All the best, Hamish

---

1 *Daily Worker*, Communist Party newspaper.

2 G.S. Fraser's *Vision of Scotland*, with drawings by Barbara Jones: 'The book was a kind of high-class tourist guide; George had sent me proofs and asked for comment' (H.H.).

3 The late David Foggie's portrait of MacDiarmid was presented to the poet by the Makars Club and other friends and admirers, in a ceremony held in the Scotia Hotel on 28 August 1948.

1949

24 John Lehmann to Hamish Henderson

[London, 8 February 1949]

Dear Hamish,

Many thanks for your letter. I was so glad Lorne Campbell[1] wrote so appreciatively. I now enclose a comic little note we had from Wavell.[2]

I wish I could report any movement from the booksellers, but they practically laugh in one's face when one mentions poetry now. It is a great shame and you deserve a better fate. I am, however, of the opinion that, as reviews accumulate, interest will grow, even if it is slow. We shall keep our eye on all this, go on advertising in one or two appropriate places, and do all else we can. Did you, by the way, see Elizabeth Bowen's really movingly sympathetic notice in *The Tatler*?

Gavin[3] told me it was *not* him in the *TLS* . . . ?

I am sending the Scottish BBC thing to our northern traveller. I am pretty certain Book Clubs do *not* take 3 weeks to deliver. I'm afraid some booksellers do not hesitate to stoop to any excuses when they have been careless. Will keep cracking, Hamish.

     Love from John

---

1 Brigadier Lorne Maclaine Campbell of Airds, VC; see Letter 27.
2 General Wavell commanded the British Army in the Libyan campaign of 1940. Wavell also edited the famous poetry anthology *Other Men's Flowers*. He wrote Lehmann a note about Henderson's *Elegies*.
3 Gavin Ewart (b. 1916), poet.

25 E.P. Thompson to Hamish Henderson

[10 February 1949]

Dear Hamish,[1]

. . . I also proffer you some heavy advice which I hope you will take as carefully considered and deeply felt – not dismiss as Marxist phrase-mongering.

But that is not the essential thing. I greet you with humility, compagno, for you are that rare man, a poet. You have achieved poems out of our dead century. I hope you have had bad reviews from the culture boys, because their approval today is cause only for shame. But you must remain a poet. Remember always who you are writing for: the people of Glasgow, of Halifax, of Dublin . . . I don't mean always today, or for all of them – but for the vanguard of the people, the most thoughtful ones. You will know Mayakovski's[2] reflections on the difficulty of writing 'big poetry – poetry genuinely created' which can be understood by the people.

I think this is your greatest danger and you must never let yourself, by the possible insensitivity or even hostility of those who should be your greatest allies, be driven into the arms of the 'culture boys' who 'appreciate' pretentiousness and posturing. They would kill your writing, because you, more than any other poet I know, are an instrument through which thousands of others can become articulate. And you must not forget that your songs and ballads are not trivialities – they are quite as important as the *Elegies*.

---

1 This extract was first published in the Afterword of the new edition of *Elegies for the Dead in Cyrenaica* (Edinburgh University Student Publications Board 1977, reprinted by Polygon 1990). The original is no longer extant.
2 Vladimir Mayakovsky (1893–1930), Russian poet; associated with Futurism, attempted to create an epic proletarian poetry.

26 Hugh MacDiarmid to Hamish Henderson
[*EUL*]

[Glasgow, 21 March 1949]

My dear Hamish,

Heartiest congratulations, in which all here join. I was just reading of the award in the *Bulletin* and *Glasgow Herald*, when your letter arrived. Wish I'd been in Belfast to join in the celebration.[1]

Many thanks, too, for the good work you put in with Paul Robeson,[2] with whom we had a splendid night here. He sang half-a-dozen songs at the reception – also gave us a long and most moving speech in reply to my address of welcome. We presented him with all F.G. Scott's songs (including George Hay's 'Old Fisherman'[3] etc.).

Since then I addressed the Saltire Society in Edinburgh and had a big audience. Prior to that I had a great time in Oxford and, on the way back, in Manchester with the Theatre Workshop people.[4]

Sorry I have been so long in getting your book reviewed,[5] but I've been having a desperately busy time. However, the review should be in either this week's – or next week's – *National Weekly* (which is beginning to go very well). Also, I'll be reviewing it in the *Voice*, which should be out in a week or so.

I am all for the Irish number[6] you suggest. Will you collect the material for me over there? Also, ask Sean O'Casey.[7] I've just done a page review of his 'Inishfallen fare thee well' for *New Theatre*; it is, I think, by far the best of his four autobiographical books, and I enjoyed it immensely.

Regards to Hewitt,[8] Davie,[9] and all. Any word yet when you want me to speak to the Socialist Club.

All the best,

Yours, Chris

PS Note enclosed cuttings re Maurice Lindsay's[10] address to London Saltire. I've sent letters to *Bulletin, Glasgow Herald* etc putting him in his place. They haven't appeared yet, but probably will tomorrow, I think.

Congratulations, Hamish – this will be a smack on the kisser for little Maurice. By the way do I get my scarf – *not green* – I'm superstitious.[11]

Love, Valda

---

1 This is the first extant letter from MacDiarmid to Henderson, who was employed in Belfast as District Secretary of the Workers Educational Association during 1948–9. Henderson's *Elegies for the Dead in Cyrenaica* was awarded the Somerset Maugham Award for Literature in 1949.

2 Paul Robeson (1898–1976), famous Black American singer and actor. Henderson met Robeson in Belfast: 'I got into his hotel in Royal Avenue, and signed him up to sing in Glasgow for the Scottish/USSR Society' (H.H.).

3 'The Old Fisherman', a setting of George Campbell Hay's poem by Francis George Scott: 'Robeson did in fact learn "The Old Fisherman", but I don't know if he ever performed it much' (H.H.).

4 Theatre Workshop, the experimental company run by Joan Littlewood and her husband Ewan MacColl.

5 MacDiarmid included a review of Henderson's *Elegies* as part of a longer article in the *National Weekly*, I.30, April 1949; no review ever appeared in *Voice of Scotland*.

6 Henderson collected material for an Irish number of the *Voice of Scotland*; however, because of a disagreement between MacDiarmid and the Caledonian Press, this never appeared.

7 Sean O'Casey (1880–1964), Irish dramatist, best known for *Juno and the Paycock* and *The Plough and the Stars*. For Sean O'Casey's reply, see Letter 29.

8 John Hewitt (1907–87), Northern Irish poet, author of *No Rebel Word* (Muller Ltd: London, 1948).

9 George Elder Davie (b. 1912), Scottish philosopher, then lecturing at Queen's University in Belfast, and a close friend of Henderson's and MacDiarmid's. Author of *The Democratic Intellect* (Edinburgh University Press, 1961), and *The Crisis of the Democratic Intellect* (Polygon: Edinburgh, 1986).

10 Although MacDiarmid admired some of Maurice Lindsay's poetry, they often disagreed on political grounds.

11 Note added by Valda Grieve. 'Little Maurice'; Maurice Lindsay.

27 **To Marian Sugden**[1]

[Belfast, March 1949]

[2]Many thanks for your kind words about the *Elegies*. I enclose Alex Scott's[3] radio review, which Norman Arnold[4] wants. Tell him I'm also sending him Naomi Mitchison's[5] review in *Forward*.[6] Geordie Fraser[7] in the *Times Lit. Sup.* was skittish about the 'English directness' of the poems (English my tartan filabeg!) but very good for all that.

This morning I was surprised and delighted to get a letter from Brigadier Lorne Maclean Campbell, the VC of Wadi Akarit, who commanded the 7th Argylls in the Highland Div. He writes:

> I find your poems give a voice to all the queer and, for me, quite inarticulate feelings one had in the desert, the sort of feeling I got for example on first hearing 'Lili Marlene', and that it was the song of the Afrika Korps. The song seemed to me one of the most tragic I had heard, wholly appropriate to a doomed Army bumping along in their trucks in the desert, the desert you describe. I still can't express what I mean, but your poems do it for me. So I am delighted to have the book and will treasure it as a reminder of great events which we both experienced and to which you give expression.

It was Lorne Campbell who accepted the VC not in his own name but in that of his battalion. (He, of course, is not the J.L.C.[8] to whom I dedicate the Fifth Elegy — that's the Gaelic scholar, 'Young Inverneil', the present Laird of Canna.) There's a picture of him in *Alba*, Maclellan's Gaelic periodical which came out for the Edinburgh Mod.

> Up wi' the carles o' Dysart
>   an' the lads o' Buckhaven
> And the kimmers o' Largo
>   and the lasses o' Leven
>
> Hey ca' thro, ca' thro
> For we hae mickle a do
> Hey ca' thro, ca' thro
> For we hae mickle a do
>
> We hae tales to tell
>   And we hae sangs to sing
> We hae pennies to spend
>   And we hae pints to bring.

We'll live a' our days
   And them that comes behin'
Let them do the like
   And spend the gear they win.

(That's a song Burns collected.[9])

Love to all and – up the rebels!

   Yours, Hamish

---

1 Marian Sugden, wife of the distinguished biochemist Morris Sugden, who later became Master of Trinity Hall, Cambridge. Henderson met her at Cambridge in 1946, and they have remained close friends ever since.
2 The first two pages of this letter are missing.
3 Alexander Scott (1920–89), poet, journalist and broadcaster; head of the Department of Scottish Literature at Glasgow University.
4 Norman Arnold, a fellow student and friend of Henderson's at Cambridge.
5 Naomi Mitchison (b. 1897), novelist and poet. Henderson stayed at her home in Carradale, Kintyre, while he was completing the *Elegies*.
6 *Forward*, a socialist weekly published in Glasgow.
7 G.S. Fraser.
8 John Lorne Campbell, Laird of Canna. Campbell was a collector of traditional Gaelic stories and songs, and it was in 1946, while staying on Canna as his guest, working on his *Elegies*, that Henderson met Calum I. MacLean and Seamus Ennis, who were collecting for the Irish Folklore Commission.
9 The title of the song is 'Hey Ca' Thro'.

28 To Hugh MacDiarmid
[*EUL*]

[Belfast, 3 April 1949]

Dear Chris,

Séan O'Casey has written to me explaining why he can't do the article I suggested on 'Scottish–Irish Relations: Past and Future'. The letter includes a warm tribute to yourself, and I've written asking him if we may print it in the Irish number.

This is the paragraph:

But even were I idle; even were the children away, I wouldn't undertake the job. I am not equipped well enough to do it. Hugh evidently has the sweet grace of humility when he thinks my mind is as brilliant as his own. Well, it isn't; and I could never sit down (or stand up) to write such a Foreword as his in his *Scottish*

Treasury of Poetry, or that which introduces Ewan MacColl's play *Uranium 235*.
Compared with his intellectual gifts and his scholarly equipment, my mind is as a
planeteen whizzing around a fine sun – to say nothing about his gift as a poet.[1]

Did wee Maurice (most minuscule of makars) reply to your letter?[2] And if so,
did you savage him?
Love to Valda,

    Yours ever, Hamish

---

1 See MacDiarmid's letter to O'Casey, *The Letters of Hugh MacDiarmid*, edited
  by Alan Bold (Hamish Hamilton: London, 1984, 635).
2 This refers to a public disagreement between MacDiarmid and Maurice
  Lindsay, the result of some critical remarks Lindsay had made concerning the
  'linking of the Scottish literary revival with Communist propaganda . . .'.
  Letter from Hugh MacDiarmid to Maurice Lindsay, March 1949, *The Letters
  of Hugh MacDiarmid*, [619–21].

29 From Sean O'Casey to Hamish Henderson

[Totnes, 21 April 1949]

Dear Hamish Henderson

Good man – a grand book,[1] thank you for sending it to me. I get in it the brown
snarly rocks, the suffocating sand, the sigh of all the Laochraies, German & Eng,
Scots & Irish, falling forever into the stifling sand, falling forever from the hills, the
dales, the streets they knew, and the warm kiss from a favoured lass when the
times were quiet. Na laochrai Eireann [agus] na Laochrai Alban. I am so glad you
got the Maugham Award for the work: it deserves it.

And I hear a cry in it that the desert which has buried so many of our dead, should
now itself be buried by the living, that we might see the blossoming of the rose.

The book is sturdily and gracefully turned out – not always the case with the
format for poems. For all that Belfast did, I reckon Rinty's[2] fight & the winning of
the Rugby Crown[3] as victories for Ireland. Yours is, of course, one for the Gauls o'
Scotland. I'm writing this in bed where I've been thrust by influenza. I dodged it
grandly while it was at its height, &, then, when it had near waned away, I loitered
to look at a shop window, and was caught.

Confined as I am, I'm bright enough to rejoice with you in the winning of the
Somerset Maugham Award. May it be but the beginning of a great time for you.

Perhaps, one day, we may be able to have a talk about Thistle and Shamrock;
and even the Leek and Rose too.

I'll get one of my boys to address the envelope to you – the hand is very shaky at the moment.

My best wishes as ucht mo chroidhe to you[4]

> Sean O'Casey

---

1 *Elegies for the Dead in Cyrenaica.*
2 Rinty Monaghan, Irish boxer.
3 The Irish rugby team won the 1949 Five Nations championship.
4 'From the bottom of my heart' (H.H.).

30 To Hugh MacDiarmid
[*EUL*]

[Belfast, 28 April 1949]

Dear Chris,

I've just returned from the Peace Congress[1] in Paris, where a blow was struck quite effectively for Scotland's identity. We got the name SCOTLAND put up in the salle where the conference was held, in company with the other nations present. I'm going to do a long feature article on the conference for next week's *Weekly*.

In London I had lunch with Lehmann,[2] who told me of your project to re-issue the *Hymns to Lenin*. He admires the poems very much, but you know yourself how poetry's in the doldrums these days. A much better bet would be Jack Lindsay,[3] who is a great MacDiarmid fan, and might bring out a grand edition of them as an adjunct to his *Arena*.

(Incidentally, as you'll remember, he's reprinting 'Yet hae I Silence left'[4] in the first number of *Arena*. It's undoubtedly the best thing in the collection.)

He also wants to know whether an official invitation to the Congress was sent to you by the British Cultural Committee, because he submitted your name in his list. If no invitation was sent he guarantees to raise Hades. I said I was sure you'll have had an invitation, it's unthinkable that even English CP [Communist Party] chauvinists shouldn't send you one.

Séan O'Casey has sent me another letter, this time about the *Elegies*, which he's now read. He gives them heart-warming words of praise & encouragement . . . I saw your review in *New Theatre*, very good: excellent that you confirm his verdict on Cathal Brugha[5] etc. Poor old A E ![6]

Another possibility for the *Hymns to Lenin*:

Dennis Dobson,[7]
12 Park Place,
St James's,
London SW1

He's turned down the Maclean[8] book as too ticklish a commercial proposition, but might readily fall for the *Hymns*.

Then there's Lawrence and Wishart,[9] who might do 'em: I used to know one of the directors, a namesake of mine; I think maybe I could persuade her. Anyway, the most distinguished Communist poetry in Europe is a re-publishing 'must' for 1949!

Love to Valda and Mike,[10]

All the best, Hamish

---

1 The Peace Congress was organized by 'Partisans of Peace', a Communist Party organization.

2 John Lehmann, Henderson's publisher.

3 Jack Lindsay, Australian left-wing poet and translator, editor of *Arena* poetry magazine.

4 From the final passage of MacDiarmid's *A Drunk Man looks at the Thistle* (Blackwood: Edinburgh, 1926).

5 Cathal Brugha (1874–1922), Irish Republican; killed in action during the early stages of the Civil War. Brugha was a strenuous opponent of the Treaty of 1922.

6 A E (1867–1935), pseudonym of George Russell, Irish poet and mystic.

7 Dennis Dobson, London publisher.

8 John Maclean (1879–1923), Scottish Marxist radical, founded the Scottish Workers Republican Party. The anthology was a selection of his political writings.

9 Lawrence and Wishart, Communist Party publishing firm.

10 Michael Grieve.

1950

31 To Sorley MacLean

[Cambridge, 24 February 1950]

Dear Sam,

I'd forgotten I still had your own copy of *Dain do Eimhir*.[1] Anyway here it is now, with many thanks for the loan.

I enclose also:

a) Two copies of the *Communist Review*, which contain interesting articles on Ireland by my friend Andrew Boyd.[2]

b) The rough draft of an article I wrote for Forward on the Nat. question[3] – but never published, as the CP asked me to do a special essay on the N.Q. for the Pollittburo. (This last was very well received, and is still going the rounds. Now Willie Gallacher is out, the Party is going to do a lot of revaluing – and – unless I'm off the track altogether – there will be a big advance on the Scottish front before the year's out.)

c) A spare copy of the *Worker* article[4] on yourself, in case you would like to have this.

James Macdonald[5] tells me he's going to talk about the Cuillin to the Celtic society of the University. In spite of the language problem I think he should do this fairly sensibly, for he's an intelligent lad.

A rivederci! Hamish

[PS] Yesterday I had lunch with Piero Sraffa[6] in Trinity.

---

1 *Dain do Eimhir agus Dain Eile* (*'Poems to Eimhir'*), MacLean's second book. (William MacLellan: Glasgow, 1943).

2 Andrew Boyd, Northern Irish journalist; 'a Protestant Republican' (H.H.).

3 An article on 'the National question' written for the internal consumption of the Politburo of the Communist Party of Great Britain. Henderson makes a play on Harry Pollitt's name: Pollitt was Chairman of the Communist Party.

4 'There's a Fine Poet in Gaelic', *Daily Worker*, 24 November 1949; reprinted in *Alias MacAlias*.

5 James Macdonald, student at Edinburgh University. 'The Cuillin', MacLean's incomplete 'heroic' poem, written in 1939 when the poet was closest to Communism (*O Choille gu Bearradh*, 'From Wood to Ridge', Carcanet Press: Manchester, 1989).

6 Piero Sraffa (1898–1983), Italian Marxist and economics lecturer at Cambridge from 1927. Sraffa had been a friend of Antonio Gramsci's; he gave Henderson much support and advice in his translation of Gramsci's *Prison Letters*. Sraffa was a close friend of Ludwig Wittgenstein's at Cambridge.

32 To Sorley MacLean

[Paris,[1] 11 March 1950]

Dear Sam,

In this number of *Soviet Literature*,[2] a particularly good one, you will find an article on Pablo Neruda[3] which I'm sure will interest you.

I'm installed in a little hotel in the rue Hachette, which is Elliot Paul's[4] 'narrow street'. Being in Paris again is marvellous – especially as I can afford the occasional meal! (My life here before the war can be well summed up in the celebrated Marx Brothers' crack: 'Will you be able to live in New York on three dollars a day? Why brother you'll live like a prince – of course, you won't be able to eat . . . But you'll live like a prince.')

Another advantage is that the prestige of the Scots – always high – seems actually to have risen. This is partly due to the fact that the narrow defeat of Churchill in the elections is attributed here to the last minute intervention of Scotland . . . The relieving pipes of Sir Colin Campbell weren't in it![5]

But the real reason is that Paris is still the finest capital in Europe. As the literate Irish tenor James Joyce remarked, it's 'a lamp lit for lovers in the wood of the world'.

My best wishes to all the mucking makars and especially to the Bard – 'The holy, the high-born, the just one, the Bard, the cypress, the peacock, the lion, the Bard – from the Cafe to the Coogate one Bullshine, the Bard'.[6]

Yours ever, Hamish

[PS] Don't write to above address, as I'm moving on shortly. At the Brasserie Sarah Bernhardt you can get (but for 90 francs, i.e. about 2/-) as nice a bottle of Dublin-brewed Guinness as I've tasted outside McDades.[7]

---

1 Henderson visited Paris en route to Italy.

2 *Soviet Literature*, literary magazine published in English in Moscow.

3 Pablo Neruda (1905–73), Chilean poet.

4 Elliot Paul (1891–1958), author of *A Narrow Street* (London, 1942); a reminiscence of Paris.

5 'This refers to Sir Colin Campbell, the reliever of Lucknow. A Scots girl, Jessie Brown, is supposed to have heard the pipes of the relieving army before anyone else' (H.H.).

6 Parody of the 'Soldier's Song' in James Elroy Flecker's *Hassan*.

7 McDade's, a famous 'literary' pub in Dublin.

33 To Marian Sugden

[Paris, 16 March 1950]

Dear Marian,

Thawing rapidly in the bright Spring sunshine, I have begun to write up my story of Dylan in Bloomsbury under the title of 'that dolphin-torn, that gong-tormented face'.[1] It's libellous, of course, but Edward[2] will likely leap at it. You remember — Niagara from the balcony!

I am writing this in a little café near the Odéon station of the métro. Over the way is the fine statue which the city of Paris put up to Danton. And looking at it fixedly — the bulky body, the broad intransigent face, the imperious little snout — I realized who it's like. None but our old friend Marshal Tito! . . . And oddly enough, in the mass of papers beside me, I found in a moment a passage in *Les Nouvelles Yougoslaves* (even more lavish than its English counterpart) which sounds like Danton in 1792:

Que les hommes envisagent la réalité avec audace, qu'ils ne craignent pas les difficultés, et nous triompherons . . . Nous vivons en pleine transformation révolutionnaire de la société de notre pays, et la révolution ne plaisante pas, la révolution ne peut jouer avec des concessions.[3]

Who was that? Tito — just a month ago.

But don't get me wrong — I'm sure the policy of the Jacobins, the policy of Robespierre was the right one in 1794 . . . (By the way, did you ever read *Danton's Death* by Georg Büchner? — one of the very few German writers for whose intellect I have any respect.)

Rooting around yesterday in the book-stalls along the river I found an old collection of Scottish and Irish songs which contained 'The Lark in the Clear Air'[4] — I wonder if I ever sang it to you:

Dear thoughts are in my mind
And my soul soars enchanted[5]

---

1 This reminiscence, 'that dolphin torn, that gong-tormented face', was published in *Cencrastus* no. 47, Spring 1994.

2 E.P. Thompson.

3 Trans. 'Let men face up to reality, with boldness, let them not fear difficulties, and we shall triumph — we are living in the midst of a complete revolutionary transformation of the society in our country — and the revolution doesn't joke; the revolution cannot play around with concessions' (H.H.).

4 The author of the song was Sir Samuel Ferguson. Henderson recalls it was one of his mother's favourite songs; he refers to it in his discussion of

MacDiarmid's poem 'The Watergaw' in his article 'The Laverock I' The Caller Lift', *Cencrastus* no. 50, Winter 1994.

5 The rest of this letter is missing.

34 To Hugh MacDiarmid
[*EUL*]

[Milan, 13 April 1950]

My dear Chris,

I've just heard from James Macdonald that you've been given an annual pension of £150. Many congratulations! It's grand news. After all, money is money — whether it's Somerset Maugham's or the House of Hanover's.

There is a certain irony, of course, in the fact that the amount of the pension is exactly the same as a parliamentary deposit[1] — however, I'll leave it to your biographers to find the right formula! The main thing is have the dough, a solid advantage in these difficult days.

Here in Italy I've made a certain hit with my revelations of the last days of Mussolini — *l'Unità*[2] is paying me generously, so life is lovelier on the Henderson front. Italy, indeed, is very nice — especially at meal-times. And also in the evenings, in the public gardens . . . they call it easing the Spring!

Bill Lauchlan[3] — or rather Bob Horne[4] of the cultural committee — is chivvying me for the text of the *Hymns of Lenin*.[5] Before I send them this, I would like to have the text of three poems in *Lucky Poet* — the three I mentioned in a previous letter. If I do not receive them fairly shortly I will assume that you do not want to include them, and prepare the text of the poems already received.

The controversy on my *Worker* articles[6] continues sporadically. I include the cutting of a letter recently sent to the *Worker* by Marian,[7] my 'amie' of the idyllic weeks in Chesterton — also an article in which you are mentioned.

Some time ago I asked Calum[8] for two copies of the number of the *Voice* which contained the Neruda poems. So far there is no sign of these . . . and no sign of the Irish number.

Best wishes, Hamish

[PS] Love to Valda & Mike.

1 MacDiarmid stood for Parliament as an Independent Scottish Nationalist candidate for the Kelvingrove constituency in the 1950 General Election.

2 Henderson wrote a series of articles for *L'Unità*, the Italian Communist Party newspaper, describing his experiences with Partisans and the surrender of Marshal Graziani in April 1945, which he witnessed.

3 Bill Lauchlan, Secretary of the Scottish Committee of the Communist Party of Great Britain.

4 Bob Horne, official of the Communist Party of Great Britain.

5 The Scottish Committee of the Communist Party proposed publishing a
 selection of MacDiarmid's poetry, edited by Henderson. This never appeared;
 the contents are listed in Letter 49.
6 *Daily Worker.*
7 Marian Sugden.
8 Calum Campbell of the Caledonian Press.

35 Hugh MacDiarmid to Hamish Henderson

[Dungavel, by Strathaven, 18 April 1950]

My dear Hamish,

Many thanks for your various letters etc. and for the copies of *l'Unità*. I am very
glad you have been able to get these articles published and that payment has been
adequate to ease your position.

Th Civil List Pension will certainly make a big difference to us here. I had of
course no hesitation in accepting it, tho' some of the fool newspapers were anxious
to know how I reconciled acceptance of it with my Republicanism. However the
matter is not supposed to be public until the Honours List is published next month.
The *Daily Mail* got hold of it by a gross breach of confidence (which may yet give
me trouble – tho' I was in no way personally to blame – with the Prime Minister's
office). So I have put off the enquiring journalists who have been buzzing round me
until then – after which I do not think I will have the slightest difficulty in showing
that I can quite easily reconcile the two things!

Have you heard from Jack Lindsay about the Lenin poems? He wanted them for
some new poetry series Fore Publications are to publish, but I told him you had
them.

I am enclosing now the poems you mentioned – at least I think so. The trouble is
I've mislaid your previous letter in which you listed them, so I'm having to go by
my not-too-good memory.

This is just a hasty note to get them off to you now. I'll write you a longer and
more interesting letter soon – I hope! – taking it for granted that the address to
which I am sending this will continue to find you.

As you probably know, Wilkie[1] took over and now edits the National Weekly –
under its changed name, *The Nationalist*. This change-over was a fait accompli
before Kenneth, Calum, Wilkie or anybody told me anything about it. Wilkie, it
seems, is only prepared to guarantee it personally for 6 weeks to see how it does –
but 6 weeks isn't long enough for any attempt to increase circulation or secure
adverts to bear fruit. It seems that if he gives it up then, Kenneth is not prepared to
carry it on.

Altho' Kenneth did not breathe a word to me of above impending change he
spent the weekend prior to it out here, and we discussed the Irish number of the
Voice of Scotland. He said he'd have it out by Easter. Well, Easter has come and

gone and there is no sign of it. I feel, like yourself, extremely sore about the whole thing. I cannot understand Kenneth's attitude at all nor does he seem willing to give me any explanation. The whole business is quite disappointing and – on any charitable assumption – quite inexplicable.

I haven't been into Glasgow for a week or two now, but I'll try to get in this week or, at latest, next, and clear the whole position up. At the same time I'll try to get hold of a couple of copies of the issue with the Neruda, and send them to you.

Excuse this very scrappy and worried epistle. Better luck next time! Valda and Mike (who is on holiday here just now) are O.K. and physically at least so am I. All of us send you our affectionate greetings and best wishes.

Yours, Chris

---

1 Robert Blair Wilkie; Blair stood as an Independent Scottish Nationalist in the Camlachie by-election in 1947. Henderson, who was working on the *Elegies* at Carradale, gave a speech of support during the campaign.

36 To Marian Sugden

[Milan, undated May 1950]

Dear Marian,

I went back to Milan for 25 April, which was celebrated in grand style[1] – *Viva Milano, capitale dell' Insurrezione!* There met Bobi, an Austrian Partisan, who fought with the Division Potente in Tuscany: we celebrated the 25th with a glorious reunion at Luigi's.[2] Also present, Antonio Salari who came forward with us into the Apennines after fighting in Florence.

On the back of this you'll see the *cose pazzesche*[3] which I wrote the other day on a brand-new Olivetti teleprinter – the first time I'd used one.

Today I met Rocco Scotellaro[4], who is not only a poet of some note but also *sindaco* of his own *paese* near Matera (Lucania). It was nice to meet a *meridionale* among all these sophisticated northerners – R. has the odd mixture of taciturnity and exuberance usually shown by Hielandmen when out of their depth, or at any rate away from their native heath.

Here is a translation of the opening of John Donne's 'Hymn to God' given me yesterday by a bloke called de Francesco.

Poi che già scorgo la tua sacra stanza
Ed il coro di santi ove per sempre
Io diverro tua musica; fin d'ora
Qui l'istrumento intorno àlle tue tempre,
Médito, qui alle porte, ora, l'Allora.

Mentre per zelo i Medici si fanno
Cosmografi e disteso io Planisferio
In questo letto; se mi diano sorte
Che qui si scopra il Passo di Sud-Ovest
Per fretum febris – per angustiè, morte,
Godrò: per queste angustìe è il mio Occidente.

Any more news of the McBane of Glasgie?
Saluti to everyone.

Love, Hamish

---

1 Anniversary of the Partisan insurrection which coincided with the final assault
   on the Axis lines in the north of Italy.
2 Luigi Castigliano.
3 Trans. 'stupid things' (H.H.).
4 Rocco Scotellaro (1923–53), Italian poet, associated with Neo-realism.

37 To Hugh MacDiarmid
[*EUL*]

[Milan, 2 May 1950]

Dear Chris,

Thanks for the poems. The only ones now missing are: the one on Edinburgh from *Lucky Poet*, and 'If there are bounds to any man' (*2nd Hymn to Lenin*).[1]

I am working hard on Antonio Gramsci's[2] 'Letters from Prison', a book of the first importance. G. was certainly the most important Marxist thinker outside Russia in the period 1920–35. His *Machiavelli and the Modern State* (just published) is a book which will certainly take its place among Marxist classics.

What you tell me about the Irish number[3] is not very encouraging. Remember this, that the work of collecting material was started over a year ago in full agreement with yourself. If the Irish number fails to come out, our name will be mud all over green Erin. This will not help the Scottish cause in any way that I can see.

Please put one or two numbers of *The Nationalist* in the post for me, as well as the copies of the *Voice*. I'd like to see what way the wee breath of Wilkie wind is now blowing.

All the best to Valda and Mike,

Yours, Hamish

[PS] If Kenny decides not to produce the Irish number, get the material from him and get another printer to produce it. I think I can maybe borrow enough dough to cover the expenses.

H.

1 The poems were to be included in the proposed *Selected Poems* referred to in Letters 34 and 49; *Lucky Poet: A Self-Study in Literature and Political Ideas, being the Autobiography of Hugh MacDiarmid* (Methuen: London, 1943).

2 Antonio Gramsci (1891–1937), Italian Marxist philosopher. Henderson had first heard of Gramsci through his comrades in the Partisans in 1944. His friend Amleto Micozzi sent him copies of Gramsci's writings, including the 1947 edition of the *Lettere dal Carcere*, as they appeared, see Letters 145 and 185. He began his translations in Belfast in 1948, and used the prize money from the Somerset Maugham Award to travel to Italy to research the book further. He completed his translation in 1951; however, it was not published until 1974, when it appeared in *New Edinburgh Review* nos 25 and 26 (reprinted by Zwan Publications: London, 1988).

3 The Irish number of *Voice of Scotland*.

38 Piero Sraffa to Hamish Henderson

[Trinity College Cambridge, 17 June 1950]

Dear Hamish,

I was thrown into a panic by your letter for, instead of asking me as I expected for help in understanding the Italian, all your questions are about how to say it in English!

I enclose such answers as, with the help of others, & some search in the Library (largely fruitless) I have been able to put together. As regards Croce's philosophical terms however one must take the English translations of his works, read a good deal of them & find out how they are rendered: this I cannot bring myself to do. On English philosophical jargon however Ambrogio Donini[1] whom no doubt you will meet in Rome (at the Gramsci Foundation) can help you more than I can.

I entirely agree with your plan of paragraphing and saying so in the Preface.

As regards 'filosofia della prassi'[2] this was in many cases a cryptogram to avoid such words as 'marxism' or 'historical materialism' which would have caused trouble with the prison authorities. Before deciding how to handle this, read the reference to this matter in the Preface to Gramsci's 'Materialismo storico e filosofia di Croce' second half of p. xix.[3]

I am keepng your letter & shall try to find the answer to some more of your queries.

Hope to see you in Milan this summer (end of July?).

Best wishes to Carlo[4] and Al.[5]

Yours, Piero Sraffa

---

1 Ambrogio Donini, left-wing Professor of English at the University of Rome.
2 'Philosophy of praxis'.

3 *Historical Materialism and the Philosophy of Croce*, Antonio Gramsci (Einaudi: Milan, 1948). The passage referred to by Sraffa elaborates on the severe censorship of the prison authorities, and Gramsci's strategy of avoiding Marxist terminology, especially at the beginning of a new notebook.

4 Carlo Gramsci, youngest brother of Antonio Gramsci; Henderson met him in Italy and he provided useful information about his family's Sardinian background, as well as helping Henderson to translate some of the Sardinian expressions in the Prison Letters.

5 Al; (ex-) Prince Aldovrandi, who ran a left-wing bookshop in Milan.

39 Hugh MacDiarmid to Hamish Henderson

[Dunvagel, by Strathaven, 19 July 1950]

Dear Hamish,

Sorry to have been so long in writing you, but I have had — and have — worries enough. The National Coal Board have bought this estate and we have to be out of it by the end of August, so are again engaged in the desperate business of trying to get a house — so far without success.[1]

I was getting on well too with all sorts of writing before this upset: but Heaven knows now when I'll be able to get working conditions again. However I've got a lot done.

Re the 'Voice' I think we'll manage this yet. I tried various other printers but the cost was prohibitive. You know Wilkie tried over the 'National Weekly' — and lost about £350 on it. Kenneth's still putting it out as a single sheet, but that's no use at all, and the circulation is down to zero. But I think we'll get it going again ere long on the old basis, and also restart the 'Voice'. I quite appreciate how the Irish writers must feel, but it has simply been impossible to do anything yet. If I had understood sooner what was happening I could have seen to it — but Kenneth kept assuring me that he had the matter in hand and that it would be published all right soon. That misled me entirely — and then the ruinous change in the 'National Weekly', with Wilkie taking over, was carried through without a word to me at all.

Many thanks for your letters, stamps for Mike, *Unità* cuttings etc. I was particularly glad to get the Italian translation of Stalin on the linguistic controversy[2], which as you say settles the hash of our Anglicisers.

I hope all is well with you. Pity you are not to be in Scotland for the PEN Congress. There's a racket there in collaboration with Unesco, where I'll be fighting a lone battle, unless there are one or two of the foreign delegates I don't know of yet on my side. Valda and I will be in Edinburgh for the last fortnight of August for that.

I enclose copies of the two poems you want.

Yours, Chris

1 The Grieves had moved to a laundry cottage on the Dunvagel estate, offered to them by the Duke of Hamilton; in June 1950 the Estate was bought by the Scottish National Coal Board, and MacDiarmid was forced to look for a new home.

2 A translation of Stalin's essay 'On Linguistics'.

40 To Marian Sugden

[Milan, 4 September 1950]

Dear Marian,

I'm very sorry for this long delay in writing – chiefly due to marathon work on my Gramsci translation, which is now properly taking shape. Also a number of other things, such as correction of the Iti [*sic*] translation of my own *Elegies*, coping with the problems of the translator (a clerk in the Roman office of the CIT[1] who's finding life very difficult) and acting as a *cicerone* to several groups of CP members who've holidayed in Italy. The result is I've taken refuge in Tuscany,[2] and I'm going to try and stay here until the translation is finished.

Your letter in *Reynolds*[3] had all sorts of unexpected consequences. In the first place, it put me in touch again with Andy Boyd, a very decent lad: and through him I met the cast of the Liverpool Unity[4] who were camping out in an unfurnished villa near Lecco. I spent several days with them, bathing in the lake and exchanging songs. I also learnt several new Alpine songs from the local lads – such as 'Quando saremo fora fora dalla Valsugana',[5] and a first-rate satirical parody of the 'Stornello del Marinaio'.[6]

Verra un di . . . finirà . . .
La cucagna dei democristian
Ed allora marciamo compatti
Col nostro TOGLIATTI per la libertà[7]

1 The Italian Tourist Board.
2 Henderson stayed in a villa near Siena belonging to the philosopher Leone Vivante.
3 *Reynolds News*, left-wing Sunday newspaper.
4 Liverpool Unity, left-wing theatre group.
5 Trans. 'When we'll be away from the Valsugana' (H.H.).
6 Trans. 'Song of the Sailor' (H.H.).
7 Trans. 'The day will come, when the Christian Democrats' antics will finish – and then we shall march in good order, with our Togliatti* for freedom' (H.H.).

* Togliatti, leader of the Italian Communist Party.

This was a popular political song of the time.
The rest of this letter is missing.

1951

41 Carlo Gramsci[1] to Hamish Henderson

[30 January 1951]

Caro Hamish —

Solo ieri Al mi ha dato il tuo indirizzo-voglio ringraziarti degli auguri che mi hai inviato tempo fa e ricambiarli con viva cordialità.

Sono stato lieto di apprendere che ti sei sistemato a Cambridge con un lavoro di soddisfazione.

E le "Lettere"? Quando si pubblicheranno? Io ho cambiato l'impiego all' [illegible] purtroppo sento un po il disaggio della nuova situazione. Sto però bene di salute. Considerami sempre buon amico. Ricorda che avrò sempre con interesse tue notizie. Una stretta di mano.

Carlo Gramsci

---

1 Trans. 'Dear Hamish. Only yesterday Al gave me your address. I'd like to thank you for all the good wishes you sent me some time ago, and to reciprocate heartily. I was glad to know that you've got settled in, in Cambridge and have work that satisfies you.

And the "Letters"? When will they be published? I've changed the job I had at the [illegible]; unfortunately I'm not really settled into my new position, but my health is all right. Always consider me your good friend. I'll always be glad to get your news. A firm handshake, Carlo Gramsci. (H.H.).

42 Ewan MacColl[1] to Hamish Henderson

[Cheshire, 16 February 1951]

Dear Hamish,

Just a brief note — there is a character wandering around this sceptred isle at the moment yclept Alan Lomax.[2] He is a Texan and the none the worse for that, he is also just about the most important name in American folksong circles. He is over here with a super recording unit and a girl, Robin Roberts, who sings like an angel. Columbia gramophone Co. are financing his trip. The idea is that he will record the folk-singers of a group of countries (he has already covered Africa — America — the West Indies — the Central European countries). And Columbia will produce an album of discs — an hour for each country. He is not interested in trained singers or refined versions of the folksongs. He wants to record traditional-style singers doing ballads, work songs, political satires etc. It occurred to me that you could help him in two ways.

1. Record some of your soldier songs and any other songs you know. You sang some to me in the little cafe opposite the Epworth Hall.

2. Introduce him to other Scots folk-singers.

You know the kind of thing he wants: bothy songs, street songs, soldier songs, mouth music, the big Gaelic stuff, weavers' and miners' songs, etc.

This is important, Hamish. It is vital that Scotland is well represented in this collection. It would be fatal if the 'folksy' boys were to cash in.

If you can help, write to him – Alan Lomax c/o BBC, London. He intends coming to Scotland in about a week's time.

Do try and help.

Yours aye, Ewan

PS If and when you meet him, get him to sing some of his American coal miners' songs. They are terrific.

---

1 Ewan MacColl (1915–89), pseudonym of Jimmy Miller; folk-singer, collector, playwright, author, and political activist. Henderson met MacColl in 1946 on Theatre Workshop's first visit to Scotland.

2 Alan Lomax (b. 1915), American folklorist, collector and author, son of the folklorist John A. Lomax. For more details of the collecting tours with Lomax in the Summer of 1951, on which Henderson acted as guide, see Letters 52 and 53.

43 Ewan MacColl to Hamish Henderson

[Manchester, 12 April 1951]

Dear Hamish,

We are back from a very successful Scandinavian tour and next week are off to do a month of one-night stands in the Durham and Northumberland coal fields.

How are things with you? Have you finished the book of the Gracci [sic] letters yet?[1] More important from our point of view, have you access to any literary periodicals at the moment?

In spite of our tremendous success in Scandinavia we are still meeting with a fair amount of political discrimination. We find it extremely difficult to book theatres in the big centres like London, Manchester, Glasgow, Edinburgh etc. We are consequently attempting to launch some kind of publicity campaign which we hope will have sufficient cumulative effect to open the doors of the theatres which are at present closed to us. The only kind of campaign which [is] worth a damn is articles in the national press and widely circulating magazines. If you have any spare time at all you would be helping us enormously by doing an article on us. You would also be striking a good blow for peace.

I seem always to be bothering you with requests and demands, few of which are ever realized. Hope, however, springs eternal, even in our breasts.

Love from everybody, Ewan

---

1 Gramsci's *Prison Letters*.

44 To Marian Sugden

The news about poor Angelina[1] was heart-rending. How dreadful you must have felt! I wondered if you would like a coronach for her, but I hadn't the heart to write it.

[Edinburgh, 12 May 1951]

Dear Marian,

Congratulations on the third broadsheet,[2] esp. from François Joseph Cariglioli, a mercurial little architect from Algeria who's married to a Scots lass. He says the Greek poem is 'from the heart'. A bouquet also from members of the Scottish Cultural Committee,[3] most mentioning the Tom McGrath poem. (And the Greek.)

The Maclean March[4] is selling in Edin., Glasgow, Dundee, Aberdeen, Oban, Kilmarnock, Paisley and ither landwart pairts. Just now I'm writing a new ballad, the Ballad of the Gillie More,[5] I'll send it to you when it's finished. The idea was suggested by an announcement during the Congress of the Scottish—USSR Soc. that a greeting message had been sent 'from the blacksmiths of Leith to the blacksmiths of Kiev'.

Gramsci. Lehmann has become distinctly difficult,[6] wants to cut 20%, and breathes ominous words about the Circe letters. I think they cut a little too deep into his soft underbelly. If necessary I can bring the big guns of Einaudi[7] to bear on him (Sraffa is au courant with developments, leaves for a few days in Italy at the end of this month) but am chary of doing so in case it queers the whole project.

Edward Haliburton[8] is now re-united to his wife, and is in much better fettle. Erich Geiringer[9] tells me that he would not have believed the improvement could be so great . . . As for the Countess,[10] she is cavorting through the USA out-gospelling the hot gospellers. I enclose a pamphlet which should give you both a happy 'quart d'heure'. I bet she becomes a Mother Divine before she's through!

Thanks a million for the corduroy breeks, damned useful. I'll send you the dough shortly. The Scottish BBC is doing a series of talks and features by me which'll bring me in a fair amount, but they're unwilling to sign me on in any permanent capacity. The finger still hovers it seems.

Last weekend I was out at Newbattle Abbey[11] (College for Adult Education) giving a talk on 'Highlands & Lowlands'. It was a weekend course organized by Edwin Muir[12] and the British Council for both foreign and Scottish students. After it I had a long talk with both Willa and Edwin over some excellent vermouth. If the worst comes to the worst and I have to retreat back into adult ed. I think I could always land a job out at Newbattle.

So far I haven't had time to see MacDiarmid (he's now in a cottage at Biggar[13]) but I saw Valda at the première of 'Spindrift', a play about the Kintyre fishermen by Naomi M.[14] and Danny Macintosh. Valda gave me all the gen: MacD. was treated royally in the Soviet Union, gave an uncenscred talk on Scottish nationalism over Moscow radio, and was knocked blind with vodka on several occasions. The Russians took to him, it seems, in no uncertain manner.

The Covenant[15] is organizing itself as a political party, country audiences singing the 23rd Psalm with great fervour. The CP[16] is still vacillating, congratulating the Stone reivers[17] one moment and condemning them for 'adventurism' the next. The Congress[18] (anti recall, civil disobedience are its planks) is gaining supporters (incidentally, it bought 200 copies of the Maclean March outright). The Catholic clique inside the Covenant seems to be gaining in strength . . . it looks as if MacCormick's[19] clever game has succeeded and that the Stone will come north again after all. (And Brer Fox — *per adesso sta zitto*[20]). All the best to Morris.[21]

Love, Hamish

---

1 A cat belonging to Marion Sugden.

2 *Poetry Broadsheet*, edited and published by Marian Sugden.

3 A committee of the Communist Party of Great Britain.

4 Henderson's 'John Maclean March', composed in 1948, published as a broadsheet by the Scottish Workers Music Association in 1951.

5 'The Gillie More', song written by Henderson in 1948 to the tune of 'Whistle o'er the Lave o't'.

6 An ongoing disagreement with his publisher: 'Lehmann had not realized there was so much (to him, dry) political matter in the [Gramsci] letters' (H.H.).

7 Einaudi, Italian publishers of Gramsci's work; Piero Sraffa.

8 Edward Haliburton, son of the Countess of Mayo; founded the Porch Philosophical Club in Edinburgh; meeting place for philosophical debates and gambling, and venue for numerous ceilidhs. It closed after a police raid in 1953.

9 Erich Geiringer, psychoanalyst; member of the Porch Club.

10 The Countess of Mayo, who formed her own 'fringe' religion.

11 Newbattle Abbey, Adult Education College in Edinburgh; see Letter 228.

12 Edwin Muir (1887–1957), Scottish poet and translator; Warden of Newbattle Abbey College from 1950 to 1955.

13 MacDiarmid moved to Brownsbank Cottage at Candymill, just outside Biggar, in January 1951, and lived there for the rest of his life.

14 Naomi Mitchison.

15 The Scottish Covenant, a petition demanding a Scottish Parliament, signed
   by over two million people.
16 Communist Party of Great Britain.
17 Henderson is referring to the 'liberation' of the Stone of Destiny from
   Westminster Abbey in 1948.
18 The Scottish National Congress was a political grouping to the left of the
   Scottish National Party, founded by Oliver Brown.
19 John MacCormick (1904–61); Nationalist politician; chairman of the SNP
   from 1934 to 1942. He left the SNP to found, and become Chairman of,
   the National Assembly and the Scottish Convention, also responsible for
   organizing the Scottish Covenant.
20 Trans. 'Brer Fox – him keeps quiet – for now' (H.H.).
21 Morris Sugden, Marian's husband.

45 Dominic Behan[1] to Hamish Henderson

[Dublin, 5 June 1951]

My Dear Hamish,

It is indeed with amazement that I realize it is now over a year since I heard from you, but for the fact of having received your 'John Maclean March', and that I read a letter of yours in the *Daily Worker*, plus the fact that a couple of people told me to the contrary, I should have given you up as dead.

What the bloody Hell (may I ask?) is wrong with you?, that you couldn't sit down and write a letter to an old friend.

However, all is forgiven and besides, your spake on Rabbie Burns in the *Worker* is nearly enough to save you from hanging for murder let alone not writing. I read your song a few times and the more I read it the more I like it, and I'm just waiting on Freddy May to come out of hospital to give me the proper air? so that I can sing it. By the way, my singing has improved remarkably since I gave up smoking (or so I am told), so I will probably be able to do justice to it.

No doubt you read about the Workers League[2] putting up a candidate in the recent election in Dublin South West. He only received 295 first preference votes, but this cannot be regarded as a true reflection of the popularity or such of the League in Dublin, as the church come out and attacked him from the pulpits, telling the people that should they vote for him they would be damned in Hell forever, in fact I personally consider him to have done very well, and the very fact that the Maynooth Maniacs think him sufficiently dangerous to come out so strongly against him, justifies me saying that the League is an organization of no little force in Irish politics and that things were not better for years, plus the fact that the IRA has swung very much to the left recently, and are preparing a very progressive public statement on America's war aims with regard to McBride's bargaining over partition and the Atlantic Pact, as well as the fact that Clann na

Poblachta[3] contested this election on a pull us in with America against Russia policy and were decisively beaten (they lost eight seats out of ten).

All this seems to me a pointer to a new development of class and national consciousness on the part of the people, and suggests that we are on the eve of a triumphant mass swing to the left.

Well Dear Friend, I don't think I have much more to say at the moment except to impress on you the necessity to my believing that I have not done anything wrong in not hearing from you. So please write as soon as you possibly can.

Yours faithfully, Dominic

1 Dominic Behan (1928–89), author and poet; younger brother of Brendan Behan. Henderson first met the Behan family in Dublin in 1948.
2 The Irish Workers League, the Irish equivalent of the Communist Party.
3 Clann na Poblachta (Children of the Republic); political party founded by Sean MacBride, son of Maud Gonne and Captain John MacBride.

46 To Hugh MacDiarmid
[*EUL*]

[Edinburgh, 12 June 1951]

Dear Chris,

A.E. Coppard has sent me the enclosed gen about the Authors Peace Appeal,[1] for onward transmission to yourself. So here it is.

I'm coming down to Biggar to see you one of these fine June days, because there are a lot of things I want to talk over with you, and get your ideas on.

First of all, the *Hymns to Lenin*, which are now being typed for me in three fair copies by Mrs Ashton of Aberdeen. I've made some small emendations which I'll show you. If things go according to plan, I'll have them out by the end of the year.

Secondly, the Gramsci. Lehmann has all the stuff now, but some difficulties have arisen which I'll explain to you when I come down.

And thirdly to fifty-sixthly, the present political set-up in Scotland, which I've been appraising since I returned from Italy.

I was up in Aberdeen recently: sang the Maclean March at the Miners' Congress Social. Both Abe Moffat and Bill Pearson[2] seemed to take to it.

Will you be at the Assembly[3] on the 23rd?

Love to Valda and Mike,

Yours ever, Hamish

1 The Authors Peace Appeal was inspired by the Communist Party of Great Britain.
2 Moffat and Pearson; leaders of the National Union of Mineworkers in Scotland.

3 The National Assembly, organized by John McCormick's Scottish Covenant
association.

47 Hugh MacDiarmid to Hamish Henderson
[*EUL*]

[Brownsbank, near Biggar, 14 June 1951]

Dear Hamish,

I had heard you were back in Alba, but could hear nothing about your
whereabouts and plans. I got the copy of the Maclean March all right, of
course, and would have written you at once – if I'd known where to write to.

I am sending Coppard a supporting message etc.

I'll look forward to hearing all about the Gramsci, the *Hymns to Lenin* etc, in due
course – but be sure to let me know in advance when you are coming down, as
both Valda and I are a great deal away and it is not safe just to chance it. The cottage
is about four miles on the Edinburgh side of Biggar and bus times are at hourly
intervals. One of the troubles is that we have no spare accommodation whatever in
this wee place, so you'd have to arrange matters to be sure of getting a return bus
or you'd be stranded. Fortunately it is handier for Edinburgh than for Glasgow –
about an hour's run to Edin^r whereas to go to Glasgow means about 10 minutes'
run into Biggar, half an hour's wait there for [the] Glasgow bus, then two hours'
run to Glasgow via Lanark, Carluke, Motherwell etc.

Yes, I intend to be at the Assembly on 23rd all right.

Every good wish,

Yours, Chris

48 To the Edinburgh *Evening Dispatch*

[Edinburgh, published 7 July 1951]

A Scottish Protestant by birth and upbringing, I feel it my duty to protest in the
most unequivocal terms against the march of the Orange Order through the streets
of our capital.

That this march is an unwarranted and gratuitous insult to the considerable
Catholic population of the city is bad enough. But far worse is the fact that this
episode marks a further encroachment on the Scottish scene of one of the least
edifying brands of virulent religious fanaticism.

Orangeism is alien to the Scottish tradition. Its mythology is a farrago of
unhistorical balderdash. The songs which its leaders still encourage their followers
to sing are not only so many ludicrous anachronisms – they are also recognizable
encouragements to violence.

'King Billy', the fetish of the Orange Order, was one of the most unpopular kings Scotland ever groaned under. His reign was disfigured by the infamous massacre of Glencoe. And as for the Battle of the Boyne, it was merely a phase in the struggle for European hegemony between Louis XIV and 'the rest' — 'the rest' including both William of Orange and the pope of the day.

I wonder how many Orangemen know that when news of the Boyne reached Rome, the Vatican blazed with light in honour of a victory of the Pope's Protestant ally?

Hamish Henderson

49 To Hugh MacDiarmid
[*EUL*]

[Edinburgh, 11 July 1951]

Dear Chris,

Here's the contents page[1] of the *Hymns to Lenin* — now all typed out, and about to be dispatched to Bill Lauchlan.

I've made one or two cuts for reasons of space — I'm sure you'll agree to them.[2] But nothing like as many cuts as Lehmann wants to make in the Gramsci: however, there his motive is clear — he wants to jettison all the intellectual content of the book and merely leave the picture of Gramsci as a suffering martyr.

Needless to say, I'm fighting him on this issue, and the Italian publisher is taking a strong line as well.

Just now I'm engaged in a running fight with Protestant Action over the Orange Walk in the columns of the *Evening Dispatch*.[3] My first letter went in on Saturday, roundly condemning the 'City Fathers' for permitting the March and asserting that Orangeism was alien to the Scottish tradition. Monday's issue (which contained a poem of your own, incidentally) had four letters supporting my line. But yesterday Cormack[4] and his jackals were in full cry, so I've just written another letter to bang their snouts a bit.

Love to Valda,

All the best, Hamish

[PS] Helen Cruickshank[5] has been a great help, for she has given me access to her complete MacDiarmid library.

What is the meaning of *Etika Preobrazhennavo Erosa*?[6]

Contents

Foreword .... (H.H.)

(53

3   The Seamless Garment ....

4   Second Hymn to Lenin ....

5   The Dead Liebknecht ....

6   Third Hymn to Lenin ....

7   To the Immortal Memory of John Maclean.................................

8   To the Young Poets of the World Today ....

9   Lo! A Child is born ....

10 Reflections in an Ironworks (from 2d Hymn) ....

11 In the Slaughterhouse (from 2d Hymn) ....

12 The Belly-grip ....

13 Ein Mann aus dem Volke (from 'Depth & the Chthonian Image')...........

14 Etika Preobrazhennavo Erosa...

15 Another Epitaph on an Army of Mercenaries..............................

16 Auld Reekie ....

17 Lamh Dearg Aboo ....

18 In the Slums of Glasgow ....

19 The Skeleton of the Future (at Lenin's Tomb)............................

---

1 This contents page refers to the proposed 'Selected Poems', edited by
   Henderson, and to be published by the Scottish Committee of the
   Communist Party, which never appeared.

2 The cuts were made in some of the longer poems, including 'On a Raised
   Beach' and 'Lament for the Great Music'.

3 See Letter 48.

4 John Cormack, Protestant activist; see Letters 212 and 213.

5 Helen B. Cruickshank (1886–1965), poet, born in Montrose; served as the
   Secretary of Scottish PEN. Cruickshank was a loyal supporter of
   MacDiarmid's and a lifelong friend of Henderson's.

6 Explained in Letter 50.

50 Hugh MacDiarmid to Hamish Henderson
[*EUL*]

[Broomsbank, near Biggar, 12 July 1951]

Dear Hamish,

Many thanks for your letter and for the contents list, which is O.K. As to the cuts which you have made there will of course be no question about these so long as they are just cuts (which may be indicated in the usual way by a few dots?). Alterations might have been more debatable. I am glad you had access to H.B.C.'s[1] collection of my books. All my own copies are in America at the moment, so if questions had arisen I myself could hardly have answered them.

Etika Preobrazhennavo Erosa = the ethics of brotherly love, but the phrase has a religious overlay, the basis of the brotherliness being a presumed Heavenly Father.

I hope your own dispute with Lehmann is satisfactorily settled. I fully appreciate the vital importance of not allowing the intellectual element to be excised and the whole thing confined to a sensational level.

I read the letters re Protestant Action in Monday's *Dispatch* but did not identify yours (was it the 'Disgusted Protestant' one[?]). That does not matter however; what does matter is that the issue has been joined and must be completely fought out. I am glad to see letters of protest in the *Scotsman* too. More power to your elbow.

YCL[2] Education Committee in London have just asked me to be one of the judges of the literary competitions on the Youth pamphlet, and I have of course agreed.

Since Tom Murray[3] went, I have heard scarcely anything about the Scottish USSR Society. I do not know MacAllister.[4] He wrote me weeks ago asking if I'd address meetings on my visit to the USSR and I replied in the affirmative. But I haven't heard another cheep from him.

My article on Ewan MacColl will be in this week's *Forward*.

Hope all is well with you. Will you still be in Edin[r] when Theatre Workshop are there? I hope so. I'll be through then too. Since the short season they have in Edin[r] will not leave them with any dough after defraying their expenses it has been requested that they also have a number of ceilidhs and if you are on the spot you might help to organize these.[4] I have already written to Norman MacCaig[5] about this and asked him to enlist Sorley too. Alan Lomax will take part and I understand Flora MacNeil and Calum Johnstone[6] have also agreed.

Kindest regards to Neil MacCallum of whom I have heard nothing for a long time. If you see him you might tell him I have been having an active correspondence with Geoffrey Wagner[7] and all seems to be going well in that quarter – I mean in regard to his work on Lewis Grassic Gibbon.

Valda joins me in all the best.

Yours, Chris

---

1 Helen B. Cruickshank.

2 Young Communist League.

3 Tom Murray, retiring secretary of the Scottish USSR Society; George MacAllister, newly appointed secretary of the Scottish USSR Society.

4 Henderson had already been put in charge of arranging this ceilidh by the People's Festival Committee, sponsored by the Labour Party.

5 Norman MacCaig (1910–96), poet; his first collection appeared in 1943, associated with the New Apocalypse poets; his *Collected Poems* appeared in 1990 (Chatto & Windus: London). MacCaig became a close friend of MacDiarmid's.

6 Flora MacNeil, Gaelic singer from Barra; Calum Johnstone, piper and singer.

7 Geoffrey Wagner, American academic writing a study of the works of the Scottish novelist Lewis Grassic Gibbon (Leslie Mitchell). His bibliography of Gibbon was published in Bibliothec no.1. It was at Henderson's suggestion that Wagner wrote to MacDiarmid, who had known and collaborated with Gibbon in the 1930s.

51 To Hugh MacDiarmid
[*EUL*]

[Edinburgh, 17 September 1951]

Dear Chris,

If you can locate that copy of my 'Notes on the National Question'[1] I'd like to have it as soon as possible.

Poetry Broadsheets (edited from Hill House, High St, Chesterton, Cambridge) is devoting its next number to a little MacDiarmid anthology. This will include 'In Memoriam Liam Mac 'Ille Iosa', the 'Mavis o' Paible' [sic] (from *To Circumjack Cencrastus*) and 'Staoiligary'[2]. I'll ask Marian Sugden to send you half a dozen copies.

The People's Festival Committee has asked me to arrange another ceilidh to be held in December[3] — meanwhile, there's a 'Harvest Ceilidh' at Bo'ness on the 22nd, arranged to go with the Young Scots' weekend school. I'm trying to rout up some singers for it. Will you be there?

Kingsley Martin[4] was up here at the weekend speaking on China and trying to size up the Scottish situation. I gave him plenty of gen — though what he'll do with it Christ only knows. What I tried to get into his head was that the Labour Party may forfeit enough support in Scotland to lose the election unless it makes a definite gesture over Home Rule.

Love to Valda,

Yours ever, Hamish

[PS] Honor Arundel[5] gave the Ceilidh a very good review in the *Worker*.[6] The only thing she found to criticize about the People's Festival Week was that it hadn't devoted an evening to the works of 'that veteran fighter for Scottish independence, Hugh MacDiarmid'.

---

1 These notes formed the basis of a lecture Henderson gave to local branches of the Communist Party.

2 'In Memoriam Liam Mac Ille Iosa appears in *Stony Limits and Other Poems* (Gollancz: London, 1934); 'Staoiligary' appears in *To Circumjack Cencrastus* (Blackwood: Edinburgh, 1930).

3 The Festival Ceilidh held in August 1951 was a great success, and another was held to raise funds for the following year's events.

4 Editor of the *New Statesman and Nation*.

5 Honor Arundel, Marxist critic and author, wife of the actor Alex McCrindle
(best known for his role as 'Dick Barton: Special Agent'); the McCrindles
were close friends of MacDiarmid's.

6 *Daily Worker*.

52 Alan Lomax to Hamish Henderson

[c/o The BBC, Glasgow, 20 September 1951]

Dear Hamish Henderson,

I've been travelling the roads of the world, hitting the high places and low
places, the rough and the smooth, for about twenty years, recording folksongs and
ballads from all sorts of people, but I have never had such kind and warm-hearted
treatment from anywhere as from the people of Scotland, and I just wanted to
write you this letter and tell you how much I appreciated this. It makes all kinds of
difference when you're a long way from home, to be treated like you were a
member of the family.

What you have done, however, is to help the folksongs of your country to be
better known. Thank you for your songs, which will be listened to by scholars and
just ordinary people with the greatest interest and pleasure.

The people of Scotland recorded about 25 hours of their folksongs this summer.
The whole set will go to the University of Edinburgh folklore archive[1] for the
permanent benefit of the Scottish people. Some will go to the BBC Permanent
Records Library, and some will be published by the Columbia Recording Company
in New York City, and some will be used in my BBC broadcasts. And all will be
deposited in a museum in the USA. No use will be made of the records by me
without first obtaining your written permission.

'Tail Toddle' and 'Wap and Row'[2] of the folklore you recorded for me are
being incorporated in the album of Scots folksongs I am preparing for publication
by Columbia Recording Company in the States this year. There is a money order
for the token fee paid for your permission to permit Columbia to put this Folklore
of the Scots Album in the World Library of Folk Music. This does not limit any
other use you make of it. I hope you will be as generous with the next collector as
you have been with me.

Please sign the attached form and return it to me.

Yours cordially, Alan Lomax

1 These recordings became the first deposits in the archives of the School of
Scottish Studies, Edinburgh University.

2 Henderson's performances of these traditional songs appeared on vol. VI
(Scotland) of the Columbia World Albums of Folk and Primitive Song, edited
and produced by Alan Lomax.

53 Alan Lomax to Hamish Henderson

[c/o The BBC, London, 22 October 1951]

Dear Hamish,

I did my best in two rather uncomfortable conversations with Gordon Gildard and Hugh McPhee[1] to get your excellent ceilidh on the air, but in tune with the sometimes timorous policy of Glasgow, they turned it down. I made quite a scene about it – but that's it. I am planning to try again here in London when the moment is right, in the meantime if you people can arrange to make your own copy of it there, I will send you the tapes. A copy of these tapes is deposited with the rest of my collection in Edinburgh University, in charge of Dr Newman,[2] and this letter will serve as authorization for you and the committee to be allowed to get to those copies if you want to.

I called you a couple of times on my last visit to Edinburgh, but never got you in. I am sorry I didn't see you again, for you were certainly most kind to me, and to you belongs the major share of credit in an interesting, if difficult summer. Perhaps the fee enclosed will seem low, but that is a bit more than your share of the cash I am allowed by Columbia to spend on the album. As you know, this thing is still in its experimental stage.

The various fees for which you sent me a receipt sometime since, all came out of my own pocket so you have been recompensed, at least so far as I could afford it.

I hope your job plan has worked out. If I were you, I would write to Gildard and suggest that a part-time collector of Scots ballads and songs would be a useful addition to the Glasgow staff. I would certainly back you up in such an application, or indeed in any other enterprise of yours in which I could help.

All the best,

     Yours, Alan Lomax

---

1 Hugh McPhee, head of the Gaelic Department of BBC Scotland.
2 Professor S.T.M. Newman, Reid Professor of Music at Edinburgh University.

54 To Marian Sugden

[Edinburgh, 29 November 1951]

Dear Marian,

There's an Alan Lomax programme on Tuesday called *I Heard Scotland Sing* (Sc. Home Service, and I think London regional too, at 8 p.m.). Listen in to it; it's really good. A lot of the singers took part in the People's Festival ceilidh I told you about. Highlights: Mary Morrison (of Barra) mimicking the pipes in superb mouth-music, Jimmy MacBeath[1] the tinker-singer discussing Shakespeare's *Macbeth*, and a ceilidh we had up in Aberdeenshire during which I sing 'Tail Toddle'! Also bits from the People's Festival ceilidh.

From 1 January I shall be on a three months' tour of the north financed by the School of Scottish Studies, Edin. University, collecting ballads and finding singers. God's own job — and hospitality money provided. The truth is that the University people were so impressed by Lomax's achievements (the amount of fine singing we collected in a short time clear bowled 'em over) that they've disregarded my suspect politics at long last and offered me a job!

Mica male![2] About time too. (The 'hospitality money' means that I'm entitled to put down as expenses the occasional drop of the immortal cratur for adding the edge to fiddle tune or song.)

> And sae at last this bonnie cat
> he had a stroke o' luck . . .

The Gramsci position is the same as before, it appears. Bloody annoying. All the best to you both (and regards to maters, paters etc.).

> Love, Hamish

---

1 Jimmy MacBeath (1894–1972), one of the most charismatic folk-singers to emerge during the folksong revival; known as the last great 'King of the Corn-kisters'. See Henderson's obituary in *Tocher* no. 12, Winter 1973, reprinted in *Alias MacAlias*.
2 Trans. 'Not bad' (H.H.).

55 To Marian Sugden

[Edinburgh, 12 December 1951]

Dear Marian,

When I saw Julian Rea at Monty Slater's party the other night, I was fearing that I couldn't come down for Christmas — but now my departure for Banffshire is delayed till 3 Jan., so you'll be seeing me again a day or two before Christmas — maybe the 21st or 22nd. *E poi — Evviva!*[1]

I was in London helping Lomax to prepare the notes for his Scottish album. It was hard work keeping his sloppy prose from spilling all over them. He wanted to call Kate Nicolson's milking song a 'Cow's Croon'! I asked him: did you ever hear a cow croon? But the album itself is 'mighty fine'.

Some of the waulking songs he has have grand poetry in them:

> Eho hao hì ó
> Tonight is the first night of Autumn
> Eho hao ri ǹ o hógo
>
> Last night I heard them talking
> Between the head of the bay and the flood-tide.

It was not the voice of bitch or hound
It was the voice of a woman on the height of her ecstasy

O it was herself that made the decision:
She took the worthless and left the choice
She took the prudent sensible youth . . .[2]

Lehmann had renegued on the Gramsci.[3] Carogna! I'll tell you all about it when
I come down.
   All the best,

      Love, Hamish

[PS] Einaudi has just sent me *Passato e Presente*,[4] the latest Gramsci volume and the
last in the *Quaderni del Carcere* series. The next volume ('L'Ordine Nuovo'[5]) will
cover his writings and speeches between 1913 and 1926.
   I'm now negotiating with Dennis Dobson[6] for publication of the 'Letters'.

---

1 Trans. 'And then Yipee!' (H.H.).
2 From the waulking song, 'Nochd a' chiad oidhche an fhoghair' ('Tonight is
   the first night of Autumn . . .'). This song appears on vol. 6 of the
   Columbia World Library of Folk and Primitive Music, edited and produced
   by Alan Lomax, performed by women on Benbecula in the Outer Hebrides.
3 Lehmann had finally turned down *Prison Letters*.
4 *Past and Present*.
5 *New Order*.
6 Henderson met the publisher Dennis Dobson in Cambridge; the projected
   publication of the *Prison Letters* came to nothing as Dobson's firm went
   bankrupt.

1953

56 **To the** *Scotsman*

Sir,

Your correspondent, Mr A.J. Aitken, has summed up the linguistic problems facing Scotland with admirable lucidity. May I add one or two points by way of amplifying and documenting his general line of argument?

That upper-class southern English speech is very unlike Scottish speech is obvious. What is less often realized is that the dialects of North Oxford and South Kensington have altered a great deal in this present century and that certain features of these dialects which to an educated Scotsman have all the appearance of linguistic abuses have become more common even in the last ten years or so. The intrusive 'r' is an obvious example: it was heard much less frequently in the speech of BBC announcers before the war than it is today.

Fifty or sixty years ago the phrase 'at home' was pronounced in southern English very much as it was pronounced by Scots school masters (although the 'h' tended to be elided, and not only by 'Cockneys'). Nowadays a very usual pronunciation of this phrase is something like 'et heowm', an attempt to ape the prestige speech of Oxford and the English public schools. This tendency is carried to absurdity and (for me at least) to nausea in the 'refained' speech of certain pathetic creatures both north and south of the Border who imagine that they are counterfeiting a 'good-class accent'.

Realization that southern English speech is in a period of fairly rapid transition cannot fail to illuminate the plight of BBC announcers in Scotland. It is claimed that they are all conversant with the 'guid Scots tongue'. This may be so, but it is very difficult to move straight from a language in which certain organs of speech seem to be deliberately atrophied to a language in which, as in Italian, every part of the vocal apparatus is called into play.

One word to Mr Aitken. He is wrong if he thinks I want to 'impose' a granite-hard standard of Scottish-English speech. I went out of my way to emphasize that I want a flexible line which would encourage regionalisms. But in order to counter the present policy of forcible anglicization we must draw the line somewhere.

Let me put it like this. If an announcer pronounces 'Boer War' with the accent of Barra or the accent of Buchan, fair enough, but if he pronounces 'Boer War' as if he were a Pekingese barking defiance (*baw waw! baw waw!*), he should be out on his neck.

I am etc., Hamish Henderson

57 To the *Scotsman*
[*EUL*]

[Edinburgh, 17 February 1953]

Sir,

When I referred to the tape-recordings of Scots folksong, housed in the archives of the School of Scottish Studies, as a 'reference library', I certainly did not mean to imply that that was their only function. I only meant that where Scottish linguistic problems are concerned they constitute a court of appeal considerably more reliable than the average textbook.

It would be a great irony if your readers assumed that I did not want my recordings of Scots folksongs to be broadcast. On the contrary, I believe that the broadcasting of them would be an event of great cultural significance in Scotland.

The decision as to whether or not they should be broadcast does not, however, rest with me. It rests, I need hardly say, with the BBC and with the School of Scottish Studies, which owns the tapes.

It is possible that either one or both of these organizations may oppose the broadcasting of the great traditional songs which I have collected, but I consider it very unlikely. These songs lie near the heart of the older Scottish tradition; they are beyond doubt the genuine article as preserved and sung by people to whom it is still a living part of reality. As for the quality of performance, it has been described by individuals well qualified to judge – for example, Professor S.T.M. Newman, Dr Herbert Wiseman, and Mr William Montgomerie[1] – as on the whole exceedingly high.

One of the functions of a university is surely to inspire the people. And what is the most reasonable function of a broadcasting system if it is not to entertain the people (and provide them *viva voce* with some stimulating food for thought)? I cannot imagine a project in which these various aims and functions could be more happily combined than in the broadcasting of genuine Scots folksong to the Scottish people.

The singers, I might add, are all for it: they fail to see why second-rate performances and battered 'lyric gems' should monopolize the air for ever.

Needless to say, they seldom clear the hurdle. Even when announcing the names of the tunes in programmes of Scottish dance music, they usually pronounce the Scots words as if they were speaking a foreign language for which they felt a slight distaste. I often wish they could somehow get relayed back to them the vivid comments of a certain Aberdeenshire folk-singer who makes his croft ring with Lallans abuse at moments such as these.

It is not so long back since I heard 'The Muckin' o' Geordie's Byre' referred to as 'The Meukin of Jawdie's Beye-a' – the most gruesome blood-bath of vowels that ever savaged a living language!

What is the solution? The BBC has a great opportunity. If it rose to the occasion it could arrest the process of wholesale anglicization and give fresh dignity and currency, not only to Gaelic and Lallans, but also the traditional Scots-English of an older generation: an infinitely more pleasing speech, I may say, than the usual run of announcers' English. What is needed is an accepted standard of Scots-English pronunciation – not a hard and fast standard, but a flexible line which would permit, and indeed encourage, deviations to Highland and to Lowland. If we could get provisional agreement on the need for this – and the correspondence in your columns shows that there is widespread feeling in favour of such a move – we would shortly find, I think, that other parts of the English-speaking world would increasingly come to accept it as a standard. (I am thinking especially of the northern English of Tyne, Humber, and Tees, who would certainly prefer Scots-English to the Hampstead–Surbiton variety.)

The Italians say that the best Italian is *lingua toscana in bocca romana* (the Tuscan speech on Roman lips). Could we not have a shot at proving that the best English is *lingua inglese in bocca scozzese?*

It may be objected that we would have difficulty in agreeing on a standard. I do not think that there are any formidable obstacles. Use might well be made of the tape recordings in the archives of the School of Scottish Studies of Edinburgh University, which are not only an incomparable treasure house of the folksong of our country, as preserved by real folk-singers, but also a linguistic 'reference library' of the first importance.

> I am etc., Hamish Henderson

---

1 William Montgomerie (1904–94), poet and folklorist.

58 To Hugh MacDiarmid

[*EUL*]

[Edinburgh, 27 April 1953]

Dear Chris,

I've written a letter to the *New Statesman* (as from the writers interested in the Edin. Labour Festival Committee) protesting against the Labour Party ban.[1] Sydney[2] has signed it, and I've added your signature too, confident that you'd give the okay.

See you at the Makars meeting[3] on Friday.

> All the best, Hamish

[PS] The Porch Ceilidh[4] will be better than I at first thought it would be.

1 The Labour Party withdrew its support from the People's Festival; the specific reason was their objections to the pro-Stalinist line of Ewan MacColl's play *The Travellers*, performed during the 1952 People's Festival. See Letter 99.
2 Sydney Goodsir Smith (1915–75), poet; best known for his work in Lallans; member of the Makars Club.
3 The Makars Club met in the Abbotsford Bar.
4 The Porch Club.

59 John McDonald[1] to Hamish Henderson

[Elgin, 3 November 1953]

Dear Mr Henderson,

I was very pleased you wrote to me & first let me say I enjoyed your Broadcast last Sunday morning at 10.30. The old singers are wearin' awa' I'm sorry to say Jimmy McBeth[2] will be about the best of the 'old timers' left. I don't have a great many songs I prefer to have a few & sing them good & play my melodeon at the same time. I am also a comedian. I have for years been presenting at concerts as 'the Orra chiel' & 'Auld Donal' the Hielanman'. Some of my favourite old songs are 'The Rovin' Ploughboy' I like the air & words (I sing it) also 'The Haughs o' Cromdale' & 'The Banks & Braes o' Dunphail', this was composed by the late Jamie MacQueen of Forres, Jamie made many songs but I am sorry to say they didn't get the popularity they should have done.

Jamie had a privilege to play his violin on the old Highland railway to amuse the passengers he was a grand fiddler. My daughter has a fine voice & sings a few songs along with me 'Lord Randal' 'Leezie Lindsay' 'Mormond Braes' & 'Hunting Tower' etc etc. Have you heard 'The Shepherd Lad of Rhynie' sung & 'Bonnie Udny'; a song I would like very much to get all the words of is 'Farewell Tomintoul' if you have them I would be delighted if you could let me have a copy. I know the air but only a verse or two. I also sing 'Jimmy Rose' & 'The Mains o' Foggieloan', I give concerts in aid of Aberlour Orphanage, I will be very pleased to see you anytime & if I come across any old singers I will take a note of them.

Hoping to hear further from you I am

Yours sincerely, John McDonald

[PS] Some of the so-called ballad singers we get on some of the radio-programmes are too stagefied (excuse the word). I prefer them like old Jimmy McBeth.

---

1 John McDonald, mole and ratcatcher and folk-singer.
2 Jimmy MacBeath.

1954

60 **To the *Manchester Guardian***

[Edinburgh, 20 May 1954]

Sir,

The oaths and ceremonies of early trade unionism, as Mr Asa Briggs reminds us, mostly derived from those of the secret craft societies of earlier days. It would be quite incorrect, however, to assume that all this died out over a century ago. In the north-east of Scotland, the secret society of agricultural labourers, known as the 'Horseman's Word',[1] continued to employ the shibboleths of the witch-cult to safeguard itself until well on into this century.

The 'Horseman's Word', in its heyday, was a mass organization, and the Kirk was powerless to interfere with it. At its initiation ceremonies the blindfolded novices had to 'hae a shak' o' auld Hornie' ('shake of the Devil's hand'). The 'Devil' was usually a calf or a goat, and the novice had to 'shake' its hoof. As late as 1914, a goat was kept year in and year out in an isolated Aberdeenshire bothy, for no other purpose than to take part in the ceremonies of the 'Horseman's Word'.

Sometimes the young lads were badly maltreated at these ceremonies: if they could be tricked into breaking part of the initiation oath, they were beaten with a 'nickie tam' (leather thong), or the back-chain of a cart. Many old men are still alive in the north of Scotland who carry on their bodies marks of this ordeal. The ceremonies of the Horseman's Word ended in what can properly be described as orgies. Toasts were drunk, defying Kirk and State, and exalting the world, the flesh, and the Deil. The newly elected novices each contributed a bottle of whisky, and the horseman staggered out into the early dawn all 'bleezin' drunk'. There is an old man alive today, in a mental hospital in the north of Scotland who, when a boy, was driven out of his wits by the well stage-managed effects at one of these ceremonies. I am reluctant for obvious reasons to mention the names in the case, but I am in possession of the facts.

On the other hand, the 'Horseman's Word' served, before the building of the Farm Servants' Union in the north-east, as a bulwark against the exploitation by the farmers. The initiated horsemen were pledged to give the younger members every help that lay in their power. If a laddie at the start of his service was inefficient, he could be sure that the older 'horsemen' would tutor him and would pull him through.

The songs which the horsemen sang at their meetings are very interesting and revealing; they ranged from versions of the classical ballads, full of supernatural folklore, to bothy songs which were explicitly anti-farmer.

> 'Come all ye jolly ploughman lads
>   That labour far and wide
> And I'll sing you a bothy sang
>   To lay the farmer's pride.'

The farmers concerned, it should be noted, were not of a different race like the Kenya settlers, but would in many cases bear the same name as their own farm-servants. The ballads are full of stanzas with direct political implication:

> 'The time has come to end my sang
>   And I will end wi' this –
> May the ploughman get mair wages,
>   It is my earnest wish.
> It is my heart-felt wish, I say!
>   It is the ploughman's due,
> For he sustains baith rich and peer
>   Wi' the handling o' the ploo.'

'Fyvie's Lands' has the following concluding stanza:

> 'Remember well, ye farmers,
>   Your men's as guid as ye!
> Dinna think ye're obligin' them
>   When they are servin' thee.
> There's fields o' speculation
>   All round, as you may see.
> And there's plenty emigration
>   To tak them owre the sea.'

In the 1890s, as the Farm Servants' Union increased in membership and prestige in the north-east under the leadership of Joe Duncan, of Tullycorthy, Udny – 'that beggar o' a mannie Duncan', as the farmers used to call him – the Horseman's Word gradually declined. The tractor superseded the horse, and the bothy system withered away. But the cult is not wholly extinct even yet. The problems that human communities have to solve are fundamentally similar, whether the communities concerned lie 'facing Mount Kenya' or 'at the back o' Benachie'.

    Yours etc., Hamish Henderson

---

1 'This letter was written to show that the rituals of the Mau Mau insurgents in
   Kenya had fairly close relatives in North East Scotland' (HH). See also Henderson's
   essay 'The Horseman's Word', *Scots Magazine*, vol. 87, no. 2, May 1967.

1955

61 To Hugh MacDiarmid

[*EUL*]

[Edinburgh, 5 October 1955]

Dear Chris,

Just a line to say that I've been reading *In Memoriam James Joyce*,[1] and enjoying it greatly. I was especially pleased to see the reference to Gramsci[2] – both 'heroic' and 'genius' are *mots justes*.

Are you replying to Fraser's[3] last letter in the *NS and N*?[4] Your earlier letter (and that glorious bolt from the blue) was so effective that it seems a shame not to get in another blow.

Why not outflank him by saying something like: 'Is it to be expected that anyone will write a poem in honour of Joyce, and not make use of what Mr Fraser evidently doesn't possess – a sense of humour.'

I'm quoting from your *1st Hymn to Lenin* in a talk on Scottish Life and Letters on Sunday night at 6.45.

Love to Valda,

    Best wishes, Hamish

[PS] I was up at the Mod in Aberdeen: it was wonderful (as a spree, I mean, not as a musical festival).

---

1 Hugh MacDiarmid, *In Memoriam James Joyce* (William MacLellan: Glasgow, 1955). The most famous of MacDiarmid's later epic poems, drawing on linguistic and scientific sources.

2 See Letter 113.

3 G.S. Fraser.

4 The *New Statesman and Nation*.

1957

62 Jeannie Robertson[1] to Hamish Henderson
[*EUL*]

[Aberdeen, 21 February 1957]

Dear Hamish,

Just a Note to Let you know That we Received your kind and welcome Letter alright and we are very Glad That you are Safe and, Not in the Hornie's[2] hands, well Hamish, I am a Good Deal Better now although I had a Bad Time of it For a while, I think this is your Song Hamish.

> The night it is Good hallowe-en
> > when Fairy Folk will Ride
> And She That would her True Love win
> > at Miles cross she maun Bide

The last verse

> Had I But the wit yestereen
> > That I ha'e coft This day
> I'd paid my Kane Seven Times to hell,
> > ere you'd Been won away,

Also King Henrie:

> Now, swear, Now swear, ye King Henrie
> > To Take me for your Bride!
> oh! God forbid, King Henrie said
> > That e'er the Like Betide:
> That e'er The Fiend that wons in hell
> > Shou'ld Streek Down By My Side.

(also Sir James The Ross.)

> His growth was as The Tufted Fir,
> > That crowns The Mountains Brow:
> and waving o'er his Shoulders Broad,
> > his Locks of yellow Flew.

She Lean'd The hilt against the Ground
    and Bared her Snowy Breast,
Then Fell upon her Lover's Face,
    and Sunk to endless Rest.[3]

Well Hamish sometime when you are in Aberdeen you May Record My Bonnie Blake ee[4] — of course I have a Good Many More Songs That you have Not Recorded yet. I have the whole, of Lord Donald[5] in the way my mother Sung it, I also have a Dottered auld carle cam ower The Lea, I wonder if you have ever heard The Song called willie's Fate[6]. It's a very nice old Song.

    as willie gaed o'er yon high, high hills,
        and down yon Dowie Den.
    Oh, there he saw a Grievous Ghost,
        would Fear Ten Thousand Men!

    as he Gaed in by Mary Kirk,
        and in by Mary Stile,
    wan and weary was The Ghost
        on him did Grimly Smile,

    oft ha'e ye Travell'd this Road, willie,
        oft ha'e ye Travell'd in sin,
    nor Thought what would come of your puir Soul,
        when your Sinfu' Life was Done.

    oft ha'e ye Travell'd this Road willie,
        your Bonnie New Love To See,
    oft ha'e ye Travell'd This Road, willie,
        Nor Thought of puir wranged me.

    oft ha'e ye Travell'd This Road, willie,
        your Bonnie New Love To See,
    But ye'll Never Travel This Road again,
        For this night avenged I'll Be.

    Then She has Ta'en her perjured Love,
        and Rave him gair By gair,
    and on Ilka side of Mary's Stile
        of him She hung a share.

His Father and Maither Baith made moan
  his New Love Meikle Mair,
His Father and Maither Baith made moan
  his New Love Rave her hair

Tell Farnham and ann That we asking For Them, also Tell Ella and Simon and Faimly That we are asking For Them, and I Send Best Regards to all my Edinburgh Friends. Donald and Isaac and Lizzie are all asking For you,

      Yours ever, Jeannie

21 Causewayend, Aberdeen
[PS]   Ask Ella if she could send me on Jobie and Isabel's[8] address they sent a card with their address on it, but was burned by mistake or if you could get it for me from Ella.

---

1 Jeannie Robertson (1908–75), folk-singer. The greatest of the singers to come to the fore during the Revival; her extensive knowledge of traditional songs and stories and her interpretations of the great ballads had an enormous influence. Alan Lomax described her as 'a monumental figure of world folksong', and A.L. Lloyd as a 'singer sweet and heroic'; see also Henderson's essay 'Jeannie Robertson as a Storyteller', *Tocher* no. 6, reprinted in *Alias MacAlias*.
    Note: all of Jeannie Robertson's letters included here were dictated to her husband, Donald Higgins.
2 'Hornie's; police's.
3 Verses from 'Tam Lin', Child Ballad no. 39.
4 One of Jeannie Robertson's own songs.
5 'Lord Donald', more often known as 'Lord Randal', Child Ballad no. 12.
6 'Willie's Fate', 'Willie's Vital Visit', Child Ballad no. 255.
7 Farnham and Ann Rehfisch; Fanham Rehfisch was an American anthropologist studying the travelling people in Scotland (at Henderson's suggestion).
8 Jobie Blanshard, husband of Isabel Sutherland, friends of Joan Littlewood's. Jeannie stayed with them when she sang at the Singers' Club in London.

63 To the *Scotsman*

                    [Edinburgh, 5 December 1957]
Sir,
    Since the days of John Gibson Lockhart,[1] bynamed 'the Scorpion', Scottish criticism has often earned a reputation for stinging and even brutal acerbity, but your unsigned review (November 28) of the second number of *Scottish Studies* seems a pretty remote by-blow of this formidable tradition.
    Reference to Mr C.I. MacLean's[2] contribution – a version of 'The Birth and Youthful Exploits of Fionn', one of the oldest hero-tales in European folk tradition

— as 'a tall story from the Gaelic', provides one straight away with a yardstick for the standard of criticism. It comes as no surprise after that to find that this contribution, together with Dr Wm. Montgomerie's[3] and my own, is regarded as belonging to the 'folksy' department of the journal.

As for the north-east songs collected by myself, these are written off as 'variations on the favourite theme of the rural muse'; it puzzles your reviewer that 'so much enthusiasm goes into their study'. Well, seduction is admittedly a frequently encountered theme in folksong, but it is also a common theme in world literature as a whole from the Heinrich and Gretchen scenes in *Faust* to *Manon Lescaut*. Or maybe your reviewer regards Goethe, Boccaccio, and the Abbé Prévost as typical country bumpkins of European letters?

I am etc., Hamish Henderson

1 John Gibson Lockhart (1794–1854), novelist, biographer and editor; son-in-law of Sir Walter Scott.
2 Calum I. MacLean, brother of Sorley MacLean; first full-time appointee to the School of Scottish Studies.
3 William Montgomerie.

64 To Hugh MacDiarmid
[*EUL*]

[Edinburgh, 18 December 1957]

Dear Chris,

Last Sunday I gave a lecture for the WEA[1] to a day-school of trades unionists, and read them a number of poems from *Stony Limits*[2] — as an example of direct political poetry in the line of Byron's 'Ode on the Framers of the Frame Bill', and the old popular broadsheets. You'll be pleased to hear that they had a terrific direct impact — especially 'The Belly-grip' and 'John Maclean'.

I hear from Dominic Behan that the WMA[3] want to record a Burns Supper this year, and I've told him that their best bet would be the Bowhill People's Burns Club. However, I don't know who they've got this year to propose the 'Immortal Memory', and I was hoping it might be yourself. Or, failing you, Martin Milligan.[4] Do you happen to know who's doing it?

I do not want to get in touch with Murdoch[5] if there's any possibility that the speaker isn't much cop. (By the way, could you let me have Murdoch's address — I had it, but Jasus knows where I've stuck it.)

When I was in London, Dominic sang me a ballad he has made on the shooting of Feargal O'Hanlon[6] last Spring — the ballad is first rate. He also gave me a poem which I'll leave you to judge for yourself — I told him I would forward it to you. Needless to say, he wants to get it published — is there any periodical that would provide an appropriate home for it? 'Whether or no', I'm sure he would listen sensibly to your judgement if you sent it back to him.*

Best Christmas and Hogmanay wishes to Valda, Mike and yourself.

Yours aye, Hamish

* His address is: D. Behan,
  77 Sternhold Avenue,
  London SW2

1 Workers Education Association.
2 Hugh MacDiarmid, *Stony Limits, and Other Poems* (Gollancz: London, 1934); reprinted as *Stony Limits and Scots Unbound, and Other Poems* (Castle Wynd: Edinburgh, 1956).
3 Workers Music Association.
4 Martin Milligan, Communist and philosopher; Lecturer in Philosophy at Oxford.
5 John Murdoch, secretary of the Bowhill Burns Club; the members were coal miners.
6 'The Patriot Game' by Dominic Behan, a song based on the shooting of a young member of the IRA, Feargal O'Hanlon.

1958

65 Jeannie Robertson to Hamish Henderson
[*EUL*]

[Aberdeen, 8 January 1958]

Dear Hamish,

I Recived a Letter From Doctor Macmachon[1] Today, and a copy of the One that he sent To you. He says we ought to Let Things Lie as They are untill at Least he has had a chance To Meet <u>You</u> and Discuss Matters with you. You see the First Time I Met Doctor Macmahon in Birmingham, I did not have Mutch Time To speak To him as The Lady I Stayed with had not Mutch Time to wait as she lived a long way out of Birmingham. He knew I was leaving For aberdeen The Next Morning at 11 AM so there he was at the Station waiting For Me, and asked me to cancel My Train For a Later one. My voice was in Good Form and I went with Them To The Birmingham Studioes and sung several songs when he Told me the <u>hopes</u> he had for the song as I never sung before & had a Determination, To Go Forward, For My own sake, and you to Be proud of Me when I Got a Letter From Doctor Macmachon a week latter he was more than pleased with me, I know Hamish you have Done a Lot of Things For Me, and I know that you would Do more if you could But There is Something I don't understand. By his letter he seems to have changed and Leaving Me in your hands To Do the Things That he wanted To Do For Me himself. Not that I mind Being in your hands Hamish. But I Thought That Doctor Macmachon could Do Bigger Things For Me, as I know he is able To Do, That Sort of Thing. I would Be very Disappointed if I did Not Get That chance. I had a Note From the Topic[2] with a chque £3 2s 4d ending September 30th. Tell my friends in Edinburgh That I am asking for Them all Not Forgetting yourself. I wish you all a very guid New Year.

    Yours ever, Jeannie.

---

1 Dr MacMahon, editor of folksong collections for schools.
2 Topic Records were the first British company to release material gathered during the Folk Revival.

66 Hugh MacDiarmid to Hamish Henderson
[*EUL*]

[Brownsbank, 15 January 1958]

Dear Hamish,

Many thanks for your letter. I've no doubt Murdoch will agree, and I am of course perfectly willing to propose toast to the Friends of the People.[1] But I wish I had more material by me about them. Have you any handy? Or can you refer me to any book or pamphlet giving a good account of them? I am desperately busy all this month and won't be able to hunt out stuff myself. On the other hand, if this toast is to be given – and recorded – it must be done well, worthy of its theme. So I'll be glad if you can send me anything.

All the best. Hope you are OK. Valda joins me in every kind regard.

Yours, Chris

---

1 Henderson had suggested this as the subject of the toast in a previous letter, dated 11 January 1958, not included here. The Friends of the People; radical political grouping with which Burns was sympathetic.

67 To Hugh MacDiarmid
[*EUL*]

[Edinburgh, 21 January 1958]

Dear Chris,

Today I am getting Meikle's *Scotland and the French Revolution*[1] out of our University Library, and will send it to you at once.

John Murdoch writes to say he is very pleased with the idea, and indeed it seems to me a great idea that the first Burns Supper ever to be put on an L.P. should be one run by the Scottish miners. We're pulling a fast one on the official Burns cult with a vengeance!

Incidentally, Topic has another excellent idea – namely, the issuing of records of Scots poetry. I suggested to them that the first of these should be your *Hymns to Lenin* – or rather, the first two *Hymns to Lenin*, plus a number of other poems which I would select myself. As readers, I suggested yourself (for the First Hymn), Norman McCaig, Alex McCrindle and Tom Scott.[2] We can discuss this more fully when I see you at Bowhill.

Le gach dùrachd[3], Hamish

[PS] Love to Valda and Mike.

---

1 Henry W. Meikle (1880–1958), *Scotland and the French Revolution*
  (J. MacLehose & Sons: Glasgow, 1912).
2 Tom Scott (1918–95), poet and anthologist; studied at Newbattle Abbey
  College, worked as a transcriber for the School of Scottish Studies in late

1950s. His *Collected Shorter Poems* appeared in 1993 (Chapman/Agenda).
Editor of *The Penguin Book of Scottish Verse* (1970); and, with John MacQueen,
of *The Oxford Book of Scottish Verse* (1966).

3 Trans; 'with every good wish'.

68 To the *Weekly Scotsman*

[Edinburgh, November 1958]

Sir,

I am interested to learn from W. Gordon Smith's column of 23 November that
'it took Roy Guest[1] to bring folk-singing into the marketplace – or the coffee-den'.

If Mr Gordon Smith is referring to folk-singing in Edinburgh, he should know
that it has been going on in howffs, dens, open spaces, and even in private houses
for several hundred years. The modern folksong revival, as far as Auld Reekie is
concerned, began not with Roy Guest but with Ewan MacColl and Joan Littlewood
of Theatre Workshop, in 1947, the year of the first Edinburgh Festival. We even
served coffee with it!

Roy Guest arrived in Scotland at the invitation of the 'Sporranslitters', in August
1960. The Howff (their name, not his) was already in existence. While it lasted, it
provided a congenial central meeting place for all interested in folk-music, and Roy
himself was undoubtedly a major attraction. Unfortunately, as it turned out,
neither the 'Sporranslitters' – a most promising and enterprising Scottish cultural
society – nor their experimental Howff survived Roy's picaresque tap-and-run raid
on the Scottish folk scene.

I don't want to 'knock' a talented folk-singer, but one must get the facts right in
these cases.

Hamish Henderson

---

1 The folk-singer Roy Guest ran a folk-club in The Howff, opposite St Giles
  Cathedral in Edinburgh.

1959

69 **To the** *Weekly Scotsman*

[Edinburgh, 2 April 1959]

Sir,

Your readers may be interested to hear the 'pedigree' of the fine song 'The Rovin' Ploughboy', which you printed (Bothy Ballads).

The man who has preserved it is John MacDonald of Pitgaveny, Elgin, who is — among other things — a molecatcher, a puppet-master, and a notable balladmaker. John first heard it 'when he was a laddie' from a ploughman, Donald MacLeod, who was fee'd on his father's farm at Dava. According to John, it was Donald's father who composed it.

Like most 'composed' songs in the folk idiom, however, it has its roots in another song, and internal evidence shows that this can only be the famous classical ballad 'The Gypsy'. When I played Jeannie Robertson a recording of John singing 'The Rovin' Ploughboy', she recognized this immediately, and began to sing the traditional 'Gypsy Laddies' words she had from her own people to the 'Ploughboy' tune.

The new setting rapidly gained a wide currency, and this explains why the tunes you publish for the two songs are practically identical.

The 'Ploughboy' is not only a fascinating example of the sort of lyric lovesong which, in the nineteenth century and on both sides of the Atlantic, began to sprout from shattered versions of the old ballads: it is also welcome evidence (having in this century given a 'new look' to its parent ballad) that folksong in Scotland is still a carrying stream.

Hamish Henderson

70 **Jeannie Robertson to Hamish Henderson**
[*EUL*]

[Aberdeen, 13 November 1939]

Dear Hamish and Katzel,[1]

Just a Note to Let you Know that we are all Keeping well Just now. well I am Going up To Cambridge. To Sing on The 30th of this Month. I will Be Staying with Helena Shire.[2] while I am up There. I have also Go To a Dinner the Same Evening with The Saltire people. I wonder if you have heard from Colin pomeroy[3] and if so, what Do you Think of his New Contract. I know I Thought Bloody Little of it, you might Tell the [?] Brothers that me and Donald are asking For Them, also we are asking for, Ian Macarthur[4] his wife and his Sister and his Family. we Do Send Them our Kind Regards, and Good wishes. Tell wee Calum, Sandy and Hamish Ross, and Stewardie[5] and all the Rest of the Clan that we are asking for them all, we have not seen this M[r] Goldstein.[6] c. The Last Time that I was in London. I Got £21. From Colin you see My Next Record, is a Long player Record. So he Give me £21 advanced money on the L.p. Now this £21 is For 600 Records that works out at about 3 and 1/2 per cent and if I Do Not Signe This New Contract I get 2 and 1/2 per cent, and That is what I Get For all my Records. From Colin, all Told he advanced me, on my Little Records since I started to sing for him, was the sum of £22-10/- and he said I was £4-10/- overdrawn on The Little Records. So he said I had no Royalties to Come For The Little Record yet for a while. So, we had a Grand old Row, over it. The First Record I Made For him you were there. The next Time it was in London I give him 18 songs enough to make 4 or 5 Records. Now this Last Time That I was up in London, I only Sung him 6 songs. Now he is Going To Take This Last 6 Songs and Make Them into a Long playing Record — why I didn't Sing him any more Songs, you see he wanted To Keep the Recording For 2 Days and this I found out — that he was Not Going To pay any of my Expences. I had to pay even the Taxi over to his place myself, 7/-6. They came the same Raket The Next Day.

But when paul phoned[7] me to come over I told him I had not so mutch money To pay Taxis so he had to pay it That Time; so he paid the Taxi and hired the Studio, and I Refused to sing; and then he wanted me To Signe this New Exclucive Contract not For 4 years, But For 5 years and then he Tried to Tempt Me, with paying Me another £29 — within 3 weeks if I would signe the New Contract. Now I had no proof that he would send me that £29 as it was <u>not</u> on the Contract, only word of mouth. Then I asked him why he Did Not write to you, and Let you know what was going on and then I got a Bit of a Shoke when they said they had Been writing To you and you would not answer them, and at the same Time They Told Me My New 3rd Record had Been Sent on To Me about 3 weeks Before. But it never came, so I knew it was only a pack of lies That They were telling all along — and Then he Started Running Down, My L.p. Record in The U.S.A. and that was why I would not sing For him. I told him why the hell Did he know about My Record in the U.S.A. Belive Hamish I know he is selling plenty of my Records he has plenty of outputs for Them. I know a lot More Than They Think, I am no Fool. Then we had lunch with Roy Guest, and then Roy Guest Came Down To The Studio with me, and then Roy and Colin had a very heated disput over The way Colin was paying me For my Records and then there was several things pointed out By Roy Guest, and then I Began to understand a few things I did not know Before. Because Roy was Triping him up, and Roy demanded To See The Contract — But

Colin would not Let him see The Contract and That Started The Row. But he had to show Roy Guest The Contract, and then Roy left, I knew By the Look on Roys Face, That he was not pleased with the Terms of The Contract. It <u>was</u> Roy Guest That Got Me the £21 From Colin. But some time Hamish when I see you, I will give you the whole Story, as one Cannot write every thing down. I Really think everyone of that Crowed of Record Makers are all the Bloody Same. I have a Feeling That a Lot of our eneameys have a Lot To Do with it. I was singing in The Recitel Room of the Royal Festavial hall and it was that very Big. But every seat was sold out. Roy sent me £10 For My Fare, and he paid me £10 for my fee, and Roy had to pay a heavy Bill For My hotel.

Roy wamts Me to Come To London on 30th Jan. 1960. To Do a Show, and I Can Tell you, That Night at The Royal Festivial hall I sang as I never Sung Before, and Roy was very very pleased indeed. In Fact so was everyone. I sang 9. songs. We saw peter Kennedy[8] and his wife. They were there. Tell Katzel we are asking for her and we all send her our Kind Regards.

> Aye, Jeannie R. Higgins

---

1 Henderson married Kätzel Schmidt in Coburg, May 1959.

2 Jeannie Robertson was invited to perform at Cambridge by the distinguished scholar Helena Shire.

3 Colin Pomeroy, director at Collector Records, who offered her a contract which she accepted.

4 Ian MacArthur organized the Linburn ceilidhs for the war blinded in 1960.

5 Calum I. MacLean; Sandy Folkard, a technician at the School of Scottish Studies; Hamish (James) Ross, lecturer and collector at the School; Stewardi, Stuart MacGregor, student doctor, novelist and founder member of the Edinburgh University Folksong Society (see letter 179).

6 Kenneth Goldstein, American postgraduate doing research on folksong in Aberdeen. Some of the songs he collected appear on the *Folk Songs of Britain* series (Topic Records).

7 Paul [?], the other director of Collector Records.

8 Peter Kennedy, folklorist; son of Douglas Kennedy, president of the English Folk Dance and Song Society; he accompanied Henderson on the important collecting trip to the Sutherland travellers in 1957.

The 'Honor'd Shade Flyting'

> MacCaig has githered 'neath Arts Cooncil shelter
> A wheen o' scrievin' chiels whase wordy welter
> Bamboozles fowk (plain men an' simple wenches)
> Wi' antran verse an' prose-in-ells-an-inches;
> An' chief o' a' thir clever scrievin' race
> Is oor ain Hughoc, splargin' intae space
> Spangled wi' Latin, French an' German words
> An' names o' furrin freends in droves an' herds
> Tae shaw the commonalty Burns has loed
> We're juist a witless wanderin' waefu' crood.
>
> Noo, wha dis Hughoc think he can impress
> Wi's fremit learnin'? Fegs, wha is't unless
> It's Chambers' Brithers, whase braw Dictionar'
> Supplied the borrowed words he writes wi' v-r,
> An' sae tae their Appendix tae, I gang,
> 'Risum teneatis, amici?'* ends my sang.

Helen B. Cruickshank, poem sent to the *Scotsman*, 7 December 1959.

* 'Could you keep from laughing, friends?'

Honor'd Shade: An Anthology of New Scottish Poetry To Mark the Bicentenary of the Birth of Robert Burns, edited by Norman McCaig (Chambers: Edinburgh, 1959). All of Henderson and MacDiarmid's letters, along with a selection of letters by other correspondents, have been included.

The anonymous reviewer for the *Scotsman* drew attention to the absence of Henderson, Alan Riddell, T.S. Law and David McEwan from the anthology:

> There are certainly fine pieces in the anthology, but the editor does not seem to have ranged very far in making his selection . . . As perhaps might be expected, Hugh MacDiarmid is given most space . . . The anthology itself, which of course neither mainly nor chiefly consists of poems in Lallans, might perhaps almost have been called like one of the poems it contains, 'The Muse in Rose Street'.
> [The author of the poem titled 'The Muse in Rose Street' was Sydney Goodsir Smith.] The *Scotsman*, 19 November 1959.

As well as the anonymous reviewers' comments, and those of Henderson, MacDiarmid, and the other correspondents, the Anthology was criticized by a group of younger poets, largely on the grounds that it showed an editorial bias towards Lallans. In February 1960 a tape titled *Dishonour'd Shade: Seven non-Abbotsford Poets* was produced, including reading from their work by seven of the poets: Ian Hamilton Finlay, W. Price Turner, Tom Wright, Stewart Conn, Shaun Fitzsimon, Anne Turner, and Tom Buchan.

71 Hugh MacDiarmid to the *Scotsman*

[Edinburgh, 20 November 1959]

Sir,

The reviewer of the anthology of Scottish poetry sponsored by the Scottish Committee of the Arts Council thinks the book might well have been entitled 'The Muse in Rose Street'. Well, why not? The Rose Street group of contributors are certainly head and shoulders above all the contemporary Scottish versifiers and several of them, in the opinion of leading critics in England and other countries, are of very high rank indeed.

Probably what lies behind your reviewer's suggestion, however, is the common, and utterly stupid, objection to 'a clique'. Why, however, should poets be excluded from the rule that 'birds of a feather flock together'? Most of the best work in literature and the other arts has generally been done by such groups – and has always been bitterly resented by the inferiors excluded from such groups.

Your reviewer does not think this anthology fully representative of the best recent Scottish poetry. Strength might have accrued to his contention if he had named other and better poems not included in it which meet the express condition of not having already been included in any of their authors' books. I know none such.

So far as I am concerned I would like to say that I am satisfied that no contemporary Scottish poet deserving inclusion has been excluded. I have the highest opinion of some of Mr T.S. Law's work but I doubt very much if he had any poems available which met the condition on which the anthology rested as stated above.

I am etc., Hugh MacDiarmid

72 Douglas Young[1] to the *Scotsman*

[Tayport, 21 November 1959]

Sir,

Mr Hugh MacDiarmid rightly stresses one limitation under which Mr Norman MacCaig worked in editing the Arts Council's anthology to mark the Burns Centenary – namely, that it was confined to poems not previously published in book form. But I disagree with Mr MacDiarmid's expression of satisfaction 'that no contemporary Scottish poet deserving inclusion has been excluded'. There is, for example, not a single woman poet represented here – or should I say poetess, or makaress? – among the 27 men occupying 117 pages. Burns, whose shade is being honoured, was not one to disregard the lassies' contribution to Scots song, and I hope some publisher will mobilize two or three lady editors to prepare a representative collection of poems by Scotswomen of this century, many of whom do not frequent megalopolitan dram shops.

Burns would relish a good few of the pieces in this selection, but he must be wandering a little bumbazedly through the Elysian Fields after seeing, in a volume commemorative of him, so much dullish prose in an artificial dialect of English, which would be at least less irritating if it did not masquerade on the elegant pages as verse. The publishers' dust-jacket has no justification in claiming that 'the book as a whole presents a picture of the widely various ways in which Scottish writers find it natural to express themselves'. Neither Sir John McEwen, in his foreword, nor Mr MacCaig makes any such sweeping claim.

I am etc., Douglas Young

1   Douglas Young (1913–73), poet and literary critic, leader of the SNP (elected 1942); founding member of the Makars Club. Author of popular verse translations of Aristophanes, *The Puddocks* and *The Burdies*. Editor of *Scottish Verse: 1851–1951* (Thomas Nelson & Sons: London, 1952). This anthology includes an extract from Henderson's poem 'The Highlanders at Alamein', an early version of the 'Interlude: Opening of an Offensive' from the *Elegies for the Dead of Cyrenaica*, first published in *The New Alliance*, June/July 1943.

73 'Your Reviewer' to the *Scotsman*

[22 November 1959]

Sir,

Mr MacDiarmid is naturally critical of my review of *Honour'd Shade*, but the ex cathedra tone of his letter in Saturday's *Scotsman* compels me to reply to some of his more sweeping generalizations. On the question of cliques – Mr MacDiarmid's word, not mine – I do not feel strongly one way or the other, though one cannot, in the nature of things, expect unbiased criticism from their members. Unfortunately, it would seem that such groups in Scotland spend too much of their time denigrating the work of those outside them, as is regrettably borne out by Mr MacDiarmid's contemptuous reference to 'inferiors'.

One of the poets whose omission from the anthology I regretted was Tom Law,[1] and I am gratified that Mr MacDiarmid has the 'highest opinion' of some of his work, though that does not prevent him from saying that no contemporary poet worthy (in whose opinion?) of inclusion has been excluded from the selection. He 'doubts very much' whether Mr Law had any eligible poems available; does he know this for a fact? If he does not, then these two statements are mutually contradictory. Alan Riddell[2] and Hamish Henderson, two others who were not included, are also poets of a certain stature, and, whether Mr MacDiarmid likes their work or not, deserved inclusion in such a collection.

His assertion that 'most of the best work in art and literature has generally been done by such groups' is difficult to take seriously. A certain proportion perhaps, but what cliques did Shakespeare, da Vinci, Rembrandt, El Greco, Racine, Rimbaud, Eliot, Stravinsky – the list is endless – belong to? Setting aside Auden, Spender and Isherwood, in the thirties, a typical example of such cliques is La Pléiade – one major luminary surrounded by satellites of lesser and varying brilliance.

As for Mr MacDiarmid's suggestion that I should have named 'other and better poems' not included in the anthology to support my opinion that it is not fully representative of the best recent Scottish poetry, I am certainly not, and I doubt if Mr MacDiarmid is, in a position to know every single poem eligible for consideration; that was the editor's duty. I listed certain poets whose omission surprised me; if they were not represented because they had no poems available, this should have been stated, instead of the subject being dismissed in an unilluminating editorial note, which might perhaps convey the impression that 'notable names' were not included because someone did not think highly enough of their work.

In conclusion, fine though the achievements of the Rose Street group may be – and certainly no scruples of modesty prevent Mr MacDiarmid from telling us that the group with which he is associated is 'head and shoulders' above the rest – they are not all that Scotland can offer. Perhaps Mr MacDiarmid is too closely connected with them to take a dispassionate view, and, with his allegiances, may not be the best person to decide on the composition of the anthology. He is a fine poet; he should not attempt to pontificate on the work of those whose aims are perhaps different from his own.

> I am etc., Your Reviewer

---

1 T.S. Law, poet and coal miner; associated with the 'Clyde Group'. His *Whit Tyme in the Day* appeared in 1948, with a foreword by MacDiarmid.

2 Alan Riddell (1927–70), Australian-born poet, editor of *Lines Review*. Riddell was a close friend of Henderson's from their first meeting in the Summer of 1949.

74 William Little to the *Scotsman*

[Edinburgh, 23 November 1959]

Sir,

As a Scotsman to whom poetry is a pleasure but not a fetish, something to be tasted and savoured for its conjured visions rather than its 'school' of origin, I can yet sympathize with Mr MacDiarmid not a little in his defence of the 'flocking together' of his poet friends in Rose Street or any other congenial venue.

When, however, he sweeps majestically on to dispose, in his oracular ultimate paragraph, of every contemporary Scottish poet not represented in the Arts Council's anthology as (by inference) 'inferiors' unworthy of the august (and often unintelligible) company there assembled, his prickly ego seems to me to deserve a little gentle deflation, and there appears no man better equipped to perform the operation than Mr MacDiarmid himself.

In August 1956, a brief review in your pages tempted me to acquire a volume of poetry which, with its successor, has given me great and abiding pleasure. The verses were by Tom Todd, and were prefaced by an appreciation written by Hugh MacDiarmid. Permit me to quote him: 'In my considered opinion – as I said in a broadcast – the poems of Tom Todd (T.T. Kilbucho)[1] are the best that have been produced in this kind since Burns and Hogg.'

High praise, but justifiably high praise, for Kilbucho's verses spring from the very heart. Yet Kilbucho does not appear in an anthology intended as a tribute to the memory of Burns, and Mr MacDiarmid now lumps him with the 'inferiors' beneath its editor's notice.

What are we to make of such an oracle who speaks with two voices? Are we to write him off as just a crazy mixed-up MacDiarmid? Or treat his inconsistency as poetic licence?

In my humble view it is patent that if Mr MacDiarmid is now right, he was wrong. If on the other hand he was right, he is wrong. What are we to believe?

If he would now don the mantle of adjudicator we might perhaps be enlightened as to which MacDiarmid (of the three), should be hearkened unto.

     I am etc., W. Little

---

1 T.T. Kilbucho (pseudonym of Tom Todd), shepherd poet.

75 Sydney Goodsir Smith to the *Scotsman*

[Edinburgh, 24 November 1959]

Sir,

Your reviewer of the Arts Council anthology of modern Scottish poetry, *Honour'd Shade*, has not chosen his 'non-clique' artists and writers very wisely. More than half those named will always be regarded in history as belonging to 'cliques'. Shakespeare, for instance, was a member of the Mermaid group – bearing a strong family likeness to the Rose Street group, surely. Rimbaud will always be associated in literary history with Verlaine; Eliot with Pound, Lewis and the Bloomsbury set; Stravinsky with Diaghilev, Picasso, Cocteau and the Russian Ballet set.

What is more interesting, surely, in your reviewer's review of *Honour'd Shade* is his snide attack on those writers using the Scottish language – an echo of his similar remarks reviewing the *Scotsman* anthology, 'A Sang at Least'. In the former, we get Scots described as 'this somewhat artificial language', and in the latter as 'a more or less artificial language'. He has evidently an axe to grind here. He is equally snooty about the Gaelic contributions to *Honour'd Shade* which he confesses he does not understand but nonetheless presumes to 'doubt their translations'. Somewhat of an intellectual somersault.

The chiefest interest to my mind is why should he be so fashed about the successful renaissance of writing in Scots and Gaelic, and I should dearly like explained how he squares this attitude with his implied admiration of his seven so-called 'non-clique' masters — da Vinci, Rembrandt, Greco, Racine, Rimbaud, Eliot, Stravinsky — all of whom were regarded in their own days as a bit odd, non-traditional, antiquarian, revolutionary, mad or 'highly artificial'.

Anyone can start swopping names and I should forbear, but cannot resist just mentioning such famous cliques as the University Wits, the Metaphysicals, the Augustans, the Kit Kat Club, the Lake School, the French Romantics of 1830, the Symbolists, the Impressionists, Les Flauves, the German Expressionists, the Cubists — to go no further into the crazy Ismism of today. All named have their places assured in literary and art history.

I am etc., Sydney Goodsir Smith

76 Hugh MacDiarmid to the *Scotsman*

[Brownsbank, Biggar, 24 November 1959]

Sir,

A great American scholar said, 'A preference for the inferior is one of the commonest disguises of envy,' and the truth of this is well exemplified in your reviewer's strictures on *Honour'd Shade*.

Underlying several of his phrases there is a suggestion that I had something to do with choosing the contents of this anthology. I had not. I have been abroad most of the year, and had no idea at all what poets were included or by what poems.

Earlier this year I was one of the adjudicators in a poetry competition. Of the hundreds of entries, I did not think any one of them deserved any prize. This is a common experience in such matters; 99 per cent. of the entries are worthless rubbish. If an anthology is to be 'fully representative' all these writers should presumably be included.

This seems to be what your reviewer contends; but 'representative' and 'all-inclusive' are not synonymous, and even if *Honour'd Shade* had been confined to half-a-dozen poets it might still be thoroughly (or even more) representative of the 'best' in contemporary Scottish poetry. There are thousands of versifiers in most countries at any time, but time is a great winnower, and it is a fortunate country that produces even one or two of any real worth in any generation.

I do not agree with Mr Douglas Young about the bevy of Scottish songstresses today, and think that perhaps his regard for them is due to his objection to modernistic trends in poetry and determination to uphold superannuated kinds of verse. He may find certain poems in Mr MacCaig's anthology 'dullish prose masquerading as verse', but literary reactionaries have condemned much modern poetry on the same ground.

This point of view is endorsed by the overwhelming majority of readers. Hence the fact that versifiers like Miss Wheeler Wilcox, Miss Wilhelmina Stitch, and Mr John Oxenford appeal to a far greater public than the poems of Mr W.B. Yeats or Mr T.S. Eliot. In other words, Mr Young and your reviewer on the one side, and I on the other, are arguing about different things altogether, and it is their kind of contention and conception of poetry that has bogged Scottish verse in ruts of worthlessness so long. But the interest of the qualified literary world, and the judgements of all critics of any international repute, lie in the opposite direction.

If I 'should not attempt to pontificate on the work of those whose aims are perhaps different from my own', what qualifications has your reviewer to pontificate about poets whose aims are different from his — or Mr Young's — and no 'perhaps' about it?

I am etc., Hugh MacDiarmid

[Our reviewer made no suggestion that Mr MacDiarmid had something to do with choosing the contents of the anthology.—Ed.]

77 'Your Reviewer' to the *Scotsman*

[26 November 1959]

Sir,

Mr Sydney Smith seems a little confused on the subject of cliques; because several artists are acquainted with each other does not mean that they form a clique. There is no evidence to show that the 'Mermaid group' was a clique in the sense that the Rose Street group is, still less that Shakespeare was a member of it. Rimbaud and Verlaine — surely two are not enough to constitute a clique, and in any case their relationship was based on more improper grounds than a purely intellectual community of interest. Eliot was never a member of the Bloomsbury group in the same way that Roger Fry, Clive Bell, and Lytton Strachey were, and the term 'Russian Ballet set' is meaningless, since many people were associated with Diaghilev — often only for a single ballet — including both Stravinsky and de Falla, two very different composers.

The instances cited in the last paragraph of Mr Smith's letter, such as the Metaphysicals, are in many cases no more than convenient names used to denote certain artists who were working along similar lines. (The 'cubist' sculptures of Jacques Lipchitz are relevant in this context.)

I described Lallans ('Scots' claims too much) as artificial because only a small minority of Scots speak a language anything like it, and, with the continuing influence of television, radio and films, that number, for good or ill, will dwindle to nothing. Poetry must be based on the natural speech of the particular country (look at Italy before Dante and Latin was still very much alive, or consider Norway today). If Mr Smith thinks it desirable that we should all speak one language while our literature is in another, I cannot argue. In that case, however, the situation would resemble present-day schoolboys' efforts to turn English poetry into Latin verse. The artists whom I instanced were all innovators, not resurrectors, and put the clock forward instead of back.

My criticism of the Gaelic poems merely means that I was too charitable to believe that the originals read as badly, from the point of view of poetic merit, as do their translations; that is why I 'doubted' the latter.

There is little to say to Mr MacDiarmid's letter, since he does not reply to the points I raised in my last letter, and contents himself with a barrage of insults and inaccuracies. He has no justification for classing me with Mr Douglas Young as being opposed to modern poetry; on the contrary, if he would read me more carefully he would see that I praised Mr MacCaig's work and implied an admiration for Eliot.

As for my qualifications, these include a keen love of poetry and a mind less blinkered than Mr MacDiarmid's. Artists generally have usually made poor critics: Mr MacDiarmid is no exception. Why does he so persistently imply that Hamish Henderson is an 'inferior' poet? He must be well aware that his 'critics of repute' have all acclaimed Mr Henderson's work.

I am etc., Your Reviewer

78 Tom Scott to the *Scotsman*

[Edinburgh, 26 November 1959]

Sir,

I have watched with considerable interest the discussion in your columns of a non-existent entity, namely, the Rose Street group of poets. This is an invention of your reviewer, and it is astonishing that anybody should have treated it as if it meant anything at all. A 'group' of writers and/or artists, as of other groups, implies a number of people with agreed aims and principles working co-operatively toward their goal. Such a group was the Pléïade in sixteenth-century France.

No such group exists in, or frequents, Rose Street. A few poets who live in Edinburgh happen occasionally to meet in certain Rose Street pubs, for want of a better social centre, and have a few drinks together with a number of non-poet friends. No two of them have any aims in common except a devotion to poetry, to Scotland (in some cases, to a Scotland that couldn't care less at that) and to doing what little they can to improve the human lot. Poets from all over Scotland, England and other parts of the world often join them when in Edinburgh, and have no other centre where they know that colleagues can be met.

Two of the poets who can be met there are Mr Norman MacCaig and Mr Sydney Goodsir Smith, say at weekends. No more unlike and disassociated poets could be imagined. Mr Smith is a writer in Scots, a nationalist, a traditionalist, and is utterly opposed to the existing Establishment in Scotland. Mr MacCaig is a writer in English, a non-nationalist, an individualist, and in the solid Establishment line from Walter Scott through Stevenson, Lord Tweedsmuir and Edwin Muir.

Both are good poets, but there is almost no ground common to them but such as I have indicated, and the fact that they use certain pubs as a central forgathering place. Mr Hugh MacDiarmid among other poets occasionally meets them there on the few occasions when he is in Edinburgh, and is different again from either of the poets mentioned.

It would have been more to the point if your reviewer had compared the work shown in this anthology with the great work of our Scottish past. Such a comparison is sobering and chastening. The sense of community, of abundant, vigorous social life has almost completely gone. There is wealth of talent, and almost any one of the best of these poets could send his work to an intelligent editor unsigned, and his signature would be on every line, but something vital has gone, or almost gone. That something is Scotland. It is enough to make the angels weep tears of blood.

I am etc., Tom Scott

79 Hamish Henderson to the *Scotsman*

[28 November 1959]

Sir,

Returning to Scotland after a short absence, I am amused to find the Rose Street tattoo going great guns in your columns.

Hugh MacDiarmid defends the 'right of association' of like-minded men of letters. No one who remembers the fruitful results for literature of similar associations in the past can doubt that in the main his contention is perfectly justified. It is also true, of course, that sometimes such groups can make life difficult for the lone wolves of literature, but probably no poet of the Western world needs less reminding of this than Mr MacDiarmid.

Stewart Conn is quite right to give the other side of the medal a close inspection.[1] Mutual admiration can be helpful and well merited, but it has obvious drawbacks. The trouble is that half the clique is sometimes nothing more than a claque. Again, nobody is more familiar with the facts here than Mr MacDiarmid, for he has frequently referred to the 'safe' Scottish cultural Establishment as a conspiracy of mediocrity against genius – and against his own undoubted genius, in particular.

Since your reviewer has displayed solicitude on behalf of my muse, I should perhaps make it clear, in justice to Norman MacCaig, that I do not believe that my patronage of bars outwith the magic Rose Street circle had anything to do with my exclusion from the present volume. Mr MacCaig did, in fact, do me the courtesy of asking me for a contribution, and it was nobody's fault but my own that I did not submit one till it was too late. However, even if I had sent a sheaf by return of post, and Mr MacCaig had rejected them holus bolus, it would not have upset me unduly. It is my opinion that few of the shorter poems I have written of late measure up to the standard that I should have felt obliged to impose if I had myself been in Mr MacCaig's position; also the final shape of a new long poem I have been working on still eludes me.

In any case I have come to set greater store by my songs 'in the idiom of the people' than by other kinds of poetry that I have tried to write. By working in the Folksong Revival, therefore, I am paying what is probably congenial tribute to the 'honour'd shade' of the most famous Crochallan Fencible.

My experience may have been misleading, but I have not found Scots writers to be particularly strong on self-criticism. Naturally, self-criticism of any kind is seldom a popular pastime, but in countries like Scotland with special literary problems – I am thinking primarily of the language question – it is all the more necessary. It would help, of course, if more Scots read poetry, and developed an informed criticism . . . Here one is reminded of Hugh MacDiarmid's homely adage, 'birds of a feather flock together' for of no craturs in the world is this truer than of those popularly known as 'culture vultures'.

I am etc., Hamish Henderson

---

1 '. . . [It] is in the long run up to the poet himself to rise above any group, to prove himself. (Otherwise the term "responsibility of the artist" becomes meaningless.) And the fact that "most of the best work in literature . . . has been done by such groups" proves not a thing – especially in a country such as our own. What of the "Caledonian antisyzygy"? And I should like to know which group gave us Robert Burns. But red herrings make cold kippers, as Mr MacDiarmaid must be fully aware.' Stewart Conn,* letter to the *Scotsman*, 22 November 1959.

* Stewart Conn, poet, producer for BBC Scotland.

80 Hugh MacDiarmid to the *Scotsman*

[Brownsbank, Biggar, 27 November 1959]

Sir,

I was very careful in what I said and broadcast about 'T.T. Kilbucho', namely that his verse was in my opinion the best of its kind being written in Scotland now, i.e. folk-poetry of the traditional post-Burnsian sort, and that he was one of the few — and certainly the best — practitioners of 'crambo-clink'[1] belonging to the same class of farmers or farmworkers still extant. The operative phrases are 'of its kind' and 'to the same class'.

There is no inconsistency such as Mr W. Little alleges between what I said then, and what I have since said about the *Honour'd Shade* anthology. One may fully appreciate the beauty of a daisy or even of a dandelion, and yet either for some special occasion or in general prefer roses or even orchids, and deem it inappropriate to add daisies or dandelions to bouquets of these.

Even if I were inconsistent some of Mr Little's expressions are quite unjustified. He is another of these ''umble, all too 'umble' people who are nevertheless so over-whelmingly conceited that they seem to think they are divinely commissioned to keep other people on the straight and narrow path of their own severely and incorrigibly limited comprehension. Witness his attribution of unintelligibility to some of the poems Mr MacCaig chose. Why should what is intelligible to him be taken as a standard?

In the same way my use of the term 'inferiors' was not offensive. It was merely exact. It cannot be denied that there are greater and lesser poets; the latter are inferior as poets to the former, and a Gresham's Law operates that to put even a little of the latter among the former is apt to reduce the value of the whole.

I am etc., Hugh MacDiarmid

---

1 'Crambo-clink': bucolic poetry.

81 Douglas Young to the *Scotsman*

[Tayport, 28 November 1959]

Sir,

Your reviewer of the Burns bicentenary anthology *Honour'd Shade* contradicts the usage of Burns himself when he differentiates Lallans from Scots. Burns, in an epistle to William Simpson, wrote of the old Ayrshire poets as speaking their thoughts in 'plain, braid Lallans', meaning simply the Scots tongue current chiefly in the Lowlands of Scotland. R.L. Stevenson continued Burns's employment of the term, and Dr Edwin Muir commended it, in a broadcast review of a book of mine in 1943, as 'a convenient term which should come into currency'. A philologist might call it Northern Insular West Teutonic.

I agree with your reviewer that Mr MacDiarmid has no justification for classing him with myself 'as being opposed to modern poetry'. I am frequently quite keen on poetry, modern as well as of any other date; but, as I believe Burns would have done, I deprecate giving to English prose space that might have been used to print verse, be it English or Gaelic, Scots or Esperanto, by Scottish contemporaries.

Your reviewer asserts that poetry 'must be' based on the natural speech of the particular country. Today the majority of Scots use colloquially a dialectal magma of Scots, English and American. It is, in a sense, 'artificial' to confine the diction of a particular poem to the Scots or English or American components; but it is not more artificial than sometimes preferring whisky neat to water or to a soft drink, or to whisky drowned in water. It is a question of taste.

I am etc., Douglas Scott

82 **Hugh MacDiarmid to the** *Scotsman*

[Brownsbank, Biggar, 28 November 1959]

Why is your reviewer so insistent on the merits of Alan Riddell and Hamish Henderson? Although he does not hesitate to accuse me of 'inaccuracies', your reviewer says I have persistently implied that Mr Hamish Henderson is an 'inferior' poet. I challenge him to cite any comments I have ever published on Mr Henderson's poems. 'Silence gives consent', perhaps, and I will not deny that Mr Henderson's work is hardly 'my cup of tea'. But the matter is beside the point so far as *Honour'd Shade* is concerned. Mr Henderson was invited to contribute but ignored the invitation until months later, by which time the anthology was already at the printer's. If Mr Henderson was one of the 'notable poets' omitted, the editor was certainly not to blame in this case. (Parenthetically, since questions have been asked about it, I think and hope the phrase in question about 'notable poets' was used ironically, meaning poets omitted who might think themselves notable!)

I am unaware — and do not believe — that any critic of international repute has praised Mr Henderson's poetry (unless Mr G.S. Fraser is to be so accounted, as I certainly do not account him!). Anyhow, whatever may be said about Messrs Riddell and Henderson, I do not think they are poets of such consequence that it matters one way or the other whether they appear or do not appear in any selection.

I am etc., Hugh MacDiarmid

83 **Hamish Henderson to the** *Scotsman*

[12 December 1959]

Sir,

Any reader unacquainted with the facts might be forgiven for assuming that Mr Hugh MacDiarmid had for years maintained a tacitly disapproving silence with regard to my *Elegies* and my poetry generally. This is not the case.

Between 1948 and 1953 Mr MacDiarmid contributed literary criticism and political articles to the *National Weekly*, the journal which was the liveliest carrier of Scottish Nationalist ideas during the period of the Covenant, the 'Stone' and the events leading up to the conspiracy trial. On 9 April 1949 there appeared in its columns a review by Mr MacDiarmid of my recently published *Elegies for the Dead in Cyrenaica*. In this review, he said, *inter alia*:

> Edwin Muir pointed out that the distinctive vision of Scottish poetry 'is profoundly alien to the spirit of English poetry – it is the product of a realistic imagination'. It is this vision which informs all Henderson's work . . . In form and substance it [my book] compares with most of the war poetry of Rupert Brooke, Sassoon and even Wilfred Owen, to say nothing of the hordes of lesser war-poets then and since, as the logistics, and political implications, and global character of the last war compare with old-fashioned militaristic sentiments about, say, the Boer War. It is, in fact, one of the few books – and the only volume of poems in English which has come my way – that expresses an adult attitude to the whole appalling business, and thoroughly deserves the honour of securing the first award of the Somerset Maugham prize.

As for my songs in the folk-idiom, Mr MacDiarmid referred to the 'John Maclean March' (*National Weekly*, 28 June 1952) as a 'splendid song'. (However, this doubtless comes under the heading of 'urban crambo-clink' and presumably doesn't count in the present argument.)

I do not hold it against Mr MacDiarmid that he has forgotten these remarks, committed to print years ago in a defunct periodical. One grows older, and one forgets things. Furthermore, it has been well said that consistency has nothing to do with genius. What does disturb me, whiles, is the whole tone and tenor of Mr MacDiarmid's approach to argument, which positively reeks of that very same self-centred provincialism which he is for ever and a day claiming to combat – he is 'satisfied' that 'no poet deserving inclusion has been excluded'. Does he really think that there was no place in 1959 under Burns' 'honour'd shade' for a single one out of the eight poets of *Fowrsom Reel*[1] and *Four Part Song*?[2]

I am etc., Hamish Henderson

---

1 *Fowrsom Reel: A Collection of New Poetry by John Kincaid, George Todd, F.J. Anderson and Thurso Berwick*, with an Introduction by Hugh MacDiarmid, printed by the Caledonian Press for the 'Clyde Group' (Glasgow, 1949). With the exception of Anderson's contributions the poems are in Scots.
2 *Four Part Song*, anthology featuring the work of Arthur James Arthur, Martin Gray, Alastair Thompson and George Kay.

84 **Hugh MacDiarmid to the** *Scotsman*

[12 December 1959]

Sir,

   I had not forgotten – nor have I altered in my opinion – what I wrote about Hamish Henderson's *Elegies for the Dead in Cyrenaica* ten years ago in the *National Weekly* and, later, about his 'John Maclean March' in the same papers and elsewhere. But *Honour'd Shade* could not use anything from the former in accordance with the express condition of the anthology, and the merits of the latter as a song, and the question of its quality as poetry are two very different matters. Like Mr Henderson, the other poets in *Fowr'som Reel* seem to have petered out, unfortunately.

   At the time I hailed their work because it seemed to me to herald a long-overdue development in Scottish poetry. That has not materialized, however. I am glad to hear that Mr Henderson is engaged on another long poem and hope it will justify my anticipations poetically and politically. All this, however, is irrelevant to *Honour'd Shade*, Mr Henderson's exclusion from which was, as he has told us, his own fault.

   Miss Cruickshank's letter expresses a point of view which I have been fighting against as strenuously as I could for the past forty years. The foreign writers and artists I listed may be 'caviare to the general' but they have had a great deal to do with modern achievements and tendencies in literature and the other arts in Europe, and to cite them in substantiation of my claim regarding cliques was certainly relevant. Scottish literature has suffered sufficiently from restriction to the kailyard and I need make no apology for my internationalism. In any case, all my work has been activated by the principle enunciated by J.R. Lowe when he wrote: 'Not failure but low aim is crime.'

   As to Chambers' 'Dictionary', all our words are borrowed from somewhere or other – we do not invent them – and all that matters is how and to what end we use them. It is a pity more people do not have recourse to dictionaries for the extension and subtilization of their vocabularies. Miss Cruickshank asks for whom I write and the answer is: Certainly not for those who, in discussing literary matters, are proud of their ignorance and fain to use it as a Procrustean bed, or for those (and Scotland is full of them) who reduce discussions on artistic matters to a question of 'scoring cheap laughs' or think they can dispose of great issues by remarks on the level of a gamin's cry: 'Get your hair cut' and ignore all the real problems raised in a lengthy correspondence in favour of an inane giggle which lets loose more than a whiff of sour grapes.

   I am etc., Hugh MacDiarmid

85 **Hamish Henderson to the** *Scotsman*

[Edinburgh, 21 December 1959]

Sir,

In his, to my taste, somewhat over-ponderous answer to Miss Cruickshank's persiflage, Hugh MacDiarmid objects to the 'gamin cry' being heard in lieu of argument.

Although as a professional folklorist, I have no small sympathy with (as well as interest in) the razory epigrammatic derision which this phrase connotes, I quite see the force of Mr MacDiarmid's objection. There is a witless philistinism of the streets which can be very galling. But there is also a philistinism of the boudoir (and even of the Rose Street pub) which can be considerably more dangerous, since it more often than not camouflages itself as a protective interest in literature and the arts.

Every country gets the 'culture vultures' it deserves: in Scotland, they are familiar figures, sticking around with necrophilous animation, and waiting to feast on the body of the stricken Bard. Hugh MacDiarmid has lived long enough north of the Tweed to know the glint of a beady eye when he sees one.

On the political side, since Mr MacDiarmid has mentioned it, I hope you will allow me space to make one brief point. Of late a new school of Socialist thinking has grown up around *Universities and Left Review, The New Reasoner*,[1] Hoggart's *The Uses of Literacy* and Raymond Williams's *Culture and Society*, a school which is not afraid of sociological revaluations, and goes out into the streets to hear not only the 'gamin cry', but the voice and song of the people.

Groups like Lawrence Daly's[2] Fife Socialist League have broken loose from the big combines and started re-thinking our political problems from the ground up: recovering some of the spirit of the early Labour pioneers, they are facing up to world issues like nuclear disarmament, and at the same time getting to grips with some neglected but important questions – recalling, for instance, that men like John Maclean and Keir Hardie were Scottish Home Rulers.

It is strange to find the author of 'A Seamless Garment' and *Second Hymn to Lenin* officially enrolled not among the sponsors of *New Left Review* but among the British representatives of what is now, in the Western world, a withered and archaic political spent force.[3]

I am etc., Hamish Henderson

---

1 *Universities and Left Review*, left-wing journal. *The New Reasoner*, left-wing political and cultural periodical, edited by E.P. Thompson. [Richard Hoggart] *The Uses of Literacy* (London, 1957); [Raymond Williams] *Culture and Society: 1780–1950, Coleridge to Orwell* (Hogarth Press: London, 1958).

2 Lawrence Daly, Fife coal miners' leader; founder of the Fife Socialist League, a progressive left-wing grouping.

3 Following the Soviet Union's invasion of Hungary in 1956, MacDiarmid rejoined the Communist Party of Great Britain.

1960

86 Hugh MacDiarmid to the *Scotsman*

[Brownsbank, Biggar, 4 January 1960]

Sir,

Mr Hamish Henderson is quite right in supposing that I have lived long enough north of the Tweed to know the glint of a beady eye when I see one, but it is not my experience that that glint is to be found more frequently – or more hungrily ruthless – among the 'ins' rather than among the 'outs' in any connection. Mr Henderson's sympathy for the 'razory epigrammatic derision' of the teddy boy type is not shared by me at all and evokes nothing but my contempt and opposition. The adjective 'razory' is particularly well chosen and should be taken literally.

What Mr Henderson's argument amounts to is equivalent to that impatience with the better educated so often manifested by the less educated and generally justified on the ground that it is just 'human nature'. But I was one of the objectors to the sacrifice of the Third Programme to the admass and I know very well that as the BBC's recent publication, *The Public and the Programme*, says, 'the higher your cultural level the less you tend to watch television or listen to the radio, and the more likely you are to be choosy when you do'.

The philistinism I oppose is that which attacks literature and the arts for not appealing to the big public, but does not expect science to do anything of the sort. As to a 'protective interest in literature and the arts', this was never more necessary than today when all values are being swamped under the rising tide of subhumanity, and is not to be looked for among the hordes of football enthusiasts, readers of the big circulation press, patrons of rock 'n' roll and all the rest of it.

Ignorance and apathy are the greatest enemies of mankind and even folksong is not today 'the voice and song of the people'. That is most accurately heard in those outside broadcasts in which mill-girls and old-age pensioners are asked such questions as 'Are yer coortin'?' and 'What's yer most embarrassing moment, luv?'

I do not believe that the salvation of literature will be secured by a fresh wallowing in a mud-bath of ignorance. I would only be interested in such a re-immersion in illiterate doggerel if I were satisfied that it represented a case of *reculer pour mieux sauter*,[1] but I have no such assurance. Very much to the contrary indeed! No doubt over the years I have been guilty of various inconsistencies. But I am still sure, as I wrote over thirty years ago, that the 'causes' which engage me are one cause, and whatever my lacunae or inconsistencies, though I am not prepared to concede that I could not reconcile them all right, I must be content in the meantime simply to say that I believe that the summa of the future will probably adjust the various parts of my work and demonstrate their compatibility.

In any case my guiding principle has always been, and remains, that expressed by Lenin when he said: 'It would be a very serious mistake to suppose that one can become a Communist without making one's own the treasures of human knowledge. It would be mistaken to imagine that it is enough to adopt the Communist formulas and conclusions of Communist science without mastering that sum-total of different branches of knowledge, the final outcome of which is Communism . . . Communism becomes an empty phrase, a mere façade, and the Communist a mere bluffer, if he has not worked over in his consciousness the whole inheritance of human knowledge . . . made his own, and worked over anew, all that was of value in the more than two thousand years of development of human thought.'

I might very well have allowed my name to be used as a sponsor of the *New Left Review* but if I had done so it would have been just on similar grounds to those which led me to vote Labour at the last election, and I have no doubt I could have justified such an action well enough in terms of the dialectic of a changing situation without for one moment losing my ultimate confidence in that 'withered and archaic political spent force' my allegiance to which not only remains unshaken but strengthened afresh by the antics of that 'new school of Socialist thinking' to whom Mr Henderson refers and who, after all, are sucklings of that mother they are now seeking to devour, an ambition which has done and is likely to do little more than change them from sucklings into suckers.

I am etc., Hugh MacDiarmid

---

1 Trans. 'To draw back in order to go forward' (H.H.).

87 Hamish Henderson to the *Scotsman*

[Edinburgh, 13 January 1960]

Sir,

Hugh MacDiarmid clearly doesn't 'want Heaven crammed', he champions the 'ins' of literature and life, and consigns the 'outs' to outer limbo. Odd categories indeed! The rebels to whom Mr MacDiarmid has written a moving ode may do a bit of barracking, but he will be consoled by hearty applause from all the ranks of glorious unknowns of the Académie.

Mr MacDiarmid affects to despise the folksong revival. Yet in the *Second Hymn to Lenin*, he wrote:

Are my poems spoken in the factories and fields.
  In the streets o' the toon?
Gin they're no', then I'm failin' to dae
  What I ocht to ha' dune.

The problems implicit in these lines do not admit of easy solutions, but I have no doubt that in the long run it is the folksong revival which offers the best hope for a genuine popular poetry, a poetry which, when it gathers strength, will make many of the raucous booths of Tin Pan Alley shut up shop. Our own poets, in particular, will feel a real thrill of liberation when they realize that the primary question facing them is not so much one of language as one of idiom; realize, too, that all resources of a folk-poetry of unrivalled beauty and power are there at their elbow, to help and sustain them – resources hardly comprehended as yet, let alone tapped.

Because it sheds light on the language question, and suggests a way out of the Lallans impasse, the folksong revival has much to offer Scots writers. But Mr MacDiarmid sees things differently. Self-criticism can safely be shelved, because the 'summa of the future' will adjust everything. And the widespread interest in folksong which is beginning to affect urban culture all over the world can be written off as 'a fresh wallowing in a mud-bath of ignorance'. Mr MacDiarmid is like some feudal Balkan grandee who continues to exercise his *droit de seigneur*, oblivious of the fact that a revolution is building up all round him.

On the political side, I wonder how many readers in all Scotland, even inside the Pollitt-bureaucracy,[1] will take seriously his Grand Guignol picture of the *New Left Review* partisans as ex-sucklings intent on devouring their mother? The dastards! However, I am all in favour of bold figures of speech in polemical correspondence, so here is my contribution to the series: The CPGB is a shrivelled limb on the tree of British Socialism, and Hugh MacDiarmid is out on it.

I am etc., Hamish Henderson

---

1 Reference to Harry Pollitt, leader of the Communist Party of Great Britain.

88 Hugh MacDiarmid to the *Scotsman*

[19 January 1960]

Sir,

In 1938 one of the earliest commentators[1] on my poetry wrote in the *Aberdeen University Review*:

> Always he [Hugh MacDiarmid] sees man 'filled with lightness and exaltation', living to the full reach of his potentialities. In that clear world 'all that has been born deserved birth'.

> Man 'will flash with the immortal fire,' will rise
> To the full height of the imaginative act
> That wins to the reality in the fact'
> until all life flames in the vision of
> 'the light that breaks

From the whole earth seen as a star again
In the general life of man.'[2]

The actuality is different. Men are obtuse, dull, complacent, vulgar. They love
the third-rate, live on the cheapest terms with themselves, 'the engagement
betwixt man and being forsaken', their 'incredible variation nipped in the bud'.
They refuse to explore the largeness of life. This refusal he sees as a cowardice. If
for the mass of men this picture is true, he believes that human society is
wrongly ordered. Therefore the poet demands a political change that will give
men such living conditions as may make the finer potentialities actual:

'And have one glimpse of my beloved Scotland yet
As the land I have dreamt of where the supreme values
Which our people recognise are states of mind
Their ruling passion the attainment of higher consciousness.'[3]

In the intervening twenty-two years that has continued to be the animating spirit of
my poetry. Mr Henderson, on the contrary, seems to find his ideal man in the
'muckle sumph', and to wish to scrap all learning and all literature as hitherto defined
in favour of the boring doggerel of analphabetic and ineducable farm-labourers,
tinkers, and the like. He is presumably at home among beatniks and beatchiks.
Personally, I continue to think Dante, for example, or Goethe greater poets – and
more creditable specimens of homo sapiens – than McGonagall[4] or the authors of any
– and all – of the 'folksongs' Mr Henderson and his colleagues so assiduously collect.
I do not envy the task of whoever may ultimately have to go through the great mass of
indiscriminate tape-recordings accumulated by the School of Scottish Studies in
order to find any elements of real value. Looking for a needle in a haystack will be a
far easier job. Such collecting is a waste of time and money.

The degree of literacy in most people as a result of our educational system may
leave a great deal to be desired, but there is some hope for the future surely in the
fact that although trashy newspapers and periodicals still command immense sales
there has recently been a considerable turning-away from tabloids and 'the yellow
press' in favour of more serious journals; or, again, in the production and wide
circulation of paperbacks of excellent quality.

Mr Henderson quotes a few lines from my *Second Hymn to Lenin*, but to wrest a
small portion of a poem out of context in this way can be made to prove anything,
and Mr Henderson ought to have considered the significance of the fact that the
lines he quotes occur in a poem of an essentially non-popular kind, the main burden
of which is, in the question of the primacy of 'life' or literature, to come down
emphatically on the side of the latter. The lines he quotes simply express a counsel
of perfection – an ultimate (and perhaps unrealizable) aim, and certainly one no
poet anywhere, at any time, has succeeded in achieving.

In addition to that, 'highbrow' although my work may be, and certainly at the furthest remove from 'folk-poetry', it ought to be pointed out that no Scottish poet since Burns has commanded anything like the sales and recognition I have done, while through radio and TV I have reached many millions of listeners in this and several other countries.

But, Mr Henderson may say, my readers must have been mainly if not wholly, in the 'upper classes'. That is not the case. When ultimately my correspondence is lodged with the National Library of Scotland he may be surprised to find that a very considerable proportion of my correspondents are working men and women in this and other countries who testify, often in the most moving terms, to the inspiration and encouragement they have derived from my poems. That influence has been directed all along to an 'unqualified onward and upward', whereas Mr Henderson evidently wants to stabilize people at a low level corresponding to a state of society which has virtually ceased to exist, and which will disappear completely and finally with the increasing introduction of automation, with its demand for ever more highly skilled workers, and its concomitant of vastly increased leisure which will certainly not be profitably filled listening to unlettered ballad-singers yowling like so many cats on the tiles in moonlight. Mr Henderson's claim is preposterous at this time of vastly accelerated change and increasing complexity in all connections.

This correspondence began apropos the anthology *Honour'd Shade*. Let me remind Mr Henderson and others of something written by John Davidson[5] with which I completely agree, viz., 'The want of poetical power is the impelling force in the case of most versifiers. They would fain be poets, and imagine that the best way is to try to write poetry, and to publish what they write. They will never see their mistake. Equus asinus still believes that the possession of an organ of noise is sufficient, with a little practice, to enable him to sing like a nightingale.'

> I am etc., Hugh MacDiarmid

---

1 From Nan Shepherd's essay 'The Poetry of Hugh MacDiarmid', published in the *Aberdeen University Review*, vol. 26, November 1938. MacDiarmid also refers to this essay in *Lucky Poet* (Methuen: London, 1943).

2 The quotation, which is taken from Shepherd's essay, is made up of lines from various poems of MacDiarmid's:

[Man] '*will flash with the immortal fire*, [*will rise*]'; from 'Genethliacon for the New World Order', '*To the full height of the imaginative act/That wins to the reality in the fact*'; from 'The Progress of Poetry'; '*the light that breaks/From the whole earth seen as a star again/In the general life of man*'; from 'Genethliacon for the New World Order'.

3 From MacDiarmid's 'Lament for the Great Music'; note that in the *Complete*

Poems the third line reads 'Which the people recognise are states of mind'.
Shepherd would have seen these three poems in *Stony Limits and Other Poems*
(Gollancz: London, 1934) where they were first collected.

4 William McGonagall (1830–1902), poet; author of *Poetic Gems* (1890). See
MacDiarmid's essay 'The Great McGonagall (1936); *Hugh MacDiarmid: Selected
Prose* (Carcanet Press: Manchester, 1992); and Henderson's essay
'MacGonagall the What' (1965), *Alias MacAlias*.

5 John Davidson (1857–1909), poet, novelist and playwright.

89 Thomas Crawford[1] to the *Scotsman*

[25 January 1960]

Sir,

It is perhaps ill-mannered for a visitor to intervene in a debate between two such
masters of 'flyting' (surely a folk-art in itself) as Mr Henderson and Mr
MacDiarmid. I am, however, surprised to find the greatest makar of modern
times questioning the value of the School of Scottish Studies.

Far from being a parochial affair, the School of Scottish Studies is an institution
of world importance and influence. As a New Zealand university teacher of English
literature, I have known of its work, for years past, and have made considerable use
of its periodical *Scottish Studies*, as have also my colleagues in the departments of
history, geography, anthropology, and modern languages at the University of
Auckland. Obviously, what is true of Auckland is probably true of every other
university in the English-speaking world. We all have a deep respect for the School
of Scottish Studies, which we regard as a pioneering body, from which we can learn
a great deal.

For example, the work of the school has stimulated some New Zealanders to
press for the establishment of a School of Pacific Studies, which would co-ordinate
research into Maori and Polynesian customs, folk-art and linguistics. One of the
most interesting things that has happened in New Zealand in the last two or three
years has been the emergence of a group of Maori writers. These young men and
women write their poems, short stories and novels in English, not Maori – and, for
the most part, on contemporary, not traditional, subjects: but the academic
collection and recording of Maori chants and customs (corresponding to the sort of
impulse which produced the School of Scottish Studies here) has in practice
sharpened the Maori writer's awareness of the world of today, rather than the
reverse.

Mr MacDiarmid calls 'indiscriminate' folksong collecting a waste of time and
money. But the School of Scottish Studies works on a shoe-string, as compared
with the institutes of Rumania, Bulgaria, and Hungary, where expenditure on such
collecting is really lavish. Perhaps Mr MacDiarmid would answer that in those
countries folksong collecting is 'discriminate', in which case I would reply that it is

safer to gather in all available specimens before evaluating them, than to begin with the arbitrary assumption that only such-and-such songs are worth recording. Any other procedure allows too much scope to the researcher's prejudices and unconscious preconceptions.

Folksong and some 'high poetry' may be more closely connected than Mr MacDiarmid thinks. Is there not a relationship between the songs in Shakespeare's plays and previously existing folksongs? Were not the lyrics of Goethe's *Faust* influenced by the folksong revival of the late eighteenth century? Does not Blake's imagery owe something to the symbolic traditions of English folksong, which have recently been investigated by members of the English Folk Song and Dance Society? Did not Wordsworth inaugurate a poetic revolution by studying the art and literature of the 'muckle sumphs', and was he not reviled for it in his own day? Finally, did not the greatest English-speaking poet of the present century, W.B. Yeats, a poet for highbrows if ever there was one, owe a great deal to the singing habits of the Irish peasantry?

    I am etc., Thomas Crawford

1 Thomas Crawford, Scottish-born academic, lecturer in English Literature at the University of Auckland, New Zealand, and latterly at Aberdeen University.

90 Hugh MacDiarmid to the *Scotsman*[1]

                       [Brownsbank, Biggar, 25 January 1960]

Sir,

I am very sorry indeed if my last letter conveyed the impression that I question the value of the School of Scottish Studies. That is very far from the case. I was solely concerned in my argument with Mr Henderson with the question of literary value, but I do not for a moment question the value of such collecting to history, geography, anthropology and linguistics. I am fully aware that the school's work is indeed conducted 'on a shoestring'.

But the ecological situation out of which our ballads and folksongs came has practically ceased to exist, and I, for one, hope, and believe, there can be no recurrence to it. The hangover of our past rural life has had most deplorable effects in the vast body of post-Burnsian doggerel, and, in my experience, the present folksong cult plays into the hands of the great number of people who are hostile to all intellectual distinction and to experimental and *avant-garde* work generally, and I regard their attitude as a menace to the arts not less serious than, and closely connected with, the pressure to reduce all the arts to the level of mere entertainment.

    I am etc., Hugh MacDiarmid

1 This was the final letter in the 'Honor'd Shade Flyting'.

91 Arthur Argo[1] to Hamish Henderson

[Elgin, undated 1959/60]

Dear Hamish,

Just a wee note to let you know I got back safely, although unwillingly, to the North and to work. But before arriving here I had a couple of days in Leven where I did some recording with Jean[2] and her parents. Her father plays dulcimer and her mother seems to have quite a deal of folklore. Unfortunately, I had not the time to make any sort of survey of her repertoire.

In Aberdeen, I made a flying visit to Jeannie[3] – there I got her daughter[4] to sing 'My Bonnie Bonnie Boy' and 'Bonnie Bogieside' – and when I got home I paid a flying visit to Lucy and to Willie Robbie.[5] Apparently Ken[6] has not returned some piece that Mrs Robbie gave him on loan and although they say they are not overworried I get the impression that they are not altogether overjoyed.

One thing I want to bring to your notice. Peter Kennedy has done to Lucy what he did to John McDonald – got her under contract at two guineas for THREE songs. And again there is this ten-year clause. Perhaps you could let me know what you think of this. I told Lucy I would consult you and let her know what you thought. To me, two guineas does not seem a lot for three songs especially with this ten-year clause.

Didn't get a chance to go past and see Jimmy.[7] Time just seemed to run away. Have you made any progress with his tangled web of contracts?

Suppose by now you'll just be about set for your departure to Germany. Hope you have a fine time.

Any word of the tape you are going to get done for me. I'm glad that you hope to get it done soon. It will be a big worry off my mind.

If, as you say, it may be ready before you go off, that will be really great.

Well, Hamish, that seems to be about all for now. In case you are off to Germany before I get my Christmas cards off to the mail, all the season's greetings to both you and Ketzel [*sic*]. I hope it won't be too long before I see you both again.

Yours aye, Arthur

1 Arthur Argo, great-grandson of Gavin Greig; folk-singer, journalist, broadcaster and folklorist. Argo edited *Chapbook* (1965–9), for Aberdeen Folk Club, widely regarded as the best magazine published during the Revival.

2 Jean Redpath (b. 1937), folk-singer, born in Fife. Redpath began singing at the Edinburgh University Folksong Society; she lives and performs largely in America, and has lectured in music at Wesleyan University. Redpath is a renowned interpreter of traditional Scottish ballads. Her collaboration with the American composer Serge Hovey on the songs of Robert Burns is referred to in Letter 217.

3 Jeannie Robertson.

4 Lizzie Higgins, herself a great ballad singer.
5 Lucy Stewart of the Fetterangus Stewarts, ballad singer, and Willie Robbie, folk artist who specialised in painting Clydesdale horses.
6 Kenneth Goldstein.
7 Jimmy MacBeath.

92 To Hugh MacDiarmid

[*EUL*]

[Edinburgh, 20 March 1960]

Dear Chris,

I don't know whether you'll remember the writer of the enclosed letter[1] – she was a familiar figure in Edinburgh Highland society circles a few years ago, and is now the wife of a French maths teacher in Savoy.

The most distinctive thing about her was her red hair – not unlike Valda's – but she also had a very nice Shetland accent, and several attractive Shetland folksongs. (I got Alan Lomax to include her spinning song in one of his ballad-hunter programmes a two-three years back.) During my honeymoon last year I paid her a visit, and found that she now speaks perfect French with an impeccable Parisian accent: her native Shetland, however, is quite unimpaired. (In fact, if anything, it's even more pronounced – as usually happens.)

As you will see from her letter, she wants a MacDiarmid Lebenslauf with all the trimmings, so I thought I'd pass the request direct to you. I have written to her, saying that she will probably hear from you in due course.

Travelling in various parts of Scotland, I have become aware – as you probably have too – of the widespread interest in our recent flyting.[2] Some time this year I intend to write a lengthy article[3] about the whole question of literature and the oral folk art, so no doubt you will be emerging from your corner for the second round!

I hope both Valda and yourself are now completely recovered from your recent mishap.[4]

Best wishes, Hamish

1 Kitty Anderson, Shetland-born folk-singer.
2 The 'Honor'd Shade Flyting', see Letters 71–90.
3 Although this article was never published, Henderson used the material in the 'Folksong Flyting' of 1964.
4 MacDiarmid and Valda Grieve were involved in a car accident in February 1960.

93 Norman Buchan[1] to Hamish Henderson

[Glasgow, 29 March 1960]

Dear Hamish,

I have been meaning to write to you for the last two weeks to tell you about Jeannie's[2] visit here.

Following upon Professor Robin Orr's[3] praise for Jeannie's record on the *Arts Review* programme, Janey[4] got in touch with him. (She had already been helping him with the controversy over the possible disbanding of the BBC Scottish Orchestra and so the approach was easy.) She suggested that the Music Department here should invite Jeannie down for an afternoon recital. He was delighted at the idea but had little in the way of funds from the Music Department (he only has about twenty students in the whole Department). Janey then suggested involving other Departments, particularly English Literature and Scottish History, and that Edwin Morgan might give a lecture on the ballad, illustrated by Jeannie.

This was done, and the University did well by her. Professors Orr, Peter Alexander and George Pryde jointly sponsored it and brought along their Honours students. Several other members of the Senate and many of the staff attended, as did the Principal and Lady Hetherington. It was therefore quite a University occasion. More important, however, was the event itself. Jeannie sang magnificently and the whole thing was a triumph for her. About 140 students and staff attended. She received a very good fee – about five guineas more than Robin Orr thought he could muster.

Incidentally, in thanking her and Edwin Morgan,[5] Robin Orr said, 'She has provided me with an afternoon which, as a musician, I can only describe as sheer enchantment.' It's a good usable quote.

Two days before, on the Sunday, we had Jeannie singing at the Folksong Club. Their biggest attendance so far, about 200 odd, and again a triumph for Jeannie – she received a rapturous welcome. Again they managed a good fee for her. It was, for me, a high-water mark in activity in this field, and, despite what had happened between us, I felt I could not let it pass without letting you know about it.

I would have written you earlier but we had Jeannie staying for almost a week and then, right on top of that, we had Cisco Houston. His concert here was also a great success. Not perhaps a 'great' singer but certainly a 'must' for Edinburgh when he comes back. He only had a flying visit here but he definitely intends to make a proper tour some time soon.

Incidentally, I had to make three attempts before I finally got a mention of her H.M.V. record in the *W.S.*[6] I had earlier tried to get it in, associated with 'Brannan' and her 'Overgate' – for which last I again got her a 'source singer' fee. The cutting of the column in this way – a perpetual nightmare – is the reason why Jeannie was not credited with the 'Overgate'.

However . . . the real point about this letter is to tell you of Jeannie's visit to Glasgow, about which I know you will be pleased.

Best wishes, Norman B.

1 Norman Buchan (1923–90), teacher and politician. Editor of *Conflict*, the magazine of Glasgow University Socialist Society, which published Henderson's article 'Lallans And All That' (March 1949); he was a founder member of the Glasgow Folksong Club, and, as a teacher, introduced his pupils to folksongs and organized a school folksong club. Buchan's collection *101 Traditional Scottish Songs* (Collins: Glasgow, 1960) was very popular during the Revival. He was elected as Labour MP for West Renfrewshire in 1964, and served the constituency until his death.
2 Jeannie Robertson.
3 Robin Orr, Professor of Music at Glasgow University.
4 Janey Buchan, wife of Norman Buchan. MEP for Glasgow.
5 Edwin Morgan recalls the occasion with great pleasure: 'I joined Hamish in admiration for Jeannie Robertson, whose way of singing was something I had not heard before . . . Having heard, on records, many famous singers of opera or lieder straining every nerve to be *expressive*, I was fascinated by the fact that J.R.'s singing was anti-expressive, classical, often emphasizing the 'wrong' word or making a pause or link that ran counter to the sense, because that was how it had always been done.' Letter to the editor (Finlay), 31 January 1995.
6 The *Weekly Scotsman*, for which Buchan wrote a regular column on folksong.

94 Norman Buchan to Hamish Henderson

[Glasgow, undated Autumn 1960]

Dear Hamish,

A very brief note to follow up what we were doing this week.
1 The 'King Farewell' text and reference is enclosed. It is in the Kidson Collection.[1]
2 The Galloway Hills reference: by William Nicholson in *The Poetical Works of William Nicholson* published first in 1824. I have the third edition published in 1878.
Page 202. 'The Braes of Galloway' Tune: 'The White Cockade'
Chorus: Oh! Gallowa' braes they wave wi' broom,
       And heather-bells in bonnie bloom;
       There's lordly seats and livin's braw
       Amang the braes o' Gallowa'.
3 I have already spoken since my return to *Mr Foreman* of Collins. I have suggested to him that some time towards the end of the month he should phone up the School to discuss amounts to be paid to source-singers and

whether Collins should pay direct or through the School. This will give you an opportunity of letting Mr Megaw know what we are doing about it.

Here is the list of songs as from the school in whole or in part which I have given to him. I have marked XX beside those where I will tell him that Collins are under obligation to make a source-singer payment. (All will be acknowledged as from the School.)

Rhynie
Jamie Raeburn tune from the singing of Jessie Murray

	XX	Tae the beggin' tune	Edith White
	XX	Gaberlunzie Man tune...................................	Jeannie Robertson
		Wark o' the Weavers tune..........................	John Strachan
		(if used — one of those you had in mind to send)	
	XX	Bleacher Lassie o' K^2............tune Hamish Henderson and Jimmy	MacBeath (OK?)
XXX	XX	Will ye Gang, Love ....text and tune Andrew Robbie	
	XX	Twa Recruitin' Sergeants ....text and tune Jeannie Rob	
XXX	XX	The Toon o' Kelso ....text and tune George Fraser	
	XX	Rovin' Ploughboy ....text and tune John McDonald	
XXX	XX	I am a Miller tae .... Text and tune Lucy Stewart	
	XX	McPherson's Rant................ Jimmy MacBeath and Davy Stewart	
		Skippin' Barfit (if used) Jessie Murray	
	XX	Cutty's Wedding tune .... Jeannie Robertson	
	XX	Gallowa' Hills text and tune.......................... Jeannie Robertson	
		Ma Wee Gallus Bloke...Josh Shaw	
		(Leave this for me to deal with)	
	XX	Haughs o' Cromdale .... tune Hamish Henderson	
	XX	The Baron o' Brackley.......................... tune Hamish Henderson	
		Farewell tae Sicily	

The ones marked XXX XX I want to pay directly from Collins since I've spoken to them about it myself. Does this seem about right to you? The Birnie Bouzle I will also send directly to Aggie. I am sending off with this as many of the texts as I have copies to hand at the moment. My main concern is to safeguard the source-singer from the two points of view of 1) crediting 2) paying. Let me know any sins of omission in this respect in the list above.

One problem is Gipsy Laddie. I would like to use Jeannie's[3] tune (i.e. Rovin' Ploughboy). Feel awkward about asking for a fee since one already for John McDonald. Can I just acknowledge 'as sung by Jeannie R'?

I hope this is all clear to you. I am trying to pile into things very quickly.

I look forward to receiving the tapes for checking with tunes as we've done them. What happens when I prefer our own tune yet it is obviously based on the credited source-singer – credit it as 'based on the singing of'?? Anyway, that might not arise.

I am sorry our visit had to end in such difficult circumstances. I think I met Callum MacLean only once, but others, as well as yourself, have talked so much about him that I can imagine the stunning effect his death[4] must have had on all of you at the School.

Thank you again – and especially as from Ann.

    Regards, Norman B.

P.S. Rhynie/Delgaty. What did we propose about that? I seem to have left some notes in the School in Edinburgh.

---

1 The Kidson Folksong Collection, Mitchell Library, University of Glasgow.
2 Kelvinhaugh.
3 Jeannie Robertson.
4 Calum I. MacLean died of cancer in the Summer of 1960.

95 To the *Weekly Scotsman*

[undated 1960]

Sir,

It has been contended by some critics, as Norman Buchan points out, that the folk ballad of 'Harlaw' is comparatively recent in origin. There are powerful arguments against this contention.

It's true, certainly, that the ballad 're-writes' (and falsifies) history in favour of the north-east Lowlanders. But a comparative study of the balladry of war shows that it is exactly this violent and often fact-denying partisanship which is characteristic of it. The song about the battle fought on the Haughs of Cromdale in 1690 was similarly re-written to make it a Jacobite victory.

We know from the Complaynt of Scotland (1549) that a song 'The Battel of the Hayrlau' was in existence at the time. In the north-east, the battle itself, which left the flower of the Lowland chivalry dead on the field, is a folk-memory to this day. Is it conceivable that a ballad about such a famous event should, in the singing north-east, have perished utterly?

An intriguing (but likely unverifiable) possibility exists that one 'Robert Forbes, Gent,' author of Ajax's speech to the Grecian Knabbs, may have re-written a version of Harlaw to give his clan the centre of the stage (Scott was later to do the same sort of thing, and for the same reasons). Also, the great vogue of Harlaw as a printed broadsheet may have tended to stereotype the ballad and to supplant variants.

However, I'm pretty sure that 'Harlaw', as sung by Jeannie Robertson, is the lineal descendant of a much older song.

The decisive argument is probably the tune, which exhibits considerable variations as between versions, but is known up and down the north-east as the 'Harlaw' tune.

Yours etc Hamish Henderson

1961

96 To the *New Statesman*

[Edinburgh, 1 September 1961]

Sir,

Reviewing Dr George Elder Davie's *The Democratic Intellect*, Sir Charles Snow pays eloquent tribute to the Scots thinkers of the last century who were preoccupied with problems of culture, science and society — problems which confront our own generation with even greater urgency. He also reminds us that 'for over 200 years, from the end of the sixteenth century to the beginning of the nineteenth, there were four universities in Scotland and two in England.'

He does not add — and it is maybe worth while bringing the picture up to date — that in 1961 Scotland still has four universities (the same old faithfuls: youngest foundation 1583), while England now has sixteen. Furthermore, it has recently been announced that England is to have forty new ones, but Scotland is denied the fifth university for which she has been campaigning, on and off, for years.

Why? The process of *Gleichschaltung*[1] to which Sir Charles refers is now pretty well complete, so a new Scottish university would not have the disadvantage of roots in the native tradition. Indeed, like certain Scottish public schools, it might eventually make the grade, and even be regarded as socially acceptable.

Where, then, from the government's point of view, is the danger? A reading of Dr Davie's excellent book suggests one answer, at least: the Establishment may know little about the Scottish academic tradition, and care less, but it has a flawless nose for potential opposition. Certainly, having ruled us for the last decade, the government has the very best of reasons for fearing a resurgence of 'the democratic intellect'!

    Hamish Henderson

---

1 Trans. 'reduction to uniformity' (H.H.).

97 To Pete Seeger[1]

[Edinburgh, 6 October 1961]

Dear Pete,

I've just come back from a late holiday in Ireland, and found a leaning tower of letters — including your own, and one from a lad who listened to your rendering of the 'Freedom Come-All-Ye' at Carnegie Hall on 16th Sep. I'm most pleased to hear that you like the song, and that you've already begun singing it.

Of the songs in Ding Dong Dollar,[2] only two – the Freedom Come-All-Ye and the sequence called 'Anti-Polaris' on page 6 – are by me. These you are quite at liberty to print in 'Sing Out'.[3] For the others you should contact Morris Blythman, 109 Balgrayhill Rd, Glasgow, who is 'inspirer and begetter' of the whole collection, and author (or part author) of most of them.

Morris has already begun recording more material for a 12" LP, and the best thing would be for Moe Asch[4] to get in touch with him directly at his Glasgow address.

Here is a glossary for my own songs:

roch = rough   dawin = dawn
heelster-gowdie = head over heels
gar = make   rottans = rats, vermin
gallus = bold, reckless   loanins = tracks, lanes
callants = young lads ('gallants' is a misprint)
crousely craw = arrogantly crow
(Like many Scots phrases, this is most difficult to render: *crouse* can mean a lot of things, including 'conceited' and 'arrogant'; in conjunction with 'craw', it has the overtone of 'harsh' and 'raucous' as well.)
wee weans = kids   clachan = hamlet
herriet = harried   ane til ither = one to another
hoodies = crows   barley bree = whisky
geans = cherry-trees   dings doon = knocks down.

Looking forward to seeing you in November.

Yours aye, Hamish

---

1 Pete Seeger (b. 1919), American folk-singer.
2 *Ding Dong Dollar*, and album released by Folkways Records (FD 5444) featuring 15 Anti-Polaris/CND protest songs. Among the songs are 'Ding Dong Dollar', a favourite of Pete Seeger's, which is styled 'rebel-direct'; 'The Misguided Missile and the Misguided Miss' ('rebel-vaudeville'); 'Freedom Come-All-Ye' ('rebel-bardic') and 'Ye'll No Sit Here' ('rebel-burlesque'); Hamish Henderson from 'Scottish Folksong: A Select Discography', *Tocher* no.27, Winter 1977.
3 *Sing Out*, folksong magazine, edited by Irwin Silver in the USA.
4 Moe Asch; director of Folkways.

98 Jeannie Robertson to Hamish Henderson
[*EUL*]

[Aberdeen, 3 November 1961]

Dear Hamish,

I Sung at the pete Seegers Concert[1] on Sunday Night and Did very very well, indeed, and there were S.T.V. men in from the Grampain T.V. aberdeen. So I am on the Grampain all next week with a short song every Night. they told me that when the Grampain is Better organised they will give me a 1/4 of an hour show to myself with a setting of an old Clachan House, with a fire Glimmering in my face for the Big Ballads. I Let them see at pete Seegers show that I Could sing the Ballads, after all, Banjo playing is <u>Not</u> Singing Ballads. But pete was a very nice man, and so was Mrs Seeger[2] very nice.

you would have Been very proud of your singer if you had Been there. The Hall was full, there were somthing like 1,000 people there that Sunday night and they Clapped the House Down and they would <u>not</u> Let Me of the stage. Could you Be so kind as to give me a copy of yon 3 songs that you were playing yon night in your Home. I wonder if you could send me a copy of the tape so that I Could Get the Right tunes and words, you know I would <u>not</u> Let anyone Hear them. I mean the tape. we all arrived Home safe and sound, from Edinburg.

we all send Katzel our Love and Best wishes. Give her a Big Kiss for all of us.

Yours aye, Donald and Jeannie. Isaac and Lizzie.[3]
22. Montgomery Road Hayton.

---

1 The concert was held at the Music Hall in Aberdeen.
2 Peter Seeger's Japanese wife, Toshi.
3 Isaac Higgins, Jeannie Robertson's brother-in-law; Lizzie Higgins, her daughter.

1962

99 **To the** *Scotsman*

[Edinburgh, 12 May 1962]

Sir,

So Labour is once again thinking in terms of bell, book and candle.[1] How depressing! One would have thought that it might well have learned something from the cases of Cripps and Bevan in the thirties, or even – although this instance must seem incredibly parochial to the bigwig bonzes of Transport House – from the equally futile and self-defeating proscription of the Edinburgh People's Festival, which was given the treatment by the Labour Party in 1953.[2]

The writers, artists, singers and actors who had given their support to the Edinburgh People's Festival discovered, too late, that the Labour Party, one of the sponsors of the venture, was really not in the least interested in its artistic achievements, or even in its practical value as a carrier of Socialist ideas, but only in stymying what was earnestly assumed to be a Communist plot to 'take over' working-class culture. From quite early on, it seems, they were on the alert to find a pretext to wind up the venture, and the 1953 Theatre Workshop production of MacColl's *The Travellers*[3] provided one.

It is maybe worth while 'recapping' the facts about the mediocre *Tendenzstück*[4] which was used to justify the ban, because the barrenness of the official Labour point of view is strikingly revealed in the process. *The Travellers* belongs intellectually to a pre-Yevtushenko[5] – I had almost written antediluvian – Stalinist climate of ideas, which even at the height of the cold war seemed not green leaf but petrified forest. The production (by Joan Littlewood) was one of flamboyant genius, but this could not disguise the muscle-bound rigidity of the play's thought. Politically, *The Travellers* made contact only with the already converted. As propaganda, swaying the Festival public, it was nowhere. Nevertheless, it was used as a stick to break the promise of the entire People's Festival.

There is a sequel, which provides an ironic turn to the screw. A year after the ban, G.M. Thompson[6] MP, the canny middle-of-the-road editor of *Forward*, quietly and without fuss serialized *The Travellers* in his (by that time) tame and unexceptionable pink weekly. Thompson had the acumen to see that in spite of its political crudities, the play could be enjoyed purely as a thriller.

The moral is perfectly obvious. The People's Festival foundered not on Communist intrigues but on the hard rock of Scottish Labour's philistine head.

Why go over this past history? Because the psychology of Labour's present surly scapegoat-finding seems to rest on much the same false and contrived ground. Gaitskell knew that the theme of Glasgow's May Day rally was 'anti-Polaris'[7] (it was written in large letters on a banner over the platform); nevertheless, he indulged in shoddy shauchling over this life-and-death issue, attempting to ignore it. By doing so, he invited a vigorous sherricking from his Clydeside working-class audience, and this is exactly what he got.

It will take more than Alan Clayton's lachrymose split infinitives to persuade the Labour movement in Scotland that there was very much more to it than that.

I am etc., Hamish Henderson

---

1 'Bell, book and candle'; proverbial meaning, to take powers of excommunication. 'This letter was a response to a bout of McCarthyism the Labour Party was going through at the time' (H.H.).
2 See Letter 58.
3 Play by Ewan MacColl, see Letter 58.
4 Trans. 'a propagandist work of art' (H.H.).
5 Yevgeny Yevtushenko (b. 1933), Russian poet; the popularity of Yevtushenko's poetry during the early 1960s reflected the cultural thaw ushered in by the Kruschev era.
6 G.M. Thompson, editor of *Forward*; now Lord Thompson of Fleet.
7 Gaitskell, then Leader of the Labour Party, was heckled by anti-Polaris demonstrators during the 1962 May Day rally in Glasgow.

100 Pete Seeger to Hamish Henderson

[New York, 2 June 1962]

Dear Hamish,

The *Ding Dong Dollar* record has not received the explosions we had hoped. I think frankly the people who oppose it are scared to publicize it because they're afraid opposing it will simply cause many people to go out and buy it. And frankly they're right. Unfortunately, however, even people who should be supporting it are not giving it enough publicity. However, I'm going to see if I can do something about that right now. There are a number of FM radio stations in the country which should be playing it. My favorite song on the record is still the 'Freedom Come-Ye-All' [sic]. However, I must say that I sing mostly, everywhere I go, the theme song 'Ding Dong Dollar' and also 'Ye'll No Sit Here'. The chorus of 'Ding Dong Dollar' appears to me more fundamental and greater, every time I hear it. 'Ye Canna Spend a Dollar When You're Dead' – this is a theme song for the entire world these days.

Take care of yourselves.

As ever, Pete

1963

101 To Marian Sugden

Dear Marian,

Very many thanks for your letter.

I was terribly sorry to hear of your father's death. He is very much part of the vivid memories I have of successive Christmases at Hill House, and he and your mother were several times kind enough to send me letters of congratulation after there had been favourable mention of my work, one way or another.

The loss of him must have been a bad blow for you, and I'm really terribly sorry about it. Please tell your mother I feel very much for her too.

Not long back I completed a new song called 'The Flyting o' Life and Daith',[1] to a tune of my own which somewhat resembles the 'urlar' (or 'ground') of a pibroch. I've been singing it around and about, at various folksong clubs, and it seems to be 'taking' rapidly. Here it is:

> Quo life, the warld is mine.
> The floo'ers and trees, they're a' my ain.
> I am the day, and the sunshine.
> Quo life, the warld is mine.

> Quo daith, the warld is mine.
> Your lugs are deef, your een are blin.
> Your floo'ers maun dwine in my bitter win.
> Quo daith, the warld is mine.

> Quo life, the warld is mine.
> I hae saft wins, an' healin' rain.
> Aipples I hae, an' breid an' wine.
> Quo life, the warld is mine.

> Quo daith, the warld is mine.
> Whit sterts in dreid, gangs doon in pain.
> Bairns wintin' breid are makin' mane.
> Quo daith, the warld is mine.

Quo life, the warld is mine.
Your deidly wark, I ken it fine.
There's maet on earth for ilka wean.
    Quo life, the warld is mine.

    Quo daith, the warld is mine.
Your silly sheaves crine in my fire.
My worm keeks in your barn and byre.
    Quo daith, the warld is mine.

    Quo life, the warld is mine.
Dule on your een! Ae galliard hert.
Can ban tae hell your blackest airt.
    Quo life, the warld is mine.

    Quo daith, the warld is mine.
Your rantin' hert, in duddies braw,
He winna lowp my preeson wa'.
    Quo daith, the warld is mine.

    Quo life, the warld is mine.
Though ye bigg preesons o' marble stane,
Hert's luve ye cannae preeson in.
    Quo life, the warld is mine.

    Quo daith, the warld is mine.
I hae dug a grave, I hae dug it deep,
For war and the pest will gar ye sleep.
    Quo daith, the warld is mine.

    Quo life, the warld is mine.
An open grave is a furrow syne.
Ye'll no' keep my seed frae fa'in in.
    Quo life, the warld is mine.

I sang it at the 'Folksong galore' session of the weekend school (programme enclosed) and it got a great reception.[2]

Kätzel and the bairn are doing fine. Christine[3] is mostly sleeping nights, and otherwise treating us decent. The sight of Kätzel and her baby daughter can go right ahead to the finals for the loveliest sight in the world!

Also enclosed is a letter which I tried – unsuccessfully – to get to you when you were in Greece. (I think you'll agree it wasn't for want of trying!) The address is picturesque, if not maybe 100 per cent accurate.

Love to all three of you.

Slàinte mhath! Hamish, Kätzel and Christine

1 'The Flyting o' Life and Daith' was partly derived from an anonymous medieval German poem which Henderson saw in manuscript in the Library of the University of Göttingen in 1939.

2 The weekend school was put on by the Traditional Cosmology Society; Henderson gave a talk on 'duality', using this new song to illustrate his theme.

3 Hamish's first daughter, Christine, was born in 1963; his second, Janet, was born in 1966.

1964

102 **Ian Hamilton Finlay**[1] **to Hamish Henderson**

[Edinburgh, 23 February 1964]

Dear Hamish,

We'd still like a poem from you, for *Poor. Old. Tired. Horse.*[2] — if you have one available. Ironically enough, we have little difficulty in getting poems from USA, Brazil, Russia, Japan, and so on, but it seems almost impossible to get Scottish poems of a decent standard . . . Of course, it seems that a lot of the Scottish poets don't feel that Neruda, e.e. cummings, Jean Arp, Shimpei Kusano, etc. are of the *standard* they are used to . . . which is one point of view. (Not mine.) I'm sorry we can't pay, Hamish, but we don't make a profit on *POTH*. On the other hand, it does go all over the world. Please do try to let us have a poem.

I was very interested to see in today's *Scotsman* a wee report of your talk on two poet Macs.[3] Do you have any interest (it seems to me that it would be nice if people did have) in the *possibilities* of folk . . . i.e. you talk about the long folk line, of the concertina sort, with rhyme-ending, and it's true, the earlier Mac is very inventive with this. Do you know my poem, 'Angles of Stamps', in *The Dancers Inherit the Party*?[4] I tried to use the folk-long-line there, with a kind of *ironical sophistication*, and it seems to me that this *use* of folk — i.e., a deliberate use of it, putting it to use, has a lot of possibilities. As has the use of actual Scots, Glasgow Scots, and so on. Do you know any of the Russian poets of the time of the painters Larionov, Goncharova, etc.? They used street-folk-speech (such as I horrified local folk by doing in *Glasgow Beasts*),[5] and the painters, too, were crazy on folk-art and *used* it in their work. We are trying to get together a special number of *POTH* to honour the Russian *avant-garde* of that time, inc. Malevitch, Tatlin, etc., as well, and if you could do any trans. of the folk-jazzy poetry they did, I would be awfully glad, i.e. I'm sick of folk as a *dead* thing, and they never treated it as such . . . Do you know Zoschenko's[6] angry words about the people who resented his using gutter-folk-idioms to make stories from? Of course the thing is, to use — not to duplicate from outside, but to make from, by understanding. We are surely very narrow if we understand only one culture. (They talk of two cultures, but it seems to me there are twenty-two. And all of value.) Well.

Do let's hear from you, Hamish. I hope all goes well for you.

Aye, Ian H. Finlay

1 Ian Hamilton Finlay (b. 1925), poet and artist. Finlay first met Henderson in 1946. He is best known for his 'concrete poetry' and the garden he created at Little Sparta.
2 *Poor. Old. Tired. Horse.*, poetry magazine edited and published by Finlay, presenting work by Scottish poets alongside international poets.
3 'MacGonagall and MacDiarmid', a report of a talk Henderson gave to the Edinburgh University MacGonagall Society, material from which he later used in his essay 'MacGonagall the What', *Chapbook* 1965, reprinted in *Alias MacAlias*.
4 *The Dancers Inherit the Party* (Migrant Press, 1960).
5 Finlay was one of the first Scottish poets to use contemporary Glasgow dialect; *Glasgow Beasts* (Wild Flounder Press, 1961).
6 Zoschenko, Russian author of comic and satirical short stories.

The 'Folksong Flyting'

The 'Folksong Flyting' of 1964 was in many ways a continuation of the 'Honor'd Shade Flyting'. Henderson has always viewed it as the most crucial of the public disputes that he had with MacDiarmid, and certainly it is the one in which their positions are most clearly drawn. I have included all of the letters by Henderson and MacDiarmid, as well as a selection by other correspondents.

103 David Craig[1] to the *Scotsman*

[Carnforth, 4 March 1964]

Sir,

In the recent Third Programme survey of Scottish culture compiled by David Daiches, it was disappointing to hear two of our best-known poets going in for sweeping and decidedly ignorant depreciation of folksong. Perhaps there is some excuse for their ignorance: even on the Scottish Home Service our folksongs, which are the very voice of the people, are grossly underrepresented.

Scotland should be proud to have, living in Aberdeen, Jeannie Robertson, a noble singer whose huge repertoire of songs gives us in living form that great body of tales, worksongs, and irrepressible sallies of comedy with which our people have kept themselves going and nourished their imaginations from time immemorial. Yet the BBC has never given this singer one fifteen-minute programme to herself.

Norman MacCaig ended his Third Programme comments by saying that folksongs might be good enough for berry-pickers and steel mill workers, but not for him — he had read Homer. The two poems we now call Homer's are believed by modern scholars to have been pieced together out of short lays chanted by minstrels at the Aegean courts.

Scotland's lays are the ballads, and it is thus no exaggeration but the sober truth to say that in Jeannie Robertson Scotland has her Homeric-type singer, whose work is the equal in quality, in beauty and truth if not in scale, to the great European epics. If she is allowed to pass her prime without being heard to the full over 'our' national radio service, it will be an irretrievable crime done to our culture.

I am etc., David M. Craig

---

1 David Craig (b. 1932), poet, Marxist critic, lecturer in English Literature at the University of Lancaster; author of *Scottish Literature and the Scottish People, 1680–1830* (Chatto & Windus: London, 1961), co-editor with John Manson of MacDiarmid's *Selected Poems* (Penguin, 1970).

104 **Hugh MacDiarmid to the** *Scotsman*

[Brownsbank, Biggar, 7 March 1964]

Sir,

Mr David Craig's letter on depreciation of folksong is altogether beside the point. In all literatures there is a vast undergrowth of doggerel and mediocre versifying, but it is a remarkable instance of *trahison de clercs* if Dr Craig would have us believe that this is to be valued as equal to or better than acceptedly great poetry simply because, thanks to their minimal literacy and because it corresponds to their ignorant tastes and reflects the sorry condition of their lives, it is more popular among the broad masses of the people than the poems of, say, Shakespeare, Dante, Goethe, Rimbaud, Rilke, Pasternak, Montale, etc, etc.

Judged on this basis, McGonagall must be accounted a great poet, since he keeps going into edition after edition and comes only second to Burns in this respect. So must Robert Service[1] be accounted as a great poet, because he, too, achieved great popularity and made a fortune out of the millionfold sales of his books. No doubt he reflected the lives and dispositions of the Yukon pioneers, but that does not mean he ever wrote a line of poetry. He didn't.

Dr Craig does not hesitate to suggest that some of us who took part in the discussion on the Scottish Home Service underrated folksong because of ignorance. The suggestion is unworthy of him. I for one have been bored to death listening to more of it, including the renderings of Jeannie Robertson, Jimmy MacBeath, and others, than I venture to suggest Dr Craig has ever suffered, and I certainly never want to hear any more of it.

Unlike Dr Craig I think the BBC has already given much more programme prominence to 'corn-kisters'[2] than they deserve, and certainly of our great treasury of Scottish song only a small fraction has yet been broadcast. We hear the same hackneyed songs, Gaelic, Scots, or Anglo-Saxon, again and again and again, and the BBC would do well if it could induce some of its artistes to extend their repertoires. It has been estimated that of the over 200 songs of Burns the great majority are never sung at all and only about twenty are frequently (and in my view far too frequently) heard.

The demand everywhere today is for higher and higher intellectual levels. Why should we be concerned then with songs which reflect the educational limitations, the narrow lives, the poor literary abilities, of a peasantry we have happily outgrown? The study of such productions may be of some historical value, but is certainly of no literary value, in regard to which, as in every other connection in life, surely our regard and, if possible, emulation, should be given to the best and not to the lowest in past literary productivity. And above all we should not allow ourselves to be bogged in nostalgia for an irrecoverable way of life, and one, I think, in every respect fortunately irrecoverable.

I am etc., Hugh MacDiarmid

1 Robert Service (1874–1958), poet.
2 'Corn-kister', bothy ballad from the north-east of Scotland.

105 Hamish Henderson to the *Scotsman*

[Edinburgh, 15 March 1964]

Sir,

Hugh MacDiarmid claims to have been 'bored to death' by Jeannie Robertson's renderings of Scots ballads. This should not surprise us. Performances of high excellence are not seldom found boring by people not in sympathy with them. It has been known for members of audiences to yawn, and even barrack, during performances of the *Oresteia, Athalie* and *Juno and the Paycock*.

As against Mr MacDiarmid's deadly boredom, it is refreshing to recall Edwin Muir's address to the Scottish Association for the Speaking of Verse, shortly after hearing Jeannie's recordings of classic balladry in the School of Scottish Studies. He said that for the first time he had understood what the ballads were; Jeannie's renderings were 'extremely noble', and had 'wonderful dignity'. Not long after, the English folklorist A.L. Lloyd called her 'a singer sweet and heroic', and Alan Lomax (one of the most distinguished modern American collectors) called her 'the greatest ballad-singer in the world'.

Why is Scotland often so slow to do proper justice to her first-raters? As I write, Jeannie Robertson is preparing to leave for Dublin, where she has a singing engagement at the Mansion House. Since she was discovered in 1953 she has repeatedly received invitations to visit both the United States and the Soviet Union. Her records have sold thousands of copies. And yet, as Dr David Craig has pointed out, she has never been given one single fifteen-minute programme to herself on the Scottish Home Service.

Among the 'acceptedly great' poets, Mr MacDiarmid lists Montale – and rightly so, for Montale is at least as good a poet in Italian as MacDiarmid is in Scots and

English. Having introduced Mr MacDiarmid to Montale in 1947, and acted as interpreter during their conversations, I well remember how keen Mr MacDiarmid was to stress the fruitful interaction from which folksong and art-poetry have always benefited in the Scots literary tradition. He assented with enthusiasm when I explained to the Italian poet that he had drawn not only the language – half-forgotten Scots, which he revivified – but also whole lines and fragments of verses from the eighteenth-century anonyms collected by Herd and others. I pointed out that Sorley MacLean, influenced by MacDiarmid, had done the same sort of thing in Scots Gaelic. Replying, Montale compared some of MacDiarmid's lyrics, which I had translated for him, to poems of García Lorca.

There can be no doubt that by denigrating Scots popular poetry now, Mr MacDiarmid is trying to kick away from under his feet one of the ladders on which he rose to greatness.

He gave Scots folksong an unwitting but no doubt sincere tribute a few weeks ago, however. In a recorded conversation with T.T. Kilbucho on the radio, Mr MacDiarmid mentioned 'some lesser known poems' of Burns which he regarded as much superior to those for which that poet is usually praised. He then proceeded to quote three of these, viz, 'O that I had ne'er been married', 'Scroggam' and 'Wha is that at my bower door?'

Of these, the first is an old song, preserved in Herd's MSS;[1] Burns added a stanza. 'Scroggam' is recognizable at a glance as folk-poetry, 'redded up' by the bard; the first stanza is adapted from 'Will ye na, can ye na let me be' in the Merry Muses, and the third stanza (still orally current in Aberdeenshire) is in 'Blythe Will and Bessie's Wedding' – an old song, also in the Merry Muses. 'Wha is that at my bower door?' is founded on a broadside ballad, 'Who but I, Quoth Finlay', and related to a large family of international folksongs.

Mr MacDiarmid has taken exception to the term 'ignorant' applied to his comments on folksong by Dr Craig, but ignorant – in this case, at least – is unfortunately the *mot juste*.

> I am etc., Hamish Henderson

---

1 David Herd (1732–1810); folksong collector, best known for his anthology *The Ancient and Modern Scottish Songs, Heroic Ballads, etc*, 1769, 2nd edition much enlarged, 2 vols 1776.

106 **Hugh MacDiarmid to the** *Scotsman*

[Brownsbank, Biggar, 19 March 1964]

Sir,

Mr Hamish Henderson points out that on radio I quoted three lesser known poems of Burns which I regard as much better than those for which Burns is usually praised. I was quite aware of their debt to folk sources, but Mr Henderson is quite wrong in thinking that my praise of these poems contradicts what I wrote in reply to Dr Craig. One point is that in thinking these poems better than the others I do not thereby think them great poetry.

I cannot deny that in Scottish literary history there have been fruitful interactions between folksong and art-poetry, and that this happened in some of my own early lyrics. But that was nearly forty years ago, and my meeting with Montale was seventeen years ago. The folksong movement I was attacking in my letter had not then assumed its present menacing form, and in my own development as a poet I have had to abandon many of my early ideas and during the past thirty years I have been writing kinds of poetry quite unindebted to any folksong source and for the most part utterly opposed to anything of the kind.

Mr Henderson seems to have a curious idea of what constitutes a *mot juste*. The fact that I attach a certain value to some poems of Burns, based on folksong originals, does not invalidate my general condemnation of the folksong cult today, and it is quite a different thing to single out what has been achieved on such a basis by a poet of standing as opposed to approving generally of the unimproved mass of such 'songs'. In any case, a tremendous change has taken place since Burns' day, and since I wrote my own early lyrics, and apart from the fact that I think poets today have far other and much more important things to do, I do not believe that folksong sources can now supply springboards for significant work.

I am etc., Hugh MacDiarmid

107 **David Craig to the** *Scotsman*

[Carnforth, 28 March 1964]

Sir,

Mr MacDiarmid remains obdurately anti-folksong. But he deals wholly in generalization, and we must be much more specific if we are to do justice to this matter. Neither I nor, I presume, Hamish Henderson is trying to ram 'the unimproved mass of such songs' down people's throats, any more than one would recommend readers to wade through the entire library of printed poetry. What I am saying is that the folksong tradition has thrown up a great number of gems, of superb poems-to-music, that are meaningful, moving and ageless enough to claim the attention of everyone, whether steelworker, stockbroker, or teacher of Latin and Greek.

Few art-poems convey the needless suffering of warfare more poignantly than the ballad 'Edom o' Gordon',[1] the desolation of a forsaken woman is classically expressed in another ballad, 'Waly, Waly', and so on throughout the whole vast tradition.

Mr MacDiarmid speaks as though the literary situation can change basically in a few years — folk models were in thirty years ago, now they are out. Did anyone dream ten years ago that a New Wave was about to emerge that would find creative uses for the music-hall, the folksong, the vernacular tale, the tough-guy novel, and the radio documentary? Yet that is what has happened with the work of Brendan Behan, John Osborne, and Joan Littlewood, Arnold Wesker and John Arden, Alan Sillitoe and David Storey, Charles Parker, Ewan MacColl and Peggy Seeger.

Scotland's part in this is still small, yet Ewan MacColl, a great songster, is a Scottish talent, and Hamish Henderson's 'Fareweel to Sicily' and 'The Freedom Come-all-ye' — both songs to traditional airs — seem to me among the few excellent poems to have appeared in Scotland in recent times.

Mr MacDiarmid once wrote (*Second Hymn to Lenin*, 1932):

> Are my poems spoken in the factories and fields,
>   In the streets o' the toon?
> Gin they're no', then I'm failin' to dae
>   What I ocht to ha' dune.

If he has abandoned this aim, then he has abandoned the attempt to bridge the modern cultural gulfs and to reach the people with his work — an appalling lapse for a Socialist.

I know what he will reply — that it is the modern poet's duty to become ever more intellectual. This is a slogan from the days of Pound, Joyce and Eliot. Yet already their work, for the most part, looks like a pedantic aberration, as does the immensely long poem Mr MacDiarmid has been piecing together since 1934, compared with the poetry and drama of Brecht (full of debts to folksong and drama) or the cream of our New Wave. What is more, this new work, both popular and quality in its technique, has been able to reach millions in the form of songs, films and paperback novels.

If Mr MacDiarmid shuts his eyes to all this, he is not being 'advanced' — he is falling behind.

     I am etc., David M. Craig

---

1 Child Ballad no. 178.

108 Hugh MacDiarmid to the *Scotsman*

                    [Brownsbank, Biggar, 31 March 1964]

Sir,

I am very tired of the unscrupulous way in which correspondents like Dr David Craig use the few lines from my *Second Hymn to Lenin* beginning:

> Are my poems spoken in the factories and fields,

to support their anti-literary demagoguery.

In honesty, they should go on to show that my subsequent verses point out that no poet of any consequence has achieved that – not Shakespeare, Dante, Milton, Goethe, Burns – or, in fact, anyone at all worth a docken.

We all know of the great vogue and inter-traffic of European balladry. Most of it is rubbish, but in a few of our Scottish ballads it soars for a verse or two into the realm of great poetry. But all that arose out of an entirely different state of society from ours today or any ever likely to recur in 'advanced' countries.

Dr Craig knows perfectly well that I was not referring to that very small number of pieces of high literary excellence, of which 'Waly, Waly' is one; but to the bulk of the songs sung in connection with the current folksong movement, and in particular the 'corn-kisters'.

I have been a Socialist and active in various ways in the working-class movement for over half a century. One of the main factors by which I have been actuated has always been the realization of the very inadequate and seriously defective character of popular education, and I have never been – and am quite incapable of being – impressed by the preferences of the great mass of people adequately characterized by Professor Kenneth Buthlay[1] in his recently published study of my work when he says, apropos the Burns cult, that it has been, and still is, largely a matter of 'fulsome lip-service paid to his genius by people who had little but contempt for poetry in every other respect, and not even the rudiments of standards by which to judge it'.

Dr Craig attempts to dissociate himself from the promulgation of 'the unimproved mass of such songs', but his original letter was largely devoted to praise of Jeannie Robertson – and what else is she doing? And what proportion of the great collection of recordings of the School of Scottish Studies is more than rubbish? Dr Craig's tribute to the two songs he mentions by Hamish Henderson shows that he falls holus-bolus into the class defined in the final clause of my quotation from Professor Buthlay.

In any event, I have always made my position clear enough, and Dr Craig would have been fairer, if, alongside the lines he quoted, he had also quoted these (written over thirty years ago, as were those he quoted):

> I'm oot for shorter oors and higher pay
> And better conditions for a' workin' folk,
> But ken the hellish state in which they live's
> Due maistly to their ain mob ignorance.
> Yet tho' a' men were millionaires the morn,
> As they could easily be,
> They'd be nae better than maist rich folk noo
> And nocht that matters much 'ud be improved
> And micht be waur!

    I am etc., Hugh MacDiarmid

1 [Kenneth Buthlay] *Hugh MacDiarmid: Writers and Critics Series*, no. 36, (Oliver and Boyd: Edinburgh, 1964).

109 Hamish Henderson to the *Scotsman*

[Edinburgh, 3 April 1964]

Sir,

Mr MacDiarmid contends that none of the great figures of world literature have also been popular poets. This is not true. Leaving aside the special case of Burns, whose world-wide popularity maintains itself in spite of the cult and not because of it, I can provide from my own experience two cogent illustrations of the position Dante holds in the life of his countrymen. In October 1944 I asked a young Tuscan Partisan – an electrician from Florence – why he had joined the Garibaldini, and had elected to share all the dangers and hardships of life in the mountains; his answer was in the words of Dante:

> *Libertà va cercando, ch'è si cara,*
> *Come sa chi per lei vita rifiuta.*

'Freedom he is seeking, which is so precious – as they know who give up their lives for it.'

A few weeks later, when another Partisan was 'missing, presumed killed', one of his mates compared his fate to that of Buonconte, whose body was never found after the battle of Campaldino in 1289. Somewhat surprised by the recondite allusion, I asked for further information about the earlier casualty, and the red-neckerchiefed tommy-gun-toting bhoyo floored me completely by quoting from memory some fifteen to twenty lines of the 5th Canto of the *Purgatorio*.

As this correspondence is taking on with every letter more and more of the high mottled complexion of a Celtic flyting, let me come right out at this point and say that Mr MacDiarmid displays not the smallest comprehension of the difference between traditional song-poetry in the folk idiom and the lucubrations of minor or minimal scribblers who in every age are the dim also-rans of 'art-poetry'.

If Mr MacDiarmid will take a look at Douglas Young's *Scottish Verse 1851–1951*, he will find that a large part of it consists of pieces which (one feels) might have waited till doomsday for an anthologist had not Mr Young emerged as their god from the machine. But these are not folksongs; they are as far removed from the folk idiom as Canberra is from the Hudson River.

One of the few pieces in the earlier part of the anthology which merit a second or indeed a third reading is the bothy song 'The Barnyards o' Delgaty', and Mr Young included it only because he had found it in the Carswells' *The Scots Week-End*. Any reader who is doubtful about the distinction I am making should read the text of this corn-kister, as Mr Young reprints it, and then read 'My Ain Hearthstane' (p. 34) or 'The Auld Kirk o' Scotland' (p. 36).

The irony is that Mr Young could have found, among the Greig MSS,[1] in the Library of King's College, Aberdeen, or in the archives of the School of Scottish Studies, splendid racy gallus examples of full-blooded nineteenth-century folk-poetry, almost any one of which could have knocked for six his whole trayful of gormless Victorian bric-a-brac. Luckily, thanks to the folksong revival, an ever-increasing number of these Scots folksongs are becoming known to the youth of the country.

Like Dr Craig, I have no doubt that we are again in a period when folksong and art-poetry can interact fruitfully, and that it is in and through the present movement that this will come about. Anyone who looks up *The Second Hymn to Lenin* will see that the section beginning 'Are my poems spoken in the factories and fields' is an eloquent, and even poignant statement of the artist's awareness of his isolation in modern society, and of his duty to look outwards, and to attempt to communicate across the apollyon chasms. The crucial stanzas are the following:

> *Gin I canna win through to the man in the street,*
>   *The wife by the hearth,*
> *A' the cleverness on earth'll no mak' up*
>   *For the damnable dearth.*

> *Haud on, haud on; what poet's dune that?*
>   *Is Shakespeare read,*
> *Or Dante or Milton or Goethe or Burns?*
>   *— You heard what I said.*

Mr MacDiarmid is by no means the only poet who has spoken on varying occasions with two or more voices. But the meaning of these two stanzas of powerful 'direct poetry' is surely quite unequivocal.

   I am etc., Hamish Henderson

---

1 Gavin Greig (1856–1914), folklorist, collector and author; with James Bruce Duncan he collected one of the largest collections of folksong, consisting of some 3500 texts and 3000 tunes. The first volume in the complete edition of the *Greig–Duncan Folksong Collection* was published by Aberdeen University Press, 1981.

110 **David Craig to the** *Scotsman*

[Carnforth, 7 April 1964]

Sir,

Mr MacDiarmid accuses me of unscrupulously misrepresenting his *Second Hymn to Lenin*. In fact, the passage I cited – the first lyric from that long poem – can be made to mean nothing else than that the poet does want to 'win through to the man in the street'. The lines saying that no poet – not Shakespeare, Dante, Burns – had ever so won through are in inverted commas to show that they represent an imaginary objector. The poet himself replied in the magnificently downright line: 'You heard what I said'. What can this mean except that the poet reaffirms his dauntless determination to write for the people? But Mr MacDiarmid takes care to include a second line of defence – he wrote that poem thirty years ago; and it is not for me to deny him the right to repudiate his own finest work.

In any case, it is not true that no front-rank poet ever had his work spoken in the fields. Alexander Somerville, author of the *Autobiography of a Working Man*, did not know what 'poem' meant (he knew some Burns as anonymous songs) until, about 1820, a fellow harvest worker recited 'Hallowe'en' to him while they waited on a stack for the next cart; and James Hogg found his own love of poetry when a 'half-daft man' came to him on the hillside while he watched his flock, and repeated to him the whole of 'Tam O' Shanter'. As for factories, Mayakovsky was spoken there after the Revolution in Russia, and two years ago a Poetry Society was set up in the EMI factory at Hayes after Christopher Logue[1] and others had spoken poetry in the canteen during a Centre 42[2] show. Surely all this makes cultural defeatism inexcusable.

Mr MacDiarmid goes on making his assertions about the folksong tradition in general, 'What else is Jeannie Robertson doing,' he asks, but promulgating the 'unimproved mass of folksong?' Rhetorical questions are no substitute for argument. An outstanding thing about her versions of songs is precisely their unerring distinction of wording, which is constantly more vivid and poignant than the Child ballad texts: and Ewan MacColl recently collected from an old Perthshire woman's singing a version of 'The Cruel Mother' which ends with a series of metaphors for hell and guilt much more imaginative than the versions known hitherto. Thus the folk tradition improves itself.

Of course, Mr MacDiarmid means improvement by art-poets, for whom alone he has any use. Well, Brecht improved folksongs in this sense; so do those great recent works, the radio-ballads (e.g. the adaptation of 'Windy Old Weather' to describe the slump, in 'Singin' the Fishing'); and so did Mr MacDiarmid in some of his finest lyrics. The individual artists of our time could not produce such work if they were not lucky enough to have access to the tradition of song which has come to us solely through the mouths of hundreds of peasant and worker singers.

I am etc., David Craig

1 Christopher Logue (b. 1926), poet; associated with Olympia Press in Paris, Logue was active in the political counter-culture of the 1960s.
2 Centre 42, left-wing grouping of poets and playwrights, founded by Arnold Wesker.

111 Hugh MacDiarmid to the *Scotsman*

[Brownsbank, Biggar, 7 April 1964]

Sir,

Despite the efforts of Messrs David Craig, Hamish Henderson and others to demonstrate that I have resiled from my previous attitude to poetry and the people, the fact is that they are basing their 'case' on fragments of my work torn out of context, whereas if they had considered my work as a whole they would have realized that I was taking up the same position over thirty years ago and have maintained it consistently since.

For example, in an essay on 'Problems of Poetry Today' in 1934, I say, 'It is impossible to believe that the vast majority of contemporary poets, believe that poetry is vitally important, let alone the rarest and most important faculty of the human mind, or are prepared, for example, to consider the relatively enormous publicity given to some murder or divorce or stupid political 'stunt' as against the lack of "news value" considered to attach to any good new poem. They acquiesce in the socio-economic-politico-journalistic debauching of educational interests – the organized subversion and stultification of even those beginnings of popular education in which so much public money is spent: but poetry ought to be the mainstay of these educational interests.

'And it is precisely here that I reinforce my line of argument – it is the parasitical "interpreting class", those who "talk down to them" and insist that the level of utterance should be that of popular understanding, and jeer at what is not expressed in the jargon of the man-in-the-street, who are the enemies of the people, because what their attitude amounts to is "keeping the people in their place", stereotyping their stupidity. The interests of the masses and the real highbrow, the creative artist, are identical, for the function of the latter is the extension of human consciousness. The interests of poetry are diametrically opposed to whatever may be making for any robotisation or standardisation of humanity or any short-circuiting of human consciousness.'

It is significant that Dr Craig accuses me of 'cultural defeatism' and sneers at the extremely long poems with which, in lieu of my early lyrics, I have been preoccupied in the last thirty years. The trouble is that he, and other professedly Communist or left-wing advocates of regression to the simple outpourings of illiterates and backward peasants, do not know what, in fact, poets are doing in the Communist countries. Our century, our society, promotes the synthesis of the arts, synthetic thinking. The art of Communism will present us with ever more edifying artistic alloys, superior forms of Lenin's 'monumental propaganda'. Indeed, the term monumental has struck root in the theory of cinematography, the theatre, and music as well. Eisenstein's films *Battleship Potemkin, Alexander Nevski, Ivan the Terrible* are monumental, epos-like in the highest degree.

The 'epic drama' of Bertolt Brecht, an innovator through acquiring the monumental traditions of Sophocles, Shakespeare, and others, possesses the same basic character. A sonata by Enescu can also be sublime: in *Oedipus*, however, 'the work of my life', as the composer called it, the fruit of a quarter of a century's creative preoccupations and ten years' labours, the sublime is specifically monumental.

In music especially those great compositions such as operas, concertos, symphonies, symphonic poems, oratorios and cantatas can be monumental. The monumental was expressed by Bach, Beethoven, Brahms, Berlioz, Wagner, Bruckner, Mahler, Dvorak, Mussorgski, Borodin, Balakirev, Bartok, or Prokofiev. Symphonism implies vast generalizations, broad planes, comprehensive dimensions. By its very nature it quite favourably suits sharp conflicts, powerful dramatism, the combination of the epic and the dramatic genres (at times even the lyrical one).

Symphonism promotes the monumental. A recent conclusive proof is the creation of Dimitri Shostakovich. Shostakovich's symphonies form a grandiose 'musical chronicle' of the revolutionary decades. The 1905 revolution (Symphony no. 9), the Socialist revolution (Symphony no. 12), the Great Patriotic War (Symphonies no. 7 and no. 8) – these are its main stages, each of them monumental.

The grandeur of the time requires grand syntheses – not only in fine arts or music, but also in literature, not only in prose but also in poetry. Mayakovsky's poems 'Vladimir Ilyitch Lenin' and 'Harasho' ('The Poem of October') render in an impressive epic and lyrical synthesis the history of the preparation and carrying out of the first Socialist revolution in the world. The Chilean Pablo Neruda celebrates the fight for national liberation in monumental cycles of poems, such as the well-known *Canto General* or in the more recent *Cancion de gesta*, devoted to revolutionary Cuba – not unlike the huge mural frescoes painted by the Mexican painters.

Nazim Hikmet[1] worked out a colossal poetical edifice, planned in nine volumes, with more than 3000 heroes, suggestively entitled *Human Panorama*, or *History of the Twentieth Century*. Vladimir Lugovski[2] wrote, in fourteen years, the great work of his life, *The Middle of the Century*, a book of poems which he called *His Century's Autobiography*, the result of profound lyrical and philosophic meditations on man, mankind, Communism.

The passage from my *Second Hymn to Lenin* is, I think deliberately, misunderstood by Messrs Craig and Henderson. The aim of all great poetry is universalization, but in so far from attaining it, great poetry is known only to a tiny fraction of the population. The isolated cases Messrs Craig and Henderson mention prove nothing to the contrary. We even used to have an occasional shepherd in this country taking a volume of Greek poetry with him to the hills. But one swallow does not make a summer – or even a good drink! Voicing the vain desire to get through to the people, realizing that I, and all literature, were failing to do so, it is noticeable that I refer to Dante, Goethe, etc. – in other words, to the great world poets, and not to the folk-poetry broad masses of the people already know.

There is no solution to the problem via the latter: the multiplication of mediocre writers is no contribution to literature.

I do not propose to do it here, but it would be useful to consider just why Messrs Craig, Henderson and others are so concerned with inferior stuff and so indifferent to the peaks of human achievement in the arts.

As to Mr William Smith,[3] I am quite aware that I must not confuse song with poetry, but this correspondence so far as I was concerned was one regarding literary values. On the musical side of the matter I said all I needed to say in my essays on Francis George Scott and Sir Hugh Roberton in my *Contemporary Scottish Studies* in 1926. As to my own poetry, Mr Smith ought to know that a great deal of it has been set to music – and that, if his musical tastes, like mine, appreciate Schoenberg, Webern, Berg, and the like, all of it could be, albeit backward-looking people may regard it as 'not really poetry at all', and would certainly regard such possible settings as 'not music', since indeed they would be as remote from folksong as the atmosphere of any intelligent household is from 'the home-life of our dear Queen'.

I am etc., Hugh MacDiarmid

1 Nazim Hikmet, Turkish poet; jailed by the Turkish Government because of his political opinions. Henderson and MacDiarmid actively campaigned for his release.
2 Communist poet.
3 Smith argued that MacDiarmid failed to 'apply the proper standards in confusing song with poetry'.

112 William Smith to the *Scotsman*

[Redding, by Falkirk, 12 April 1964]

Sir,

What Mr MacDiarmid has to say (10 April) in reply to my earlier letter is largely irrelevant, since he must know that the point at issue was not whether or no his poetry could be set to some kind of music, but the spuriosity of applying to folksong the criteria employed in the appraisal of formal literature. He concedes that to do so would be wrong ('I am quite aware that I must not confuse song with poetry'), but goes on to say that the correspondence 'was one regarding literary values'. The fault here is only too obvious, so perhaps, after all, an example would not come amiss.

I would not dismiss out of hand the poetry of these lines from a well-known folksong:[1]

> The trees are a' ivy, the leaves they are green,
> The times are past that I hae seen.
> And I maun lie my lane the weary winter through,
> For my bonnie laddie's lang, lang a-growin'.

Nevertheless, when these words are sung, as they are intended to be, one realizes the obvious, gross and fundamental error made by those who, like Mr MacDiarmid, speak of literary values as the main consideration in assessing the merit of a folksong.

There is more even than the music of the song to be considered. A few hours after reading Mr MacDiarmid's last letter I had the pleasure of asking Jeannie Robertson to sing one of our finest ballads, 'The Laird o' Drum' (a ballad of considerable beauty and force, achieving the gentle philosophy of Burns at his humanitarian best without the brassy tub-thumpin of 'A Man's a Man' – perhaps because of this). I have heard this ballad sung with the same words and tune by a Stirlingshire man who learnt it from his mother some sixty years ago, and the difference between the two renderings was one of interpretation.

The man sang the words and tune faithfully and without modification. Jeannie Robertson used her voice – pauses, tone, volume – to express the variations of each word, to emphasize, to soften.

By far the bulk of Mr MacDiarmid's letter, however, is concerned only incidentally with folksong. It is mostly an embodiment of the astounding proposition that 'the grandeur of the times requires grand syntheses'. His illustrations do not, mercifully, constitute a proof, but the implications are grave indeed. There is no inherently greater merit in the large work per se.

It is not, moreover, the sole function of art to chronicle the upheavals of this or any other time. But there has always been implicit in the worlds of art the function – for many, a primary one – of creating beauty. If the times did indeed require that creative endeavour should be channelled towards epic production, a serious limitation would be placed upon art as intolerable as any of the restrictions of Knox's Scotland, Puritan England, or the France of Napoleon I.

Would that Mr MacDiarmid could give us some more of his lyrics!

I am etc., William Smith

---

1 Lines from 'Still Growing'; also known as 'The College Boy'.

113 Hamish Henderson to the *Scotsman*

[Edinburgh, 12 April 1964]

Sir,

Scottish literary controversy not infrequently provides occasion for sardonic humour, and never more so than at this stage in the present correspondence, when Hugh MacDiarmid tries to suggest that because Dr Craig and I are interested in folk-music we are therefore indifferent to 'the peaks of human achievement in the arts'.

This allegation comes at the end of a long letter in which Mr MacDiarmid extols the 'monumental' in all the arts. It is clear he feels that if one is going to beg the question, one might as well go the whole hog and beg it on a truly monumental scale.

Those who have read Mr MacDiarmid's *In Memoriam James Joyce* will recall that he refers to:

> That heroic genius, Antonio Gramsci,
> Studying comparative linguistics in prison.
> For, as he said in his *Lettere dal Carcere*,
> 'Nothing less. What could be more
> Disinterested and *für ewig*'.[1] (p. 27)

Gramsci, friend and antagonist of Croce,[2] was a polymath who, ranging as widely as MacDiarmid (and digging far deeper), was always ready to learn from, and appreciate, popular culture. He was also one of the few men in this century in connection with whom one can meaningfully use such terms as 'universalization'. Arrested by the Fascists in 1926 and given a twenty-year sentence, he spent the ten years which remained to him working on the grandiose prison notebooks, out of which were later quarried such works as *Notes on Machiavelli, Politics and the Modern State, Historical Materialism and the Philosophy of Benedetto Croce*, and *Intellectuals and the Organization of Culture*.

Thinker, man of action and Socialist martyr, Gramsci has left his mark indelibly on the largest Communist Party in Western Europe, and indeed on the whole Left in Italy. Yet, far from despising the folk arts, this universal genius devoted much of his time to their study, and some of the most perceptive remarks about folksong in modern European criticism are to be found in *Letteratura e Vita Nazionale* and other volumes.

In the same letter which Mr MacDiarmid quotes – it was written from Milan prison on 19 March 1927 – Gramsci outlines the projects he means to work on, and one of these is a study of popular taste in literature. What binds the various subjects together, he says, is 'the creative spirit of the people in its diverse phases'. A paper by Raimondo Manelii, read at the 1958 Rome Conference of Gramsci Studies, pays tribute to the philosopher's inspiration in this field ('Studi Gramsciani' 1958, pp. 183–7).

Why does Mr MacDiarmid despise the folk arts with such vehemence? Why does one encounter in his letters patronizing phrases like 'the simple outpourings of illiterate and backward peasants' – or even (not so long back) 'analphabetic and ineducable farm labourers, tinkers and the like'? Why this eager disparaging of Jeannie Robertson, whose magnificent classic ballad repertoire and noble singing style combine to make her in Alan Lomax's words, 'a monumental figure of the world's folksong'?

Some readers may have put Mr MacDiarmid's growlings down to mere testiness, or regarded them as understandable excrescences on a flyting which in the nature of things may tend to get a bit inflamed. In my opinion it goes much deeper than that. There are unresolved contradictions in Mr MacDiarmid's whole approach to the problems of language and the folk arts, and the passages in question represent no new development, but are the logical outcome of a train of thought which has been observable in his writings for twenty years and more.

Mr William Smith puts his finger on the trouble. Mr MacDiarmid has come to despise and reject the 'people of his country's past' with all the ardour of a seventeenth-century 'saint' outlawing the folk-singing and dancing damned to outer darkness. He has been, in fact, for years – in one of his personae, at least – the apostle of a kind of spiritual apartheid, and an acrid anti-humanist flavour in some of his writings is readily documentable.

A prime example of what I am referring to will be found in Mr MacDiarmid's 'Lewis Grassic Gibbon, James Leslie Mitchell' which appeared in *Scottish Art and Letters* no. 2 (Spring 1946). After referring to Gibbon's expulsion from the Communist Party, Mr MacDiarmid proceeds: 'As I have said, I on the other hand would sacrifice a million people any day for one immortal lyric. I am a scientific Socialist. I have no use whatever for emotional humanism.' (The reader will note that Mr MacDiarmid has unaccountably omitted the operative words from the above passage. They should be inserted after 'any day', and read: 'before breakfast'.)

Mr MacDiarmid's present broadsides against folksong are only to be understood against the background of passages such as this. Nevertheless, the anti-humanist strain which seems to parody itself here has not always borne the gree in this complex and turbulent imagination. Towards the end of *Third Hymn to Lenin*, Hugh MacDiarmid writes: 'Our concern is with human wholeness.' It is my belief that the communally shared and developed folk arts can be valuable aspects of 'human wholeness'. However, I would need another letter to do anything like justice to this theme.

I am etc., Hamish Henderson

---

1 See Letter 61. Trans, 'Für ewig', for eternity, *Complete Poems*, 745.
2 Benedetto Croce (1866–1952), Italian philosopher.

114 David Craig to the *Scotsman*

[Carnforth, 17 April 1964]

Sir,

Let me make one point absolutely clear in what will be my last contribution to this discussion. Mr MacDiarmid says that I am 'indifferent to the peaks of human achievement in the arts'. This is not true. My original purpose in writing to you was to publicize the BBC's neglect (since partly redeemed) of 'classical' Scottish folksong. This meant making the case for folksong. Obviously this does not mean depreciating other kinds of art. But it is not obvious to Mr MacDiarmid. He cracks up the 'monumental' — Shostakovich, Neruda, Brecht (who loathed the monumental) etc.

Certainly the big, comprehensive work of art is a vital thing in our culture. But why on earth has another kind of work — the more immediate, oral, sometimes extemporized — to be cried down so as to extol the big work? This is the easiest way to argue, and the most treacherous. It puts sectarian, snobbish, unnecessary barriers between forms of culture.

This is precisely what the Communist countries have not done; they have both fostered the oral side of literature (from modern, poetry-speaking in the squares of Moscow to epic singing by great peasant artists such as Jamboul of Kazakhstan and Karalayev of Kirghizia), and produced big work in modern forms such as cinema and the symphony.

For my own part, two of the 'biggest' composers (Beethoven and Shostakovich) are two whom I listen to most. In no way is this incompatible with my absorption in the unfolding of a long ballad like 'Lord Donald',[1] my relish at the sting and crack of 'The Blackleg Miners', my feelings of solidarity with 'The Durham Lockout' or my sheer delight in the zest of 'The Calton Weaver'.

The 'big' artists (such as Britten, Shostakovich and Brecht) will never turn their backs, as Mr MacDiarmid now does, on folksong — they feel its fertility for their own art, and value it as the voice of the common people.

   I am etc., David Craig

---

1 Child Ballad no. 12; also known as 'Lord Randal'.

115 Hugh MacDiarmid to the *Scotsman*

[Brownsbank, Biggar, 18 April 1964]

Sir,

How silly can Mr Hamish Henderson get? Everybody in some degree practises what he calls 'spiritual apartheid' if he or she likes one thing and dislikes another, prefers to associate with certain people and not with others, and so forth. I dislike folksong and as far as folksong concerts go simply ask, 'Include me out.' More generally, I prefer 'to be alone in my togetherness'.

But all that has little or nothing to do with the essential argument. Mr Henderson may assert, but certainly cannot show, that most of the great (as generally regarded) writers, painters and composers of Europe have owed anything decisive to folksong, and even if they had, what matters is not that, but what they did with the influence in question. At the present stage in human history, there are far more important things to do than bawl out folksongs, which, whatever function they may have had in the past, have little or no relevance to most people in advanced highly industrialized countries today. The arts grow, like apples, from the periphery, not from the core.

Folksong, and other folk-arts, may be the root from which all else has sprung, but a root is best just taken for granted, if the tree or plant is flourishing; or, as André Gide quoted, 'si le grain ne meurt . . .' The seed has died; we have the harvest. It does not matter one iota if we never see the seed (or root), nor would it matter if we just failed to realize there is one.

It is all too easy to bandy words like 'human' – they are the common stock of all demagogues and can mean anything or nothing. So far as Mr Henderson's attempt to prove me or my work 'anti-human' goes, the significance of the term is nil.

I am etc., Hugh MacDiarmid

PS Your readers will have noticed that Dr Craig and Mr Henderson tried first of all to show that I had retracted from the position expressed in a passage of my *Second Hymn to Lenin*. Now Mr Henderson has just gone to the opposite extreme and tried to show that in so far from wishing to write poetry that the people would read and repeat, I have all along expressed just the opposite attitude of contempt for the working class.

If my opponents had been capable of thinking rather more deeply, they would have realized that the two attitudes in question are just the two sides of the same penny. What they are really anxious to do, of course, is just to pull me down as many pegs as they can, and exalt instead Miss Robertson or some other folk-singer – in other words they are (naturally, I think) on the side of the merely interpretative artist and against the creative writer.

116 Hamish Henderson to the *Scotsman*

[Edinburgh, 2 April 1964]

Sir,

My only purpose in adding one more letter to this correspondence is to try to get the controversy into focus.

To oppose creative art to folk 'interpretation' is a false dichotomy. The essential difference between ethnic folksong and the commercialized folksong of the entertainers is that the former is creative and the latter is usually a dead-end.

Nobody with any sensitivity who has spent any time listening to Jeannie Robertson singing, talking or story-telling would deny that she is a creative artist in her own right.

Mr MacDiarmid is not, I think, wholly to blame for his evident failure to grasp this. The Scottish BBC must bear a substantial share of the blame for the obfuscation which obviously exists on this whole issue, and in the middle of which Mr MacDiarmid is wandering benighted. Until the present revival, the BBC relied, for 'folksong', upon art-singers who were prepared to do some occasional slumming – 'mucking the byre in white tie and tails'. If they used any near-ethnic singers, these would usually be the village concert type who could be relied on to reduce even the great tragic ballads to the scale of 'couthie wee thingies'. Alan Lomax's appearance (1951) shook things up a bit, but they soon got back to normal.

It took the BBC two whole years, after they were informed of Jeannie's existence and given samples of her performance (1953), to decide that she was good enough to be put on the radio, and it was not until after the start of the present correspondence that she was given a fifteen-minute ballad programme to herself.

Meanwhile, hours of BBC time had been devoted to the guitar-bashing popfolk performers who emerged in the wake of the revival. These entertainers were interpreting folksong with an eye to the appealing gimmick, some of them quite effectively, others pretty dimly. The uniforms had changed, but the people singing Scots folksong on the radio were still not the folk-singers. These latter had to be content with American LPs, invitations to sing at Cecil Sharp House,[1] and their modest niche in the archives of the School of Scottish Studies.

There are, needless to say, many reasons, other than literary ones, why a department such as ours assembles ethnographic material to document the folk-arts and folk-life of a country or community. Not all the singers with interesting material have good voices or singing styles, and vice versa. What impelled Dr Craig (in his original letter) to acclaim Jeannie Robertson was precisely his realization that Scotland possesses a major folk-singer whose talents cut across all such academic considerations, and whose merits warrant the sort of recognition from her native land which she has never so far received.

Mr MacDiarmid's comments on the phrase 'spiritual apartheid' are transparently disingenuous. To me, it signifies a great deal more than just preferring one pub to another, or one companion to another. It is a malady which used to be very rife among the 'justified sinners' of old-style Scots Calvinism, and it still bedevils some of their descendants. It never did us, or the world, any good.

And what on earth is one to say of Mr MacDiarmid's charge that because I drew attention to the anti-humanist flavour of certain of his writings, I was calling him and his work 'anti-human'? A person who can argue like this may not impress the

readers of a newspaper controversy, but at least he would never find any difficulty
earning a living as a professional contortionist. Is Mr MacDiarmid trying to emulate
that other MacD., whose Parliamentary performances earned him the title of 'the
boneless wonder'?[2]

          I am etc., Hamish Henderson

---

    1 Home of the English Folk Dance and Song Society.
    2 Ramsay MacDonald (1866–1937), first British Labour Party Prime Minister.

117 Douglas Young to the *Scotsman*

                          [University of Minnesota, 28 April 1964]
Sir,
     Mr Hamish Henderson, in his flyting with Mr Hugh MacDiarmid, takes a swipe
at me in his letter on 3 April, which has just reached me on the Left Bank of the
Mississippi. I am, in general, on the side of Mr Henderson and Dr Craig in the
issues they argue; but I must correct his assertion that I could have found 'in the
archives of the School of Scottish Studies' material for my anthology, *Scottish Verse
1851–1951*. At the time of its compilation there were no such archives.
     He errs also in stating that I included 'The Barnyards o' Delgaty' only because I
had found it in the Carswells' *The Scots Week-End*. I had known it before their
anthology came out, and merely took their text as a good one. From the collections
of Gavin Greig and Superintendent John Ord,[1] and other sources, I had selected
quite a few other anonymous items which Mr Henderson might reckon 'splendid
racy gallus examples of full-blooded nineteenth-century folk-poetry'; but, as rising
costs caused a downward revision of the scale of the anthology, I had to drop most
of them, apart from the suspicion that some of them really belonged before the
year 1851, my approximate starting-point.
     'The Barnyards o' Delgaty' was given as a specimen of what I termed 'those
excellent corn-kisters which flourish best in the north-east', and I look forward to
Mr Henderson's giving us a liberal anthology of such material from the archives to
which he has access and which he has himself helped to swell.

          I am etc., Douglas Young

---

    1 John Ord, folksong collector, Inspector of Police; edited *Bothy Songs and
      Ballads* (Paisley, 1930).

118 Hamish Henderson to the *Scotsman*

                          [Edinburgh, 11 May 1964]
Sir,
     I have no wish to flyte with Dr Douglas Young, especially as he is on the Left
Bank of the Mississippi, and there would be a grave danger of some of the missiles

falling short. (Those directed at Biggar mostly come back like a shot from a shovel.) However, Dr Young's letter is such a fruity example of camouflaged condescension towards folksong that we had better take a good look at what he is actually saying.

Before rising costs and misgivings about dates caused him to jettison the idea, Dr Young had selected 'quite a few' anonymous items from the Greig and Ord collections, and it had been his intention to include these in *Scottish Verse 1851– 1951*. Eventually he was obliged to drop 'most of them'. Dr Young may not have a copy of his anthology to hand on the Left Bank, but when he is able to refer to one he will see that he was obliged to drop all of them except 'The Barnyards o' Delgaty', which is presented in a shortened version. I quite agree with Dr Young that the *Scots Week-End* text, which he used, is a fairly good one, but he can hardly claim that it constitutes adequate representation of nineteenth-century folk-poetry.

When Dr Young was obliged to retrench, it was the folksong which went first. It never occurred to him to throw out the musty Victorian aspidistra leaves which clutter up the first half of his anthology, although most of these pieces would be more appropriately accommodated in an anthology of bad verse such as 'The Stuffed Owl'. (I am not referring to the item by Wm. McGonagall, whose verse – like the fiction of the Irish Ouida, Amanda McKittrick Ros – is so bad that it's good.)

Mr David Butts, BBC schools television producer, reminds me that three years ago he devoted a twenty-minute sound radio programme for schools to the life and songs of Jeannie Robertson. This had slipped my mind, and I am very happy to be able to put the record straight on this point. However, one isolated schools programme merely throws into higher relief the inexplicable BBC neglect of a great folk-singer. In his letter, the Scottish Information Officer of the BBC does not attempt to dispute this charge of neglect – for the simple reason that he cannot. As for the proportion of 'ethnic' to 'pop' folksong on BBC programmes over the last decade, that is the sort of question which could best be entrusted to a computer capable of reckoning in very small fractions, and as Mr Stewart is by no means responsible for this state of affairs, it would be unfair to press him too hard on this issue.

An article by Robert Shelton in the *New York Times* of 5 April puts the whole thing in a nutshell. Mr Shelton writes:

> The narrow-mindedness of some of the pop taste-makers concerning traditional music can be illustrated with this true story: two of the finest Southern mountain musicians, Tom Ashley and Doc Watson, did a recent guest appearance at a New York coffee-house. The audience went wild for their skilful traditional performances. The two are born showmen, professionals, at times virtuosos, with proven appeal far outside their milieu.

But the coffee-house owner wouldn't hire them. 'I'm not running an ethnic club,' he insisted, while the cheers of the listeners in his 'non-ethnic club' were reverberating for the two ethnic performers.

This sort of blind prejudice against 'ethnic' music, the misconceptions that surround all native singers, whether they are 'far out' or 'in', have simply served to rob a lot of city listeners of some of the golden moments in folk music.

The prejudices of our own pop taste-makers in this country are much the same, and the results are naturally identical.

I am etc., Hamish Henderson

119 Douglas Young to the *Scotsman*[1]

[University of Minnesota, 8 June 1964]

Sir,

Mr Hamish Henderson's renewed attack on me in your issue of 16 May has just arrived. He accuses me now of 'camouflaged condescension towards folksong', overlooking the substantial number of specimens of folksong which are to be found in my anthology of Scottish verse from 1851 to 1951.

If we accept the Webster definition of 'folksong' as 'a song originating and traditional among the common people of a country', Mr Henderson would be grossly unscientific and unhistorical if he denied that description to 'My Ain Hearthstane' by Hugh Macdonald, a man undeniably one of the 'common people' in the dictionary sense, and immensely popular on the Clydeside in his own day and long after; or to the handloom weaver's poem 'Tammie Treddlefeet'; or William Miller's 'Wee Willie Winkie', still orally current; or Ellen Johnston's 'The Last Sark'.

I am not sure where Mr Henderson wants the 'common people' to stop, but 'The Pawky Duke' is orally current as a folksong among ordinary persons who have never heard of Dr David Rorie as its author. Some great 'Anon' was inspired to compose the admirable piece entitled 'The Station-Master's Dochter', which Miss Helen Burness Cruickshank rescued from a column of *The People's Friend* of 2 April 1917. It might well be classed as folksong by analogy. I have evidence that some of Willie Soutar's 'bairn rhymes' are orally current without the name of their author, and are in course of becoming 'traditional among the common people'.

When forced to select among specimens of folksong, a wide-ranging category, I took 'The Barnyards o' Delgaty' as a favourite corn-kister from the Nor' Aist, and probably dateable after 1851; and for the folksong of other regions gave popular or at least meritorious specimens by known authors. I also gave representation to areas of what Mr Henderson terms 'nineteenth-century folk-poetry' apart from the more obviously singable, for instance, with Janet Hamilton's poems on 'The

Sunday Rail' and 'Oor Location', or John Mitchell's effusion on the St Rollox Lum. My tastes in folk-poetry seem to be broader than Mr Henderson's, and I repudiate his accusation of 'camouflaged condescension towards folksong'.

I am etc., Douglas Young

1 This was the final published letter in the 'Folksong Flyting'.

120 Hamish Henderson to the *Scotsman* (unpublished)

[Edinburgh, 20 June 1964]

Sir,

This folksong correspondence is like Finnegan's Wake; no sooner is the stiff decently laid out for burial than someone spills a drop of the cratur on him, and – lo and behold, see how he rises! Dr Douglas Young has supplied the requisite drop of Bourbon from across the water, so here we go again.

Dr Young does not deny that the items from the Gavin Greig and John Ord collections which he chose for his anthology vanished beyond recall, but claims that some of the pieces he did include can be regarded as folksong. Quoting the Webster definition ('a song originating and traditional among the common people of a country'), he offers us 'My Ain Hearthstane' by the amiable Bridgeton block-printer Hugh Macdonald, whose contributions to the Glasgow *Citizen* were very popular in their day. All right. I'll readily concede that Dr Young has named a folksong if he will answer me the following simple questions. Who sang 'My Ain Hearthstane'? Where and when was it collected? How many variants are on record? How does the tune go?

Not even the most hirsute backwoods folklorist would nowadays accept the above-mentioned Webster definition as it stands. There was once a very determined school of German ethno-musicologists which went to the other extreme, and tried to prove that what Western Europe regarded as folksong had mostly just descended from the 'higher' levels of society to the 'lower', getting all mixed up and jurmummelt on the way. Their contentions are now themselves part of the history of folksong controversy, but there can be no doubt that a fair amount of folksong which has gained wide currency and can be collected in diverse variants did not in fact originate among the 'common people'.

The Victorian rhymesters who are listed by the hundred in D.H. Edwards' *Modern Scottish Poets* were to a large extent working class – the 'occupations' section enumerates blacksmiths, weavers, miners, factory-workers, and even a railway detective ('he seems to possess inherent poetic fancy') – but they would not have thanked Dr Young for the suggestion that they were folk-poets. Here are some of the titles listed by Edwards: 'To a raindrop'; 'To an infant'; 'To an iceberg'; 'To a noble gentleman'; 'To a ruin'; 'To an old clock'. There are four poems entitled 'The Widow's Mite', and five called 'To a Snowdrop'. Among the subjects which have inspired poetic effusions are 'My auld aucht-day clock', 'My grannie's auld plate-rack' and 'My first pair of breeks'. Opening these volumes, you find yourself at once in the dimmest recesses of forgotten art-poetry, and in no time you are choking with the stour.

All this is the very antipodes of the folk-idiom as one finds it in the orally transmitted bothy songs and ballads. Folk-poets operate in a way quite different from that of bottom-echelon art-poets. They nearly always use a tune (or a variant of a tune) that's known already, and sometimes annex a line, an idea or even a whole verse from an earlier song. In fact, the song which at birth (so to speak) is already a folksong in the making has usually got something of other songs embedded in it. This is one reason why, when other folk like the song, and sing it, they don't regard it as being the exclusive property of the author, and feel at liberty to change it.

The 'folk process' is a useful shorthand phrase for what happens to songs when they begin to take on a life of their own, start shedding some things and acquiring others, and generally assuming a new form, or forms. It's not the origin of the song which really matters, but what becomes of it, and the best of the items in the Greig and Ord collections bear splendid witness to the continuing vitality of a tradition which, in the days of Scott, Ritson and Kinloch, contributed scores of famous ballad-texts to the world's folksong.

It will be clear from the above that I do not consider Hugh Macdonald's 'My Ain Hearthstane' to be folksong, although I can well understand the reasons for its immediate popularity when it appeared in the columns of the *Citizen* in 1849. Most of the other items mentioned by Dr Young are likewise minor art-poetry, not folksong. Janet Hamilton's 'Oor Location' has genuine merit; it is a charcoal sketch, done with gusto, of Scots proletarian life a hundred years ago. As for 'The Pawky Duke', it fully deserves its Bab Ballad-style popularity as a party piece. However, if one compares these items with the texts of orally transmitted folksong variants, the idiomatic difference is obvious.

Admittedly, 'Wee Willie Winkie' and 'Tammie Treddlefeet' fall into a sort of intermediate category of their own, but even if (for the sake of argument) one were to allow Dr Young's plea in these instances, would this justify his claim to have included 'a substantial number of specimens of folksong' in his anthology?

I am etc., Hamish Henderson

121 Hamish Henderson to the *Scotsman*

[Edinburgh, 24 August 1964]

Sir,

I hope that poetry written by children will not be left undiscussed at this year's Poetry Conference at the Traverse. Here is an example of considerable interest which reached me recently:

GOD

I've been told God's all around,
But when you look, he can't be found.
He's my bookcase, books as well,
A pan, a plate, a church tower-bell.
He is nought, one, you and me,
The Indian Ocean, a cup of tea.
God's the man who was first in space,
The tiny freckle on my face.
He is music, love and woe,
God is stop, get set and go.
He's my carpet and my toes,
He's just atoms, I suppose.

The above was written by Diarmid Moncrieff,[1] an eleven-year-old schoolboy.

I am etc., Hamish Henderson

_____

1 Son of Douglas and Queenie Scott Moncrieff, named in honour of MacDiarmid.

122 Letter to Hugh MacDiarmid
[EUL]

[Undated, postmark 29 August 1964]

Dear Chris,

I spoke to George Bruce[1] on the phone yesterday, and he promised me he would write and acquaint you with the true facts of the situation.

As you have made an untrue statement about me in public,[2] I rely on you to make an equally definite – and handsome – retraction before the Poetry Conference ends.

I'm going on holiday to Germany today, and won't be back for a few weeks. It's a great feeling.

Yours, Hamish

_____

1 George Bruce (b. 1909), poet, born in Fraserburgh; producer of
   documentary talks for BBC Scotland.
2 A public discussion of the issues raised during the 'Folksong Flyting' was held
   in the Traverse Theatre during the 1964 Edinburgh Festival. This was chaired
   by Magnus Magnusson, with Henderson and Craig, and MacDiarmid and
   MacCaig arguing their respective cases. Later in the International Writers
   Conference MacDiarmid delivered a talk about folksong, during which he
   made the comments Henderson took exception to. No apology was
   forthcoming.

1965

123 G.S. Fraser to Hamish Henderson

[Leicester, 28 March 1965]

My dear Hamish,

I'm writing off to David Posner today, and shall try and be as persuasive as I can. I am afraid I mislaid your earlier letter, or I would have answered you sooner and written to him sooner – but end of term, as you know, is a busy time, and the more I move about the world I seem to get letters of literary enquiry, books to review, poetic manuscripts to express an opinion on, from all over the world, so that if I kept up with my correspondence conscientiously it would be a full day's work, and leave no time for writing or teaching. Two other jobs I am doing, and am scared of falling behind-hand on, are trying to get together a posthumous volume of Jimmy Singer's[1] poems, at the request of his wife Marie; and doing my share in the collected Keith Douglas,[2] prose and verse, which Faber's want to bring out, probably with an introduction by Edmund Blunden. I often feel guilty about not answering letters from Scotland – two recently from Robin Lorimer[3] and Ian Hamilton Finlay are on my conscience. If you see either of these two, tell them that it is [because] I am kept pretty hard-worked, not (I hope) natural churlishness. One other thing I have to work on in this vacation is a couple of cantos of the *Paradiso* for the Third – I did Brunetto Latini and the sodomites and the usurers and Geryon last year, wonderful fun keeping the vividness of the detail and yet loosening up the syntax a bit for the speaking voice, but the *Paradiso* is a trickier job, not so homely or so vivid. But I mustn't tire you with these excuses.

The *Observer* rang me up the other day to ask me to do Willa Muir's ballad book,[4] but I was doing it already for the *Guardian*, so recommended you: did they get in touch? I see they have not done it yet. I found it a wonderful book for Willa's fine, tenacious character coming through it and awfully vivid and just as appreciative criticism, but I gather from Matthew Hodgart's piece in the *Spectator* that it's vulnerable from the point of view of ballad scholarship. But beautifully written, in that firm old Scottish voice.

A friend of mine, an American poet and novelist and anthologist (he also writes cook-books), with a beautiful double trochaic name, Paris Leary, is coming to Edinburgh this week, and I've taken the liberty of giving him a letter of introduction to you. He is a large man, heavy in body though not in mind, who broke his leg getting into his bath the other day, but has had it plastered up and will be able to get about, though not too far or too fast. He is a Southerner from Louisiana, with that rich, slow voice which is much pleasanter than the New York state or than most New England voices, but very sound on Civil Liberties. Paris has just brought out, or at least it's in final proof stage, a very big anthology of the American poets under forty or so. He enjoys a social glass. I hope you find some time for him, and can introduce him to some of the other poets.

The article[5] about you brought back all sorts of memories – what a lovely song and tune 'The pipie is dozy, the pipie is fey'[6] is. Are you ever going to publish the series of longish poems you were working on about the Italian Resistance?[7] I enclose a cheque for a subscription to *Scottish Studies*:[8] how about back numbers?

You look a very authoritative, professorial character – slightly Germanic – in the photograph on the first page of the article, and it contrasts with the slim kilted young figure in the Rome picture. But time goes by and I weigh literally twice as much as I did in those army days, though I am afraid I have not acquired professorial dignity!

Paddy[9] sends her best remembrances.

Yours, George

1 (James) Burns Singer (1928–64), poet.
2 Keith Douglas (1920–44), poet; fought in the Desert campaign, killed in Normandy.
3 Robin Lorimer, publisher; son of W.L. Lorimer, translator of the New Testament into Scots. Lorimer founded the Southside Publishing.
4 Willa Muir (1890–1970), author and translator; wife of the Scottish poet Edwin Muir. Her 'ballad book' was *Living With Ballads* (Hogarth Press: London, 1965).
5 *Chapbook magazine*, III.6, 1967; a feature issue on Henderson, which included two essays, 'Seumas Mor' by Maurice Fleming, and 'An Analysis' by Jack Mitchell, and six of Henderson's own songs.
6 Henderson's song 'The 51st Highland Division's Farewell to Sicily' was composed in 1943, to the tune 'Farewell to the Creeks', written by Pipe Major James Robertson of Banff.
7 'Freedom Becomes People', a long poem begun in the late 1950s; extracts of the poem and an introduction, 'The idea of the poem' written in 1968, appeared in *Chapman 42*, VIII.5, Winter 1985.
8 *Scottish Studies*, journal published by the School of Scottish Studies, Edinburgh University.
9 Paddy Fraser, wife of G.S. Fraser.

124 **To Tom Scott**

[Edinburgh, 14 April 1965]

Dear Tom,

I got a letter from Geordie Fraser[1] the other day — he asked me to give you his best wishes.

The Argo record company are using the 'Flyting o' Life and Daith' in a forthcoming LP of spoken poetry, so your 'White Cockade' prediction about its chances is getting substantiated. The only trouble is that I haven't found anyone yet who can really do it justice as a *song*. A Clydebank lad called Andy Hunter,[2] who's at present in Britanny, sent me a tape of himself singing it the other day; he makes quite a good job of it, but tends to make Life too much like an Italian general, leading his troops from a Roman villa. Life has got to be ready to do plenty of infighting, and the tune allows for this.

Argo asked me what the copyright position was in regard to the Flyting, and the position is certainly rather curious — until your Oxford book[3] appears (when will that be, incidentally?), the song will have circulated almost entirely by oral transmission. I suppose it would actually be possible for someone to print it, text plus tune, and claim the copyright. If that happens, I'll have to enlist your aid as an expert witness![4]

---

1 G.S. Fraser.

2 Andrew R. Hunter, folk-singer and lecturer in French at Heriot-Watt University, Edinburgh. See also Hunter's essay 'Hamish Henderson: The Odyssey of a Wandering King', *Aberdeen University Review*, no. 178, reprinted in *Cencrastus*, no. 47, Spring 1994.

3 *The Oxford Book of Scottish Verse*, edited by Tom Scott and John MacQueen, 1965; 'The Flyting o' Life and Daith' and the First Elegy 'End of a Campaign' are included.

4 The rest of this letter is missing.

1966

125 **To the** *Scotsman* (unpublished)

Sir,

No mention has been made so far, in the correspondence about John Maclean, of what one might call 'The Strange Case of the Great Soviet Encyclopaedia'. I refer to the 'John Maclean' entries in the volumes published in 1938 and 1954 respectively.

The 1938 volume has nothing to say about Maclean's relations with the British Communist Party, and provides no biographical details after 1918. On the other hand, the 1954 volume (published after Stalin's death, but presumably compiled during his last years) ends a much shorter entry with the categorical statement – 'In 1920 he [Maclean] joined the Communist Party of Great Britain'.

This statement, as all your correspondents will agree – whatever else they disagree on – is just not true. It would be interesting to know what the Scottish Committee of the CP (which has been conspicuous by its absence in the present correspondence) has to say about this blatant contradiction of historical fact. The error cannot be due to compression, because the two entries are curiously dissimilar, even giving different dates for Maclean's year of birth. Nor can it be due (from the Soviet point of view) to the obscurity of the subject, for Maclean was one of the two Western Socialists – the other was Karl Liebknecht – who were singled out for special praise by Lenin in 1914, on account of their courageous stand against war.

This is not just a question of academic accuracy. John Maclean was one of the few great nationally-minded Scotsmen of the present century; he was also a hero of the Labour movement, and gave his life for it. We owe it to his memory that the record should be put straight, and this correspondence has already provided some useful clarifications.

I am etc., Hamish Henderson

126 **To the** *Scotsman*

[Edinburgh, 2 May 1966]

Sir,

Would all or any of the correspondents at present holding their ritual biennial wake over the defunct Scots tongue – a corpse which just as regularly does a Finnegan on them – kindly provide answers to the following questions:

1 Why is it that when poets use words like 'sprauchle', 'stravaig', or 'breenge', they are often accused of employing unintelligible archaisms, but when these same words are used in programmes like *This Man Craig* and *Dr Finlay's Casebook* they seem to present no problem whatsoever to a television audience of millions on both sides of the Border?

2 How is it that teenage folk-singers in the clubs take so easily to the ballad-Scots (the 'folk-literary' language of such songs as 'Sir Patrick Spens', 'Clark Saunders' and 'Tamlane')?[1]

I am etc., Hamish Henderson

---

1 Child Ballad no. 58; Child Ballad no. 69; Child Ballad no. 39.

127 John Prebble[1] to the *Scotsman*

[Surrey, 27 June 1966]

Sir, ·

Though well upholstered by other material, Hamish Henderson's article in your Weekend Magazine was, in fact, his long-awaited attack on my book, *Glencoe*. Over the past few years I have developed an affectionate admiration for his persistence, but I would do myself an injustice if I did not answer him.

His attack was on two fronts – a feint upon the errors he found and a frontal assault on my manner of writing. Surprisingly, he cites two errors only – one of which I shamefully acknowledge, the other I dispute.

I apologize for the stupidity of 'below the haughs', particularly since I have always been aware of the meaning.

But what of Herd-widdiefous? My Scots dictionary defines this as 'cattle-thieves' and widdiefow as 'gallows-bird' or 'deserving to be hanged'. I do not claim that Gallows Herd was a translation. The term, in fact, is not mine, but I used it because it is more easily appreciated than the archaic Scots, and because it, too, means those who deserve to be hanged. Mr Henderson's pedestrian examination of the ballad I quoted does not alter my point – that Lowlanders believed the Lochaber men were fit for the gibbet only.

He then writes of my omissions, and not altogether correctly himself. If he looks at· the book again he will see that I acknowledge, by a footnote and in the bibliography, the source of Philip's 'Grameid'. I was also aware of John Hill's claim that MacIain went to Glengarry after his visit to Fort William. Mr Henderson makes too much of this, ridiculously so when he asks if Hill were lying. It was a simple mistake on Hill's part – the letters of the time are full of misinformation and gossip, arising from poor intelligence, lack of rapid communication, etc. Hill never referred to this again, nor did anyone else.

The rest of Mr Henderson's article is concerned with my style and with what he thinks is my attitude to Scots history. What answer can one give to cat-calls like 'glamour-whimsy', 'romantic literature' and 'pop historian', except to wish that Mr Henderson, in his disapproval of my style, had a more felicitous pen himself?

What he is really saying – and this is dangerous – is that his idea of how history should be written is the only one, the correct one, and all others are nonsense. He does not argue this, he flails at me with phrases like 'jerry-built reconstructionism' and 'costume-play posturing', stunning himself with his own ugly vocabulary. His only argument appears to be that a historian should not interpret, not make a writer's use of his MS. material, but should repeat it verbatim, in as many pages and as many appendices as may be required. Perhaps. But had I done this, my book would not have been one, but twenty volumes.

In any case, this is not how I see my obligations as a writer. History to me is the story of people, and when I tell it, as best I can, I try to demonstrate that they lived, and that, when pricked, they bled. This does not mean that I rely on what Mr Henderson calls my 'fertile imagination'. I invented no dialogue, no incident in *Glencoe*. I used no fact that is not in evidence, and I made no deductions (even as to smiles or a fire in the hearth at Fort William) that cannot be reasonably supported by fact.

I write this way because I wish my books to be read by the ordinary man and woman who have an avid thirst for knowledge about the past. I think this can be done without deception. But apparently it cannot be done without defiling the sacred cow of History which Mr Henderson worships, and which bores the ordinary man into ignorance. I find Mr Henderson's accusation of 'romantic nonsense' puzzling. My three books on the Highlands have brought down upon me the wrath of the romantics, the adherents of Celtic Twilight. They will not thank Mr Henderson for declaring me one of them.

As for his *Time-Life* taunt, it is unoriginal and incorrect. He should know that *Life*, at least, has published work by Hemingway, Churchill, English and American novelists, scholars and historians who must surely be found in his hagiocracy. But since I believe he may be open to persuasion, I will send him a year's subscription to both magazines – since plainly he does not read them – if he can secure from the editors the unlikely declaration that my writing is just what they demand from their editorial staffs.

I am etc., John Prebble

---

1 John Prebble (b. 1915), historian; author of popular histories of the '45 Rebellion and the Clearances. The correspondence between Prebble and Henderson amounts to a mini-flyting all of its own. On 25 June the *Scotsman* published an article by Henderson discussing John Buchan's *The Massacre of Glencoe* (Putnam & Sons: New York, 1933), and Prebble's recently published *Glencoe* (Secker & Warburg: London, 1966), in which Henderson praises

Prebble's version of the historical events as 'panoramic', a 'tour de force',
but criticizes him for errors of fact and a style too close to *Time-Life*
journalism. A complete version of this truncated article, 'Glencoe on our
Minds', was published in *Alias MacAlias*.

128 To the *Scotsman*

[Edinburgh, 1 July 1966]

Sir,

John Prebble has replied at length to my criticism of *Glencoe*. I have no wish to
prolong the Massacre unduly, but some points need clearing up.

He informs us that his Scots dictionary defines 'herd-widdiefous' as cattle-
thieves. The work Mr Prebble owns is Chambers's Scots Dictionary. Herd-
widdiefous is not in the Scottish National Dictionary, for the simple reason that it is
what lexicographers call a 'ghost word'. Its history can be traced back to the
Introduction which Scott wrote for 'Rob Roy' in 1829; it appears in a story which
Scott claimed to have collected from an old countryman in the Lennox. The
passage in question goes as follows: 'He expressed his confidence that the herd-
widdiefows could not have carried their booty far.' At the foot of the page Scott
glossed the word as meaning 'mad herdsmen – a name given to cattle-stealers'.

It has often been pointed out that Scott made some gross errors when dealing
with Gaelic, but it is less known that he sometimes made bad blunders with Scots.
Here he is confusing 'wud', meaning mad, with 'widdie', meaning gibbet (from
'withy halter') – a truly ludicrous error, much worse than anything Mr Prebble has
perpetuated. And where did Scott get his 'herd-widdiefows'? We know that he saw
the Skene Manuscript, which contains a version of 'The Barony of Brackley', the
ballad which Mr Prebble quoted. This is the version which refers to 'heard
widifas', and Scott probably did not realize that this was merely a free-wheeling
speller's way of writing 'hir'd widdiefous'.

If we have proved, therefore, that it is a 'ghost word', then Mr Prebble's
Gallows Herd is a spook which is the shade of a spook.

Mr Prebble avers that 'Lowlanders believed that Lochaber men were fit for the
gibbet only.' Some of them probably did, just as some Englishmen thought, then as
now, that the coolies began at Calais. However, I am quite sure that many God-
fearing, law-abiding Gaels, from Scourie to Inveraray, thought that the Scotts,
Elliots and Armstrongs would be 'nane the waur o' a hangin' ', into the bargain.

One of the less pleasing features of *Time-Life* caption-writing is the occasional
compression of texts, or the manipulation of them, in order to effect a subtle
change of emphasis. There are two good examples of this in *Glencoe*. Under the
picture of Campbell of Glenlyon the caption reads: 'I'd dirk any man if the King
gave me orders!' The source of this caption is the following passage in the Letter

from a Gentleman in Edinburgh: 'He said in the Royal Coffee House in Edinburgh that he would do it again, nay, that he would stab any man in Scotland or in England without asking the cause, if the King gave him orders.' Why 'dirk'? Because it sounds more picturesque and swashbuckling, more plaid-and-dagger. (Actually, the plain English 'stab' seems, in the context, much more formidable and sinister.) Similarly, the caption under Stair's portrait ('Be earnest, be secret and sudden, be quick') is a pasting together of three separate passages.

Although Mr Prebble lists the Scottish History Society edition of 'The Grameid' in his bibliography, he nowhere mentions the translator and editor whose work he has very freely used – though not always with perception. For example, on p. 76 he describes Claverhouse as wearing 'green leaves in his hat'. Here he has adapted Murdoch's translation, which is 'olive-crowned', but if he had looked at the Latin original, he would have realized that the poet was indulging in a harmless neo-classical flight of fancy.

I have no space here to deal with Mr Prebble's exaggeration of the psychological effects of the Highland Host of 1678, or with his quite illicit use of the phrase 'Mi-run mór nan Gall'[1] (a quotation from Alasdair MacMhaighstir Alasdair) as a peg on which to hang what is, in effect, a racialist interpretation of Scottish history.

I am etc., Hamish Henderson

---

1 Trans. 'great ill-will (or hatred) of the Lowlanders' (H.H.). The line comes from Alasdair MacMhaighstir Alasdair's poem 'The Resurrection of the Ancient Scottish Tongue' (1751).

129 To the *Scotsman*

[Edinburgh, 10 September 1966]

Sir,

According to Wilfred Taylor (A Scotsman's Log, 9 September), Bettina Jonic has stated that Lorca's[1] family believed the poet owed loyalty neither to the Republicans nor to the Nationalists. It would be interesting to know exactly to whom she is referring when she talks about Lorca's family, and also the sources (with dates) of her information.

Lorca's parents went into voluntary exile in the United States a year after the end of the Civil War; his father died in 1945, and his mother (who eventually returned to Spain) in 1959. Francisco, Lorca's younger brother, is still in the US as Professor of Spanish Philology at Columbia University; of his two sisters, only one – Isabel – is still alive. Isabel has provided the German critic, Günter W. Lorenz, with much biographical information for a book which presents quite a different picture of Lorca from that given in the abysmally poor play at the Gateway. The other sister, Concepción ('Conchita') – widow of Dr Manuel Fernandez

Montesinos, mayor of Granada, who was murdered by the Fascists on 3 August
1936 – was killed in a car crash in 1962.

It seems unlikely that Miss Jonic can be referring to Conchita's son Manuel, who
(true to the memory of his father and his uncle) demonstrated with other students
in 1956 in favour of greater freedom of speech and thought in the Spanish
universities, and as a result of this highly non-political misdemeanour spent a year
in the Carabanchel Prison in Madrid (1956–7).

Lorca was murdered because the leaders of the 'Escuadra Negra' in Granada
knew perfectly well where his political sympathies lay. They knew that he was
'essentially of the Left' (I quote Jean-Louis Schonberg), and that he was opposed to
a clerical-Fascist dictatorship. This is why he had to die, together with the flower of
the liberal intelligentsia of Granada – doctors, lawyers, professors, writers,
journalists, artists, poets. The victims, among them Federico, were forced to
dig their own graves.

Disingenuous attempts by right-wing propagandists to suggest that Lorca's death
was some sort of 'ghastly mistake' are decisively disproved by the fact that on 20
August 1936, the day after the poet was shot, the official Fascist newspaper in
Granada, *El Ideal*, published his name in the daily list of the 'executed'.

I am etc., Hamish Henderson

---

1 Federico García Lorca (1899–1936), playwright and poet, executed during
the Spanish Civil War. See Henderson's review 'Lorca and Cante Jondo',
Cencrastus, no. 26, Summer 1987, reprinted in *Alias MacAlias*. Henderson
attended a performance of Bettina Jonic's play, *Lorca*, at the Gateway Theatre
during the Edinburgh Festival Fringe. His shouted protests – 'It's a lie. Lorca
was for the Republic' – were referred to in Dorothy Young's review in the
Scotsman, 7 September 1966.

130 To the *Scotsman*

[Edinburgh, 20 September 1966]

Sir,

Commenting on my letter (14 September) about her play *Lorca*, Bettina Jonic[1]
(19 September) says: 'History is always muddled where there is more than one
observer.' Her letter, like her play, hardly tends towards clarification. Indeed,
both may be regarded (at any rate, as far as Spanish politics are concerned) as not
very successful essays in obfuscation.

Conceding that 'Lorca's sympathies may well have been with the Republic', she
adds: 'There is some evidence that he made statements to support the left and
much other evidence to show he did not.' I challenge her to produce some of this
plentiful evidence that he did not.

Meanwhile, here is one of the quite unequivocal public statements of Lorca, made on the eve of the Fascist putsch: 'I am a Spaniard through and through, and it would be impossible for me to live outside my own geographical frontiers: but I hate the Spaniard who is that and nothing else, and wants to be nothing else. I am the brother of all men, and I abhor the man who sacrifices himself for an abstract nationalistic idea, just because of a blindfolded love of his country. The good Chinese is nearer to me than the bad Spaniard. I sing Spain, and I feel it in my very marrow; but I am, above all, a citizen of the world, and a brother of all men. Therefore I do not believe in frontiers' (*El Sol*, Madrid, 10 June 1936).

This is a direct and unambiguous affirmation of patriotism and internationalism, made at a time when the shadow of Nazism was growing large across Europe, and when both Hitler and Mussolini were about to intervene in Spanish politics. Referring to this and similar statements, G.W. Lorenz writes: 'Was it strange that a man who came of a family hated by the reactionaries, who gave public expression to such views, and who in speech and writing and through his own example had fought against a world of dour stupidity and self-complacent darkness, was liquidated by a movement which acknowledged as its inspiration "Hitler, the renewer of Germany" (Pemán)?' (Lorenz, *Federico Garcia Lorca in Selbstzeugnissen und Bild-Dokumentum*, Rowohlt, 1963, p. 93).

It will not have escaped your readers that Miss Jonic passes over in discreet silence all the points I made about Lorca's family. Maybe she has learnt, too late, that Lorca's parents, although wealthy landowners, were politically opposed to the feudalistic diehards of Andalusia. The atmosphere in the Garcia Lorca family was liberal, anti-clerical and revolutionary, in the spirit of the movements of 1830 and 1840. After the tactical union, under Franco, of clerical reaction and Mussolini-inspired Fascism, the Garcia Lorca family was 'on the spot'. No wonder that it took the first opportunity, once the Civil War was over, of emigrating to the United States.

'Mr Henderson seems to forget', says Miss Jonic, 'that Lorca was staying with a prominent member of the Falange when he was arrested.' In 1946 the late Roy Campbell, who fought on Franco's side during the Civil War, spent nearly an hour at a party trying to convince me that because Lorca took refuge in the house of the Falangist Luis Rosales, his mind must have been divided about the rights and wrongs of the fratricidal struggle. As I pointed out to Campbell at the time – in an argument which became increasingly heated – this is the purest sophistry.

Luis Rosales had been a friend of Lorca's since childhood; he, too, was a poet; and Lorca's parents accepted his offer of a place of refuge for Federico, believing it was made in good faith. There is no reason to believe that it was not. Shortly after Federico left his parents' house, a squad of Fascists broke in looking for him, but for about a week he remained undetected in the house of Rosales. When Ramón Ruiz Alonso of the 'Escuadra Negra' (armed with a warrant for Lorca's arrest signed by General Valdes, the Governor of Granada) did manage eventually to track Lorca down, Luis Rosales was away from home; however, there is plenty of evidence that Luis's brother Miguel did his best to save the poet's life.

The reason for the vendetta is not in doubt. Lorca, inspired by the philosopher Don Fernando de los Rios, first Minister of Public Instruction under the Republic, had played a vital part in revolutionizing the cultural and artistic life of the Spanish masses. His travelling theatre, La Barraca (a direct forerunner of Joan Littlewood's Theatre Workshop), had played to packed houses in towns and villages all over Spain. During the Civil War, the *milicianos* on the fronts of Madrid and the Ebro sang the songs they had learned from Lorca and the student-actors of the Barraca.

Far from remaining neutral in the struggle between the entrenched reactionary old and the creative revolutionary new in Spanish life, Lorca was the inspiration and energizer of the Republic in the field of the Arts. This is the principal – if not the only – reason why the sadistic praetorians of the 'Escuadra Negra' did him in.

      I am etc., Hamish Henderson

---

1 'Unlike Mr Hamish Henderson (14 September) I do not make assumptions where there is no evidence in support. Lorca's sympathies may well have been with the Republic, and they probably were, but at a time of great commitment Lorca took no active part in politics. There is some evidence that he made statements to support the left and much other evidence to show that he did not. My play tried to maintain the ambiguity, while dramatising the anguish which is the most characteristic quality of his poetry . . . Wherever the "Escuadra Negra" believed his sympathies to lie, the bigots of Granada had many old scores to settle, because Lorca had for many years shocked and outraged them on the moral and artistic plane. Mr Henderson seems to forget that Lorca was staying with a prominent member of the Falange when he was arrested, having gone there because he knew perfectly well the quality of those who disliked him.' (Extract from Bettina Jonic's reply, *Scotsman*, 10 September 1966.)

131 To *Edinburgh Weekly*

[Edinburgh, 29 December 1966]

Sir,

I read with interest John Watt's article about an eighteenth-century execution in the Grassmarket, and the public reaction to it. The condemned man whose walk to the gallows Capt. Topham described was John Reid, a Stirlingshire sheep stealer.

Reid had the distinction of being defended by James Boswell, advocate, and anyone interested will find a lengthy account of the whole affair in *Boswell for the Defence*, the seventh volume of the Yale Edition of Boswell's private papers.

Before the execution, Boswell had a bright idea. 'After drinking a bottle of port, a curious thought struck me that I would write the case of John Reid as if dictated by himself on the day fixed for his execution. I accordingly did it, and hit off very well the thoughts and style of what such a case would have been. Nasmith took it home to get it copied and undertook to send it to Galbraith, a printer, that it might be hawked about the streets this very night; which would have a striking effect as it called on his readers to think that it was his Ghost speaking to them.'

The final sentence of this effort – which did in fact appear as a printed broadside – suggests that Boswell was well and truly under the influence of the port when he wrote it, for it reads as follows: 'May all good Christians, then, charitably pray that, as the King's heart is in the hand of the Lord, and he turneth it whithersoever he will, it may please him to save me from an ignominious death, which can do harm to no man.'

Hamish Henderson

132 **To *Tribune*[1]**

[Edinburgh, 30 December 1966]

Sir,

Gavin Kennedy writes (*Tribune*, 16 December): 'I can see no real principled reason why Labour should oppose home rule if the electorate wishes it.'

In 1949 the Scottish Covenant, a document which declared for an exceedingly moderate measure of Home Rule, was signed by over two million Scots. It got them nowhere. The Labour Government of the day had conveniently forgotten the pro-Home Rule opinions of Keir Hardie, James Maxton and other pioneers of the Labour movement: it had deliberately turned its back on its own pre-World War II policy statement on Scotland (published with a foreword by Attlee which stressed the advantages of devolution). The references to the need for a Scottish Parliament which appeared as vote catchers in the manifestoes of 1945 Labour candidates were some small embarrassment to the Government and helped to lose it Camlachie in 1947, but they were soon forgotten.

I spoke about this to John Strachey[2] during one of his visits to his Dundee constituency, and I found him quite cynical about the whole business: 'They'll have to start learning how politics work, and get a few Nationalists into Westminster.' It was obvious he was convinced this would never happen.

The Scots have learned by bitter experience that London-controlled parties talk about 'the country' but tend to think, when they come to power, very largely in terms of south-east England. It is all very well to talk glibly about subordinating everything to 'the achievement of Socialism', but Socialism will not be fashioned in a vacuum; it will be fashioned by the painful and difficult struggles of definite communities, in definite places; it will be achieved on farms and in workshops, in mines and in shipyards, and not only by courtesy of an act of the Westminster Parliament.

Also, in spite of Mr Kennedy's cheap cracks about 'sycophants of Burns', it seems likely that the inspiration of creative artists and thinkers will still count for something when we start the real job of building Socialism. Those who know the history of the left in Scotland honour John Maclean because he deserves it, and Burns because he was a 'friend of the people' as well as a great poet.

May I add that although I am not a member of the SNP, I know enough about Scottish affairs to be able to inform your readers that Mr Kennedy's references to 'a *one-party* SNP state', and to the neo-Nazi NDP, are so much idle bunkum.

Hamish Henderson

1 *Tribune*, Labour Party supporting weekly magazine.
2 John Strachey, Labour MP for Dundee.

1967

To T.S. Law[1]

[18 January 1967]

Dear Tom,

Many thanks for your letter, which I was delighted to get. I have received quite a few comments on my wee article.[2] One or two folk have drawn my attention to the fact that the same sort of thing (I mean the women more or less taking over) has happened in other places, including Africa, where a warrior caste has been destroyed and the women, so to speak, have the 'edge on the men'.

Tom Scott reminded me of the Lex Adamnani, which renewed a prohibition of St Columba's, and stopped the Caledonian tribes taking their women into battle with them. And all the bare-fist battles between the tinker women, north and south! Jeannie Robertson told me that her mother, Maria, 'was a bonnie fechter'. A week after the birth of her fourth child she fought and beat a woman nicknamed 'The Terror of the North' in a battle on the market-stance of Alford.

Here is Jeannie's own memory of what her mother said when she told the family of this famous event:

> Well, lassie, she says, I never was feared of nae woman in my life. I was a wee bittie windy, she says, but still I wouldnae show it – my bad temper wouldnae let me show it! She fought a clean fight, and I fought a clean fight wi' her. The woman had bonny hands – that was scientifically learned, ye see – but I had what she didnae; I had a terrible strength, wi' naething but the power o' bad temper!'

Have you ever met old Jock Keenan,[3] of Cardenden? He's long been a stalwart in the mining community there, spoke for Lawrence Daly and the Fife Socialist League in the 1959 election, and has 17 million ideas to rope together. He came and visited us (together with Lawrence and some others) at Hogmanay and we had a roarious time. I was answering a letter of his today, and seeing he had commented on my Clearance article himself, I told him about your letter and indeed sent him a copy of it; I hope you don't mind.

If you haven't met him you really ought to get together with him some time. All best wishes.

Yours aye, Hamish

1 T. S. Law, poet and miner, writes in Lallans.
2 Henderson's article 'Some Thoughts on the Clearances' (*Scots Magazine* vol. 86 no. 2, November 1966) discusses the role of women in resisting the evictions of the Clearances; an expanded version, 'The Women of the Glen: Some Thoughts on Highland History', was published in *The Celtic Consciousness*, edited by O'Driscoll (Canongate: Edinburgh, 1982), reprinted in *Alias MacAlias*.
3 Jock Keenan, a Fife coal miner.

134 To Jimmie MacGregor[1]

[18 January 1967]

Dear Jimmy,

I was glad to get your letter. I haven't time to make you a tape just now, but enclose photo-copies of three versions of 'The Flyting'[2]. The first is the basic tune; the second is a variant, as I sing it, and the third a variant sung by Andy Hunter.

'The Flyting' is a song for a single singer. Life and Daith are present in the one man. If it were done by two singers as a dialogue, it would be an empty dualism, and I don't think it could ever effectively be made into a group song. The tune is exceptionally exacting, and has to be sustained with decorated grace-noting (which is up to the singer) for eleven verses.

I take it you have had second thoughts about assisting me to reclaim some of the now considerable performing rights royalties which are owing to me. I am going to apply again to join the PRS[3] anyway.

Regards, Hamish

1 Jimmie MacGregor (b. 1932), folk-singer, author and broadcaster; his duo with Robin Hall was one of the most popular of the acts to emerge during the Folksong Revival, and the first of the successful commercial groups to emerge from Scotland. The two letters (134 and 137) to MacGregor illustrate the lessening of Henderson's antipathy towards 'commercialism' and 'professionalism'. Throughout the 1950s he (along with other 'father-figures' of the Revival such as Ewan MacColl and A.L. Lloyd) strongly resisted commercial pressures, which might distort the artistic achievements of the Revival, at the same time as trying to ensure that the 'source-singers' were paid. By the 1960s singers such as Jeannie Robertson had become, in effect, professional, and these distinctions became less relevant.

The duo Hall and MacGregor were responsible for the first commercial recording of 'The 51st Highland Division's Farewell to Sicily' (Collector Records, 1957). The John Maclean March and 'Freedom Come-All-Ye' are included on their final album *Songs Of Scotland*, and in the sleeve-notes MacGregor writes: 'Henderson is deservedly one of the most respected figures of the folk music revival in this country. It is impossible to estimate the value of his contribution, but his collecting and writing, combined with formidable energy and personality, have been a powerful re-energising force in Scottish traditional music. For me the 'Freedom Come-All-Ye' is, quite simply, the best song of the revival.'

In recent letters to the editor MacGregor comments: 'Not every live venue presented P.R.S. forms, but wherever they did, Hamish and indeed every other composer was credited'. 'As the revival gathered strength and the number of performers and venues increased, the whole question of copyright became a minefield, especially in the area of traditional material. People like MacColl and A.L. Lloyd tried to wrestle with the problem, but it was the agents, publishers, record producers and wheeler dealers of all kinds who reaped the benefits while the source singers were virtually ignored.' (August 1995.)

2 'The Flyting o' Life and Daith'; see Letter 101.
3 Performing Rights Society.

135 To David Rubenstein[1]

[8 January 1967]

Dear Mr Rubenstein,

Many thanks for sending me a comment on my little Clearances article.[2] By trailing my coat quite a bit I have elicited quite a number of interesting letters from historians and anthropologists. Some of the latter commenting on the role of the women point out that much the same sort of thing has happened in other parts of the world where a warrior caste has been broken and the women so to speak have the edge on the men.

My work among the Scots tinkers, who have inherited so many archaic curiosities, has convinced me that remnants of matriarchal rule must have persisted for longer in Scotland that many would imagine. Also, the tinker women (like the Celtic tribeswomen of St Columba's day) are doughty fighters both with fists and weapons. The great ballad singer Jeannie Robertson – I wonder if you know her singing – gave me a description once of a bare-fist battle on the market stance of Alford between her mother and another woman nicknamed 'the Terror of the North'. Here is Jeannie's own memory of what her mother said when she told the family of this famous event:

Well, lassie, she says, I never was feared of nae woman in my life. I was a wee bittie windy, she says, but still I wouldnae show it – my bad temper wouldnae let me show it! She fought a clean fight, and I fought a clean fight wi' her. The woman had bonny hands – that was scientifically learned, ye see – but I had what she didnae; I had a terrible strength, wi' naething but the power o' bad temper!'

Here is an essay on the great McGonagall[3] – a theme which lies somewhat nearer my own subject. I hope it will amuse you.

I always read your reviews in *Tribune* with interest.

Best wishes, Hamish Henderson

---

1 David Rubenstein, Lecturer in Economics at the University of Hull.
2 'Some Thoughts on the Clearances', *Scots Magazine*, vol. 86 no. 2, November 1966.
3 'MacGonagall the What', *Chapbook* 1965, reprinted in *Alias MacAlias*.

136 To the *New Statesman and Nation*

[Edinburgh, 3 February 1967]

Sir,

Conor Cruise O'Brien[1] enquires about the gobbet of Scots ('It'll na dee') which appears in a letter of Gladstone's. This is perfectly good north-east Doric for 'It will not do'; the more familiar 'dae' is used south of the Grampians. Presumably Gladstone preferred the Aberdeenshire form, which is found in the ballads quite often, and which is still current speech in many parts. Pithy Scots phrases appear not infrequently in nineteenth-century letters and journals written by people with Scottish antecedents. For example, the 'Scarlet Marquess' of Queensbury wrote in one of his letters to his son, Lord Alfred Douglas: 'Ye maun dree your weird' (i.e. you must suffer your destiny).

Hamish Henderson

---

1 Conor Cruise O'Brien (b. 1917), Irish historian, critic and author.

137 To Jimmie MacGregor

[Edinburgh, 10 February 1967]

Jimmy,

Thanks for your letter. I think the MCPS[1] has already collected the royalties owing to me in respect of the various television and radio programmes you mention. As I told you in the Traverse, the royalties still outstanding are performing rights royalties for 'live' performances at concerts, etc., and if the desultory information I receive from time to time is even half ways correct, there are quite a number of people in quite a number of countries who owe me a considerable amount of money.

As you know, I have taken an exceedingly liberal attitude towards performances of my own songs by the folk singers of the revival, especially the ones who are just about making a living jigging around the clubs. However, you and Robin are now in a totally different position. I don't think that you could altogether deny, furthermore, that it is partly at least due to my own work (not to mention, in the case of one of you, a fair amount of definite practical assistance) that you are in a totally different position.

As for the songs I collected and put into circulation, I did this in the context of a definite cultural strategy, and as in war one must always allow for losses of one sort or another. (I am not now referring to financial losses.) My hope — and it has been realized in quite a large number of cases — has been to encourage young folk to approach their cultural heritage with real creative elan. Some years ago M.L. Rosenthal wrote in his volume *The Modern Poets*: 'Among living English dialects it is a peculiarity of Scots that, while vigorous and full of homely and racy and humorous idioms, it also has the richness and dignity of a formal literary and even scholarly tradition.' To this one can surely add that it has an unsurpassed 'vernacular' musical tradition.

It is now a fact that many young people all over the country are aware of the implications of this statement, and even in some cases are doing creative work on the basis of them.

As far as 'A Wee Cock Sparra' is concerned, the facts are not in doubt. It is a traditional Scots item, known to many, which has been effectively copyrighted by two people. I was not referring to the rights and wrongs of the situation — in this field, they hardly seem to count, do they? — but only to what seems to me the actual legal position. I would have thought that Mr Farren knew the difference between Robin Hall and Jimmy MacGregor but one certainly does get surprises of this sort now and again.

Regards, Hamish

---

1 Mechanical Copyright Protection Society.

138 To Hugh MacDiarmid
[*EUL*]

[Edinburgh, 16 February 1967]

Dear Chris,

I enclose a copy of the new *Chapbook*. Please disregard the bouquet on pages 3 to 6, and move straight on to Jack Mitchell's[1] criticism. I'd be quite interested to know — as devastatingly frankly as you like — whether you think there is anything in Mitchell's apologia for my work, or whether you still think it is all a lot of nonsense.

Did I send you a copy of John Robert Colombo's[2] experiment with 'redeemed prose' — excerpts from the speeches and letters of Canada's early nineteenth-century rebel, William Lyon Mackenzie? He calls it 'The Mackenzie Poems'. In view of your own experiments along these lines I thought that this would be of considerable interest to you, and meant to send you one, although I may not have got round to it.

Hoping you are both keeping well.

Best wishes, Hamish

---

1 *Chapbook*, III.6, 1967.
2 John Robert Colombo (b. 1936), Canadian poet; Henderson is referring to poems of Colombo's which present 'found text', much as MacDiarmid has done in *In Memoriam James Joyce*.

139 To the *Sunday Times* (unpublished)

[25 October 1967]

Sir,

In his article 'Written in the Sand', Philip Oakes says that the poets who were actually fighting the desert war rarely wrote for the Cairo magazines. I do not think this is correct. Keith Douglas published several poems – including one of his finest, 'Dead Men' – in the monthly *Citadel*, which was edited by David Hicks and sponsored by the British Institute. *Citadel* also published, in March 1943, a remarkable poem called 'Stane Jock'[1], which was written by Lt W.H. Burt, an officer who fought at Alamein with the 51st Highland Recce Regiment.[2]

'Stane Jock' is in ballad-Scots, the old 'folk-literary' language, and – although it has been completely ignored by the various editors and anthologists who have been scraping around in the sand this year – it recently received a new lease of life in Scottish folk-clubs as spoken poetry. Here are the opening verses:

> Atween the mune an' the yird
>   There is quick steel:
> Atween the steel and the yird
>   There is quick stane!
>
> The man-trap field is fu' o' men
>   Walking saftly.
> The man-eating mandrakes scream
>   As they bite.
>
> The stane Jock o' Beaumont Hamel:
>   Is fa'en doon.
> There's nae mair pipes in France –
>   Nae mair sweet croon.
>
> But this nicht stane Jock.
>   Walks in the sand . . .

Another magazine, *Orientations*, occasionally had trouble with the military censor in Cairo. I sent it the first completed drafts of two of my elegies, but the censor felt himself obliged to axe them — as the editor explained to me, in a letter that eventually caught up with me in Sicily — on the grounds that 'such morbid writings have a depressing effect on the troops'.

I wonder if any of your readers can supply the end of a vigorous piece of folk-poetry which I saw written on the wall of a room in a *casa cantoniera* about thirty or forty miles west of Halfaya in November 1942.[3] The initial letters of this poem, read downwards, formed the words WE WILL REMEMBER THEM. I copied it down in a notebook which unfortunately went astray later in the war. The opening lines (all I can remember) went as follows:

> Wherever history is made, in this old world of strife,
> El Alamein will still remain and follow us through life.
>
> Who would not praise the glory there that our 8th Army won?
> Invincibly their unity put Rommel on the run
> Like lions at bay the guns roared on that famous 23rd.
> Living death the barrage it gave that Jerry herd.
>
> R.E.s there clearing minefields, showing courage brave and rare;
> Each lane made safe, lamps coolly lit, by CMPs placed there . . .

The armour, and the infantry divisions of 30 Corps all got their mention. The final 'M' was Montgomery.

>   Yours etc., Hamish Henderson

---

1 At Henderson's suggestion this poem was published by MacDiarmid in *Voice of Scotland*, IV.4, June 1948.

2 Lieutenant Burt was killed in Germany on 10 April 1945.

3 The missing lines have yet to be discovered. See also Henderson's essay 'The Poetry of War in the Middle East 1939–45', *Aquarius*, no. 17–18, reprinted in *Alias MacAlias*.

1968

140 To Mr C.A.R. Rayner

Dear Mr Rayner,

The Director passed your letter on to me. I have not come across songs referring directly to Thurot, but there are quite a number which refer to Paul Jones' appearance off the Scottish coast. For example there is a song called 'O Wow, Marget', which was first published in Hans Hecht's edition of David Herd's MSS (1904, p. 214). Here is one verse of it:

> For o, dear woman, o dear! o dear!
> The like o' this was never heard since Mar's year:
> The French and the 'Mericans they will a' be here,
> And we will a' be murdered, o dear, dear.

Hecht says: 'Of this spirited and clear production several versions have been published, all of them differing from Herd's which is here printed for the first time. They occur in (1) Sharpe's "Ballad Book" 1823, pp. 109–10, tune "How are ye Kimmer"; (2) Maidment's "North Countrie Garland" 1824, pp. 47–50, from R. Pitcairn's MS – collection of ballads etc. (3 vols. 1817–25) entitled "Paul Jones", tune "We're a' Noddin' " identical with "How are ye, Kimmer" for which see Johnson's Musical Museum VI no. 523; (3) Buchan's *Gleanings of Scotch English and Irish Scarce Old Ballads* 1825, pp. 147–9, as "The Sheriffmuir Amazons" – none of them as early as Herd's version, who stood in the full prime of his manhood when the events happened which gave rise to the song. Buchan remarks that since his ballad was printed he had "seen one similar to it called "Paul Jones" but what claim it has to this title I know not for it might with equal propriety be called The Apostle Paul, for it has no more connection with the one than the other" (L.C. p.202). *Pitcairn* knew better, and I may be allowed to quote a few interesting sentences on the history of the song from his MS. He says that he wrote it down from the recitation of an old lady and that it "was much sung in Edinburgh by the populace, on occasion of Paul Jones making his appearance in the Firth of Forth; and also during the strenuous opposition in Scotland, and the consequent riots which took place, during the discussion of the Papish Bill. It was afterwards revived during the threatened invasion of Britain by Bonaparte, in ridicule of the attempt" (Maidment I.c.47). It may be mentioned en passant that only in Sharpe's version the allusion to Sheriffmuir is omitted, and the powers threatening invasion are France and Ireland.

As to the history of John Paul, alias Paul Jones (1747–92) I must refer my readers to J.E. Ebsworth's remarks in *The Roxburghe Ballads*, vol. VIII pp. 330 ff. where several interesting slip-songs on this daring adventurer are reprinted from the Roxburghe and other collections: one of them, viz. 'The French Squadron', to the tune of Sheriffmuir, is very much in the strain of our song. Jones entered the Firth of Forth, after having plundered the coast of Fife, in September 1779.'

Here is the verse already quoted as it appears in Maidment's 'The North Countrie Garland' –

> Little do we see but meikle do we hear
> Frenchies and the Americans are a' comin here,
> An' we'll a' be murdered,
> An' we'll a' be murdered,
> And we'll a' be murdered,
> Before the New Year.

I hope this information is of some use to you.

> Yours sincerely, Hamish Henderson

The '1320 Club Flyting'

This brief public flyting between Henderson and MacDiarmid was to be their last. Henderson's Letter 141 supports the SNP's refusal to co-operate with the 1320 Club. This flyting is of more lasting significance primarily because Henderson draws MacDiarmid's interest in Fascist ideas in the 1920s into open discussion.

In a letter to Charles Lahr* written in March 1968, MacDiarmid described the 1320 Club as:

> . . . a group of people to conduct research into various aspects of Scottish economy, culture, etc., with a view to having these thoroughly studied and the results available when, and if, Scottish independence is achieved . . . As with other struggles against Imperialism, I do not believe that the Westminster Parliament will grant Scotland any useful measure of Self-Government no matter how strong the popular demand may be. Consequently contingency planning must include measures in case armed struggle is forced upon us.
> *The Letters of Hugh MacDiarmid*, edited by Alan Bold (Hamish Hamilton: London, 1984, 875).

---

* Charles Lahr, second-hand bookseller in London: a close friend of
  MacDiarmid. He published *Wha's Been Here Afore Me Lass* (from *A Drunk Man
  Looks at the Thistle*) as a *Blue Moon Poem* (Christmas 1931).

141 **To the** *Scotsman*

[Edinburgh, 21 February 1968]

Sir,

The mere mention of political witch-hunting is a drag to the spirit, and the less we have of it the better. However, one understands very well what Winnie Ewing[1] and George Leslie[2] are about when they draw attention to the activities of some rather dubious allies.

Groups of 'self-elected Elect' have always been the bane of Scottish Home Rule politics. Gathered in disputatious huddles on the periphery of whatever rational and coherent activity they can find to disrupt, the self-elected Elect have done much to make Scottish self-government a subject for mockery not only south of the Border but among the broad masses of the Scottish people as well. As often as not, their farcical self-important professions of secrecy arouse a healthy public mistrust as regards the intentions, capabilities and motives of the national movement as a whole.

I, for one, am absolutely convinced that about the only thing that can now seriously hinder Scotland's development into a self-respecting adult community in effective control of its own affairs is the big-headed presumption of the 'self-elected Elect'. It is surely more than ever vital that the advance to Home Rule, so urgently needed, should not only be democratic but be seen to be democratic.

Also there is no use blinking the fact that the self-elected Elect are a pure godsend to the vast army of narks, agents provocateurs and political agents of all persuasions who are a disagreeable reality of mid-twentieth-century politics. It is not hard to imagine a typical ploy. Agent A tells dupe X (one of the self-elected Elect) that his associate Y is less rigidly righteous and/or shockingly sectarian than he ought to be. X, who probably hates Y's guts anyway for ordinary mundane reasons of spite, rivalry or plain bloody-mindedness, is delighted to have this additional ideological reason for abhorring him. Of course we must keep an eye on Y, who is doubtless working for the Cheka, M.R.A.,[3] the tontons-macoute[4] or whatever. Repeat the formula with Y – and of course with Z, who is already organizing a faction. If an agent is any good, he can keep this sort of thing going indefinitely, and acres of reports (top secret, in triplicate, 'as of this time') can be dispatched to Whitehall or the Pentagon.

Of course, X and Y are probably just a pair of bumbling lunatics who couldn't start a bun fight at a kirk soiree, but for heaven's sake don't tell that to the agents who depend on them for their sustenance . . . Anyway, the whole infantile charade is no doubt officially considered to have paid off if the imperfectly muffled antics of those concerned serve to discredit the rational Home Rulers.

And now we hear that one particular group of political 'Close Brethren' are kindly offering to turn themselves into 'Open Brethren' (more or less). Mrs Ewing and her associates are surely to be congratulated for doing the necessary and no doubt harder thing, and showing them where they get off.

I am etc., Hamish Henderson

1 Winnie Ewing, Scottish National Party MEP for Hamilton.
2 George Leslie, Scottish National Party MP.
3 Moral Rearmament Association.
4 Infamous Haitian secret police.

142 Hugh MacDiarmid to the *Scotsman*

[Brownsbank, Biggar, 26 February 1968]

Sir,

It is natural that Mr Henderson should inveigh against intellectuals and dub them 'self-elected'.

His conception of 'democracy' is what concurs with majority opinion. Minorities are consequently to be vilified, and stigmatized as 'trouble makers', 'agents provocateurs' and all the rest of it. This is simply stupid abuse. Mr Henderson has no tittle of evidence to show that any of his algebraically-denoted sinister intriguers have been, or are to be, found in any of the little groups he indicates.

People do vary in intellectual status. Why deny this in favour of the undifferentiated mass, or accede to the demand of the latter that superior brains should acquiesce in the delimitation of their political and other objectives to conciliate the mass who cannot see beyond their noses?

What would Mr Henderson say to any suggestion that University Research Fellowships should be open to 'Tom, Dick and Harry' and, since there would be an unmanageable superfluity of applicants, the matter should be decided by simply putting all the names in a hat and drawing out the number required? That might be more 'democratic', in Mr Henderson's sense of the term, and I agree that in certain cases it might fill a post to better advantage than the present method.

Even Mr Henderson cannot deny that little groups of the 'self-styled intellectuals' he affects to despise have been the spearhead of all political movements. It will not be otherwise in Scotland, and if he is opposed to this Mr Henderson is perfectly free to 'self-elect' himself as the champion of the 'hoi polloi' and see how far he gets with that, not in mere abuse but in the serious intellectual discussion called for.

I am etc., Hugh MacDiarmid

143 To the *Scotsman*

[Edinburgh, 29 February 1968]

Sir,

Hugh MacDiarmid's contempt for the 'undifferentiated mass', and his pre-dilection for a kind of 'samurai sword' politics, with a high-toned élite holding sway over the common weill, are by now well and truly familiar to your readers. What may not be so widely realized is that Mr MacDiarmid has on occasion given these attitudes a quite concrete political expression. For example, in his article, 'A Programme for a Scottish Fascism' (*The Scottish Nation*, Montrose, 19 June 1923) he wrote: 'The entire Fascist programme can be readapted to Scottish national purposes and is (whether it be called Fascism or pass under any other name) the only thing that will preserve our distinctive national culture.'

Mr MacDiarmid was himself the editor of *The Scottish Nation*[1] and was, in 1923, a man of thirty, not a juvenile enthusiast. He wrote these words eight months after the march on Rome, and at a time when reports of beatings-up and castor oil dosings were causing as much public concern throughout Europe as the revolting details of torture in Greek prisons currently being investigated by Amnesty International.

A fortnight earlier (5 June) he had written in the same periodical 'A Plea for a Scottish Fascism' which contained even more outspoken deliverances on a Musso-type future for Scotland.

I am quite aware, of course, that since then Mr MacDiarmid has changed sides politically as often as a Chinese warlord during a civil war, and in the 1930s he was to write one of the outstanding anti-Fascist poems of the Spanish Civil War (*The Battle Continues*)[2]; however, if there is any single thing which gives a kind of unity to all his various tergiversations, it is precisely this authoritarian strain.

Writers like Hugo Moore (*Agenda*, Autumn/Winter, 'awesome in its tensile strength') aplomb on the subject of MacDiarmid and politics usually just butter him up ('a mental grip' etc.), without subjecting his truly awesome political career to the courtesy of detailed logical analysis. With such adulation they do him no service whatsoever, but merely encourage him in the self-gratificatory euphoria which has made so much mischief in Scottish Home Rule politics over the last few decades.

At the same time that Mr MacDiarmid was recommending Scotsmen to give Fascism a trial, Giacomo Matteotti and Antonio Gramsci were rallying the Italian working-class to combat the vicious onslaught on its living standards launched by Mussolini and his black-shirted authoritarians.

If Mr MacDiarmid would like to contemplate a true political hero and national patriot, let him look once again at the career of Gramsci, whom he mentions (quoting an unsigned article in the *TLS*[3]) at the beginning of *In Memoriam James Joyce*. Gramsci returned from Russia, leaving a wife and two small children in Moscow to fight Fascism on the soil of Italy. A man of great intellectual distinction, friend and philosophical adversary of Benedetto Croce, Gramsci as a sociologist found fruitful differences among the undifferentiated mass, and learned much from the workers of Turin and the peasants and fishermen of southern Italy, frequently acknowledging his debt to them.

He made a special study of Italian popular culture, and wrote much on that subject. His posthumous political influence in his own country is great, and still growing. Yet if there are three words which epitomize all that Gramsci was not, they are 'by invitation only'.

I am etc., Hamish Henderson

---

1 *The Scottish Nation*, monthly journal of cultural affairs edited by MacDiarmid, appearing August 1922–December 1923.

2 *The Battle Continues* (Castle Wynd Printers: Edinburgh, 1957); the poem is an attack on the South African poet Roy Campbell who eulogized Franco in *Flowering Rifle: A Poem from the Battlefield of Spain* (London, 1939).

3 See Letters 61, 113; and the note on the correspondence concerning Erich Heller's unsigned *Times Literary Supplement* article in Letter 149.

144 Hugh MacDiarmid to the *Scotsman*

[Brownsbank, Biggar, 4 March 1968]

Sir,

Mr Hamish Henderson is quite right. I was in the early twenties over-impressed by Italian Fascism, largely because of such enterprises as the draining of the Po marshes,[1] just as others believed that Hitler in Germany did well in abolishing unemployment there. But a great deal has happened in the intervening forty-odd years. My mind has not stood still during that period of unprecedented acceleration of change. I have never been one of those who having once formed an opinion are afraid to permit themselves any further intellectual development lest they be accused of inconsistency. Even Mr Henderson has had his tergiversations. It is a long time ago since he enthusiastically praised my work as a Marxist poet in *Our Time*.

It is amusing that he should use the great name of Gramsci in trying to confute me. Gramsci (in precisely that contradistinction to the SNP in Scotland which accounts for my contempt and antagonism to that body) dealt primarily with the 'superstructure' – the whole complex of political, social and cultural institutions and ideals – rather than its 'economic foundation'.

This choice was deliberate; Gramsci believed that 'cultural' problems were especially important in periods following revolutionary activity, as in Europe after 1815 and again after 1921. At such times, he said, there are no pitched battles between classes: the class struggle becomes a 'war of position' and the 'cultural front' the principal area of conflict. But a 'cultural' battle was not easy: Marxism

(167

had retained too many elements of materialism, determinism and economism.

'In its most common form of economic superstition, the philosophy of praxis loses its cultural expansiveness in the upper sphere of the intellectual group, however much it acquires among the masses and among mediocre intellectuals who do not want to tire their brains but wish to appear very shrewd.'

The quotation is from Gramsci's *Quaderni del Carcere* – as perhaps Mr Henderson knows, since he told me about twenty years ago that he had been entrusted with the translation of Gramsci's works into English – a project of which, so far as Mr Henderson is concerned, nothing quite characteristically has been heard since.

I am etc., Hugh MacDiarmid

PS Mr Henderson ought to remember, when he attempts to discredit me because of my attitude to Italian Fascism away back in 1923, that only a little earlier (in 1921) Gramsci himself attempted for some reason to establish contact with Gabriele D'Annunzio.[2] The former Comandante of Fiume had previously had vague ties with other European radicals, and in 1921 even Lenin himself thought D'Annunzio might be a 'revolutionary'.

Though evidently I sinned in 1923, it is clear that I did so in excellent company, and certainly forty years ago I never imagined I was better endowed with foresight than Lenin or Gramsci.

More to the present point of my attitude to the SNP on the one hand and the 1320 Club on the other, Mr Henderson needs to be reminded that in *Capacità politica*[3] (24, IX 20) and *L'Ordine nuovo* (10), p. 170, Gramsci denounced the then leaders of the proletarian movement for asking 'the prior consent of the masses by proceeding to consult them in the forms and at the time they [the leaders] have selected' and declared: 'A revolutionary movement can only be founded on the proletarian vanguard and must be conducted without prior consultation, without the apparatus of representative assemblies. A revolution is like a war. It must be minutely prepared by a workers' general staff, just as a war is prepared by the general staff of the army. Assemblies can only ratify what has already happened . . . no revolutionary movement will be decreed by a national workers' assembly; to convoke an assembly means to confess one's own lack of faith.'

With regard to Scottish nationalism as with the development of Italian Communism, the immediate task, as Gramsci said, is not to establish another democracy upon existing models (i.e. what the SNP is seeking to do), but to create a revolutionary vanguard of high technical competence and great freedom of initiative (i.e. the aim of the 1320 Club). Otherwise the progress of the movement will be paralysed by the inadequacies of the present.

---

1 Pontine Marshes.

2 Gabriele D'Annunzio (1863–1938), Italian poet and political leader.

3 Trans. 'political capacity' (H.H.).

145 **To the *Scotsman*** [1]

[Edinburgh, 9 March 1968]

Sir,

To clear up all the distortions and errors in Mr MacDiarmid's letter is a task comparable not so much with the mucking of the Augean stables as, in fact, with the draining of the Pontine marshes.

He alleges, for example, that I have altered my views on his Marxist poetry since I praised it in *Our Time* twenty years ago. This is quite untrue. Reviewing the Duval-Goodsir Smith Festschrift in *Lines* (no. 18, 1962), I again praised this poetry, which seems to me among the best twentieth-century European poetry known to me. I have frequently repeated this opinion in lectures.

As for Gramsci, I see I must start from square 1. Mr MacDiarmid first heard about Gramsci from me, not long after the end of World War II. I told him about the project, then under way in Italy, to publish a collection of the letters Gramsci had sent from prison to his wife and children in Russia, and to close friends. This was to be followed by selections from the 'Quaderni del Carcere' – the prison writings, 2848 tightly-packed pages in thirty-two notebooks – which had been saved from destruction by the heroic Tatiana Schucht, Gramsci's sister-in-law.

I was never 'entrusted' with the translation of these, as Mr MacDiarmid mistakenly asserts. A friend of mine in Rome – Amleto Micozzi, whom Mr MacDiarmid mentions in a 1948 number of *The Voice of Scotland* – sent me each volume as it appeared ('Letters from Prison', 1947; 'Historical Materialism and the Philosophy of Benedetto Croce', 1948; 'Notes on Machiavelli, Politics and the Modern State', 1949). The 'Letters' arrived when I was working in Ireland, and I began the translation of them straightaway, as a labour of love, and without (at first) a thought of a publisher.

The man who, with the approval of the newly founded Istituto Gramsci in Rome, embarked on a translation of extracts from the 'Quaderni' volumes was Dr Louis Marks, whom I met in London in 1950. We discussed the problems of the translation, which are exceedingly formidable ones, due to the necessarily elliptic style of much of the material. Dr Marks kept in touch with me while his work was in progress, and he sent me a complete copy of the translation before it was published (in 1957) by Lawrence & Wishart, under the title, *The Modern Prince*.

My own translation of the letters was completed in March 1951, and was sent away to John Lehmann, Ltd. Lehmann accepted it, but his firm was shortly to go out of business, and the typescript was returned to me. Since then it has been to almost as many publishers as James Joyce's *Dubliners*, and is still unpublished, although I am convinced it deserves publication, and that it will eventually achieve it.

Mr MacDiarmid is in error once again when he insinuates that the public has never had a chance of seeing a specimen of my translation. Extensive extracts from it were published in 1959 in successive numbers (9 and 10) of *The New Reasoner*, a quarterly journal of Socialist Humanism edited in Halifax by Edward Thompson.[2] The first of these brought together Gramsci's various comments on the menace of anti-Semitism. The second dealt primarily with problems of education and psycho-analysis.

I cannot possibly in the space available deal adequately with Mr MacDiarmid's remarks about the 'superstructure' in Gramsci's thinking. Mr MacDiarmid is as fond as ever of trying to blind the reader with a show of science. Deploying out of context quotes from the 'Quaderni', we could go on like this for weeks in the *Scotsman*, and nobody any the wiser. I refer Mr MacDiarmid to an article by Togliatti, 'Leninism in the Thought and Action of A. Gramsci' (*Studi Gramsciani*, 1958, especially pp. 25–8) . . . However, the only short Marxist riposte is Groucho's, not Karl's: one could say that Mr MacDiarmid had got hold of the wrong end of the stick, if only he had a stick to hang on to. And that he has not is shown conclusively by the wholly fantastic attempt to equate Gramsci's 'revolutionary vanguard' with the 1320 Club.

Gramsci's vanguard was based on the organized working-class movement, on its most intelligent and self-sacrificing cadres, on its known and trusted leaders. If Mr MacDiarmid thinks this has anything in common with the 1320 Club, he is living in a dream world.

I am etc., Hamish Henderson

---

1 This was the final letter in the '1320 Club Flyting'. The first two paragraphs were cut from this letter:

Among the Fascist exploits which impressed Hugh MacDiarmid in the early twenties was, he tells us, the 'draining of the Po marshes'. (I suppose he means the Pontine marshes, which are quite a long way from the Po valley, but let that pass.) This information is not surprising; it just means that Mr MacDiarmid was one of several millions among the petit-bourgeois masses of urbanised Western Europe who swallowed Mussolini's well-packaged propaganda. While the Duce was draining the Pontine marshes and the Italian trains were still running on time, the Bolsheviks weren't getting it all their own way.

(Historical note: the plan which the Fascists utilized was drawn up in 1919 by the Genio Civile – the Engineering Dept of the Civil Service in Rome – four years before Mussolini seized power. The Fascist 'drive', accompanied by countless publicity fanfares, did not take place until 1932, nine years after Mr MacDiarmid wrote 'A Programme for a Scottish Fascism').

2 E.P. Thompson.

146 To the *Scotsman* (unpublished)

[Edinburgh, 3 April 1968]

Sir,

While Labour is still wondering what hit it in the English byelection debacle, we need to take a cool look at what the Wilsonite fiasco means for Scotland. The message could hardly be clearer. There is now one thing and one thing only which can prevent Scotland from being at the receiving end of Tory policies for a renewed stretch of five or maybe even ten years, and that is a decisive SNP victory north of the border at the next General Election.

The Ayr conference has demonstrated that the Labour Party in Scotland is now in the process of committing hara-kiri. It was nothing short of gruesome (and fearsome) to read the speeches made at this conference, and to realize that the bulk of the delegates have understood nothing, but nothing, of what Harold Wilson has done in recent years to the Labour movement by failing to challenge the power of international finance, and also by his servile complicity in the Vietnam war, the first war in history (as Lord MacLeod of Fuinary[1] has recently pointed out) in which civilian casualties account for over 90 per cent of the total.

In May 1965 Tom Nairn[2] published an article in *The Week* entitled 'The Fetish and the Menace'. This accurately diagnosed the nature of the malady, and forecast the results of the failure to treat it radically. One of the passages about British imperialism should have been printed in gold caps and handed out to every delegate at Ayr. It reads as follows: 'The City and its complex of institutions for the financing of overseas trade and investment displaced the industrial north. The Pound sterling replaced the railway engine as the national fetish-object. The way had been found to make money reproduce itself without end. The secret of this magic lay in the labour of hordes of men in far-away lands, and its corollary was the decline of the British industrial economy. But what did these facts matter, to the high-priests of the Pound in London, or the ruling elite and the nation blinded by the sorcery? Out of this possession, the final form of British imperial power, there arose a chronic disequilibrium of the British economy: the sacrifice of industrial capital to financial capital became a way of life. Now, under the utterly different conditions of the 1960s it has become a way of death.'

This puts the problem in a nutshell. The question is: who suffers, and where? London-controlled parties talk about 'the country', but tend to think, when they come to power, very largely in terms of south-east England. The Wilsonites of Ayr are quite happy that Scotland should continue to occupy its familiar windy nook, sheltered only by the flapping moth-eaten blanket of Britain as a whole'. For this they will deserve all they get at the coming Election, and it does not need a seer to foretell that it will be annihilation.

Some Socialists obviously think that support for a Scottish Parliament would run counter to their internationalism. However, as Lawrence Daly has pointed out (*New Left Review*, no. 17), 'they enthusiastically support every movement for national independence overseas. Scotsmen watch the emergent nations, on the morrow of their freedom, taking their place in the world parliament, while Scotland, with a record of many centuries as an independent nation, becomes an economic and political backwater. They are aware of ludicrously small attendances in the House of Commons when Scottish affairs are being debated; of the extremely limited powers of the Scottish Departments in St Andrew's House, Edinburgh; of the time-wasting coming and going by armies of bureaucrats between there and London. They see small nations like Denmark, Norway, Switzerland and New Zealand match political independence with economic viability.'

On top of all this they are obliged to watch Harold Wilson butcher Socialism's future in order to placate Zurich and Washington.

The remedy is obvious. As soon as it gets a chance, the electorate will undoubtedly bid a 'soldier's farewell' to the raddled rump of the Labour Party in Scotland, and entrust the SNP with the job of negotiating our necessary and long-overdue autonomy.

Yours etc., Hamish Henderson

---

1 Baron George MacLeod of Fuinary (1895–1991), Moderator of the General Assembly (1957–8); founder of the Iona Community.

2 Tom Nairn (b. 1932), sociologist, author and columnist.

3 *The Week*, political weekly.

147 Jeannie Robertson to Hamish Henderson
[*EUL*]

[Aberdeen, 3 May 1968]

Dear Hamish and Katzel,

Just a Note to Let you know I Received a Letter today from White Hall N° 10, Downing Street London. Harlod willson prime Minister stating that I am getting the M.B.E. there was a form in the Letter that I had to fill up. well I filled it up and Sent it Back to Downing Street. you see it was urgent. tell Katzel and the two Children that we all Send them all our Love.

Yours aye, Jeannie Donald Isaac Lizzie

P.S. I and Donald will have to go to London. No Doubt I will have to Go Before the Queen to get My M.B.E. But I dont know when But they will write and Let Me know. I think it will Be on her Birthday.

148 To Willie Mitchell[1]

[29 August 1968]

Dear Willie,

It was marvellous seeing you again at Blair.[2] It is ages since I enjoyed a ceilidh as much as the one we had in the sun lounge of the Angus on Saturday night. Ever since then Machrihanish Bright and Bonnie has been a deep ground swell in my consciousness.[3]

I saw Arthur Argo the other day and he told me that he wants to use Stewarton Corner in a half-hour programme on Radio 4 on 30 August. No doubt he has written to you about this already. Isn't it ironical that the very song which the BBC big-wigs found too dissipated for their liking in 1957 is the one chosen to appear in this new BBC programme?

Have you had any more thoughts about the Bill Leader LP?[4] Quite a lot of folk I saw at Blair have been asking if there are any records of you. I know you would find Bill Leader an easy person to get on with, and that there would be little or no strain about the recordings.

I am enclosing a copy of *Chapbook*[5] which contains a number of my own songs. I meant to send this to you a long while ago, but better late than never! You will find that the first article in it is a wee bit over-enthusiastic, but please overlook that and pass straight on to Jack Mitchell's analysis of the songs.

I also enclose a short article on the old ploughman cult of The Horseman's Word.[6] Did you ever hear of this in Kintyre?

I do hope your wife is now keeping better. It was nice hearing her singing again in the sun lounge.

With all best wishes to the whole family,

Yours aye, Hamish

---

1 Willie Mitchell, folk-singer, collector and butcher, from Campbeltown in Kintyre.
2 Blairgowrie.
3 Henderson described the evening in his broadcast talk 'The Midnight Ceilidh in the Sun Lounge of the Angus', BBC Scotland, reprinted in *Alias MacAlias*.
4 Bill Leader worked with Topic Records in the early 1960s, and then formed his own company, Leader Records.
5 *Chapbook*, III.6, 1967.
6 Published in *Scots Magazine*, vol. 87 no. 2, May 1967.

1969

149 To Hugh MacDiarmid
[EUL]

[Bavaria, Germany, 5 July 1969]

Dear Chris,

As you may recall, I told you in the Traverse last year that I've been working on an essay – or rather a series of essays – which attempts to survey your later poetry through the eyes (so to speak) of the people who have contributed to it, e.g. Gramsci, Karl Kraus, etc.[1]

I have often wondered if you know (or have guessed?) who wrote the unsigned article in the *TLS* ('Satirist in the Modern World', 8 May 1953) which you turned into a poem in *In Memoriam James Joyce*?

There are two reasons why, continuing to work on one of these essays in the quiet of the Bavarian countryside, I've suddenly decided to ask you this direct question. The first is just natural curiosity, which you may feel like satisfying, or not, just as you wish. The second, however, springs from an extensive reading – and re-reading – of Karl Kraus himself, which I've undertaken in connection with this work. I don't know how familiar you are with Kraus's own work; not very familiar, I imagine, because of the paucity of translations. Much of his best work has to be sought out, in the pages of *Die Fackel* and other magazines. But it is really astounding at how many points the life and work of Karl Kraus touch the life and work of Hugh MacDiarmid.

It would take a longish letter to do anything like justice to this theme; however, here are a few general headings: attitude to religion, politics and the state; overmastering interest in linguistics and the power of the word; assaults on a philistine late-capitalist society; neglect (sometimes total) by the press, even when his name was put forward by Sorbonne professors for the Nobel Prize; sharp-edged polemics; fine poetry.

Here is one incident, which ties up with the general line of my essay 'Alias MacAlias' in the last *Scottish International*. When Brecht's *Dreigroschenoper* was staged in Berlin, the dramatic critic Alfred Kerr accused Brecht of plagiarism, because he had used twenty-five lines of a Villon ballade, and had credited the poet but not the German translator. Karl Kraus leapt to the defence of Brecht, saying (in *Die Fackel*) that Brecht had more originality in the little finger of the hand which had lifted twenty-five lines of Ammer's translation of Villon than Kerr (the critic) had in his whole body . . . He then carried the war into the enemy's camp by recalling that during World War I this same Alfred Kerr had published a lot of drum-thumping chauvinistic rhymes under the pseudonym 'Gottlieb', and added, 'Kerr has had worse luck than Brecht, in that it has never occurred to anyone to reveal that he *didn't* write the rhymes signed "Gottlieb" '.

There is even a parallel to your own early flirting with Catholicism, for Karl Kraus was actually received into the Catholic Church in 1911, although he left it again a few years later.

For me, the most interesting thing about Kraus is his championship of spoken poetry; he was an early wave in the carrying stream which has given poetry back to the spoken (and sung) word in the last three decades As Paul Schick has pointed out: 'His readings influenced his own creative work . . The unity of word, sound and content explains the enormous effectiveness of his language – an effectiveness which even his enemies could not call in question'.

The main difference between Karl Kraus and Chris Grieve resides in the languages with which they have had to cope. Chris Grieve has operated, in the main, through the English language, that great estuary on which so many craft can ride; although, of course, he also did his famous salmon-leap upstream in the Lallans peat-burn. Karl Kraus, on the other hand, had to deal with the German language, that extraordinary mixture of the angelic and the diabolic; the language which, more than any other I know, seems to have taken off, and to have enjoyed a separate existence over and above the life and tradition which brought it into being. His life-long struggle with this sinuous word-monster invites comparison with your own half-century long *Ringkampf*[2] with intractable Scottish philistinism.

Best wishes to Valda.

Yours aye, Hamish

---

1 These essays never appeared. Henderson used this material in a paper he gave at the MacDiarmid Symposium in 1972, and also in his article, 'The Langholm Byspale' which appeared in *Edinburgh City Lynx* magazine, 1978. The correspondence which follows between Henderson, Heller, MacDiarmid and David Wright discusses MacDiarmid's unacknowledged use of the German literary critic Erich Heller's unsigned *Times Literary Supplement* review (8 May 1953) of *Die Dritte Walpurgisnacht* by the Austrian satirist Karl Kraus. The review was itself an extract from Heller's seminal study *The Disinherited Mind: Essays in Modern German Literature and Thought* (Cambridge, 1952). The transcription appears in the 'And above all Karl Kraus' section of *In Memoriam James Joyce*. Alan Bold's edition of MacDiarmid's *Letters* quotes the following explanatory remarks from Heller's Preface to the fourth edition of *The Disinherited Mind* (London, 1975):

   Part of my essay on Karl Kraus was originally written for the *Times Literary Supplement*. It appeared anonymously . . . I was surprised as well as flattered to discover much later that with this article I had contributed not only to the *TLS* but also to the poetry of Hugh MacDiarmid (Dr C.M. Grieve), the renowned Scots poet. His poem 'And above all Karl Kraus', from his cycle *In Memoriam James Joyce*, consists of 157 lines of which 149 are taken from my essay – with their essential identity preserved – even though they suffer a little breakage in the process of being lifted into the poetic mode. My slight anxiety that this transference might be detected by some readers and ascribed to me as plagiarism is caused by the (may I say deserved) notoriety of Hugh MacDiarmid's poem. It was selected without acknowledgement of my *TLS* essay for the Penguin book *The Mid-century English Poetry 1940–1960*, which enjoys wide circulation.

    See *The Letters of Hugh MacDiarmid*, edited by Alan Bold (Hamish Hamilton: London, 1984, 832).

2 Trans. 'struggle; wrestling-match' (H.H.).

150 **To Erich Heller**
[Northwestern University, Evanston (USA)]

[Bavaria, 5 July 1969]

Dear Erich Heller,

Many thanks for your letter. It arrived just as I was leaving for Germany myself – hence the delay in replying, for which I'm very sorry.

The anthology in which the Hugh MacDiarmid poem appeared was David Wright's Penguin *Mid-Century English Poetry*. The last thing I did in the School before leaving was to put a copy of this in the post for you, and I imagine it should arrive about the same time as this letter.

The following quotation from Kenneth Buthlay's *Hugh MacDiarmid (C.M. Grieve)* (Oliver and Boyd, *Writers and Critics Series*, Edinburgh, 1964) will explain my interest in both your article and what MacDiarmid made of it:

> If one takes a piece of some one else's prose and distributes it in verse-lines, one is contributing *something*, rhythmically speaking. The question is 'how much?' – and the answer in MacDiarmid's case is 'generally far too little for a creative artist'. There are exceptions, however, one of the best of which is to be found in the passage about Karl Kraus in the first part of *In Memoriam James Joyce*.

> This passage occupies about half-a-dozen pages of the book. It is taken from a long unsigned article in the *TLS* to which MacDiarmid directs the reader in a footnote – an article written by a fine stylist with a very unusual feeling for rhythm. Anyone can see this, going from MacD. to his original; the point is that MacD. saw it first, and brought out the rhythmical pattern of some parts of the prose by cutting them into verse-lines:

What was the inspiration of his vast productivity?
The answer is Hamlet's: 'Words, Words, Words!',
And the commas between them
And the deeds they beget,
And the deeds they leave undone;
And the word that was at the beginning,
And, above all, the words that were at the end.

Any-one who looks closely at the little changes, including word-substitutions, that have been made in the original will recognize that the hand of the poet has not lost its old cunning.

Other examples appear from time to time, as always in MacD., even when the prospects seem to be at their dimmest; and several of these he has himself selected from *In Memoriam James Joyce* for preservation in the *Collected Poems*. Among them is the wonderful interpolation of a piece of scientific information as an analogy at the point in the Karl Kraus passage where the original refers to Hölderlin, who 'sought, and often miraculously found, the word with which silence speaks its own silence without breaking it':

(Silence supervening at poetry's height,
Like the haemolytic streptococcus
In the sore throat preceding rheumatic fever
But which, at the height of the sickness,
Is no longer there, but has been and gone!
Or as 'laughter is the representative of tragedy
When tragedy is away')

Not thus preserved by MacD., but equally fine, is the factual description of the growth of nerves, muscles, bones, lungs, and so on, in the foetus:

A pseudo-aquatic parasite, voiceless as a fish,
Yet containing within itself an instrument of voice
Against the time when it *will* talk —

which he suddenly makes analogous to the later work of James Joyce, 'vastly outrunning present needs . . . but providing for the developments to come'.
To MacD., Joyce, Doughty and himself are 'harbingers of the epical age of Communism', when everyone will have followed the directive of Lenin and 'worked over in his consciousness the whole inheritance of human knowledge'.

All this is a quote from Buthlay's study of MacDiarmid; you'll find it on pp. 105–107 of the book.

It was most kind of you to write to me, and you may be assured that I'll not divulge this confidential information. May I add that I'm full of admiration for MacD.'s inspired plagiarism, and I am sure you will not mind finding yourself part of the English poetry of the mid-century. (Although there should undoubtedly have been a footnote in David Wright's anthology too.)

Best wishes – and, again, many thanks, Hamish Henderson

PS I saw an article of yours called 'The Last Days of Mankind' in the *Cambridge Journal* just after the war, so that you'll understand that I had a 'hunch' about the passage in question.

151 Erich Heller to Hamish Henderson

[Germany, 4 August 1969]

Dear Hamish Henderson,

It was good to have your kind letter of 5 July. It was forwarded to Germany. Unfortunately, I shall not be able to inspect *Mid-century English Poetry* before my return to Evanston: I have asked my secretary not to send any printed matter after me. But to you my thanks now for your great kindness. May I ask for another one? Should you be in touch with David Wright, the editor, would you be good enough to ask him to supply, in a second printing, the missing footnote and [credit] my authorship; there is nothing anonymous or confidential about it, for the plagiarized *TLS* article has been included in the *German* edition of my book *The Disinherited Mind* (the English edition has only the piece you once read in the *Cambridge Journal*) *and* in a little volume called *Studien zur Modernen Literatur* (Suhrkamp Verlag, Frankfurt a. M.). Half-a-dozen pages (if Mr Buthlay – whom you quote – is correct in his statement) of unacknowledged quotation is a bit much.[1]

---

1 The final part of this letter is missing.

152 To Hugh MacDiarmid
[*EUL*]

[Edinburgh, 27 August 1969]

Dear Chris,

Many thanks for your letter. I would have answered it before, but I did not know your holiday address, and of late I have had a great deal to do in connection with the International Folk Music Council Conference in Edinburgh, the Blairgowrie Festival of Traditional Music, and other things. However, things are a bit easier now, so I thought I would get in touch with you again about the author of the Karl Kraus article.

I should have made it clear to you, when I wrote from Germany, that I did not write this article myself. The reason why I know who wrote it is because I have done a great deal of work on Karl Kraus over the years, and naturally, having access to a number of critical works in German, I pretty soon guessed who the author was. I wrote to him some while back, and asked him if my supposition was correct, and he wrote back confirming it. He also drew my attention to the fact that the article has in fact been published under his own name in Germany, and I thought you might be interested to see some of the passages as they appear in the original. I think you will agree that the process by which this German article became a poem in English is one of the utmost fascination for students of literature. At the present moment I do not think it would be correct for me to reveal the name of the author; at any rate I think I ought to get his explicit permission before doing so. Sooner or later I would like to write a full-length essay on the whole subject, and I will have to get his permission eventually if I am to do this. However, I will certainly not have this completed for quite some time.

I don't know whether you noticed the correspondence in the *Scotsman* about the proposal in Germany to call the new University of Düsseldorf the Heinrich Heine University. In view of the rise of neo-Nazism and the need to act against the resurgence of many backward-looking and sinister elements in modern German life, the idea of a Heinrich Heine University has got immediate practical importance as well as symbolic significance. The Committee in Düsseldorf would be very pleased and honoured to have a message of support from you. If you would like to send them one, the man to write to is Otto Schönfeldt, 4 Düsseldorf, Grunerstr. 26.

I am very sorry indeed to hear that you have been ill, and I do hope you are on the road to recovery.

With best wishes to Valda.

Yours aye, Hamish

Extracts from the German original.

Man fragte Konfutse einmal, womit er beginnen würde, wenn er ein Land zu verwalten hätte. «Ich würde den Sprachgebrauch verbessern», antwortete der Meister. Seine Zuhörer waren erstaunt. «Das hat doch nichts mit unserer Frage zu tun», sagten sie, «was soll die Verbesserung des Sprachgebrauchs?» Der Meister antwortete: «Wenn die Sprache nicht stimmt, so ist das, was gesagt wird, nicht das, was gemeint ist; ist das, was gesagt wird, nicht das, was gemeint is, so kommen die Werke nicht zustande; kommen die Werke nicht zustande, so gedeihen Moral und Kunst nicht; gedeihen Moral und Kunst nicht, so trifft die Justiz nicht, trifft die Justiz nicht, so weiss die Nation nicht, wohin Hand und Fuss setzen. Also dulde man keine Willkürlichkeit in den Worten. Das ist es, worauf alles ankommt.»

Das war es, worauf auch dem Wiener Satiriker Karl Kraus alles ankam.[1] Er prüfte die Sprache, die seine Zeitgenossen sprachen und schrieben, und fand, dass sie nach falschen Ideen lebten. Er hörte, was sie sagten, und entdeckte die unreinen Quellen ihres Tuns. Er las, was sie schrieben, und wusste, dass sie einem Unheil entgegengingen. Die Sprachgestalt der Zeitungsberichte über eine diplomatische Konferenz enthüllte ihm die wahre politische Situation genauer, als es das so berichtete Ereignis tat. Die Diplomaten mögen Grund gehabt haben, optimistisch zu sein; schlimme Vorzeichen aber erschienen in ihren gedruckten Reden: falsche Konjunktive und substanzlose Substantiva. Die Hoffnungen der Welt, verkündet in Manifesten guten Willens, zerbrachen an einem falsch gesetzten Komma, und die höchsten Erwartungen der Menschheit wurden vereitelt durch ihre Wort-Allianz mit einem Klischee. Sätze und Phrasen gaben Karl Kraus besseren Aufschluss über die Aussichten von Krieg und Frieden als die Rüstungen beider Seiten, und während er den Prognosen der Politiker misstraute, sah er eine besondere Vorsehung über den Fall eines Relativsatzes walten.

Karl Kraus' Satire wäre undenkbar in einem anderen Sprachmedium als dem deutschen. «Die deutsche Sprache ist die tiefste», sagte er, «die deutsche Rede die seichteste.» Aus diesem Kontrast zwischem dem Glauben an die Sprache und der Rede der Sprachabtrünnigen – einem Kontrast, der in keiner Sprache so gross sein kann wie in der deutschen – kam seine Inspiration.

Sein Denken war eine Entdeckungsreise in einer Landschaft von Worten. Keine andere Sprache gestattet ähnliche Abenteuer, denn jede andere Sprache ist gründlicher erforscht, gemeistert und geordnet. Was im Englischen etwa ein Handgemenge mit Worten sein mag, ist ein Weltkrieg im Deutschen, dessen Siege gewaltiger und dessen Niederlagen vernichtender sind. Und was im Alltagsleben der Sprache ein geruhsamer Spaziergang durch einen englischen Park ist, das ist auf deutsch ein Auszug in gefährdetes Gebiet. Während der englische Schriftsteller über weite Strecken seines Sprachunternehmens unter dem Schutz der taktvollen Weisheit sprachlicher Konvention steht, setzt sich der deutsche sogleich der Gefahr aus, vom Tonfall und Rhythmus seines ersten Satzes als Schuft oder Dummkopf überführt zu werden. Wären Hitlers Reden der Welt im unsagbaren Original zugänglich gewesen, so wäre uns vielleicht ein Krieg erspart geblieben. Denn diesen Krieg haben Hitlers Übersetzer mitverschuldet, deren zivilisierterem Sprachgebrauch sich die Resonanz des diabolishen Raums entzog. Trotz ihrer notorischen Weitschweifigkeit kennt nur die deutsche Sprache solche Abkürzungs-wege zu den Endstationen der Menschheit. Karl Kraus kannte sie alle.

Die Leute schwätzten über den Krieg; er hörte sie den Verlust ihrer Seelen beklagen. An jeder Strassenecke wurden Akte des Hochverrats am Geiste begangen. Die Rufe der Zeitungsjungen die in geheimnisvollen Vokalen die letzten Ausgaben anpriesen, wurden zur ungeheuerlichen Bedrohung der geistli-chen Sicherheit oder zu Schreien der ewigen Verdammnis.

So lehrt denn Karl Kraus von Anfang bis zu Ende die Lektion der Sprache und des Schweigens. Die Sprache verstummt am Gestade des dunklen Wassers der Verzweiflung und weist nur schweigend nach dem anderen Ufer. Dort aber, und nur dort ist Hoffnung. Sie is gewiss nicht bei denjenigen, die nie sprachlos waren, sondern – Denker des Un-Heils, Schreiber des Un-Sinns – sich ihre Redseligkeit bewahrten, als das Wort entschlief.

---

1 Margin note by Henderson: *your quotes start here.*

153 To Helen B. Cruickshank
[*EUL*]

[Edinburgh, 5 November 1969]

Dear Helen,

I'm sorry to have been so long in replying to two perfectly simple questions, but I had a lot of things to do just before we went to Perthshire, and – as usual – found a great mass of new chores on my desk when I got back.

'Williamina' is one of those rather awkward names to write in Gaelic – it is, of course, not really Gaelic at all, but the diminutive of English William. (The Gaelic diminutive is 'ag', as in 'Morag', which means little Sarah.) However, it *is* possible to write it in a sort of Gaelic, and what probably appeared above the door of the Inn was

UILLEAMINA.

The coo's name, on the other hand, is much easier: the Gaelic for 'Primrose' is:

SOBHRACH
OR
SEOBHRAG
(OR, less often, SOBHRAG)

If the phonetic rendering would be Shorak, I imagine SEOBHRAG would be the best form to use.

We had a very nice time in Killiecrankie with the MacMartins[1] – Donald, the husband, was a native of Strathtay, and I recorded him just before his death in 1965. Morag, his elder daughter, is now schoolmistress in Killiecrankie, and Tinky[2] loves going up and becoming part of her flock for the time being. She was in school with the rest of the gang on the 31st, which meant that she took part in dookin' for aipples, and a lot of other Halloween ploys. Then in the evening she joined the local bairns who went out guising – they were a marvellously photogenic lot: a scarifying Deil with a wooden pitchfork, an even more eldritch-looking witch with 'mony a cornelian and cairngorm pimple', and one or two gibbering sheeted ghaisties. Tinky was in a sort of Flora MacDonald costume with a Royal Stewart sash, and Janet[3] was a wee fox, complete with bushy tail. Kätzel joined the ghaistie brigade with a white sheet, which was very useful in the darkness – all cars gave us a wide berth!

Mary Brooksbank,[4] the Dundee folk-singer who wrote the best-known version of the 'Jute Mill Song' (O Dear me, the mill's gaen fast), has also been writing her autobiography – it's mainly about the working-class movement in Dundee, and in places makes quite interesting reading. The School now has a copy of the manuscript.

We are all looking forward to seeing you again soon, and were wondering when it would be convenient for us to come round. I'll give you a ring in a day or two, and maybe you could suggest a date.

Love from us all,

      Yours aye, Hamish and Kätzel

PS Do you ever see *Stand* (Jon Silkin's magazine, which is based on Newcastle on Tyne)? The most recent number has an article by Robin Fulton on Edwin Morgan and Iain Crichton Smith, and also a general article by Stewart Conn on the Scottish Literary Revival.

---

1 'Morag MacMartin, schoolmistress in Killiecrankie, is the daughter of Donald MacMartin, whose ancestors were the armourers of Clan Cameron in Lochaber' (H.H.).

2 Tinky; Henderson's elder daughter Christine, then 6 years of age.

3 Janet; Henderson's younger daughter, then 3½.

4 Mary Brooksbank, poet, song-writer and folk-singer.

154 **To the** *Scotsman*

                         [Edinburgh, 26 November 1969]

Sir,

Referring to the South African troops who fought in the Middle East and elsewhere during Hitler's war, Mr Hector I.C. Maclean asks: 'What has become of the British tradition of fair play?'

It would take all of Voltaire's pity and irony to supply an adequate answer to that one. As a Scot who found himself attached to the 1st South African Division during the Alamein period, and who is also an opponent of apartheid and a committed supporter of the present very necessary demonstrations, may I try to get clear some of the facts behind this particular desert dust-cloud.

Unlike the ill-fated 2nd SA Division, which was obliged to surrender at Tobruk, the 1st SA Division played a major part in our desert victory. When the Germans attempted to break through to the Nile Delta on 1 July 1942, they were decisively halted at Alamein by the 1st South African Division, and at Deir el Shein by the 18th Indian Brigade. Paul Carell, author of a German history of the African campaigns, has compared the importance of this bitterly-fought engagement to that of the Marne in September 1914. According to Carell, the famous German 90th Light Division 'suffered fearful losses' at the hands of the South Africans.

At the time this was all happening, the present Prime Minister of South Africa was interned as a Nazi sympathizer. Confined with him was a prize assortment of malignant racialist crackpots, the ideologues and political strategists of the Broederbond, the secret society which now effectively runs South Africa.

I remember the 1st SA Division well. Its commander, Major-General Dan Pienaar, was universally respected in the Eighth Army. Of its nine battalions, three bore Scottish names. The padre at Division HQ was not a member of what James Robertson-Justice has aptly dubbed the 'Much Deformed Church'; he was a Gaelic-speaking Highlander from Ledaig, the Rev. Ian Kennedy, and I clearly remember an open-air service conducted by him just before the Alamein offensive at which Cape Coloured auxiliaries sat side by side with white troops.

Furthermore, there was no question of apartheid on the battlefield. The South Africans were glad enough to have the support of 4th Indian Division on their left flank on the night of 23 October 1942! And I never heard any objections, either from Springbok or Pommie, to the presence on our side of the New Zealanders' Maori battalion under its half-Maori CO, Fred Baker.

Who would have thought in 1942 that a quarter of a century after the victory of Alamein, the Broederbond would succeed not only in getting South Africa completely by the thrapple but even of carrying apartheid-controlled sport on to the soil of Britain, with the tacit connivance of a Labour Government? It is this utterly shameful thing we are opposing, and I hope, for Scotland's sake, as well as for the sake of Alan Paton's 'beloved country', that 6 December will see the biggest turn-out to date of anti-apartheid demonstrators.

　　　　I am etc., Hamish Henderson

155 To *Tribune*

　　　　　　　　　　　　　　　　　　[Edinburgh, 12 December 1969]

Sir,

Anyone who goes to a demonstration such as the one at Murrayfield[1] is prepared to accept a bit of pulling and hauling. More important, all the demonstrators had accepted that they would be arrested for an illegal act if they stepped on to the pitch. But the action of some policemen and stewards went far beyond what could reasonably be expected.

Previous British practice would have suggested some such course of action as the following: police linking arms to create a strong cordon along the one vulnerable front and, in the event of the cordon's being broken, arresting and removing demonstrators.

What we witnessed was this. The police had erected a high steel barricade, itself in the context of a football crowd a positive danger to spectators. Police, reinforced by Rugby Union stewards, mounted benches to face the crowd over the barricades.

When, as everyone had been forewarned, the demonstrators moved forward, the response was positive violence. This violence was quite clearly distinguishable from the force exerted by demonstrators pushing forward on a cordon. To push is one thing; to use fists and feet as many of the police and stewards did is quite another.

Demonstrators were grabbed by the hair, kicked and punched by police and stewards towering over them. It was not long before some demonstrators, apparently arbitrarily selected, were being hauled by the hair through the ranks of police and stewards and thrown on to the benches, in some cases with extreme violence.

The reason there were not more rushes by demonstrators was that they could not hope to gain their objectives without themselves exerting unjustifiable force and because they saw a very real danger of someone getting crippled, badly maimed or even killed as police and stewards knocked people down into the crush at the barricades.

Some specific cases of improper behaviour witnessed included the following. A sergeant harassed a young photographer recording these scenes by snatching at his camera and, when he couldn't take it by force, warning him off. A spectator, who had nothing to do with the demonstration whatsoever (Stephen McAndrew), has complained that he was assaulted by a policeman in a totally unjustifiable manner and that, when he attempted to get the policeman's number, he was refused both by the policeman and by the sergeant in charge of that part of the terrace.

There have also been complaints by visibly bruised demonstrators – including girls – that they were made to run a gauntlet of kicks and punches in a tunnel leading off the pitch. We know of cases of people being hindered when they tried to make for the advertised complaints bureau, and senior police officials consistently refused to take complaints on the spot. We know many instances of policemen refusing to identify themselves or to be identified to an extent that this seemed official policy.

The impression of police behaviour left in one's mind was by and large one of ugly truculence. It was plain that to demonstrate against apartheid within the ground at Murrayfield was, in the eyes of the police, to forfeit many of one's rights as a citizen.

Hamish Henderson, Robert Tait, Robert D. Waugh

---

1 The controversial 1969/70 Springboks Rugby Union tour of Great Britain was opposed by the anti-apartheid campaign.

156 **To the** *Scotsman*

[Edinburgh, 23 December 1969]

Sir,

Mr Donald Campbell[1] seeks to show (11 and 19 December) that militant anti-apartheid demonstrations are counter-productive. According to him, they only succeed in convincing the South African bosses that British opposition to their policy of white supremacy 'is very slight and limited to a tiny minority of crackpots'.

Events are already proving him wrong. If there is one thing which emerges with any clarity from the welter of rattled and sometimes contradictory statements in Johannesburg and Pretoria, it is that our demonstrations have got the South African Government seriously worried. Experienced observers and commentators are virtually unanimous on this point. For example, John Arlott wrote in the *Guardian* on 9 December, 'It must now seem that the demonstrators, by their actions against the Springbok rugby tour, have in a few months achieved more than the cricket officials have done by fifteen years of polite acquiescence. The South African Government has cause to understand that a thousand active demonstrators probably bespeak a hundred times as many silent objectors.'

Mr Campbell fears that these militant demonstrators will give ease and comfort to British racialists by helping to provoke a bigot backlash from the 'Alf Garnetts of the New Right'. It is obvious that any political activity which is seen to be having an effect will in some degree 'rally' and energize its opponents. But the opponents, in this case, have already been summoned to the field by that devious demagogue Enoch Powell, and we are convinced that our comrades both inside and outside the Scottish universities who have the intelligence and the heart to see racialism for the evil and destructive thing it is, and are resolved to combat it, have everything to gain and nothing to lose, as far as their cause is concerned, by intensifying their efforts at this critical juncture.

How often have we been told in the past that it is politic to placate the infamous! Many will remember the glutinous editorials of the thirties in *The Times* and the *Observer* (then under the editorship of J.L. Garvin) urging us to sympathetic understanding of the problems of Nazi Germany, and deprecating the irresponsible utterances of anti-Fascist 'agitators'. If we would only be polite to Herr Hitler, one almost felt, he would gradually turn into an English gentleman and we might even see him playing cricket at The Oval.

Herr Hitler . . . your younger readers would hardly believe how infernally polite we were in those days! One wonders if any German politician, before or since, has had Herr attached to his name as often as Hitler in those same *Times* and *Observer* editorials. And as for Low, with his disrespectful cartoons showing the myopic Führer wearing his specs – the Blimps thought he was rocking the boat of good relations, and actually wrote in to the *Evening Standard* to say so.

In the period of Tory euphoria after Munich it got even worse. *The Times* mocked the veteran war correspondent H.W. Nevinson for going to a university Popular Front rally and applauding the student activists of those days when they said that the Munich agreement was a sham, that we would still have to fight Fascism, that it was still possible to save the Spanish Republic etc, etc. Poor old Nevinson, the incurable romantic, sitting among these juvenile parlour-pinks, and clapping a mention of 'heroic Madrid still untaken!'. After all, we were now safe, thanks to Mr Chamberlain: after Munich there just couldn't be a Nazi backlash.

It is now well known, of course — from Halder, Speer and dozens of other sources — what an opportunity was lost in 1938 of calling Hitler's bluff and giving heart to the anti-Nazi opposition inside Germany.

Freedom is never, but never, a gift from above; it invariably has to be won anew by its own exercises.

We are etc., Hamish Henderson, Robert Tait

---

1 Donald Campbell (b. 1940), poet and dramatist, author of *Playing for Scotland: A History of the Scottish Stage, 1715–1965*, (Mercat Press: Edinburgh, 1996).

1970

157 **To the** *Scotsman*

Sir,

Mr George E. Wingate's memory of demonstrations and student activity in the thirties is 'all for such as no arms, and peace at any price'. One wonders in what remote seclusion he spent these years. Does he really remember nothing of the massive demonstrations in support of the Spanish Republic in its fight against native Fascism and German and Italian invasion? While the appeasers of Whitehall and the Quai d'Orsay were well and truly giving Hitler the green light to continue his career of aggression, men like John Cornford, Christopher Caudwell and Ralph Fox[1] were giving Fascism an uncompromising red light, in the university city of Madrid, at Brunete and in the valley of Jarama. This, the 'militant demonstration' of the century, lasted for nearly three years.

The student right wing was not exactly silent in those years, either. In November 1938, just after the 'crystal night' of anti-Jewish pogroms in Germany, Attlee came to Cambridge to speak on the grave international situation. He was greeted at the Guildhall by hundreds of young Tories chanting 'We want Attlee's pants.' This was their current political ambition, apparently! (Nowadays, reading the correspondence columns of the press, one surmises that the lads who wanted Attlee's pants are probably still with us; only what they want now – by proxy, of course – is the demonstrators' hair.)

As for the Peace Pledge Union and the Oxford 'King and Country' debate, Hitler was far too shrewd a politician to attach any real importance to these. The people who can't do without them are right-wing propagandists who want to divert the public's attention from the real 'guilty men' – Neville Chamberlain, and his fellow-appeasers – who in September 1938 allowed Hitler to think that he could get away with murder.

On Mr Wingate's final point – there is war in Southern Africa, and while the doctrine of white supremacy exists it will certainly continue.

We are etc., Hamish Henderson, Robert Tait

---

1 John Cornford (1915–36), poet; fought with the POUM (Partido Obrero de Unificación Marxista) in Spain, killed in December 1936. Christopher Caudwell, see Letter 12; Ralph Fox, left-wing writer who also fought in Spain.

158 **To David Wright**[1]

[Edinburgh, 4 March 1970]

Dear David,

How are you keeping? I greatly enjoyed that session in Leeds, when I met you after delivering a lecture to their Folk-song Society. It was a magnanimous do, and it took me some while to recover from it!

The reason I am writing is because I have received a letter from Erich Heller, author of *The Disinherited Mind* (published by Bowes and Bowes, Cambridge, 1952). Erich Heller was the author of the unsigned article in the *Times Literary Supplement* which Hugh MacDiarmid used in *In Memoriam James Joyce*. MacDiarmid's use of this particular article is one of the most extraordinary examples of his 'feel' for material written by others which can serve his literary purpose, particularly in long poems. However, as is understandable, the original author can sometimes be forgiven if he is not completely in sympathy with this particular mode of literary construction.

I have been in touch with Heller for quite a long time, because I was exceedingly interested just after the war in the articles on Thomas Mann, Kafka and Karl Kraus which appeared in successive numbers of the *Cambridge Journal*. It was the one on Karl Kraus – published, if I remember rightly, in 1948 – which first made me suspect that Heller was the author of the unsigned article. The article on Karl Kraus in *The Disinherited Mind* is not identical with that used by MacDiarmid, but in the German version (*Enterbter Geist*) which was published by Suhrkamp in 1954 the text is almost identical with that used in *In Memoriam James Joyce*.

Erich Heller is interested in MacDiarmid's use of his work, but he feels that it would be only right and proper that his authorship of the article used by MacDiarmid should be explicitly credited in any forthcoming edition or printing of *Mid-century English Poetry*. He adds: 'There is nothing anonymous or confidential about it, for the *TLS* article has been included in the German edition of my book *The Disinherited Mind* (the English edition has only the piece you once read in the *Cambridge Journal*) *and* in a little volume called *Studien zu Modernen Literatur*, Suhrkampverlag, Frankfurt a. M.'

The last thing I want to do, in view of the long correspondence about the poem 'Perfect'[2] in the *TLS* some years ago is to embarrass MacDiarmid unnecessarily, so I thought I would just write to you direct, and tell you what Erich Heller requests. If you want to get in touch with him direct, his address is: Department of German, Northwestern University, Evanston, Illinois 60201, USA).

With best wishes,

Yours sincerely, Hamish Henderson

---

1 David Wright, poet and critic; Lecturer in English Literature at the University of Leeds.

2 This controversy concerned MacDiarmid's poem 'Perfect' which consisted of eight lines, the first by MacDiarmid and the rest transcribed from a short story by the Welsh author Glyn Jones. In the wake of a letter from Jones to the *TLS* a flurry of letters appeared citing other examples of unacknowledged 'borrowings' in MacDiarmid's work, including the 'And above all, Karl Kraus' section of *In Memoriam James Joyce*; see *The Letters of Hugh MacDiarmid*, edited by Alan Bold (Hamish Hamilton: London, 1984, 828–33).

159 To Hugh MacDiarmid
[*EUL*]

[Edinburgh, 4 March 1970]

Dear Chris,

I enclose a copy of a letter to David Wright which is self-explanatory. I'm sure you'd have no objection to the addition of the sort of footnote which Erich Heller suggests.

How are you keeping these days? We're all in fairly good form, although flu took its toll a few weeks ago. The children are both quite good singers!

Best wishes to Valda,

Yours aye, Hamish

160 Hugh MacDiarmid to Hamish Henderson
[*EUL*]

[Brownsbank, Biggar, 12 March 1970]

Dear Hamish,

Many thanks for your letter.

Of course I quite agree that the addition you suggest – and Prof. Erich Heller also suggests – should be made in the Penguin book.

However I don't know what stage it has reached and whether that can be done now. I believe the book is almost ready, i.e. that the printing off has now taken place.

I wrote at once on receipt of your letter to David Craig[1] but have had no word from him yet.

You'll have seen the long correspondence on Copyright Permissions which has been running for several weeks in the *Times Literary Supplement*. The disclosures have certainly upset the common understanding on this matter and blown sky-high the charge of plagiarism in such matters.

Re the poem 'Perfect', this has recently appeared in several anthologies – not at my instance but at that of the Welsh author a passage from one of whose stories I used; and now at his suggestion it is accredited to both of us.

All the best,

Yours, Chris

---

1 See Letters 158 and 161.

161 To Hugh MacDiarmid
[*EUL*]

[Edinburgh, 16 March 1970]

Dear Chris,

Thank you for your letter. You say you have written to David Craig, and have had no word from him; no doubt this is a slip of the pen for David Wright, but just on the off-chance that it is not, I thought I would write at once and draw your attention to the error. It has happened to me in the past that I have written a letter to one person, and because of a similarity of name or surname have been on the point of sending it to somebody else.

As you probably know, there has been a split on the editorial board of *The Black Dwarf*. Tariq Ali now edits a magazine called *The Red Mole*,[1] and if you are interested in obtaining it, the address is 182 Pentonville Road, London, N1.

The trials of the Murrayfield demonstrators have been going on this month, but the press has not given them much publicity.[2] A young Dundee doctor was fined £40 for a non-existent assault – a scandalous business. However, one or two of the others have been found not guilty because of the scrappy nature (or complete absence) of police evidence. One of these, I am glad to say, was Iain Lindsay, a good friend of ours, who wrote the article on the 1968 'Paris Spring' in the last number of *Student*[3] before the end of term.

I was very glad to see the *Akros*[4] double number about you and your work, and I have read most of it with great interest. G.S. Fraser has some good points in his article on 'On a Raised Beach'.[5] I don't know whether I ever told you that I gave a talk about 'On a Raised Beach' to a school literary society when I was a sixth-former myself in 1938. I compared it to 'Water Music',[6] and remember commenting that it was 'the stone in the midst of all'. There is an account of this lecture in the school magazine; sometime I must dig it out and send it to J.K. Annand[7] or one of the other people interested in MacDiarmid bibliography. I also remember reading it to Jimmy Singer[8] in his parents' flat in Ruthven Street, not long after I first met him.

I enclose a copy of my song 'Rivonia',[9] which was sung on the terracing at Murrayfield.

With all best wishes to Valda and yourself,

      Yours aye, Hamish

PS I enclose a photostat of the complete Karl Kraus article in *Enterbter Geist*, for I am sure you would like to see it.

---

1 *The Black Dwarf* and *The Red Mole*, left-wing Trotskyist periodicals.
2 See Letter 155.
3 *Student*, newspaper published by Edinburgh University Students Association.

4 *Akros*, V.13–14, April 1970, edited by Duncan Glen; the title of G.S. Fraser's essay is 'Hugh MacDiarmid: the Later Poetry'.

5 'On a Raised Beach', *Stony Limits and Other Poems* (Stanley Nott, 1935).

6 'Water Music', *Scots Unbound and Other Poems* (Gollancz: London, 1934).

7 J.K. Annand (1908–93), poet; wrote mainly in Scots.

8 (James) Burns Singer.

9 Henderson's song 'Rivonia', composed in 1964, became a popular anthem of the Scottish anti-apartheid movement; Nelson Mandela heard it when he was imprisoned in Robben Island, and Henderson sang it for Mandela when he was awarded the Freedom of the City of Glasgow in 1993.

162 To Hugh MacDiarmid

[*EUL*]

[Edinburgh, 17 March 1970]

Dear Chris,

I got a letter from David Wright this morning; he tells me he has written to Erich Heller along the lines suggested. I enclose a copy of the relevant paras.

The note he has drafted is not quite accurate – the *TLS* article appeared *after The Disinherited Mind* was published, which was in 1952. The book reprints the article in the *Cambridge Journal*, which I read in 1948. It was in the *German* version of the book (*Enterbter Geist*) that the *TLS* article was reprinted.

Textual analysis would suggest, in any case, that the German version of the article preceded the English one, although I have not yet asked Heller to confirm this.

In any case, the use you have made of this article is clearly its own justification.

I hope you are keeping well, and that we may have a chance of a reunion before long.

Best wishes to Valda,

Yours aye, Hamish

163 To Professor Erich Heller

[Northwestern University, Evanston, USA]

[Edinburgh, 19 March 1970]

Dear Professor Heller,

You have probably heard by now from David Wright, who edited the Penguin anthology containing parts of your *TLS* article on Karl Kraus set out in verse form by MacDiarmid. He informed me recently that he had sent you a draft of a footnote to be inserted in future printings of the anthology. I have pointed out to him that what he says is not quite accurate, in that the *TLS* article appeared after *The Disinherited Mind* was published – which, if I remember rightly, was in 1952. Furthermore, as you pointed out, in a letter last year, *The Disinherited Mind* reprinted the article in the *Cambridge Journal* which I read (and greatly admired) in 1948 or '49. I have since got hold of a copy of *Enterbter Geist* and read the German version of the *TLS* article, and so am almost in a position to write a 'Road to Xanadu' on the extraordinary route by which your original Karl Kraus article became a much admired poem in the English language. David Wright says in his letter: 'I must get hold of Heller's *Disinherited Mind* – I know no German, but have been exceedingly interested in Kraus since reading about him in *In Memoriam James Joyce* – and that is really thanks to Heller!'

I well understand what you must feel about MacDiarmid's 'Border reiver' attitude to the work of others, but one must also remember that because of his rather high-handed action in appropriating sections of your fine article, he made the name of Karl Kraus known to hundreds – maybe thousands – of people who would otherwise never have heard his name. David Wright tells me that his anthology has in fact been very popular, and will certainly be reprinted in the future.

In the case of MacDiarmid, the whole question of plagiarism is an exceedingly difficult one. Lifting your Karl Kraus article for *In Memoriam James Joyce*, he made practically no alterations, and so it is only right and proper that your name should appear with his in the anthology – in fact, should precede it. But in the case of other quotations – even lengthy quotations – used by MacDiarmid, one can see a definite creative hand at work, and I personally find it very difficult to know where to draw the line. I should be interested to hear what you feel about this.

With all best wishes,

Yours sincerely, Hamish Henderson

PS Reading the German text the other day, I noted that 'false inflections' in English appears as *substanzlose Substantiva*, which seems to me to have a much better ring in context. It also made me wonder which really came first – the German text printed in *Enterbter Geist*, or the English version in the *TLS*. Were you in fact thinking in German or in English when you wrote this article? Or maybe a mixture of both?

164 **Hugh MacDiarmid to Hamish Henderson**
[*EUL*]

[Brownsbank, Biggar, 6 April 1970]

Dear Hamish,

Many thanks for the reproductions of Heller's essays.

I have now heard from David Wright and this should put the matter of my use of the Kraus essay in order. I did not know of course that a new edition of David Wright's Penguin was coming out. I wrote to David Craig, as I told you, because he is co-editor of my *Selected Poems* which Penguin is publishing. I could not remember if I'd included in that the Kraus sections from the Joyce poem but concluded that I had never thought of David Wright's anthology at all.

With best wishes,

Yours, Christopher Grieve

165 **To the** *Scotsman*[1]

[Edinburgh, 13 April 1970]

Sir,

Mr Berresford Ellis and Mr Mac a' Ghobhainn have done much valuable research for their book on the 1820 rising, but there are important omissions which ought to be noted. For example, they make no mention of Orangeism, although this was already an influence to be reckoned with on our side of the water. It is a curious fact, not mentioned by the authors, that the infantry battalion stationed at Glasgow at the start of the rising – the 1st Battalion of the Rifle Brigade, earlier known as the 95th Regiment of Foot – was one of the units in which an Orange Lodge 'cell' had existed as early as 1811. (It still had one, complete with secret oaths, rituals and passwords, in 1830: see H. Senior, *Orangeism in Ireland and Britain 1795-1836*, Appendix B). Ironically, it was in the '95th' that John Baird had himself served for a number of years as a 'lichtbob'.

The counter-revolutionary role of Orangeism is part of the submerged history of those years. The Lodges were willing and eager to serve the repressive policies of successive Tory Governments, quite irrespective of the religious persuasion of their adversaries. The Irish Grand Lodge even made the magniloquent claim (in a declaration dated 12 July 1813) that the Order had saved Britain from Luddism:

> The seditious agitators are stung to madness by the knowledge of the Union between the British and Irish Orangemen, which every day acquires new power and more wide extension. Following your loyal example, the British Orangemen have saved their country by suppressing the treasonable bands calling themselves Luddites.

It is also on record that Orange bravos, willing hatchet-men for Sidmouth and Castlereagh, served as special constables at Peterloo – they made 'Orator' Hunt run the gauntlet between their staves – while the ultra-reactionary Col Fletcher of Bolton, who (according to E.P. Thompson, *The Making of the English Working Class*, p. 536) 'often had fuller sources of information on the Manchester reformers than the local bench', was actually Deputy Grand Master of the British Grand Lodge based in Manchester.

What I am getting at is that there may well have been more than one major spy ring in Scotland, for the complete disappearance of the committee arrested on 21 March in the Gallowgate takes a lot of explaining. What about their wives, relatives, dependants? Why don't we hear anything of them? . . . One is reminded almost of the fantasy world of G.K. Chesterton's 'The Man who was Thursday', in which all the conspirators turn out to be double agents.

One thing is perfectly obvious, however, and that is that the more sophisticated type of spy – the direct emissary of Sidmouth, with access to the Home Office files – would have been at a grave disadvantage when trying to infiltrate working-class organizations. The Orangemen, being themselves in the main ordinary working men, would have been much better suited to this task.

According to the authors, the folk memory of the rising was soon lost. This is to do the tenacious folk memories of the Scottish working class less than justice. It was precisely along the line of folk tradition in the west of Scotland – by means of the 'underground press' of broadsides and chapbooks, and of oral transmission – that the memory of Baird, Hardie and 'Pearly' Wilson[2] was kept green. In 1947 I bought in Glasgow a pamphlet costing 2d which contained a brief history of the insurrection; the text had appeared earlier the same year in the *Springburn Pioneer News*. Much of it was a reprint of nineteenth-century chapbooks describing the executions in gory detail, and exhorting the reader to 'remember Baird and Hardie'.

I am etc., Hamish Henderson

---

1 The first four paragraphs of this letter were cut on publication:

The importance of the 1820 rising resides not so much in what it was as in what the ruling class thought it was. The evidence at our disposal shows that the Scottish (and particularly the Edinburgh) bourgeoisie got such an almighty scare from the events of April 1820 that the long-range results of this most singular of conspiracies might even be said to be still with us.

Thomas Carlyle has left a vivid description of the scene on the bourgeois side of the barricades:

A time of great rages and absurd terrors and expectations; a very fierce Radical and Anti-Radical time. Edinburgh endlessly agitated all around me by it (not to mention Glasgow in the distance); gentry people full of zeal and foolish terror and fury, and looking disgustingly busy and important: courier hussars would come in from the Glasgow region, covered with mud, breathless for head-quarters as you took your walk in Princes Street; and you would hear old powdered gentlemen in silver spectacles talking with low-toned but exultant voice about 'cordon of troops, Sir' as you went along.

Among the well-fed Yeomen who rode west to do or die in combat with the 'Rad rabble' was J.G. Lockhart, who described his experiences in a letter to his fiancée (Scott's daughter Sophia):

There seems now to be no doubt that there had been a serious and well-arranged plan on Monday last. On Wednesday evening, the greater part of the roads leading from Glasgow were in the hands of the Radicals, and various places of encampment in the neighbourhood were resorted to by the weavers from the villages. The drum was beat, such was their audacity, within a mile of the Barracks. The numerous executions which must occur in a very few weeks may be expected to produce a salutary effect, but meantime, till they are over, there is no prospect of entire tranquillity.

Many such passages could be cited to show with what vindictive energy the class war was fought by the haves against the have-nots in the years . following Waterloo:

Prodded forward by agents provocateurs, our west country weavers went to their doomed rising as an ox to the shambles. There was no planning and no co-ordination – except, of course, such co-ordination as was provided by their enemies. No wonder those who came out did so with wary diffidence, like Covenanters uncertain of Divine sanction. Nothing could have been less like the mood of the pike-toting croppies who had ridden in an heroic savage jacquerie twenty-two years earlier. Nevertheless, when it came to the bit, they stood their ground at Bonnymuir, and their leaders – or rather the scapegoats selected as their leaders – died bravely enough on the scaffold.

2 John Baird (1787/8–1820) and Andrew Hardie (1791/2–1820), martyrs of the Scottish Labour movement. Baird and Hardie were weavers; they led the insurrection which resulted in the 'battle of Bonnymuir', both were executed for high treason. Pearly Wilson (1757–1820), a weaver from Strathaven, was also executed for his part in the 1820 rising.

166 To Tom Scott

[Edinburgh, 26 May 1970]

Dear Tom,

I've just bought a copy of your Penguin book and had a look through it. My first impression is that it is a very good selection indeed. Although I naturally regret to see your remarks about 'pseudo folksongs'[1] – 'Banks of Sicily'[2] has circulated as freely and anonymously as Besom Jimmy's,[3] 'Tramps and Hawkers', and so has 'The Men of Knoydart'[4] – I was glad to see a few genuinely popular items from the folksong revival included in the book.

The omissions I find really regrettable are poets like Tom Law[5] and Thurso Berwick who seem to me more interesting poets – and, at their best, better poets – than (shall we say) Douglas Young, Alec Scott and Geordie Fraser.[6]

As you may remember, we have always tried to secure a fee for the source-singers when items like Jimmy MacBeath's 'Come A' Ye Tramps and Hawkers' are used in collections, or by professional singers. Maybe you have taken care of this already, but if not, would you like to arrange it? Jimmy, incidentally, still lives in his Aberdeen model lodging-house; address:

33 East North St,
Aberdeen.

Love to the family,

   Yours, Hamish

PS There are one or two errors in the glossing of Jimmy's song which ought to be corrected. 'Blaw' is not packman's goods; it is the meal — oat-meal or bear-meal — which travelling folk carried in bags or satchels. 'Nethy' is not Abernethy; it is the river Nethy, a tributary of the Spey, which rises in the Cairngorms, and joins the Spey near Nethy Bridge. 'Braxie ham' (not glossed) is mutton from the carcase of a sheep that has died of the braxie. Jimmy does not sing 'a toorin tae the mune' — he sings 'awa too'erin tae the mune', a much nicer phrase, in my opinion.

Also, there is no acknowledgement to the School of Scottish Studies, and there should be.

---

1 Scott's comments in the Introduction, 'The post-war scene in Scotland has seen a revival of interest in, and singing of, folksongs — songs written in the folk idiom by highly educated poets. I have included here one or two which seem genuine' (pp. 53–4), were, it would seem, implicitly aimed at Henderson. The three folksongs included in the anthology are 'Johnnie Lad', 'Come A' Ye Tramps and Hawkers' and 'The Barnyards o' Delgatie'. Nothing of Henderson's is included in the anthology.
2 'The 51st Highland Division's Farewell to Sicily.'
3 Jimmy MacBeath: also the nickname of an earlier folk-poet sometimes credited with the authoring of the song.
4 'The Men of Knoydart', folk-song written by Henderson in 1949.
5 T.S. Law.
6 Alexander Scott; G.S. Fraser.

167 To Hugh MacDiarmid
[*EUL*]

[Edinburgh, 9 June 1970]

Dear Chris,

Thank you for your letter about the Karl Kraus passage. I imagine you will have heard from David Wright by now, and I hope that everything has been 'redded up' to Erich Heller's satisfaction, and your own.

As I think I mentioned in an earlier letter, I now have enough material to do a sort of mini-'Road to Xanadu' on the origins of the whole business — including passages from articles by Kraus which appeared originally in his magazine *Die Fackel* and were reprinted in collections like *Die Chinesische Mauer* (the Chinese Wall). As you are aware, Karl Kraus's method was often merely to *quote*, without any verbal additions of his own, except sometimes an ironic title and subtitle. For example, in his article *Die Weisse Kultur* (White Culture) which he subtitles *Warum in die Ferne schweifen?*[1] he juxtaposes an article from a Berlin newspaper about 'undesirable' pen-pal contacts between German 'Mädchen' and Negroes in the German colonies with a series of 'with a view to marriage' adverts in the German press which reveal a whole ugly world of sex and the cash nexus reminiscent of those surgical cartoons of Gross which appeared just after World War I ('Engineer with Diploma desires to meet Protestant lady of means (not under 25,000 marks)').

Last night I was re-reading the very interesting double number of *Akros*[2] about you and your work, and I noticed a reference (in your conversation with Duncan Glen) to the 'draining of the Po marshes' as one of the achievements of Mussolini which impressed people outside Italy. (You also mentioned this in a letter to the *Scotsman* a couple of years ago, and I alluded to your statement in my reply, but unfortunately the para was cut in the published letter.)[3]

No doubt, when you refer to the 'Po marshes', you mean the Pontine marshes, which are — or rather were — between Rome and Naples. This is a minor point. However, it should be remembered that the plan which the Fascists utilized was drawn up in 1919 by the 'Genio Civile' — the Engineering Dept of the Civil Service in Rome — four years before Mussolini seized power. Furthermore, the Fascist 'drive', accompanied by countless publicity fanfares, did not take place till 1932 — nine years *after* you wrote the two articles 'A Plea for a Scottish Fascism' and 'A Programme for a Scottish Fascism'. It seems to me a matter of some importance that this obfuscation should be cleared up, for Italian Fascism obviously impressed you as an *idea* when it emerged in the early 1920s; it is therefore regrettable that political and social events should be hauled in to confuse the issue, which is surely the demonstrable and revealing influence which a political ideology had on you.

This influence is, of course, very understandable, given the conditions in Scotland after World War I. Wouldn't you agree that the key to your 'Fascist' articles is to be found rather 'in the slums of Glasgow' than in the Pontine marshes?

Best wishes,

Yours aye, Hamish

PS I have often wondered if you came across the books of the philosopher Giovanni Gentile[4] in the thirties, and if so, what you thought of them.

---

1 Trans. 'Why roam around in foreign parts' (H.H.).

2 *Akros*, V.13–14, April 1970, edited by Duncan Glen.

3 See Letter 145.

4 Giovanni Gentile, Italian philosopher; executed by Partisans in 1944.

168 **To the** *Scotsman*

[Edinburgh, 6 July 1970]

Sir,

At a time when everyone who wishes Ireland well must hope that 12 July celebrations will be cancelled, it is maybe opportune to draw attention to some historical facts which the Orange Order invariably does its best to obscure behind the all too familiar smokescreen of bigotry and rancour.

First, the official Orange mythology about 1690 conveniently forgets that during the War of the League of Augsburg the Pope of the day was William's ally against the French King, Louis XIV, and that news of the Battle of the Boyne was greeted with enthusiasm in Rome.

Second, in 1798, the 'Year of Liberty', the leaders of the Republicans were in the main Protestants, and Ulster was the heart of the United Irish movement.

Third, the Orange 'loyalists' were willing enough to be rebels in 1914, when they defied the British Government over Home Rule, and by a secret deal got arms from the Germans.

It is amazing what the Orangemen have been allowed to get away with in the distorting of history; they must be the most successful mystagogic con-men who have ever gulled the admittedly gullible British public. Last Friday Captain Laurence Orr,[1] speaking in the House of Commons, called 12 July 'a national day', and Bernadette Devlin[2] was not there to contradict him. However, the gallant captain knows perfectly well that the 'Twalfth' is neither national nor sacrosanct; it has been banned before, and it ought to be banned again.

When Lord Wellesley (elder brother of the Duke of Wellington and himself an Irishman) arrived in Ireland as Viceroy in 1822, one of his first political acts was to ban 12 July celebrations. The Orange bravos did not like it, but they had to lump it. The worst that happened, by way of reprisals, was that when Wellesley went to see a performance of *She Stoops to Conquer*, an assortment of objects was thrown at the Vice-regal lodge, including an empty bottle and an orange labelled 'No Popery'.

This was only one of hundreds of occasions when these loud-mouthed 'loyalists' were viewed with justified mistrust by the Government. Almost immediately after the Order was founded, an ex-Viceroy, Lord Buckingham, referred in scathing terms to 'the very violent Orangemen, who have formed a very dangerous society, professing very loyal principles'. By 1836 the Orange Order had become such an intolerable nuisance that the lodges were dissolved after what amounted to a direct order from King William IV.

As for the military, successive commanders-in-chief and other officers have found themselves obliged to cope with the menace of Orange cells in British regiments stationed in Ireland. General Sir John Moore ('Moore of Corunna') ended one address to the troops on this subject with the words: 'For a man to boast of his religion is absurd.' (One could wish that these words had been carved an inch deep on the front of all public buildings in the North of Ireland.)

The cream of it is that close on two centuries of intrigue and mayhem are presented to the public as in some mysterious way connected with religion. It is time the truth got around. The Orange Order is a sort of Protestant mafia which exists to protect the wealth, power and privilege of the Anglo-Irish (and Scoto-Irish) ruling class, but which all too frequently gets out of hand. Lord O'Neil wore a sash, and employed 'Protestants only', but when he went against the Order he got the boot. What we need in this country is a government willing and able to call this sinister organization's bluff. It is the world's pity, and a real tragedy for Ireland, that we haven't got one.

I am etc., Hamish Henderson

1 Captain Laurence Orr, Unionist MP.
2 Bernadette Devlin, Nationalist MP.

169 **To the** *Scotsman*

[Edinburgh, 10 July 1970]

Sir,

Mr James G. MacLean, the secretary of the Loyal Orange Institution of Scotland, County Grand Lodge of Stirlingshire, the Lothians and Fife, seeks to assure your readers that 'the participants in Orange parades have always acted in accordance with law'.

This is the sort of outrageous statement which one gets used to from people connected with the Orange Order. Mr MacLean states that among other 'historical irrelevancies', I referred to the anti-Home Rule agitation of 1911. What I actually mentioned was the Strangford Lough gun-running of 1914, as anyone can verify by looking up my letter. However, Orange gun-running is not the sort of subject Mr MacLean and his law-abiding colleagues are likely to mention, if they can possibly help it.

As for Orange parades and the law, Mr MacLean must know that Orangemen have often defied bans and marched illegally. Far from denying this, their folklore positively glories in it, as it does in the number of Catholic victims in various 'battles'. (At the notorious battle of Dolly's Brae, there were almost as many victims as in the Massacre of Glencoe. Not a single Orangeman was wounded in this action, let alone killed.)

Mr MacLean talks about respect for the law, but the record does not support him. The Orange Order is an organization whose central ethos is one of uninhibited prepotent violence. When Catholics hear Orange Order tunes, they know that the texts (as actually sung) are quite unambiguous incitements to sectarian rammies.

Here is one of the less obscene of these ditties which put the Orange point of view in a nutshell:

> Now, Croppies, ye'd better lie aisy and still,
> Ye won't get your liberty do what ye will.
> As long as salt water is found in the deep,
> Our foot on the neck of the Croppy we'll keep.

The appalling thing about Mr MacLean's letter is that not a line of it suggests an even partial awareness of how dreadfully close Northern Ireland is to real civil war. One can well understand why Mr MacLean dislikes references to history, for he and his colleagues have learned nothing from it. Here is another quotation from the past which Captain Orr would do well to heed in the present. Towards the end of his successful campaign to achieve Catholic emancipation, the Duke of Wellington said these words in the House of Lords: 'I am one of those who have probably passed a longer period of my life engaged in war than most men, and principally in civil war; and I must say this, that if I could avoid, by any sacrifice whatever, even one month of civil war in the country to which I was attached, I would sacrifice my life in order to do it.'

I am etc., Hamish Henderson

PS Now that Mr MacLean has found out that '1690 and all that' is an 'historical irrelevance', one hopes that he will take steps to pass on this priceless information to the rest of the Orange Order. If he does so, he will be well advised to take it in easy stages. For one presumes he would not wish a substantial proportion of his senior membership to die of shock.

170 To the *Scotsman*

[Edinburgh, 20 July 1970]

Sir,

Mr J.G. MacLean reminds us of the views of the Duke of Wellington on the Reformation and religious toleration. One can only say that our system of religious toleration must indeed be in a sorry shape if it has to depend on the Orange Order for protection. The order itself is and always has been one of the principal drags on the – at all times – slow and difficult development and consolidation of civil and religious liberties in Britain.

If the turning of every town and village in the North of Ireland into an orange and green donnybrook within twenty years of coming into existence was a service to religious toleration, then the Orange Order must be accounted liberty's most intrepid standard-bearer. Its services to religious toleration, in fact, can only be compared to those of the Ku Klux Klan to anti-racialism.

Mr MacLean repeats Lincoln's adjuration, 'Never forget history', so let us subject orange history to what is obviously a necessary scrutiny. The cult of King Billy, however ludicrous some of its manifestations may be, does have a certain historical justification. 'In 1688' – I quote John Carswell's excellent book on Whiggism, *The Old Cause* – 'the threat from France and Popery to both liberty and property was all too real: the ceaseless reiteration that it was so enabled the Whigs eventually to separate from its shell of Toryism the native, hereditary and divine crown that was its kernel.' Thus Dutch William became king, and started on that curious road which was to lead, a century later, to grotesque apotheosis as the royal and tribal totem of the Orange Order. The truly sick joke is that by the time the order was founded (1795), the threat of the counter-Reformation had long since ceased to have any concrete political reality, and the foreign country – France – to which the united Irishmen looked for help was just about to carry the Revolution's 'Tree of Liberty' into Italy by force of arms, thereby causing a paroxysm of fury and horror in the Vatican. Thus Ireland's capacity for being permanently two moves behind in the European game of political checkers had really landed her in Queer Street, with the foundation of the Orange Order; so much so that in 1970 Northern Ireland is the last place in Europe where you can start a real religious pogrom more or less at the drop of a hat.

Mr MacLean adds a touch of comedy to this rather grisly subject by implying that the Ulstermen who fought at the Somme did so with arms previously smuggled into Ireland from Germany. Again, he must know perfectly well that the Irishmen who fought at the Somme:

> The mad Mulvaneys of the line,
> All that delirium of the brave

included both Catholics and Protestants, and it is an ignoble thought to suggest otherwise.

When Mr MacLean states that the Orange Walk which took in Dolly's Brae in 1864 was a 'lawful parade', he is in error. The Orangemen were marching in direct contravention of the anti-processions Acts which were passed by Parliament in the years following Catholic emancipation, and which remained on the Statute Book till 1871. The song 'Dolly's Brae' appears in the *Crimson Banner Song Book* (sub-titled: *A Collection of Popular Songs and Poems for all True Orangemen*), which was published at Omagh, Co. Tyrone, circa 1910. Here are the lines to which I referred:

> They prayed to Lady Mary, but their prayers were all in vain,
> For in spite of all their Popish schemes one hundred there was slain.

This, incidentally, was an over-enthusiastic 'corpse-count'; the total number of Catholic dead was actually between thirty and forty. As for the 'battle' itself, this is how the song describes it:

We loosed our guns upon them, and we gave them no time to pray,
And we kicked the Virgin Mary right over Dolly's Brae.

Why should not the Orangemen march? Because these two lines represent what their parades mean to one-third of the Northern Irish population. It is farcical to compare an orange parade with, say, the Civil Rights march from Belfast to Derry which was ambushed at Burntollet. The Orange Order, for all its public prancings, is a secret society which has much more in common with the Ku Klux Klan than with a normal political organization or pressure group. This is the fact that British politicians are now, at long last, beginning to comprehend.

I have no sympathy with political gangsterism on either side of the religious fence. A plague on both your bowseys! However, our most urgent problem is to identify the real sources of the violence. Until the British Government realizes just what the Orange Order is, and proceeds to act on that realization without fear, there will be no lasting cure for the maladies of Northern Ireland.

I am etc., Hamish Henderson

171 To Hugh MacDiarmid
[*EUL*]

[Edinburgh, 16 September 1970]

Dear Chris,

Just a line to tell you that I have an article in the Campbell–Collinson edition of Donald MacCormick's 1893 collection of Uist waulking songs in this week's *TLS*.[1] If you have any comments on it – pro or contra – I'd be most interested to hear them.

By now I imagine you'll have got everything straightened out with Erich Heller about the Karl Kraus quote. I enclose the latest 'communiqué' from the Heinrich Heine University Citizens Committee. If you wish to contact them the address is:

Otto Schönfeldt,
4000 Düsseldorf
Grunerstr. 26.

Regards to Valda.

Best wishes, Hamish

---

1 *Hebridean Folksongs: A Collection of Waulking Songs* (Clarendon Press: Oxford, 1970). The review 'Scottish Songs at Work' appeared in the *Times Literary Supplement*, 29 May 1970, reprinted in *Alias MacAlias*.

1971

172 To Hugh MacDiarmid
[*EUL*]

[Edinburgh, 22 May 1971]

Dear Chris,

Here's the first number of *Tocher*,[1] which I hope you'll like.

The last time I heard from you, you told me you were going to write to Erich Heller (this was shortly after I had identified him as the author of the Karl Kraus article used by you in *In Memoriam James Joyce*). Did you ever hear from him? I've been meaning to write to him myself for ages, but thought that I'd wait till I heard from you first.

As I think I told you then, I have gradually amassed a lot of information about the route which led (from Karl Kraus himself) to the *TLS*, via the *Cambridge Journal*, and then on into *I.M.J.J.*[2] It's a sort of mini 'Road to Xanadu'. The German text (in *Enterbter Geist*) is exceedingly interesting. If you'd like to see a xerox copy of this, I can easily make one for you.

Best wishes, Hamish

---

1 *Tocher*, quarterly journal of tales, songs and traditional material selected from the archives of the School of Scottish Studies; issue 43 (1991) is devoted to Henderson's work.

2 *In Memoriam James Joyce* (William MacLellan: Glasgow, 1955).

173 To the *Scotsman* (unpublished)

[Edinburgh, 25 June 1971]

Sir,

I hope no futile internecine bickering between militants and 'Fabians' on the sexual liberation front will be allowed to obscure the fact that a lot of hoary misconceptions and prejudices relating to homosexuality are in process of being dynamited all over the Western world right now.

Are homosexuals sick? Well, let's face it, a lot of homosexuals are sick – but then so are a lot of heterosexuals. Our society, lumbered with the great ruined four-poster of the family, and obscurely conscious all the time that owing to the misuse of science its own extinction is by no means out of the question, is a natural breeding ground for sicknesses of all sorts. All the more reason then for pressing forward on the front of personal sexual happiness, and if revolutionary acts are needed to create a new situation, then we should surely be consequent, and applaud those who have the courage to be revolutionaries.

It is when one encounters irrational prejudices among people who are otherwise intelligent and cultivated individuals that one realizes what the liberationists are up against. Some years ago I heard Edwin Muir deliver a lecture at Newbattle Abbey during the course of which he referred to Thomas Mann's novella *Death in Venice* as 'a Walpurgisnacht[1] of lust and perversion'. And this of a grave tragic idyll in which the protagonists never as much as speak to each other! I suggested to Muir that his remarks did not tell us much about the book, but did tell us a good deal about the panic fear of homosexuality which seems endemic in puritan patrist societies.

About the same time I offered a Scottish literary magazine[2] two translations (one from German and the other from modern Greek) which seemed to me to display an interesting contrast in the handling of what was essentially the same theme, namely the evocation of Roman and Greek antiquity by means of the voices of dead homosexual boys. The first of these was Stefan George's[3] 'Porta Nigra' and the other C.P. Cavafy's[4] 'Favour of Alexander Balas' – this last now justly famous in the French-speaking world in the translation of Georges Papoutsakis.

> (Je suis l'adolescent le plus glorifié.
> Je suis de Balas le plus cher souci, son adoré.)

My own translations were rejected by the editor, although he did make it clear to me that he was motivated by strictly non-literary considerations.

Incidentally, I was afforded an insight into what Cavafy himself must have had to go through in the Greek community in Egypt when I heard (in the summer of 1942) that the headmaster of a boys' school in Alexandria had vetoed a production of *The Importance of Being Earnest* – not, as anyone might have been forgiven for assuming at the time, because Rommel was just up the road, but because the name of its author was Oscar Wilde.

One remembers too, in this context, the lonely courage of the Austrian satirist Karl Kraus, whose articles against the infamous vendetta conducted by the self-advertising publicist Maximilian Harden[5] against certain chosen victims must surely add up to the most brilliant sustained flyting in the German language. Referring to the campaign of vilification run by the German press of the day – which had absolutely nothing to learn from Hearst and Northcliffe[6] – Karl Kraus remarked that it amounted to a 'victory of information over civilization'. Let us hope that on this particular battle-field, information is going to come to the aid of civilization at long last.

I am etc., Hamish Henderson

1 'Walpurgisnacht'; 'night when the witches ride' (HH).
2 *Lines Review*, then under the editorship of Alan Riddell.
3 Stefan George (1868–1933), German poet. Symbolist in influence, his work is prophetic in character.
4 C.P. Cavafy (1868–1933), amongst the foremost of modern Greek poets. Henderson includes a translation of lines from Cavafy's 'The God Leaves Anthony' in the 3rd Elegy: 'Leaving the City'. Cavafy's use of Alexandria as a symbol of life itself also recurs in Lawrence Durrell's *The Alexandria Quartet*.

An echo of the unpublished poems referred to here is found in *Chapman 42*, in which Henderson published a translation of Cavafy's 'Tomb of Iasis' alongside a translation of Dino Campana's 'Chimaera', under the heading '*Androgyne mon amour*', with an explanatory note: 'These two translations together form a kind of janus-poem. I seldom think of one without thinking of the other. They seem to me to express the psychological ambivalence of much poetic activity, the interpretative ambiguity of its very nature' (pp. 19–20).
5 Maximilian Harden mounted a campaign against Count Kuno Moltke and Prince Ehrenburg on account of Moltke's homosexuality. These events are referred to in Karl Kraus's *Die Chinesische Mauer* (*The Chinese Wall*).
6 Hearst and Northcliffe; American and English press barons.

174 To Kätzel Henderson[1]

[Edinburgh, 8 July 1971]

Lovely small Mama,

I'm so glad the weather seems to have changed for the better at exactly the right moment. The last few days in Edinburgh have been almost too hot – I've taken to getting up early in the morning (it's now 7 a.m.) in order to get as much work as possible done before the heat of the day makes it difficult to think. (I'm not joking: yesterday I sat in my office at mid-day mopping my brow, and trying in vain to get my thoughts assembled in order to write one of the sections of my paper on Scott[2] and folksong.)

Now, I imagine, you will all be getting ready for the wedding – please wish them both all the best from me.

The two Dutch students are here, and I am having to devote a good deal of time to them: this week they are coming into the School every day to familiarize themselves with north-east dialects, so that they don't run into the same problems that Ken Goldstein[3] encountered at the start of his field-work. (In his case, of course, there was plenty of time to make good the damage, but the Dutch will only be here for six weeks.)

Garech Browne and Paddy[4] have just returned to Ireland after making recordings in Edinburgh and Orkney. Sorley Maclean came down from Plockton, and we made some splendid recordings of him in the School. The Dutch kids met him, and were tremendously impressed. There was also an absolutely wonderful session in Sandy's[5] on their first day here, with Paddy playing the tin whistle – and joined by musician after musician, until there were about a dozen performing: a sort of impromptu Scottish Chieftains! Jimmy Greenan[6] also playing the whistle, Tom Ward[7] on concertina, the Bitter Withy, Biff Bailey[8] on 'spoons' – I tried to phone Alastair Clark (who does the mid-day folk programme for the BBC) to come over from the *Scotsman* office, but unfortunately couldn't get hold of him.

Marita (the Dutch girl) gazed at this scene with incredulous eyes, and asked me 'Is it always like this in here?'

I eventually extracted a sizeable cheque from Claddagh[9] in recognition of my help, so I send you five pounds of it herewith to add to your funds.

The production of the Bothy Ballads[10] record is proceeding apace, and we hope to have it on sale by the time of the Scott Bicentenary Conference. I've written very long and detailed notes on the various items for the booklet: in fact, this will be the first time in LP history that a folk record will go out with such exhaustive documentation, plus photos etc. Also, I have written the notes as well as I could – Peter Cooke[11] was kind enough to say that he thought the booklet was a work of art in itself . . . which naturally pleased your Dada, after all the work he has put into it!

I'm sure Tina[12] and Sand[13] are having a great time – how are they getting on with the ponies? I'd love to see two girls on pony-back – remembering Portobello beach last year, and that exceedingly staid and broad-backed quadruped on which Sand was perched, as if on a young elephant!

I enclose the Indian stamps for Opa, plus a few of the others. Also, rather a nice Marmaduke,[14] which was in the *News* the other night. What do you think those girls would do if Marmaduke got in ahead of them every time Dada got home with Smarties or Maltesers?

Pretty small Mama-wink, Dada is missing his three ladies, and sorry he isn't with them right now.

Lots of love and plenty of big tussners[15] to all three of you,

    Euer Dada

[PS] Love to Opa and Oma,[16] and the rest of the family.

---

1 Henderson's wife; she was attending a family wedding in Germany.
2 Sir Walter Scott (1771–1832), poet, novelist, collector.
3 Kenneth Goldstein.
4 The Hon. Garech Browne, founder of Claddagh Records; Paddy Moloney, Irish piper.
5 Sandy Bell's, an Edinburgh pub famous for folk-music.
6 Jimmy Greenan, tin-whistle-player and 'Sandy Bell's man'.

7 Tom Ward, concertina player.

8 Biff Bailey, singer.

9 Claddagh Record Company, Eire.

10 Bothy Ballads; the first of the Scottish tradition series released by Tangent (TNGM 109).

11 Peter Cooke, musicologist at the School of Scottish Studies.

12 Tina: Henderson's daughter, Christine.

13 Sand: Janet, Henderson's youngest daughter.

14 'Marmaduke', cartoon-strip in the Edinburgh *Evening News*.

15 Kisses.

16 'Grand-dad' and 'Grannie', Henderson's parents-in-law.

1972

175 Hugh MacDiarmid to Hamish Henderson
[*EUL*]

[Brownsbank, Biggar, 30 June 1972]

Dear Hamish,

Many thanks for sending on the Golden Treasury. McKechnie must have borrowed it over 20 years ago — when I was living in Victoria Crescent Road. I haven't seen or heard from him since then, and did not know he was dead. Please thank Freddie Anderson on my behalf. A lot of books of mine, and Valda's, must be in all sorts of hands. I loaned them pretty freely and did not keep a record, but I can think of at least twenty books missing from my shelves which I'd gladly — but do not expect to — have back.

Thanks also for the two copies of *Tocher*. Full of interesting stuff.

I thought the Symposium[1] went off very well. I did not attend, of course, because I am too deaf to hear. I only heard bits of David Daiches' lecture tho' I sat as near his lectern as I could.

Several friends have told me that Garioch's[2] remarks were obviously derogatory. He apparently said some things about Grant Taylor and I am told suggested I owed Taylor a great deal.[3] That is absolute nonsense, Taylor — even if he had the necessary knowledge — was in no condition to do more to help me than simply type my stuff. I do not know what mare's nest Garioch was herrying, but his intention was apparently malicious.

Hope all goes well with you and yours.

I'll be glad when my 80th[4] birthday is over. Exhibitions in Edinburgh, Glasgow and Aberdeen — two films — Tom Fleming's reading of The Drunk Man on Radio 4 etc etc. I have made up my mind never to have another 80th birthday!

Glad HBC[5] is still able to get about and do a little gardening.

Yours, Chris

---

1 The MacDiarmid Symposium was held in the David Hume Tower of Edinburgh University, on 27 May.

2 Robert Garioch, pen name of Robert Garioch Sutherland (1909–81), poet; his best work was written in Scots. His long poem, 'Embro to the Ploy', gives a feeling for the Edinburgh of the early Festivals and Folk Revival ceilidhs. Garioch fought in the North African Desert campaign.

3 Henry Grant Taylor (b. 1914); Taylor worked for MacDiarmid as a personal assistant/secretary during the latter part of his stay on Shetland. In his article 'Tangling with the Langholm Byspale', Henderson describes Garioch's role in securing Taylor's help for MacDiarmid in 1937:

> The link between this young man, whom one might call without hyperbole, the providential *deus ex machina*, and the beleaguered Grieve family, was the poet Robert Garioch, who bumped into Taylor one day and told him that Grieve was 'living in Whalsay and on his uppers, as you might say, pretty well broke' . . . Bob was therefore self-evidently a potent agent of benefaction, and through his intervention he secured MacDiarmid two and a half years' devoted service from Grant Taylor. *Cencrastus* no. 48, Summer 1994.

4 Exhibitions were held in honour of MacDiarmid's birthday in Edinburgh University Library and the Old Glasgow Museum. The BBC broadcast a film *Rebel Poet*.

5 Helen B. Cruickshank.

176 To the *Scotsman*

[Edinburgh, 14 July 1972]

Sir,

Can there be another subject on earth about which more nonsense is written and spoken than homosexuality? (In Scotland the language mix-up probably beats it by a shrunken head.)

People who talk about 'bastions of morality' all too often turn out themselves to be merely bastions of prejudice and outmoded myth and tabu. The sexual tabu which the Reverend Malcolm H. MacRae wishes to uphold surely has about as much relevance for us in this country today as the Hindu tabu on the eating of beef or the Jewish tabu on pork. Man is an inherently pansexual creature, capable of responding to a variety of sexual stimuli, and the dichotomy of 'homosexual' and 'heterosexual' is therefore highly artificial.

Those who challenge irrational and oppressive tabus need all the help they can get from men of goodwill. Your correspondents are naive, however, if they expect to get much assistance from ministers of religion when lifting the mines in this difficult and bedevilled territory. Here and there you get 'the auntran guid ane', but in the main they are just the same old pack of self-elected elect who see sex as one of the comparatively few areas in which they can still have the occasional field day, doing their self-important thing and interfering with other people's lives. And, let us face it, there is an unhealthy Puritan strain in a broad stretch of Christian tradition which crosses the frontiers of individual sects and denominations and which is deeply suspicious not only of homosexuality but of sexuality, tout court.

It is high time the ignominious role of the clergy in most of the humanitarian campaigns of the last 150 years was brought right out into the open. In the early nineteenth century the attempts of reformers such as Sir Samuel Romilly to bring to an end some of the horrors of the English 'hanging code' – a starving mother of 17 with an infant at her breast executed for lifting a yard of linen from a shop counter; the hanging of children (two sisters of eight and 11 strung up at Lynn in 1808); 13 people hanged at a single session for being found in the company of Gypsies – were met with resolute opposition from the Archbishop of Canterbury, most of the bishops and the vast majority of the clergy of the Church of England. By the same token, the comparatively more humane and liberal Scottish criminal code was brought into being and defended by courageous laymen against vehement and often virulent opposition from the Calvinist clergy. It should surprise nobody, therefore, that in the much needed and long overdue sexual revolution – which, as Norman Mailer has suggested, is by far the most 'meaningful and natural' revolution of our time – the same general pattern can be discerned.

Latter-day Puritans like Malcolm Muggeridge try to pillory liberal-minded clergymen by calling them 'trendy', etc., but the fact is that such clergymen are a tiny minority as against the conservatives.

People like the Rev. Malcolm MacRae may try to stem the tide, but they will not succeed, because public opinion is now getting adjusted to the self-evident truth that the homosexually oriented person has as undeniable a right to personal sexual happiness as anyone else. Chastity may suit some people, and it may even sometimes burgeon into saintliness, but it can also be one of the 'roots of evil': the unholy flowering, in this case – from the auto da fe to the fantasy (or practices) of celibate floggers – being punitive sadism.

Luckily the views of psychologists like Dr Mark Freedman are rapidly gaining widespread acceptance. In his book *Homosexuality and Psychological Functioning*, Dr Freedman writes: 'Social attitudes to sexuality have to be changed, or else an atmosphere of fear, negation and restrictiveness will continue to pervade society. Some theorists – notably Marshall McLuhan – maintain that the world is rapidly changing because of the speed of communication fostered by the electronics media, and that these changes include a new tolerance for and interest in differentness. This appreciation of differentness includes acceptance of people formerly discriminated against according to social, ethnic, religious and sexual distinctions. Hopefully, then, a new climate of respect for diversity and acceptance of individual differences is arriving.' With human relationships still resulting in individual chaos because of these divisions and discriminations, I hope this change arrives soon.

I am etc., Hamish Henderson

177 To Hugh MacDiarmid
[*EUL*]

[Edinburgh, 16 July 1972]

Dear Chris,

Many thanks for your letter. When I next see Freddie Anderson,[1] I'll pass on your thanks to him.

The enclosed is by way of being a small birthday present – sent off early, because I shall be away for most of the rest of the Summer. I don't know if you've read Hesse's *Das Glasperlenspiel*[2] – it first appeared in English (under the title *Magister Ludi*) in 1948 or thereabouts – but I am told this translation is very much better.

Das Glasperlenspiel is (in one of its aspects, at least) a kind of Karl Kraus-type satire on the whole idea of an intellectual élite. If you want to get something of its flavour, read pages 132–133 and 156–157.

Last weekend I was down in Newcastleton for the village's annual folk festival. It was a very enjoyable occasion – almost as good as the Langholm Common Riding – though hardly as old, of course. While I was there, I met two young blokes, one of whom comes from Langholm and the other from Longtown. They both, apparently, work in the mills in your home town. As there had been quite a bit of poetry, as well as song, at the folk festival, I asked them if they had read 'The Seamless Garment', and, as of course they hadn't, I recited it to them in the street, then and there. The upshot was that they wanted copies of it, so today I photostatted it (from my own copy of the *First Hymn to Lenin*) and dispatched the copies. I tell you this little story to show you that – by courtesy of the folk revival – 'the guid wark gangs bonnilie on'.

I read with regret what you wrote about Robert Garioch's contribution to the Symposium. I can assure you that 'malicious' is just about the last word I would use to describe it. What he said was in the context of a discussion touching on all aspects of your encyclopaedic interests, and your techniques of assembling and mastering such diverse material as appears in the long poems (or poem) of the last thirty years are obviously going to be interesting to scholars (and other poets) for a long time. There was a good deal of discussion about this whole question, and I contributed to it myself with much greater forthrightness (I would say) than Bob Sutherland.[3] Bob mentioned this fellow Taylor[4] – of whom I had never heard – and asked for information about the work he had done for you. It was suggested, if I remember rightly, that Taylor had acted as a sort of volunteer archivist for you, putting cuttings etc into order, and generally doing secretarial work for you. That, to my recollection, is a fair summary of that part of the discussion.

The friend or friends of yours who have suggested that Bob's remarks were malicious have themselves been guilty, in my opinion, of seriously misleading you. I don't want to start bandying around adjectives of that sort myself, but I can think of one which would describe their conduct. I have no use, and never have had, for this internecine nonsense and try to knock it on the head whenever I come across it.

I hope you have a pleasant Summer – and a not too strenuous eightieth birthday, when it comes. If the world gets too clamant, you can always retire to Castalia[5] and take refuge in the Glass Bead Game!

Love to Valda,

Yours aye, Hamish

---

1 Freddie Anderson, poet and playwright, member of the 'Clyde Group'.
2 Hermann Hesse (1877–1962), German-born author and poet, later assumed Swiss nationality. *Das Glasperlenspiel* was translated as *The Glass Bead Game* in 1970.
3 Robert Garioch Sutherland.
4 Henry Grant Taylor, see letter 175.
5 Castalia, an imaginary country dedicated to the intellectual pursuits of *The Glass Bead Game*.

178 To Robert Sutherland (Robert Garioch)

[*NLS*]

[Edinburgh, 17 July 1972]

Dear Bob,

The other day I heard from Bob Tait[1] that somebody – Alex Scott?[2] – had been giving Chris Grieve what was plainly a badly distorted account of what you said at the Symposium.[3]

He even said that he had threatened to sue you!

Anyway, I thought it might be useful to let him know, in no uncertain terms, what I felt about this sort of nonsense. The 'malice' wass assuredly not on your side. I enclose a copy of a letter I have just sent to Chris. I hope you will approve of it.

All the best, Hamish

[PS] To make the necessary point without bitterness, I enclosed the letter with a copy of Hesse's *Glass Bead Game*, which I'm giving the old boy for his eightieth birthday.

---

1 Robert Tait, poet and critic; editor of *Scottish International*.
2 Alexander Scott.
3 The Symposium in honour of MacDiarmid's eightieth birthday.

1973

179 **To Tom Scott**

[Edinburgh, 23 February 1973]

Dear Tom,

Many thanks for your letter, and for the poem about Stuart.[1] His death certainly hit us hard; as you know, I valued him greatly as a friend, and on top of that he was for long my most resourceful ally in the Scottish folk revival.

If you ever make your way to Sandy Bell's[2] these days, you will find a portrait of Stuart installed in a place of honour, together with the text and tune of 'The Sandy Bell's Man'. Gordon Wright[3] is responsible for this. Managers may come and managers may go, but I am pretty sure that Stuart's portrait will stay on the wall of Sandy's for quite a long time. (Probably till Judgement Day in the afternoon — or even later, if we get a late licence!)

Jane[4] and the children have taken it amazingly well, but it is probably just coming home to them now. The children are back at school in Edinburgh, and I believe Jane intends to start teaching again. The suggestion in your letter is a very practical one, and I have passed it over to Donald Archie[5] (Stuart's brother-in-law).

I have not heard recently from Germany myself, and I am really wondering what has happened to Schönfeldt.[6] I think I will drop him a note today. One thing that may have annoyed him was the design of the Heine stamp which was issued on the anniversary. As you may know, the Heine Committee had been pressing for well over a year to have a Heine stamp issued, and submitted a number of excellent designs. The stamp which was finally produced was unspeakable: it made Heine look not so much dreamy and woozy, as positively half-witted. This stamp is a real insult, and I am sure there must have been a lot of annoyance about it in Germany. It really made me sick at heart to see it, and I well imagine it must have distressed Schönfeldt and his comrades terribly. As my father-in-law pointed out, the stamps of the Bundesrepublik have tended to be for some reason uglier than practically any of the others issued in Europe, but the Heine stamp is an all-time low. It would really make you think that some swastika'd gremlin was sitting permanently in the designer's office.

Anyway, I am sure your reference to Pound[7] would have absolutely nothing to do with Schönfeldt's silence — which as I say, has hit me too.

With best wishes, Hamish

1 Stuart MacGregor, poet and novelist, doctor; a close friend of Henderson's and,
   as a student in the 1950s, one of the founding members of the Edinburgh
   University Folksong Society. The character of Hector Gunn in MacGregor's
   novel *The Myrtle and Ivy* (Macdonald: Edinburgh, 1967) is based on Henderson.
   His song 'Sandy Bell's Man' is still popular. He left for Jamaica in March 1972
   to take up a temporary medical post, and was tragically killed in a car crash in
   January 1973. Henderson's song 'To Stuart – On His Leaving For Jamaica', a
   Burns pastiche, is included in *Chapman 42*. Tom Scott's poem, 'Morningside
   Cemetery: Burial O Stuart MacGregor' was included in his *Collected Shorter Poems*
   (Chapman/Agenda: Edinburgh, 1993). The following is an extract:

   > The day dowie, dowie the fowk aa roon,
   > I myndit, Stuart, the days we baith had seen
   > No that langsyne when you were just a loon
   > In Sandy Bell's, in folk-song ceilidhs gien
   > By Hamish and yoursel, whaur I wad sing
   > Some auld Scots sang or twa amang the lave . . .

2 Sandy Bell's, an Edinburgh pub famous for folk-music.
3 Gordon Wright, Edinburgh publisher.
4 Jane MacGregor, Stuart MacGregor's widow.
5 Donald Archie MacDonald, Lecturer in the School of Scottish Studies.
6 Henderson and Scott wrote letters of support to Schönfeldt, who was
   organizing the campaign to have the University of Düsseldorf renamed the
   Heinrich Heine University.
7 Ezra Pound (1885–1972), American poet.

180 To the *Scotsman*

[Edinburgh, 15 May 1973]

Sir,

Referring to Bob Tait's resignation as editor of *Scottish International*, Tom Scott
makes the following rather oddly expressed admission: 'It is true that Mr Tait has
said that he is resigning for private reasons.'

Surely Mr Scott is not taking it upon himself to question the veracity of Mr
Tait's perfectly straightforward statement, when many people in addition to
Robert Garioch are in a position to corroborate it.

Having been a very infrequent contributor to *Scottish International* (twice in five
years), I am possibly better placed than Mr Tait to comment on the charges
levelled against his editorial policies, the majority of which seem to me to range
from the rancorous-malicious to the patently untrue and unjust.

What, I'd like to ask, does Mr Scott consider so 'anti-national' about the
magazine? Stephen Maxwell, maybe? One wonders sometimes whether the people
who are so voluptuously free with their brickbats have ever actually read the paper
they are so quick to denigrate.

It is about time somebody told the real truth, which is that *Scottish International* is only the latest victim of a long and dishonourable 'nesty Scotch' tradition of bitching, girning and traducing which, at its worst, can strike life (and art) 'like a black frost'. Hugh MacDiarmid (archetypal executioner-victim) gave an accurate if hardly dispassionate account of this often lethal syndrome when he wrote ('The Company I've Kept', p. 275):

'Modern Scots are adept at disparagement — there is nothing they hate more than a man getting 'a little above himself' and rising above the ruck. They are quick to prick the balloon of any such pretensions, and Lewis Grassic Gibbon and many other Scottish writers have had bitter cause to complain of the way in which the deadly phrase 'I kent his faither' is used to reduce them to their proper level, the implication being that coming from the background they did, it was impossible that they should become of any more consequence than any other people.

Who would have thought, twenty years ago, when a pitiful handful of subscribers and helpers (including myself) witnessed Alan Riddell's agonizing attempt to get *Lines Review* off the ground — the genteel bosses of International House, the British Council's club in Princes Street, would not even let him sell it on the premises, let alone support it financially — that in 1973 we would have a professionally produced monthly (facing up to the realities of Scottish life and politics, as well as Scottish art and letters) which would stand comparison with any similar publication in Western Europe?

Well, we have one, and we had better defend it here and now, with money and moral support and more money, if the most promising Scottish journalistic venture for many years is not to founder.

Hamish Henderson

1974

181 **To the** *Scotsman*

[Edinburgh, 31 January 1974]

Sir,

I was glad to see, from your report of the debate in the House of Lords on 'a taxing problem for the oldest profession', that we now – at long last – have the answer to one of the questions which preoccupied Robert Burns when he was composing his epistle 'to a gentleman who had sent a newspaper, and offered to continue it free of expense':

> How cesses, stents and fees were rax'd,
> And if bare arses yet were tax'd.

Hamish Henderson

182 **To the** *New Statesman and Nation*

[Edinburgh, 6 June 1974]

Sir,

Referring to the scurrilous anti-Catholic publications which circulate in Northern Ireland, Fr Herbert McCabe writes: 'Nobody has even found it worthwhile trying to exploit such bigotry among the products of Catholic schools.' This is unfortunately not correct.

When I was working in Northern Ireland several years before the present Troubles started,[1] I assembled a fair-sized collection of sectarian publications originating on both sides of the religious divide. Some of these were obviously aimed at secondary school children. The prize exhibit is a school story called 'The Beefy Saint', written by the Rev. Fergal McGrath, S.J., and published in 1950 by Veritas Company Ltd, Veritas House, Dublin. On the surface, this is merely a rather ludicrous imitation of the sort of school story that used to appear in weeklies like *The Magnet* and *The Gem*, but on closer examination it can be shown to pack quite a powerful charge of lethal sectarian animus.

The hero is a boy from Portadown, Co. Armagh, who is at 'St Ronan's', a Catholic boarding school in the south. When he goes home for the summer holidays, after his first year there, he gets involved in a rough-house on the Twelfth of July, and dies of his wounds. Later the same day his best friend reads about what has happened in the Dublin *Evening Herald*:

DASTARDLY OUTRAGE IN PORTADOWN

About one o'clock today a shameful assault was perpetrated on the outskirts of Portadown. Two Sisters of Mercy, on their way to the work house, were assailed in a threatening manner by a party of Orange rowdies. A young man named O'Hagan who happened to be passing on a bicycle interfered on behalf of the nuns. He was thereupon attacked, and so badly beaten that his life is despaired of. The police were shortly on the scene, and the nuns reached their destination in safety. The victim of this outrage, who is only seventeen years of age, is a son of Mr W.J. O'Hagan, manager of the Leinster Bank.

The fact that no incident of the sort described — two nuns assailed by Protestants, and a youth killed as a result of intervening — has ever happened in Northern Ireland on the Twelfth of July need not worry either the author or the publishers. Catholic school children who have never so much as spoken to a Protestant child will merely be confirmed in the sterile rituals of their archaic private mythology, and adults brought up in the same tradition will be unlikely to enlighten them. (And of course the same ugly pattern can be observed perpetuating itself on the other side of the sectarian divide.)

Here is another short passage which effectively gives the flavour of this curious tract. The hero is in a tight spot, earlier in the story, when he tries to stop a dormitory rag. 'Ryan was a different proposition . . . Jim's mind went back to the stable at home in Portadown. He could see the sack of bran hung up and Andy McLafferty, the gardener, his big fists thumping the sack vigorously. "Yon's it, Master Jimmie," he would say contentedly. "Ye have it fine. The Falls Road uppercut they call it, and a queer useful punch it is".'

The sad truth is that the folklorist is often better placed than the politician when it comes to exploring the deeper roots of evil in Ireland.

Hamish Henderson

---

1 Henderson worked in Belfast for the Workers Education Association from 1948 to 1949.

183 To the *Scotsman*

[Edinburgh, 14 June 1974]

Sir,

Commenting on the television version of *The Cheviot, the Stag, and the Black, Black Oil*,[1] Wilfred Taylor suggests that 'it would be far more dramatically exciting if some writer were to cast Patrick Sellar[2] in a favourable, heroic light', and adds: 'Originality and unpredictability in the theatre are never lightly to be dismissed.'

It would be quite possible, I suppose, to write a play in which Burke and Hare were portrayed as intrepid pioneers in the field of medical research; Gilles de Retz given his due as a forerunner of revolutionary advances in tackling juvenile delinquency; and Reinhardt Heydrich depicted as a martyr in the cause of European unity. These are, of course, just ordinary old paradoxes; sometimes, in art, they do come off, but much more often they fall flat, and – as Chesterton addicts know to their cost – there is nothing in art so boring as a boring paradox.

Highland folk tradition is, however, solidly behind John McGrath in the matter of Patrick Sellar, and there can be little doubt that – in this case, at any rate – art can only benefit by listening with respect to the voice of popular tradition.

The following is an attempt to render into Scots verse the devastating final stanza of a Gaelic song about the Sutherland Clearances; the original – which is a variant of a song said to have been composed by Ewen Robertson of Tongue – was recorded in 1958 from Andrew Stewart, a native of Melness, by my colleague John MacInnes:[3]

> Sellar, daith has ye in his grip;
> Ye needna think he'll let ye slip.
> Justice ye've earned, and, by the Book,
> A warm assize ye winna jouk.
> The fires ye lit to gut Strathnaver
> Ye'll feel them noo – and roast forever.

Hamish Henderson

---

1 *The Cheviot, the Stag, and the Black, Black Oil*, by the Scottish playwright John McGrath.
2 Patrick Sellar (1780–1851), lawyer and factor for the Duke of Sutherland during the Clearances; he was despised for his brutality.
3 John MacInnes, Lecturer and collector in the School of Scottish Studies.

184 To the *Scotsman*

[Edinburgh, 16 July 1974]

Sir,

It may be worth pointing out that the individuals responsible for the best organized and most thorough orgies of 'queer-bashing' in history were Hitler and Stalin. Overwhelming proof exists that the Nazis selected homosexuals as the preferred victims in some of the more fiendish of their pseudo-medical experiments. In so doing they were, of course, merely carrying society's irrational hatreds to their logical final solution.

The Stalinists, for their part, used prostituted psychiatry as a bogus justification for penal measures which to all intents and purposes equated sexual with political deviancy. As Karl Kraus remarked earlier in the case of Germany, there is without doubt a plentiful dose of hypocrisy and cynicism in this whole revolting set-up, in which the prepotent State takes it out on selected scapegoats in order to safeguard absolute political power.

The sheer size of these 'operations' has – like the extermination of gypsies and other travelling people – tended to be forgotten because of the much greater enormities perpetrated against the Jews; the latter being so colossal and so horrible that they quite literally baffle the imagination, and reduce other human crimes to seeming insignificance.

Hitler and Stalin were both, of course, 'mature' adult heterosexuals, and therefore presumably – for some of your correspondents at least – more balanced and fulfilled personalities than (say) Kit Marlowe or Michelangelo, or any of the other famous exemplars of 'Socratic love' in world history.

It is hard to know which is most to be deplored – the smug complacency of some of your letter writers ('we are not as these other human beings are') or their intemperate stridency ('the Lord Provost should resign,' etc.). It is hardly necessary to remind your readers that the psychologist is sometimes able to offer a clue as to the hidden causes of both these ugsome manifestations.

Hamish Henderson

185 To the *Times Literary Supplement*

[Edinburgh, 23 July 1974]

Sir,

Referring to the translation I made, shortly after it was published, of the first (1947) edition of Gramsci's *Lettere dal Carcere*, you state (Commentary, 3 July) that 'apart from a few passages, no steps were taken to publish it for twenty-five years, until Gramsci became a subject of interest – indeed, almost a cult figure – among the English-speaking left'.

As this might well leave your readers with the erroneous impression that I did not make much of an effort at the time to get my translation published, I feel it necessary – in justice not only to myself, but also to several helpers and well-wishers – to set the record straight.

The first publisher to take an interest in the translation was John Lehmann, who had published a book of my poems. Lehmann gave me a considerable amount of assistance and encouragement, but when the translation was completed he found himself unable – for reasons quite unconnected with the book itself – to publish it and he returned the typescript to me. In the succeeding four or five years I tried publisher after publisher without success. Then, in the mid-1950s, Mary

Ringsleben[1] of Leeds University formed a small ad hoc committee which took over from me the thankless task of hawking the typescript around. This committee did its best; however, Mary was eventually obliged to report that she had had no more success than I had.

As I had spent the best part of a literary award on the translation, and had really tried to make a good job of it – seeking out Gramsci's relatives in Italy, and doing a fair amount of original research – this failure to get it published was naturally very frustrating. It was some satisfaction to me, therefore, that E.P. Thompson decided to publish a few extracts in *The New Reasoner*: these extracts, which were from the letters dealing with anti-semitism, psychoanalysis and child psychology, appeared in two successive numbers of the magazine in 1959.

Meanwhile Sergio Caprioglio in Turin was keeping me posted on the progress of his work (with Elsa Fubini)[2] on a greatly enlarged edition of the letters. This splendid collection, which appeared in 1965, is furnished with a vastly superior commentary and critical apparatus, and all the texts have been checked with the most scrupulous accuracy from the original manuscripts; it is rightly held, therefore, to have superseded the 1947 edition which I had translated.

I do not think, in spite of this, that my own work has – as your commentator suggests – been likewise 'superseded'. The 1947 edition, which was awarded the Viareggio Prize when it appeared, remains a literary and historical document of considerable importance. The rather drastic editing, which expunged all references to the disgraced former leader Amadeo Bordiga, has its own political interest. Furthermore, as Tom Nairn points out in the bibliography appended to his translation of Fiori's biography of Gramsci, published by New Left Books in 1970, 'it [the 1947 edition] presented a clear enough intellectual and moral portrait of Gramsci, and it is still worth reading today by anyone looking for an outline sketch of his personality'. It was because the editor of the *New Edinburgh Review* considered this statement to be correct that he decided to publish my work alongside the other documents which reflect the period.

Hamish Henderson

---

1 Mary Ringsleben, librarian at Leeds University.
2 Caprioglio and Fubini, editors of the 1965 edition of Gramsci's *Lettere dal Carcere*.

1975

186 To Hugh MacDiarmid
[*EUL*]

[Edinburgh, 21 February 1975]

Dear Chris,

I forgot to tell you last night that 'The Muckle Sangs'[1] – the School's double album of Scots classic ballads – will be out on 1 March. You will find some familiar quotations – from yourself[2] – tucked away among the documentation. I've asked Mike Steyn (boss of the record company) to send you a complimentary copy.

The recordings I made of the reading sound pretty good. This double bill of yourself and Sorley was truly an historic occasion.

Best wishes, Hamish

[PS] I hear *Calgacus*,[3] which has been having printer trouble, will be out some time next week – probably coinciding with Gramsci III!

---

1 Scottish Tradition 5, *The Muckle Sangs: Classic Scots Ballads*, Tangent Records (TNGM 119/D). This record was part of a series featuring recordings of Scottish folk and traditional music from the archives of the School of Scottish Studies.

2 The three quotations included in Henderson's sleeve notes are:

(i) As life to death, as man to God, sae stands
This ruined mill* to your great aumrie then.
This ruined mill – and every rinnin' mill?

from 'Depth and the Chthonian Image'

(ii) Descendant o' the unkent bards wha made
Sangs peerless through a' post-anonymous days,
I glimpse again in you that mightier poo'er
Than fashes wi' the laurels and the bays
But kens that it is shared by ilka man
Since time began.

from 'First Hymn to Lenin'

(iii) *Ein Mann aus dem Volke*** – weel I ken
Nae man or movement's worth a damn unless

The movement 'ud gang on withoot him if
He de'ed the morn. Wherefore in you I bless
My sense o' the greatest man can typify
And universalize himsel' maist fully by.

from 'Depth and the Chthonian Image'

The first quotation is repeated again at the conclusion of Henderson's
Introduction.

* The cover of the record features a photo of the ruins of the 'Mill o Tifty', which features in the
last of the ballads on the album, 'Andrew Lammie' (Child ballad 233).

** *'Ein Mann aus dem Volke'* (A Man out of the People); from 'Depth and the Chthonian Image',
published in *Scots Unbound and Other Poems* (Eneas MacKay: Stirling, 1932). Ironically the phrase is
an unattributed quotation from Wyndham Lewis's book *Hitler* (London, 1931).

3 *Calgacus*, Scottish cultural review, edited by Ray Burnett. 'Gramsci III'; *New
Edinburgh Review* (no. 27, 1975) published a selection of the papers given to a
conference on Gramsci organized by the *New Edinburgh Review*, in the David
Hume Tower, Edinburgh University, June 1974.

187 Hugh MacDiarmid to Hamish Henderson

[Brownsbank, Biggar, 26 February 1975]

Dear Hamish,

Many thanks for sending me the Calgacus folder, tho' I am a bit peeved that the
long list of prospective contributors doesn't include my name, as I still regard
myself, and am regarded elsewhere, as a Communist writer. However I'll certainly
subscribe.

Both Valda and I greatly enjoyed the Poetry Reading. Sorley and Renée[1] invited us
home, after an interlude in the University Staff Club. I thought you'd come along
there too, but realize that you've probably to be very careful still after your illness.

Two friends of mine are arranging to start a magazine in Irvine, basically of
Ayrshire local interest, but concerned with the Arts. They are asking to contact,
and receive articles from, people who knew the two artists, Colquhoun and
MacBride.[2] I mentioned that you had known them and also that a friend of yours, a
Scott Moncrieff, knew them. So they are hoping you might write a short article
about McBride and Colquhoun for them and put them in touch with Scott
Moncrieff[3] in the expectation he may also do so.

The man to write to about this is:

Clement Caldwell,

32 Glenconner Row,

Ayr.

All the best.

Yours, Chris

1 Sorley and Renée MacLean.
2 Robert Colquhoun (1914–62) and Robert MacBryde (1913–66); known as
   'the two Roberts', born in Kilmarnock and Maybole, Ayrshire. Both were
   important artists, who explored contemporary European currents in art. They
   sustained a long relationship, living out most of their artistic careers in or
   near London, where MacDiarmid met them in the 1930s; Henderson first
   met them during the early years of the war, but did not know either of
   them well.
3 Douglas Scott Moncrieff (b. 1917) and Queenie Scott Moncrieff (1920–90).
   Douglas worked as a civil-servant. One of their three sons (Diarmid Hugh,
   who was named after MacDiarmid) wrote the 'poem by a child' which
   Henderson praises in a letter to the *Scotsman*, see Letter 121.

188 Hugh MacDiarmid to Hamish Henderson

[Brownsbank, Biggar, 13 March 1975]

Dear Hamish,

Many thanks for the Muckle Sangs record and accompanying material. The
various quotations from my poems are very relevant and no matter how what I've
said on occasions may have been interpreted I of course stand by what I wrote in
these quotations.[1]

The record is a splendid one and the whole programme of records to come
represents a great achievement.

With every kind regard to Mrs Henderson and yourself.

Yours, Chris

---

1 These conciliatory remarks refer to their flytings of 1959 and 1964.

189 Queenie Scott Moncrieff to Hamish Henderson

[London, 14 March 1975]

Dear Hamish,

Thank you for your letter and for the leaflet about the records. We'll certainly
keep them in mind. Trouble is, we listen to records so rarely. There's so little
time.

About Colquhoun and MacBryde[1] – the twa Roberts – and having mulled things
over with Douggie this morning, I hardly think our reminiscences will help. We
hadn't met them before and haven't met them since and there they were with a
number of other people we didn't know. We were all hard up at that time. £2 was
all we allowed ourselves for a party – that was 4 bottles of San Vito @ 5/6 from
Parmigiani's, a miniature of rum, some chopped fruit and 4 bottles of lemonade
with which you made the resultant punch more dilute as the evening progressed.
So there were we with these unexpected guests, who arrived some time after you

and Chris, who had trailed you in some mysterious manner, who were critical of the lack of liquor. One suggested we telephone our wine merchant, one offered a cheque and Douggie thinks one actually went and got some more booze.

So, Chris[2] in his kilt, sitting in an armchair in a corner, with an attractive, well-tanned girl (whom Douggie thinks was a journalist) in a low-cut dress, on his knee. The Nut-Brown Maid. Short chap standing on tip-toe to try and see down the front of the dress.

Chris very complimentary about John McLean[3] and asking you to sing it and a row, Douggie says, as a result. I think you tried to chuck a chap over the balcony and Douggie told him to leave, but thinks he probably came back in after.

And Paul Potts[4] the People's Poet was there. I heard later that he regularly stole things from people he visited which could explain that a new giant tablet of soap was missing after the evening. I was assured that I should regard it as evidence of favour that no more was gone.

Since I was heavily pregnant with Diarmid it must have been early June in '52. Chris recited a part of one of his poems. A little fat man sang The Bold Fenian Men. And I sang an Italian song you'd taught me. A chap, who obviously regarded me as a sort of Mother Earth symbol, full of child as I was, was on his knees in front of me.

So the only hope is that these scraps might spark off more meaningful memories. You were always so good at remembering detail. We were obviously preoccupied with management problems. 'Hosting' I heard it described by an American recently. We would have had two kids asleep upstairs and would have concern about the neighbours.

We hope you're fully recovered and that Kätzel and the kids are well.

Love, Queenie

---

1 See Letter 187; Henderson had written to the Scott Moncrieffs at MacDiarmid's suggestion.

2 Christopher Grieve (Hugh MacDiarmid).

3 Henderson's song 'The John Maclean March'.

4 Paul Potts, 'self-styled "Canadian Hick poet" ' (H.H.), Henderson first met Potts in the Spring of 1940 when he visited Cambridge to read his poetry and give a talk on Mayakovsky to the Cambridge University Socialist Club. They met again later in June of the same year, when Henderson stayed with Potts in the studio of the Irish painter Eric O'Dea in Great Ormond Street. This was the occasion of Henderson's first meeting with Dylan Thomas, an episode described in 'That Dolphin Torn, That Gong-Tormented Face: Dylan in Bloomsbury', *Cencrastus* no. 47, Spring 1994.

190 Hugh MacDiarmid to Hamish Henderson[1]
[*EUL*]

[Brownsbank, Biggar, 29 March 1975]

Dear Hamish,

I gather that the Red Book[2] is now out but I have nowhere seen where it can be obtained or what the price is etc. I am anxious not to miss getting a copy, as also of Gramsci III which from your last letter I think must be published by now.

Can you send me copies of each of these and a note telling me the prices and postal costs, and I'll recoup you at once.

I was pleased to have a visit from Arthur Argo the other day and recorded for him a brief tribute to Jeannie Robertson[3] and to the Muckle Sangs and other promised records from the School of Scottish Studies.

With every kind regard.

Yours, Christopher Grieve

---

1 This was the last letter MacDiarmid wrote to Henderson.

2 *The Red Paper for Scotland*, an anthology of contemporary political writings, edited by Gordon Brown, published by Edinburgh University Student Publications Board, 1975.

3 MacDiarmid's comments were included in the tribute to Jeannie Robertson who died earlier in this year, aged 67, broadcast on BBC Radio Scotland.

191 To Hugh MacDiarmid
[*EUL*]

[Edinburgh, 3 April 1975]

Dear Chris,

I've asked John Forsyth, of the E.U. Student Publications Board, to send you complimentary copies of the Red Book and of Gramsci III (which arrived from the printers this afternoon).

We were naturally very glad to have your tribute for the Jeannie programme. Did you hear it? In addition to yours, there were tributes from Alan Lomax, Pete Seeger, and some of the younger singers who met Jeannie and learned from her.

Best wishes, Hamish

192 **To the** *Times Educational Supplement*

[Edinburgh, 2 May 1975]

Sir,

I was glad to see Michael Grosvenor Myer's largely favourable review of our double album of Scots Classic Ballads *The Muckle Sangs* (Tangent TNGM 119/D), but his reference to what he calls my 'uncritical adulation of the works of the portentous Hugh MacDiarmid' really can't be allowed to get away without comment.

In the introduction to the booklet accompanying the records I called MacDiarmid 'the greatest living Scots art-poet — who is also, by general consent, one of our best poets ever'. But this is nowadays quite a commonplace critical assessment; Yeats thought so, and few critics who have occupied themselves with the Scottish literary tradition in recent years would quarrel with his judgement. And surely it would be hard to find a single epithet more inept than 'portentous' to characterize the work of a poet as many-sided as Burns or Brecht.

There is another and highly ironical turn of the screw, as far as I am concerned. Far from indulging in 'uncritical adulation' of the bard, I have been engaged for nearly twenty years in running battles with him on a variety of subjects: one of the more energetic of these being exactly on this same subject of traditional music and song. The contestants were described, in the immediate aftermath of the battle, as 'blasting away at point-blank range in a manner reminiscent of the old Scottish "flyting" tradition'. Any of your readers who are interested can verify this by looking up the correspondence columns of the *Scotsman* for March and April 1964.

This does not of course alter the fact that there are a number of deeply percipient passages in MacDiarmid's poetry which illuminate the nature of Scots balladry, and of folksong generally; that is the reason why I quoted one or two of them in the notes to *The Muckle Sangs*.

Hamish Henderson

1976

193 **To the** *Scotsman*

[Edinburgh, 2 November 1976]

Sir,

If the witch-hunt which disfigured the Scottish Labour Party Congress in Stirling,[1] and nearly put paid to the party itself, was not the most ineptly staged 'happening' in political history, it will do until the most ineptly staged happening comes along − if it ever does.

The International Marxist Group [IMG] presence in the Scottish Labour Party was neither big enough nor powerful enough to warrant the treatment it got. The sledgehammer blow dealt by the party leadership certainly made contact with the IMG, but unfortunately it made a sorry mess of the party's limbs into the bargain.

The question-begging word, used insistently by those supporting the platform line, was 'revolutionary'. Any Socialist worthy of the name wants, and works for, a revolutionary transformation of society. That is what he is striving for, that is his ultimate aim. If it is not so, then he − or she − should fly different colours.

There are some who hold that the IMG are the modern equivalents of the 'primitive rebels' of earlier days − the present-day counterparts of the soldiers of that avenging 'Army of Redressers' commanded by Captain Swing and General Ludd. This is an arguable proposition. It is not, however, the point at issue here. If individuals who may previously have been members of the IMG − or indeed of other political groupings, such as the Scottish Workers Republican Party − decide to join a new party, it is surely quite unfair to them, as well as impolitic generally, to assume from the word go that they will not accept party disciplines.

If, having participated in congress debates, and argued for their point of view, they do not accept congress decisions, and are seen to be working actively against such decisions, disciplinary action is bound to follow, once the evidence has been properly sifted. But in this case nothing resembling hard evidence was ever brought forward.

As first chairman of the Edinburgh Scottish Labour Party I got to know most of the people concerned personally. Indeed, in the case of one of them − if I may be forgiven a familiar homely expression − 'I kent his faither.' I marched side by side with his father in the demonstrations protesting against Chamberlain's betrayal of Czechoslovakia to Hitler in 1938. I respect him now as I respected his father then, and know him to be a sincere and devoted man, willing to sacrifice much for what he believes in. Nothing, but nothing, will stop me regarding him as a comrade.

It is not too late to heal this lamentable breach. The import of Neal Ascherson's article today – 'Exit the entrists' should be *exeunt*, but we'll let that flea stick by the wa' – is only too clearly that the leadership over-reacted to a largely imaginary threat, and that the whole ghastly business was unnecessary. Jim Sillars and Alex Neil have already admitted an error of judgement with regard to one press conference. If they can have the consequence, and the strength of mind and character, to admit that they made a major error of judgement when confronted by the existence of a small but vocal left minority in the party – and act on that recognition – the two conferences due to take place in Stirling in a fortnight's time can be one congress.

And Alex Neil and Jim Sillars will reassume their rightful position as leaders of a healthy, vigorous and united party, eager to get to grips with the problems and opportunities facing a Scotland moving forward towards independence.

Hamish Henderson

---

1 At the 2nd Congress of the Scottish Labour Party, the party's leader Jim Sillars refused admittance to 'Trotskyist' left-wingers.

1977

194 To the *Scotsman*

[Edinburgh, 13 January 1977]

Dear Muckle Toun,

Last year I had, once again, the pleasure and privilege of attending your Common Riding – as ever, one of the truly prodigious events of the Scottish calendar. I have often told visitors from the South (and other airts) that if they are desirous of witnessing what is just about the most gallus manifestation of *ingenium perfervidum Scotorum*[1] that the country can offer, they have no need to proceed farther than a mere eight miles this side of the Border.

All that's necessary, usually, is to play them a few tape-recordings made over the years – the flute band playing reveille by the Esk in the early morning; the wild gallop of the Cornet and hundreds of horsemen up the steep brae of Kirk Wynd; the crying of the Fair (by a crier standing on horseback), and the marching and counter-marching of pipe, flute and brass bands – and the date duly goes down in their diaries. In 1976 a Swedish television team joined the column as well, and added a valuable film record to the archives.

However, the experience itself invariably surpasses memories and anticipations. For me, the most thrilling moment is always when the Cornet and his mounted followers appear once again at the top of Kirk Wynd, after climbing to the summit of Whita Hill and performing the ceremonial ride-around of its landmark monument. The pipe-major gives the word of command to his men, when he sees the horsemen, and the children who have formed up behind the band lift their heather besoms with the roses entwined in them, and cheer as they march forward into the square.

Then there's the moment when the walloping outsize thistle, with its prickly tentacles capering in the air, joins the procession of emblems. First comes the 'bannock and saut herrin', its escort linking arms and singing 'The Bonny Wood o' Craigielea'; then there's the spade, decorated with heather 'lately pulled frae Whitaside', which has been used for cutting sods on the common land by men able and willing 'to gang oot in defence of their property'; then there's the Crown of Roses bobbing in the lift; and last of all, the 'breenging growth' itself, the contumacious camsteerie national symbol, greeted all along the route with a special cheer.

Last year a small boy of nine or ten was sitting on a window ledge, just behind where I was standing, and I heard him exclaim 'the thistle!' as those great jigging green antlers hove into view. Any lucky spectator witnessing that incident would have learned a lot in a moment about the Borders, and about Scotland – the old Scotland, and the renascent new.

'The aucht-fit thistle wallops on hie'[2] . . . and that reminds me, Muckle Toun, why I am writing you this open letter today.

Your Common Riding is indeed a noble occasion, but you possess another and, some would say, greater glory than the Common Riding, although you've aye been gey sweir to admit it. I refer, of course, to Christopher Murray Grieve, alias Hugh MacDiarmid, who is now universally acknowledged to be one of the greatest poets we have ever had in this country, and also one of the foremost poets now living in the world.

Muckle Toun o' the Langholm, I'm hardly revealing any secrets when I say that this particular prophet has been all too long without honour in his own home town. There have been attempts, off and on, to give him the 'Freedom', but they never got anywhere. And although I know Chris Grieve was given a presentation by your citizens on his eightieth birthday, I gather that all the subscriptions barring a very few came from outwith your boundaries.

I'm not contending, of course, that in this troubled relationship the fault has aye been on your side. In the rammies of life Chris Grieve has given at least as many blows as he has taken, and seeing that he would not wish us, in mim-mou'd Southron style, to be 'nice' with him, let us freely admit that he can be a rale coorse carnaptious auld blellum, when the mood takes him. I, too, have had my share of flytings with him over the years, and I am quite sure that he would be game for another one right now, at the drop of a hat.

However, this alters nocht of the undoubted fact that he is one of the splendours of our literature, a man of rare genius, and (like Johnnie Armstrong o' Gilnockie) a true hero of Border history. He deserves better of you than he has got.

So, Muckle Toun – what about it? I know that the reorganization of local government has robbed you of the power to make Chris a Freeman of Langholm. However, this is of no account. (I very much doubt, anyway, if Chris would wish to be accommodated in the same galère as a mere astronaut.) May I, with respect, offer a suggestion? Every year, for the last twenty-five years, Chris has visited Langholm as a private visitor on the occasion of the Common Riding. Why not make him a guest of honour in 1977? Alternatively, you could invite him to a birthday celebration on 11 August, when he will be 85, and do him proud in traditional Border style.

It would be very appropriate, let alone the anniversary, that this should happen in 1977, for this is undoubtedly the year that Scotland will make a major step forward towards independence – the goal that Christopher Murray Grieve has devoted his life to help bring about. And, Muckle Toun, when he thought of Scotland, and Scotland's potential, it's plain he often thought of you.

Are you equal to life as to the loom?
   Turnin' oot shoddy or what? . . .
Lenin and Rilke baith gied still mair skill,
   Coopers o' Stobo, to a greater concern
Than you devote to claith in the mill.
   Wad it be ill to learn
To keep a bit eye on their looms as weel,
And no' be hailly ta'en up wi' your 'tweel'?[3]

Muckle Toun, I have to admit that I got the idea of writing you this letter on another birthday that came up for celebration recently — namely that of the 'bon sansculotte Jésus',[4] around whose mystery so many of Chris Grieve's own poems dip and circle like seabirds. I'd like, therefore, to end with some lines written by Chris's old friend and benefactor, the late Helen B. Cruickshank — who was not only a marvellous person, but also a much better poet than the lazy anthologist, repeating and repeating 'Shy Geordie', would ever have you believe. Here are the concluding lines of the epistle she wrote for C.M. Grieve (whom she described as 'chief pillydacus o' the haill clanjamfrie') when he reached the age of seventy-five.

I mind o' ane that bore in wind an weather
A sacred load thro' cataracts o' thocht.
Na, *Christopher*, yer faither an yer mither
They didna wale *that* wechty name for nocht.[5]

I am, Muckle Toun, your maist leal, devote and obleeged servitour.

   Hamish Henderson

---

1 Trans. 'perfervid spirit of the Scots' (H.H.).
2 From *A Drunk Man Looks At the Thistle* (Blackwood: Edinburgh, 1926).
3 Lines from 'The Seamless Garment', *First Hymn to Lenin, and Other Poems* (Unicorn Press: London, 1931).
4 Expression used by the French revolutionary Camille Desmoulins when he was arrested in 1794.
5 Helen B. Cruickshank's 'Epistle for C.M.G. on his 75th birthday', *Poems Addressed to Hugh MacDiarmid and Presented to him on his Seventy-Fifth Birthday*, edited by Duncan Glen (Akros Publications, 11 August 1967).

195 **To Sorley MacLean**

[Edinburgh, 15 March 1977]

Dear Sam,

   I've found — and transcribed — the letter from Lorne Maclaine Campbell[1] and have put it in a folder, together with a few other things, so that you can see it when you want to.

Meanwhile I thought I'd send you the enclosed, which is his VC citation.[2] I remember thinking, when I heard from swaddies in the 7th Argylls of the doings of their C.O. on that day, that Alasdair at Auldearn was no bad parallel. It seemed he'd been everywhere.

Cheers, Hamish

1 Lt Colonel Lorne Maclaine Campbell of Airds VC
2 The quotation was included in the Afterword to the new edition of *Elegies for the Dead in Cyrenaica*, with an introduction by Sorley MacLean (Edinburgh University Student Publications Board, 1977, reprinted by Polygon, 1990), see Letter 27.

1978

196 To Eddie Linden[1]

[Edinburgh, 28 September 1978]

Dear Eddie,

Thanks for your letter. I'm glad you liked my short article. I have in fact done a lot of research on the 'found poems', and presented some of my findings in a lecture at the MacDiarmid conference last year[2]. The origins of the Kraus passage can be traced back to an article by Heller in *The Cambridge Review* in 1948. (I happened to see it then when on a visit to Cambridge — Piero Sraffa the friend of Gramsci had a copy.) It surfaced again in the *TLS*, and — somewhat altered and re-arranged — in *The Disinherited Mind*. (The German original is in the 'translation' of that work which appeared later as *Enterbter Geist*).

Buthlay pointed out in his *Writers and Critics*[3] book that the author of the *TLS* article had an unusual style and feeling for words, but he had not twigged that the first draft of the article was in German.

In my lecture I listed numerous sources for passages in MacDiarmid's poetry — sources as disparate as Ibsen and Coventry Patmore — and discussed the whole question of MacDiarmid's creative plagiarism. Bill Montgomerie[4] invited me to publish the paper — or an extended summary of it — in *Lines*, but I decided not to, while the old man was still alive. Although in the main I was justifying (or attempting to justify) what he had done, I felt that he would misunderstand this, and that the whole thing would embarrass him. Also, he was too old to remember exactly what he *had* done, and publication of my paper would probably have led to him getting queries which he couldn't answer. Now he is dead, the situation is quite different, and I'll probably publish the whole thing next year — maybe in *The New Edinburgh Review*.

The fact that some of the most interesting borrowings appear embedded in some of his finest poems — e.g. 'Lament for the Great Music'[5] — presents some pretty problems . . . But in the long run, what does it matter? Plagiarists of genius are the justified sinners of literature. Apart from being everything else, MacDiarmid was also a sort of folk poet, and in nothing was he more Scottish than in his acquisitive attitude to the property of others! Incidentally, as you may know, there was much more to the feud with the Langholmers than a few mildly risqué passages in *Lucky Poet*.[6]

After the funeral, four drunk men (including me) called in at Crowdieknowe,

and gey near got our own deaths declaiming poetry under a real 'second flood'
onding.

Cheers, Hamish

[PS] If you run into Alec Scott,[7] I'd be grateful if you'd lend him your copy of *Lynx*.
He'd probably be interested to see it – the photo, anyway.

---

1 Eddie Linden (b. 1935), poet; author of *City of Razors* (Landesman: London,
  1980), editor of *Aquarius* literary magazine.
2 MacDiarmid died on 9 September 1978, aged 86. Henderson's contribution
  to the 1977 conference was the basis of his article, 'The Langholm Byspale',
  published in *Edinburgh City Lynx* shortly after MacDiarmid's death.
3 [Kenneth Buthlay], *Hugh MacDiarmid: Writers and Critics Series*, no. 36, (Oliver
  and Boyd: Edinburgh, 1964).
4 William Montgomerie.
5 'Lament for the Great Music', *Stony Limits and Other Poems* (Gollancz:
  London, 1934).
6 *Lucky Poet: A Self-Study in Literature and Political Ideas, Being the Autobiography of
  Hugh MacDiarmid (Christopher Murray Grieve)* (Methuen: London, 1943).
7 Alexander Scott.

1979

197 Willie Mitchell to Hamish Henderson

[Argyll, 14 November 1979]

Dear Hamish,

When I glanced over *Tocher*[1] without reading it, I went to read thoroughly *First Elegy on the Dead in Cyrenaica*. When I dried my eyes I read *Tocher* thinking if I am half the man I am portrayed, I am twice the man I thought to be. Then I thought of dear Katharine Tynan and of words she said. I thought also of that other dear Catherine with her artistry, so you have my portrayal as I am to me.

You are showered by congratulations which can only be sincere because you know that they are true.

Sorry to note in *Tocher* obituary the passing of Sean O'Boyle[2] and John McKeith[3] of Saddell. In Kintyre the name was pronounced M'Keech (gh). I have known them for about fifty years.

Minor detail: author of *M'Kinnon and the Bards* 1898 was *John* Mactaggart, not James. He also wrote a volume of verse *Our Land*. He was uncle to my mother (Mary Keith) and I attended his funeral in 1923.

Your other letter just to hand. I will pass it on to Agnes. If you can make your visit before Xmas or after New Year. Hectic & hectic times 24 hours a day. Clear of that this house is yours at any time.

Enclosed programme of Bonnie Green Braes of Kintyre, performed Tuesday night 13/11/79 and went [down] a bomb, the old songs got a grand reception.

Best wishes, Willie Mitchell

---

1 An issue of *Tocher* (no. 31) dedicated to the work of Willie Mitchell, with an introduction by Henderson, was published by the School of Scottish Studies in 1979.

2 Sean O'Boyle, Northern Irish folksong collector; Lecturer at St Patrick's College in Armagh.

3 John McKeith, Kintyre Gaelic speaker.

1980

198 **To the** *Scotsman*

[Edinburgh, 23 September 1980]

Sir,

In his article 'The Influence of MacDiarmid' in the recently published symposium *The Age of MacDiarmid* — reprinted in the *Weekend Scotsman* of 20 September as 'In praise of a pioneer loner' — Tom Scott writes (about MacDiarmid and myself): 'That their attitudes were incompatible is one thing, but they need not have led to such desperate enmity as in fact occurred.'

I cannot speak for Chris Grieve, who can no longer speak for himself, but I would like to think that the phrase 'desperate enmity' has minimal contact with the reality of our relationship.

Certainly I felt no such sentiment towards MacDiarmid, and I very much doubt — on the evidence of the many private letters that passed between us over the years — if he felt anything remotely similar towards me.

It is true there were profound differences in our attitudes towards the folk revival, and the altercation had to be fought out; the first 'whiff of grapeshot' was followed by heavier and more damaging carronades, and in no time the letters in the *Scotsman* which served as missiles had taken on the high mottled complexion of a medieval flyting.

But this was in accord with the rules of a traditional native bloodsport which neither of us (I am sure) would have disavowed, and of which furthermore we were both — although in vastly differing degrees of talent and aptitude — by no means unwilling practitioners.

Hamish Henderson

199 **Robert Sutherland (Robert Garioch) to Hamish Henderson**[1]

[Edinburgh, 9 November 1980]

Dear Hamish,

That was a remarkably fine and unusual television programme,[2] especially unusual, I mean, in being built around and upon your *Elegies*, sort of, poems plus illustrations, not the other way about, and similarly it is rather uncommon to have books of poetry with illustrations, though Alastair Mackie's new book, *Back-Green Odyssey*, has drawings that add to the effect of the book. All the same, to have illustrations from the Desert is really something. And anyone could see from the pictures what the Desert was like; there was no need for you to rub it in, and neither you did. That made what you had to say about the massacre in Rome that much more powerful. The production moved very fast, too, with Cambridge in about two scenes, and those pictures of the Pioneers, and all the way to Rome. I liked that cheerful party of former Partisans. It upset me a lot to see that inscription on the modern traffic-sign: very effective television to spot it and get it into the picture, but it did make me wish I hadn't seen it, and could have gone on thinking swastikas belonged to long ago.[3] Curious it was the Jerry sign, in Italy, still. 'The Banks of Sicily' came into its place in fine style, and the story belonging to it, in the place where it happened.

Well, anyway, it was a quite extraordinary programme, I mean, compared with the patterns of television. And yet there was nothing unusual in taking a writer to talk in the places he wrote about. But this one was different.

yours, etc . . .
Hamish Henderson

PS You may wonder at it, but I was extraordinarily affected by the view of King's College, remembering Peg[4] there with me on holiday. Right enough, though it came at the beginning of the film, not after all those big events.

---

1 This letter was first published in *A Garioch Miscellany*, selected and edited by Robin Fulton (Lines Review Editions, Macdonald: Edinburgh, 1986).

2 The film was *The Dead, the Innocent*, a television documentary based around Henderson's wartime experiences and his wartime poems and songs, first broadcast on BBC2 on 8 November 1980. The massacre Garioch refers to was the murder of 335 Italians in the Ardeatine caves, in March 1944, carried out by the SS.

3 When filming in Sicily, Henderson spotted a swastika and the words 'Viva Kappler' daubed on a roadside traffic sign. Kappler was the SS Colonel who commanded the death-squads at the Ardeatine caves – see letter 6.

4 Peg, Robert Sutherland's wife.

1982

200 **To the** *Scotsman*

[Edinburgh, 12 October 1982]

Sir,

The canonization in Rome of the heroic priest Father Maximilian Kolbe who at Auschwitz accepted an agonizing death to save the life of a fellow-prisoner recalled to my mind statements made to me after the war by a Polish Jew whom I met through the Sue Ryder Organization.

This chap told me that the Auschwitz camp guards seemed to have a greater animus against Catholic priests than against almost any other category of prisoner, because of their courage, dignity and quiet moral authority. He had personally witnessed the punishment meted out to one priest — he did not know his name — who was ordered to take a shower, and then to stand at attention naked in the open air in freezing weather.

While he was standing there the SS guards came out of their warm mess with glasses of schnapps in their hands and taunted him: 'We are the gods now.'

Luckily the SS State did not last the thousand years predicted by Hitler.

As a non-Catholic I am very happy to be able to put on record these recollections of a survivor.

Hamish Henderson

1983

201 **To the** *Scotsman*

[Edinburgh, 22 February 1983]

Sir,

In his challenging letter in support of Stephen Maxwell's article 'Edinburgh's celebration of provincialism' — an article with whose general argument I personally have a great deal of sympathy — Peter Chiene muddies the issue by taking a gratuitous side-swipe at the department of which I am now the longest-serving member.

He writes: 'The time has now passed when we can be fobbed off by being told that to pay proper attention to Scottish cultural problems we need but be shunted into the bothy-ballad sidetracks of the School of Scottish Studies.'

I really thought that we in the School had heard the last of this sort of coat-trailing disingenuous blarney. I have no doubt that Mr Chiene knows perfectly well that the charge that the School of Scottish Studies is dabbling in cultural backwaters is a modern 'Scotch myth' — and by no means the least odious.

The traditional arts are, and always have been, central to Scottish aesthetic experience. The poetry of Sorley MacLean — hardly to be regarded, here or elsewhere, as provincial backyard dubs — draws very largely on the splendid Gaelic anonyms of which his brother Calum (one of the earliest full-time members of the School's staff) made a collection in the forties and fifties, of unrivalled beauty and magnitude.

Our collection of song-poetry in Scots consists, I need hardly say, not only of bothy ballads — although the bothy ballads are by no means to be despised and rejected, being at their best gorgeous humorous flytings against the intractable stony reality of an under-paid hired hand's life-style — but also hundreds of versions of the great classic ballads, of which the American critic Stanley Hyman[1] wrote that they constituted 'a folk literature unsurpassed by any in the world'.

We have also a large body of exquisite lyric love songs which rival the best in the vast Greig–Duncan collection harvested in the north-east in the early years of this century — and maybe the best in the folk literature of many other countries. I have no space to mention with more than a passing reference the School's important achievements in the ethnographical, anthropological and sociological fields, and its pioneering work in the realm of Scots folk-tale.

Mr Chiene talks about 'predicating an issue of Scottishness'. One wonders sometimes what the hell people like him actually *mean* by 'Scottishness'.

Not long back there was a reference in your columns to the magazine *Scottish International* (1968–76), which, according to the writer, 'eschewed Scottishness'. This of a magazine which published about as wide a range of Scottish art criticism and political analysis (including Stephen Maxwell, on various occasions) as anyone could have hoped, and which included on its editorial board Edwin Morgan and the late Robert Garioch – two 'rootless cosmopolitans', I suppose! (And, for the record, it also printed Alan Bold[2] himself, the perpetrator of that inept crack about 'eschewing Scottishness'.)

Here is something patently bogus that really needs to be brought out into the open. Was Hugh MacDiarmid 'eschewing Scottishness' when he wrote *On a Raised Beach* and *Lament for the Great Music* in English? Is Brian Holton[3] 'eschewing Scottishness' when he translates from the Chinese? or Harvey Holton 'eschewing Scottishness' when he directs satiric body-blows at that most robustly Scottish of all institutions, the Presbyterian Church?

In Italy Gramsci wrote scathingly, in his articles about the 'the land of Pulcinella', about those too prone to invoke *italianità*. In the German-speaking lands Bert Brecht and the great Viennese satirist Karl Kraus waged unremitting war against the cultural 'drummers for Deutschtum'. In Spain Miguel de Unamuno[4] wrote 'me duele Espana' – Spain hurts me. And yet these artists were not the betrayers but the fulfillers of their respective national traditions.

Isn't it time Scotland tried to emerge from its cosy self-satisfied cocoon? One can be sure that not until it does so will it have a chance of taking its place as a self-respecting – and respected – nation, with a reasonable chance of managing its own affairs.

> Hamish Henderson

---

1 'The Language of Scottish Poetry', *Kenyon Review*, Gambier, Ohio, Winter 1954; a key text in Henderson's critical arguments on the issue of the Scottish voice and the folk tradition.
2 Alan Bold (b. 1943), poet and critic; biographer of MacDiarmid.
3 Brian Holton, Fife poet and translator, brother of the poet Harvey Holton.
4 Miguel de Unamuno, Basque Spaniard; prestigious literary critic and Rector of Salamanca University.

202 **To the** *Scotsman*

[Edinburgh, 10 March 1983]

Sir,

In describing the great humanist Miguel de Unamuno, author of *The Tragic Sense of Life*, as a 'Basque who turned his back on the ancient language and traditions of his people', Dr John Lorne Campbell is telling only a part – and a very small part – of the story.

It is true that Unamuno's attitude to his own native culture was deeply ambivalent. In this he resembles quite a number of outstanding men from 'minority language' backgrounds who have gone through phases of doubt, rejection or even disgust. Many Scottish writers and intellectuals have done so, including – dare I say it? – Hugh MacDiarmid.

Indeed, I would think that any writer or artist of stature who found himself wrestling with this existential challenge would *need* to go through some such phase. It is only the self-complacent Kailyairdy third-rater who could conceivably take it all for granted.

MacDiarmid himself wrote (echoing Socrates at his trial, reported by Plato): 'An unexamined life is no' worth haein' ' and even Sorley MacLean could write, in an early poem:

> *Chan fhaic mi fàth mo shaothrach,*
> *Bhith cur smaointean an cainnt bhàsmhoir . . .*

'I don't see the sense of my labour, putting thoughts in a dying tongue . . .'[1]

The fact of history ensured that Unamuno should be heir not only to Basque tradition but also to Cervantes and Calderon. (Just as MacDiarmid could not but be in the line of Shakespeare and Blake as well as of Dunbar and Burns.)

Allow me to remind Dr Campbell of a scene in Unamuno's life which provides a picture very different from the one he drew in his letter. At a ceremony in the University of Salamanca on 12 October 1936, at which Unamuno (as rector) was in the chair, the Fascist general Millán Astray made a vicious attack on Catalonia and the Basque provinces, describing them as 'cancers in the body of the nation. Fascism, which is Spain's health-giver, will know how to exterminate both, cutting into the live healthy flesh like a surgeon free from false sentimentality'.

Unamuno rose to rebuke this paranoid necrophilious fanatic, and proudly reminded his bitterly hostile audience that he was himself a Basque. (It should be remembered that the Basques were especially detested in Franco's Spain because – being fervent Catholics fighting for the Republic which had granted them autonomy – they disrupted the 'official' propaganda image of a Catholic crusade against 'atheistic Communism'.)

At this 'moment of truth', therefore – and in the same speech he declared 'at times to be silent is to lie' – Unamuno did not turn his back on his origins. After a noble speech, in which he exhibited superb courage and dignity, he was placed under house arrest by the Fascists.

I hope you will allow me one short comment on Mr Peter Chiene's second letter (3 March), for I do not intend to beat about the bush. Your correspondent has chosen a time when the School of Scottish Studies has launched an appeal aimed at safeguarding its existence to make slighting and depreciating cracks about its work. He is all in favour of 'Scottishness' – whatever that may mean – but he is quite willing to take pot-shots at a department which is actually doing something about preserving the Scottish heritage, and building for the future.

Hamish Henderson

1 '*Chan fhaic mi* . . .' ('I do not see . . .'), poem LV, from *An Traigh Thathaich* (*The Haunted Ebb*): *December 1939–July 1941*, in *O Choille Gu Bearradh, From Wood to Ridge*, Collected Poems (Carcanet Press: Manchester, 1988).

203 **To the** *Scotsman*

[Edinburgh, 22 March 1983]

Sir,

As James Campbell's article on Alexander Trocchi[1] leaves the impression that he had no friends and allies in Scotland, I think it only fair to Alan Riddell, founder and first editor of *Lines Review*, to put it on record that Alan was a constant champion of Trocchi's, and that it was through him that I – and I should imagine quite a number of other people in Scotland – first learned of a major literary talent. This was long before the farcical Writers Conference of 1962 – best remembered for the naked lady 'happening' in the McEwan Hall – to which Campbell refers.

The feelings of angry revulsion which Trocchi made all too explicit in his outburst at that gathering were, of course, nothing new on the literary scene, and by no means peculiar to Scotland. In June 1951 – a year before the first number of Trocchi's *Merlin* appeared in Paris – Brendan Behan wrote a letter to the poetry editor of *Points* (a bilingual literary magazine published in the same city) giving vent to the following sentiments:

> Cultural activity in present-day Dublin is largely agricultural. They write mostly about their hungry bogs and the great scarcity of crumpet. I am a city rat. Joyce is dead and O'Casey is in Devon. The people writing here now have as much interest for me as an epic poet in Finnish or a Lapland novelist.

No one can read Trocchi's work, however, without realizing that his relation to his Scottish background was (and no doubt is) a matter of deep concern and importance to him. A quotation from Unamuno which appears on p. 59 of *Cain's Book* is very revealing:

> Don't you suppose – since I am in a confidential and confessional vein – that when they have accused me of not being a good Spaniard I have often said to myself: 'I am the only Spaniard! I – not these other men who were born and live in Spain.'

A wary Joycean eye for nets flung at the soul to hold it back from flight, and a love of literature and practice of the same, were not the only things which linked

Australian-born Alan Riddell and Glaswegian-born Alex Trocchi (who worked as a scow captain on the Hudson River between 1956 and 1959).

Among the papers which I inherited from Alan was the report of Summer 1944 on Junior Leading Cadet A. Riddell, then studying navigation at University College, Southampton. This showed that he had come first in a class of 33, and had won the prize for Best Duty Watch.

The director's remarks suggest a further link between these two intermittently nautical men of letters: 'Exceptional and outstanding work . . . always maintained a high standard of efficiency and conduct in his Duty Watch. Still too many petty crimes on his conduct sheet.'

Hamish Henderson

1 Alexander Trocchi (1925–84), novelist; editor of the influential literary magazine *Merlin*.

204 To His Excellency, the Ambassador for the Soviet Union
[Edinburgh, 11 August 1983]

Dear Sir,

I have been re-reading John Bierman's fine book *Righteous Gentile*, which describes the wartime career of Raoul Wallenberg[1] – saviour of thousands of Jewish lives in Hungary during the Nazi terror – and have naturally been wondering yet again about his fate.

I would be greatly obliged if you could possibly supply answers to the following questions:

(1) Why on earth was Wallenberg ever detained by Soviet troops? (According to Mr Dekanosov – Soviet Ambassador in Berlin right up to Hitler's invasion in 1941 – he was 'under the protection' of the Red Army in January 1945.)
(2) Why did the Soviet statement on 9 February 1957, which admitted that Wallenberg had been a prisoner in the Lubianka Prison, give no *reason* for his detention in the Lubianka Prison?
(3) Is Raoul Wallenberg dead? If so, will his family ever be given a chance to bring his body – or his ashes – back to Sweden?

Allow me to assure you that I have absolutely no ill-will towards the Soviet Union when I ask you these questions. For years I was Secretary of the Literature Section of what was then the Scottish–USSR Society, and helped to bring Samuel Marshak here to Scotland, where he got a great welcome. For years also I conducted a correspondence with VOKS, and always got courteous – though not always very prompt – replies.

I regret to say that the same courtesy has not been conspicuous when I have written to you – or other Soviet citizens – about Wallenberg. In fact (to put it bluntly) I have never received a single reply to any letter written either to you or to people in the Soviet Union about his case.

What do you think this indicates to me – and to others who, like me, were trying to maintain cultural contacts with the Soviet Union at the height of the Cold War – about respect for human rights in your country? (And it was certainly inside the USSR that Raoul Wallenberg was last heard of.)

'Acts of injustice done,
Between the rising and the setting sun,
In history lie like bones, each one.'[2]

Yours sincerely, Hamish Henderson

---

1 Raoul Wallenberg (1912–?), Swedish diplomat; he managed to save up to 100,000 Jews during the Nazi occupation of Hungary. The Soviet authorities claimed that Wallenberg had died of a heart attack while in Lubianka Prison (July 1947), but there were sightings of him in prison up to the 1970s.
2 From W.H. Auden and Christopher Isherwood's *The Ascent of F6: A Tragedy in Two Acts* (London, 1936).

205 To Mr Parshin[1]

[Edinburgh, 12 September 1983]

Dear Mr Parshin,

I listened with great interest to the David Scott programme on Saturday to which you contributed.

I – and friends who were with me – thought that you put up a very good case indeed. There's no doubt that the Reagan administration is using this tragic incident to obliterate opposition to his escalation of the arms race. And nobody I have talked to here doubts that the Americans know much more about the background to the incident than they have yet divulged.

But why on earth didn't you agree to accept questions from members of the public who phoned in? Don't you realize that your refusal to do so completely neutralized the otherwise good impression that your statement made?

There is another matter which has never ceased to preoccupy a number of people here – people, may I say, who are by no means hostile to the Soviet Union, and indeed have a consistent record of friendliness towards it. This is the fate of the noble and heroic Raoul Wallenberg, saviour of thousands of Jewish lives during the Nazi terror. Some weeks ago I wrote a letter to the Ambassador, asking three specific questions, but have received no reply. I am reluctant to think that after thirty years of work in the interests of Scottish–Soviet cultural relations, my letter is just being ignored. As I say, I am by no means the only person here who is worried about the fate of this man. I would be most grateful if you would look out my letter, and see that it gets an answer.

Yours sincerely, Hamish Henderson

(Copy of letter of 11 August enclosed.)

---

1 An official at the Soviet Embassy in London.

206 **To the** *Scotsman*

[Edinburgh, 25 October 1983]

Sir,

In his very impressive and highly idiosyncratic *The New Testament in Scots*, the late W.L. Lorimer has given us a fresh version of the Lord's Prayer (printed in the *Scotsman* on 21 October) which, like all such, is thought-provoking. Many people must have been struck, as I was, by his bold personification of the ambiguous *ponerou* (usually translated 'evil') as 'the Ill Ane'. (This is presumably the English-speaker identified in your report!)

However, I am less happy with his retention of the Authorized Version's 'Thy Kingdom come'. Admittedly this is good Scots, as it is good English, and maybe it can't be bettered, but I have always had a liking for a version which I heard as a child: 'Thy Kinrik come'.

'Kinrik', according to the *Dictionary of the Older Scottish Tongue*, used to be by far the commonest form, and it was gradually supplanted by 'kingdom' in the sixteenth century. Its appearance in this century, in a version used by an old 'Piskie' minister – who was reputedly quite a good Classical and Celtic scholar – was therefore probably a conscious archaism, but in the present context it has (especially when spoken aloud) a truly noble ring.

Furthermore, it *does* have a very old 'Biblical' lineage. I am indebted to Dr Jim Stevenson for putting me on the track of a verse translation of this same Pater Noster which appears in a manuscript written in Louvain in 1477 by a Scottish student called Magnus Makculloch. Here the text reads: 'Come mot thi Kynrik'. However, in Archbishop Hamilton's Catechism (printed in 1552) it is already: 'Thy Kyngdome mot cum'. The background influences here are probably Wyclif and his reviser Purvey.

When I was in Berlin in 1937, I went (out of political curiosity) to a service in Pastor Niemöller's[1] Dahlem Dorf Church, and heard for the first time Luther's massive-sounding translation *Dein Reich komme*. At that time it was impossible to shut out of one's mind the other connotations of the word *Reich* – *Ein Volk, ein Reich, ein Führer* – and looking at Niemöller's face, I was sure the same thought was in his mind. It was ironical indeed to be reminded in the same instant of that old Scots expression, with its closely-related Germanic roots.

(During the service, incidentally, Niemöller read out the names of the pastors who had been arrested and interned because of their opposition to the Nazis – a company he was soon to join.)

All these thoughts have been reawakened in my head by *The New Testament in Scots*, so I owe a real debt of gratitude to both Lorimers, father and son.

Hamish Henderson

---

1 Pastor Martin Niemöller (1892–1984); Lutheran pastor known for his
   courage in denouncing Hitler and Nazism. He was imprisoned in
   Sachsenhausen and Dachau concentration camps from 1937 to 1945.

207 To the *Guardian*

[Edinburgh, 15 December 1983]

Sir,

In your report (14 December) giving my reason for refusing the offer of an OBE in the forthcoming New Year honours list – namely, my total disagreement with Mrs Thatcher's highly dangerous defence policies – you state that I have 'already rejected two honorary degrees'. This is not correct. I have in fact accepted these degrees for the precise reason that they carried no political implications. I am not as great an addict of refusals as all that!

(Dr) Hamish Henderson

1984

208 **Joan Lingard to the** *Scotsman*

[Edinburgh, 10 January 1984]

Sir,

Mr V.T. Linacre (9 January) describes Hamish Henderson as 'the man who sensationally publicized himself in the most calculated fashion' when he rejected the offer of an OBE. I write to correct this misapprehension.

When turning down the OBE, Mr Henderson had no intention of making a public announcement, but on discussing the matter (a month after he had replied to Mrs Thatcher's Private Secretary) with myself and another member of the Scottish Writers Against the Bomb committee, he decided that if it would be of value to our campaign, which is supported by some 200 Scottish writers of all shades of political and non-political opinion, he would allow us to publicize it. This we did, although the press in their reporting of it did not always make this clear.

Mr Henderson was particularly anxious not to seek publicity for himself personally, but inevitably some accrued to him. He most certainly did not anticipate being elected Scot of the Year by the listeners of Radio Scotland. But we saw no reason why he should not let his rejection be made public; there was no obligation on his part to keep silent, he had not asked to be considered for an OBE, and had signed no document swearing secrecy.

As for Mr Henderson 'like all CND supporters . . . enjoying the fruits and exploiting the freedom of our capitalist society' – using a freedom is not synonymous with exploiting it. A freedom which is not used becomes value-less. We *must* raise our voices to protest against policies which we believe endanger the future of mankind, otherwise we do not deserve to have freedom of speech at all.

If the Russian people do not have the same freedom, we regret and deplore it, but that is no reason for us to remain silent. We are not pro-Russian and anti-American, or vice-versa. We are opposed to all nuclear weapons, regardless of the country of origin, or the country of deployment, but are campaigning specifically against the siting of missiles in Scotland since we are Scottish writers.

Joan Lingard, Co-ordinator,
Scottish Writers Against the Bomb

209 To the *Scotsman*

[Edinburgh, 16 January 1984]

Sir,

Mr V.T. Linacre accuses Joan Lingard and myself of 'Doublespeak', but the two letters from him which you have published recently (9 and 16 January) provide ample evidence that he is no slouch himself when it comes to verbal manipulation and artful question-begging. He even has the gall to insinuate that Joan Lingard, who is engaged on an important voluntary organizational task at a time when the country is in dire peril, might take it upon herself to 'prohibit' pro-British sentiments!

Because I have made it plain, in the most forceful manner open to me, that I regard rapprochement between the West and the Soviet Union as the all-important issue facing mankind today, and because I took the opportunity to express openly what a vast number of people, silent perforce, think of the character and performance of Ronald Reagan, Mr Linacre sees fit to pillory me as a sensation-seeking self-publicizer, and a devious Soviet apologist. Furthermore, he unworthily implies that I might 'rejoice' to hear of the plight of prisoners of conscience in the Soviet Union.

I could easily, although with extreme reluctance, produce a great mass of evidence to the contrary which even Mr Linacre would be obliged to accept as conclusive. However, I will cite one single case, which must stand for many.

For years I have been concerned about the fate of Raoul Wallenberg, the heroic Swede who saved the lives of thousands of Hungarian Jews during the Nazi terror. On 11 August 1983[1], I wrote a letter to the Soviet Ambassador in London, again raising Wallenberg's case. I quote the central paragraph:

> I would be greatly obliged if you could possibly supply answers to the following questions: (1) Why was Wallenberg detained by Soviet troops? (According to Mr Dekanosov — Soviet Ambassador in Berlin right up to Hitler's invasion in 1941 — he was 'under the protection' of the Red Army in January 1945.) (2) Why did the Soviet statement on 9 February 1957, which admitted that Wallenberg had been a prisoner in the Lubianka Prison, give no *reason* for his detention in the Lubianka Prison? (3) Is Raoul Wallenberg dead? If so, will his family ever be given a chance to bring his body — or his ashes — back to Sweden?

I concluded the letter by quoting the following lines of Auden:

> Acts of injustice done,
> Between the rising and the setting sun,
> In history lie like bones, each one.

This letter remained unanswered for nearly five months; however, by one of those curious synchronic coincidences which preoccupied Arthur Koestler in his later years, a reply arrived from a Counsellor on the same day Mr Linacre's first letter about me appeared in the *Scotsman*. Dated 5 January 1984, it contained the following statement:

> Paul Wallenberg [*sic*] was arrested in January 1945 in Budapest in the area of the Soviet troops' combat actions, where he worked as a Swedish mission's secretary. The head of the Swedish mission was informed about his arrest on 16 January 1945, in reply to his inquiry.
>
> Consequently, the question on the Wallenberg's case was on different levels raised before the Soviet side by the Swedish one. Till 1957 it was said to the Swedish side the Soviet authorities had no information about him.
>
> During the official visit to the Soviet Union in 1956 the Swedish Prime Minister personally addressed the Soviet leaders on the Wallenberg case. On 6 February 1957, the Swedish Ambassador in Moscow was officially answered that Wallenberg had died, supposedly from a heart attack, in July 1947, in the Lubyanskay prison.
>
> The USSR Ministry for Foreign Affairs memorandum said that the Wallenberg's imprisonment and misinformation about him were the results of Abakumov's criminal activity. Abakumov acted in violence of the Soviet Law and tried to inflict any possible damage to the Soviet Union. In view of his grave crimes the Supreme Court of the USSR sentenced him to death and subsequently he was executed.
>
> The Soviet Government expressed a sincere regret about the accident, and deep condolence to the Swedish Government and Wallenberg's relatives.

The Counsellor went on to regret the 'various fantasies and speculations' about Wallenberg's fate.

Well, was it worthwhile writing a letter to the Soviet Embassy, only to receive a reply of this nature? Yes, and again, yes! Not only because the actions of Raoul Wallenberg when he was a free man entitle him to the lasting concern of all of us, but also because it is surely vital that friends of the Soviet Union – and I have admired the great achievements of the Soviet people in war and in peace for about as long as I can remember – should speak with absolute frankness across the frontiers, and not allow moulds of bitterness, prejudice and silence to harden on both sides of the divide.

Letters and opinions like Mr V.T. Linacre's are of no use to us in this urgently necessary work of understanding and reconciliation.

Hamish Henderson

---

1 See Letter 204.

210 **To the** *Scotsman*

[Edinburgh, 24 January 1984]

Sir,

There seems no limits to the extent to which Mr V.T. Linacre is willing to go when it comes to exposing his own cocksure ignorance – not to mention his cheap reluctance to acknowledge the all too obvious fact that he has done someone else a blatant injustice.

He thinks that 'the death (? execution)' of Raoul Wallenberg has only just been 'formally admitted' by the Soviet authorities – presumably in the letter to me from a Counsellor at the Soviet Embassy which I quoted in your columns (20 January). What the Counsellor wrote was an almost word-for-word reiteration of statements in the Soviet Note of February 1957.

This admitted that Wallenberg *had* been a prisoner in the Lubianka Prison, but alleged that he had died in July 1947 'probably as a result of a heart attack'; it also laid the blame for 'incorrect information' about him at the door of V.S. Abakumov, Minister of State Security from 1946 to 1952, who was executed in December 1954 under Khruschev.

A detailed account of all this will be found in John Bierman's meticulously researched book *Righteous Gentile*, which was published in London in 1981 – particularly chapters 12–14.

Concern about the fate of the noble and heroic Swede has been widespread throughout the world for over three decades. The letter I wrote to the Soviet Embassy on 11 August 1983 was only the most recent in a series I have written to people inside and outside the Soviet Union for a number of years. I would not even have mentioned it had it not been necessary to show up for what it was worth Mr Linacre's base gibe that I might 'rejoice' to hear of similar violations of human rights.

None of these considerations alters the basic fact about the threat of nuclear warfare which hangs over humanity. It is no exaggeration but only plain fact to recognize that there are only two options open to us: rapprochement or self-destruction. Concern for human rights in all countries should be regarded as an essential *part* of rapprochement, not as a hindrance to it.

It is now over thirty years since the death of Stalin. This is a longer period than that which encompasses the Fall of the Bastille, the whole French Revolutionary and Napoleonic era, and the restoration of the Bourbons after Waterloo. (And for that matter a longer period than lay between the Russian Revolution of 1917 and the dropping of the two atom bombs on Hiroshima and Nagasaki.) If all that we have learned in this precious time granted to us is the gospel according to V.T. Linacre, then our prospects are bleak indeed.

I see that Mr Linacre has found a congenial yoke-fellow in that veteran Cold Warrior, Mr H.H. Goodwin; and no wonder, for they are both, on the evidence of their writings, immovably embedded in a bygone Ice Age of the planet's history. Less troglodytical individuals realize that the stark reality of our present predicament is expressed at its simplest and most urgent in Auden's line:

We must love one another or die.[1]

Hamish Henderson

1 From W.H. Auden's '1st September 1939'.

211 **To the** *Scotsman*

[Edinburgh, 1 February 1984]

Sir,

Anyone who read the letter (20 January) in which I quoted the reply I had received from the Soviet Embassy to questions put to them about Raoul Wallenberg will already have assessed at its true value Mr V.T. Linacre's pathetic statement that I then 'appeared to claim' to have elicited the truth at long last.

The widespread belief, amounting now to positive certainty, that Wallenberg was still alive long after the year (1947) which the Soviet Note had given for his alleged death has received publicity all over the world, and it is really quite astonishing that Mr Linacre was ignorant of the fact.

It reminds me of the wise remark of an English Quaker – a member of a group for which some students worked in Germany just before World War II – that one very soon gets to know who is actually interested in doing something on behalf of the victims of tyranny, and who is merely 'sounding off' about them.

I do not believe that the exchange of letters between myself and the Soviet Embassy 'accomplished nothing'. It brought to the attention of diplomats in this country – and, with any luck, some at least of their political masters back home – that a person like myself with a long record of friendly co-operation with the Soviet Union on the cultural plane is still worried enough about the violation of human rights in cases like that of Raoul Wallenberg to keep on pursuing the issue. These contacts have never been of more vital importance than they are today.

Mr Linacre refers to the 'appeasers of the the thirties'. I spoke and demonstrated against the appeasers of Hitler in the thirties, and against Chamberlain's betrayal of the Czechs at Munich; I also served in the Army during World War II. Those who remember the period will agree that to equate the appeasers of Fascism with the CND of today is mere verbal sleight of hand.

The Hitler of today *is* the bomb, and we in CND have no intention of appeasing it. Luckily, there are now welcome signs, in both West and East, that public opinion – followed, albeit grudgingly, by 'official' opinion – is moving towards a recognition of this essential political reality.

Our lives depend on the process being accelerated: hence the need to keep a meaningful dialogue going, and to counter, with all vigour possible, such views as those expressed by the Bomb-toting troglodytes.

Hamish Henderson

212 To the *Scotsman*

[Edinburgh, 20 November 1984]

Sir,

In his article (17 November) about the 'charismatic demagogue' John Cormack, Tom Gallagher states that 'on two separate occasions at the Mound, in June 1940, he was reported as saying that ''when Protestants went over the top with Roman Catholics, the Protestants should shoot them.''

In the Summer of 1951 I was one day on the edge of the crowd which had gathered around Cormack's soap-box, when he came away with a variant of this obscenity. On that occasion he said in World War I Protestant officers had had to threaten Roman Catholic 'other ranks' at pistol-point, in order to make them go 'over the top'.

Having quite recently been a member of a citizen army, recruited without discrimination between people of different creeds and colours, I found this crack more than I could take, and I called Cormack a liar. The reaction of the heavies around the soap-box was immediate. Luckily, two or three members of the University Highland Society – who were also members of the shinty team – happened to be with me.

The scene I have described took place only four years before this evil blackguard was elected a bailie by courtesy of the so-called Progressive (i.e. Tory) councillors. Surely nothing could have shown up with more devastating clarity the contempt of these gentry for their fellow citizens – not to mention their coarse malignant cynicism – than the fact they felt themselves able to share a seat on the Bench with the founder of 'Kormack's Kaledonian Klan'.

Hamish Henderson

213 To the *Scotsman*

[Edinburgh, 22 December 1984]

Sir,

The correspondence about John Cormack has elicited a truly surprising piece of information: namely, that the move in 1955 to get this notorious 'Pape-baiting' rabble-rouser elected to the grave and responsible office of bailie was initiated by two Catholic priests.

Historians and folklorists who explore the bizarre undercover life of Auld

Reekie need no longer worry about identifying the most grotesque episode in its history. Without a doubt – this is it.

It even beats the voluntary confession of Major Weir to the City Fathers in 1670 that, although one of the 'Bowhead Saints', and bynamed 'Angelical Thomas', he had all his life been a practising warlock.

(Hogmanay quiz: Why is it that Deacon Brodie and Bailie Cormack mak a bonnie couple? Answer: One was elevated to the Bench, while the other . . .)

Well, if a respectable ex-councillor gives us the aforesaid information, it must be true. All the same, it reminds me of the fact that in 1933 there was an Association (or *Bund*) of right-wing Nationalist Jews in Germany who actually thought they could strike a pact with the Führer.

In cynical Berlin (whose humour is not unlike Glasgow's) a joke went the rounds at that time: these Jews had got a banner made on which was inscribed a variant of the Nazi slogan *Die Juden sind unser Unglück* ('The Jews are our misfortune'). On the front of their banner were the words: *Wir sind unser Unglück* ('We are our misfortune') and on the back *Raus mit uns* ('Out with us').

The Hitler parallel is not as far-fetched as might at first appear. Although Cormack was a comparatively small-time local operator, and Hitler was operating on a world stage, to the bane of millions, there were in fact striking similarities between these two self-obsessed power-seekers.

Both were charismatic demagogues, and both had voices that could sound like the ripping of a topsail: both could be vulgar and virulent to the point of obscenity – and yet both could make a cosily disarming and even 'couthie' impression. And finally, as is amply documented, both had a semi-mesmeric effect on women.

This had to be seen to be believed. On Hitler's birthday in April 1937 I joined an immense crowd in the Tiergarten in Berlin to watch the procession: first a lot of military hardware, and then, standing in an open car – amazingly vulnerable by present-day standards – came the Führer, giving his familiar droopy salute. The women around me all went wild, and one of them (who had been 'heiling' like hell) suddenly fainted. In fact, it was quite like a big Beatles concert.

Not long after, I went to the cinema to see *Der alte und der junge König* ('The old and the young King') – militaristic propaganda, but with a very impressive performance by Emil Jannings as Frederick William I. Before the big film there was a newsreel, most of which was taken up with shots of Hitler relaxing on the terrace at Berchtesgaden,[1] smiling benignly into the middle distance, and occasionally patting the head of a big alsatian. This went on for rather a long time, as such things in Germany sometimes tend to do, and I was getting a bit bored – when suddenly I became aware that a girl sitting on my right had begun to weep with ecstasy.

After the show I got into conversation with her, and just to see what she would say, I remarked that it was a pity the Führer often got such a bad press abroad. I have always remembered her reply, which seemed to me a classic in its own way. She assured me, with glistening eyes, 'But he wants to harm nobody . . . nobody.'

As Tom Gallagher stated in his article, Cormack exerted the same sort of attraction. I don't want to tread on any feminist toes, for I have the highest respect for their cause, but all the same I have a hunch that it would be highly revealing if one could have a breakdown by sexes of the votes which gave Cormack's Protestant Action 31.6 per cent of the poll in the Edinburgh local government elections of 1936.

Twenty years later, at the time of the Soviet invasion of Hungary, Cormack was asked at the Mound by a medical student – now a doctor living near Darlington – what Britain should do at that moment of highly dangerous international crisis. Cormack replied that all reachable centres of population in the Soviet Union should be saturation-bombed with nuclear weapons. Later he was asked if he would like to contribute something to a collection in aid of the Hungarian refugees, but the bold bailie – for that is what he already was – brusquely waved the collecting-box away.

He was willing, in short, to advocate a course which would undoubtedly have plunged the world into unthinkable horror, but was unwilling to contribute a silver sixpence to help the very people he was claiming to be concerned about.

And does this tell us all we need to know about Johnnie Cormack? I doubt it. As Edwin Morgan has written, at the end of his fine poem about another 'Protestant' bravo of the thirties, 'King Billy of Brigton':[2]

> Deplore what is to be deplored,
>   and then find out the rest.

Hamish Henderson

---

1 Hitler's mountain retreat.
2 From 'King Billy', published in Edwin Morgan's *The Second Life* (Edinburgh University Press, 1968).

1985

214 **To the** *Scotsman*

[Edinburgh, 11 March 1985]

Sir,

David Steel states in a letter to *The Times* that *Private Eye* 'is intended to be a satirical magazine'. The intention may be there – let us give the rag the benefit of the doubt – but the performance is another story. Indeed, Richard Ingrams seems intent on proving, issue after issue, the truth of a statement by the great Austrian satirist Karl Kraus that the English do not know what satire is.

For Ingrams, satire is purulent muck-raking and clubfooted facetiousness. To find a parallel, one has got to go back eighty years to Wilhelmine Germany, and to an infamous case of sadistic journalistic persecution which Kraus himself excoriated: the remorseless hounding by Maximilian Harden of Prince Philipp Eulenburg and Count Kuno Moltke as alleged homosexuals.

This was part of Harden's campaign against Kaiser Bill's so-called 'court *camarilla*', and although Kraus had no sympathy with the intrigues of these gentry he was revolted by the use of sexual innuendo in political infighting; consequently, he took Harden apart satirically in two famous pieces (later reprinted in his collection *Die chinesische Mauer*, The Chinese Wall). One of these included a surgical parody of Harden's own style.

Kraus's real target, of course, was the limitless sexual hypocrisy of bourgeois Wilhelmine Germany, which he regarded as a much uglier and more threatening phenomenon than the antics of the *camarilla*, affording as it did disquieting evidence of a deep corroding malaise in that exceedingly unliberated society.

What we really need today is a genuine satirist like Karl Kraus who would set *Private Eye* firmly in its social/political context (and also, of course, in the context of contemporary pseudo-'sexual liberation') and then take it apart in similar fashion. The result would almost certainly be a good deal funnier than most issues of the *Eye* itself, and indeed might even have some literary interest.

A few months ago *Private Eye* printed a short 'profile' of Gordon Brown, MP (signed 'Backbiter') which was grotesquely inadequate by any standards. The hack who did this particular blunt hatchet-job had the temerity (lurking behind anonymity) to call Gordon Brown – one of the most able MPs in the present Parliament, and a brilliant man – 'mediocre'. His pathetic piece contained the usual farrago of distortions and errors of fact (including the inevitable irrelevant sex bit).

I wrote a letter to the editor correcting these, and added the following comment:

> Dennis Nilsen is on record as saying that he enjoyed a 'love-hate' relationship with your pestilence-breeding organ.
> What a pity he couldn't have invited it round for a friendly chat some evening.

It did not altogether surprise me that this letter — which I would suggest bears some resemblance to genuine satire — was not printed by the bold 'satirist'.

Hamish Henderson

215 To the *Scotsman*

[Edinburgh, 31 May 1985]

Sir,

The wish of many, inside Scotland and beyond its borders, to erect a memorial sculpture to Hugh MacDiarmid in or near the Muckle Toon o' the Langholm will be readily understandable to anyone with even a sketchy knowledge of that great poet's stature in Scottish and world literature.

It therefore came as a severe shock to the organizers of the international competition which awarded the commission to MacDiarmid's fellow Borderer Jake Harvey when the Planning Committee of Dumfries and Galloway Regional Council refused, last March, to give planning permission for the erection of his much acclaimed sculpture on the chosen site at Collins Turn, Whita Hill.[1]

The result then was a narrow victory for the objectors — six votes to five — but the reasons advanced for rejection on that occasion did not give much evidence of artistic comprehension or expertise on the part of the individuals concerned. Indeed, Councillor Robert Robinson's dismissal of Harvey's very impressive celebratory sculpture as an 'Oxo sign' certainly deserves to rank high in any *sottisier* of really egregious gaga Philistine nonsense — alongside (for example) Krushchev's famous dictum, delivered after viewing the work of a young Soviet abstract painter, that 'a man's face is better-looking than his backside'. (A very curious remark when you come to think of it, seeing that the reverse is often so obviously the case.)

Anyway, Councillor Robinson has now entered local folklore as 'Bumpkins', thanks to a mordant satirical poem by William Neill which was published in a local newspaper not long after the ignominious decision was taken.

It seems unlikely, however, that 'Bumpkin values' will bear the gree for aye. The Langholm, Ewes and Westerkirk Community Council, which has generously and enthusiastically supported the project has recently, unanimously, reiterated its wish that the memorial sculpture should stand in the poet's native place – to which, throughout his life, he remained deeply attached.

MacDiarmid was laid to rest in 1978, not in Crowcieknowe – immortalized in one of his early lyrics – but in the local graveyard on a hill above the Muckle Toon. The Scottish Sculpture Trust still hopes that the memorial will stand not far away. On Tuesday, 4 June, the planning committee will sit again in Dumfries – this time to consider the placing of the sculpture on an alternative site at Whita Yett. To coincide with this meeting, there will be a demonstration in support of the project at Dock Park, Dumfries, at 12 noon. There will be piping, singing, poems and speeches. We hope that as many people as possible will attend, and – if the application is successful – join in a celebration in honour of Scotland's greatest poet since Burns.

Hamish Henderson

1 The decision was reversed and the monument was sited at Whita Yett, Langholm.

216 **To the** *Scotsman*

[Edinburgh, 20 August 1985]

Sir,

Nobody acquainted, even superficially, with the history of armies will be in the least surprised by the recent 'revelations' about Field-Marshal Montgomery's interest in a series of youthful protégés. Indeed, an obsessive and mildly homo-erotic predilection for the company of young boys has been a well-documented characteristic of quite a number of famous soldiers: among these, General Gordon ('Chinese Gordon'), and General Sir Hector Macdonald ('Fighting Mac'), who is mentioned in Gide's *Corydon*.

These generals shared other very noticeable characteristics: they were all military mavericks, impatient with and scornful of the type of brasshat bureaucrat who gets to the top in most armies; they were all, like Suvarov,[1] charismatic 'quarefellows', much happier in the company of junior officers or other ranks than in the company of commanders of their own status; and (in the British Army) they were mostly of strongly Evangelical persuasion.

It is, of course, a commonplace that hero-worship often has a homo-erotic element as a vital component part. The well-reciprocated affection of Napoleon for his *grognards*[2] will be remembered; likewise Byron's arresting description (*Don Juan*, Canto VII) of the delight of the Russian soldiers when Suvarov ('Hero, buffoon, half-demon and half-dirt') arrived to take command before the assault on the town of Ismail:

The whole camp rung with joy; you would have thought
That they were going to a marriage feast . . .
And why? Because a little, odd, old man,
Stript to his shirt, was come to lead the van.

I can personally vouch for the fact that a not dissimilar spirit began to animate the troops after Monty arrived to take command of the 8th Army in the desert. When, on 13 August 1942, he ordered all contingency plans and instructions for a retreat to the Delta to be burnt; told the troops: 'If we can't stay here alive, then let us stay here dead'; forecast eventual complete victory over Rommel and invoked 'the Lord mighty in battle', the troops believed him.

Monty can best be seen, in fact, as one in a long line of off-beat Evangelical military charismatics, and we were darned lucky to have him. Furthermore, it is touching as well as amusing to recall that, of all writers, it was William McGonagall who really hit the nail bang on the head when — with admirable succinct directness — he wrote, referring to General Gordon:

He always took the Bible for his guide,
And he liked little boys to walk by his side.

Hamish Henderson

1 Suvarov (1729–1800), famous Russian general.
2 Trans. 'Grumblers' (Napoleon's Old Guard).

1986

217 **To Timothy Neat**[1]

Dear Tim,

Welcome home! I'm greatly looking forward to hearing about all your exploits and getting news of Serge and Esther.[2]

. . . And how better to celebrate your home-coming than by writing out the fine words spoken by Goethe about Robert Burns in his 'Conversations with Eckermann':[3]

How is he great, except through the circumstance that the whole wealth of song of his predecessors lived in the mouth of the people – that the songs were, so to speak, sung at his cradle; that, as a boy, he grew up amongst them, and the high excellence of these models so pervaded his being that he had in them a living basis on which he could proceed further. Again, why is he great, except through this, that his own songs at once found susceptible ears amongst his compatriots; that, as sung by reapers and sheaf-binders, they at once greeted him in the field; and that his boon-companions sang them to welcome him at the ale-house.

Salud, Hamish

---

1 Timothy Neat, film-maker and art critic. Since they first met at the Padstow Festival in 1967, Henderson and Neat have collaborated on seven documentaries, including *The Summer Walkers*, about the travellers, and *Journey to a Kingdom*, an autobiographical journey from Henderson's childhood home in Blairgowrie to the lands of Fyvie and beyond. Henderson also appeared in Neat's feature film *Play Me Something*, which won the 'El Premio Europa' prize at the Barcelona Film Festival in July 1989.

2 Serge and Esther Hovey: Serge Hovey, American composer who dedicated his life to composing settings for all of Robert Burns' songs. Seven albums (over eighty songs) were recorded in collaboration with Jean Redpath (who was recommended to Hovey by Henderson), before Hovey's death in 1989. The final album was produced concurrently with Neat's documentary *The Tree of Liberty* (Channel 4, 1986), which was awarded the Best Documentary/ Feature prize at the Celtic International Film and Television Festival, Inverness, April 1987.

3 From Eckermann's *Gëspräche mit Goethe*.

218 To Ewan MacColl

[Edinburgh, 10 March 1986]

Dear Ewan,

Here are the letters from the mid-fifties, plus the rest of the chronology, as far as I can remember it.[1]

I don't think there was any contact between us when I was working in Ireland – although on odd weekends in Dublin I saw a fair amount of the Behans, who were later to enter the Theatre's history in no uncertain fashion![2] After I got the Somerset Maugham Award (March '49) I resigned my job in Belfast, but stayed on until my successor had got to know the ropes. I returned to Scotland in the early Summer, and a day or two after I got back to Edinburgh, Theatre Workshop re-entered my life in the shape of 'Camel' and his girl[3] (? wife). They showed up in International House, looking for help in finding accommodation for the company during its '49 Festival visit. There was a certain irony in the situation, because at that very moment I was phoning around, trying to find some buckshee accommodation for myself. (I had the award money, of course, but I wanted to save it up for Italy, where I intended to go on translating Gramsci's prison letters with the help of the PCI.[4])

Anyway, the person who came to our mutual assistance was the old poet Helen Cruickshank; she found digs for everyone, and if anyone from the Theatre Workshop of those days wanted to contribute to her plaque (letter enclosed), I'm sure it would be much appreciated. (Alan[5] stayed with her as well a couple of years later.) ... What about sending a copy to Joan?[6]

A day or two after Camel's arrival, Dominic Behan appeared out of the blue – having just been expelled from the Irish Workers' League, apparently – and attached himself to me. I gradually got involved in Joan's plans for the Festival – she wanted me to organize some of the 'Fringe' events which in '51 blossomed into the People's Festival, and the result was that I stayed in Edinburgh until the end of September. (I remember an afternoon session with you and Joan in a cafe opposite Nicolson Square, talking and singing for quite a while.) To get money, I did several readings/singings – mostly in the west of Scotland – being at that time, because of the award, a sort of 'temporary celebrity' – much as I'd been a sort of 'temporary gent' during the later stages of the war . . . that, incidentally, was where East Kilbride came in!

Eventually I made it to Italy, and your letter of 9 Feb 1950 (copy already sent) reached me in Milan.

I had almost finished the translation when I was expelled from Italy by the CDU[7] government. (I'd been speaking at reunions of the 'Partigiani della Pace'.)[8] Back in Cambridge I got a letter from you announcing Alan's imminent arrival, and soon I was being recorded by him in London; when he finally turned up in Edinburgh in mid-'51, I had several local 'champs' lined up to meet him, viz. Calum Johnston and Flora MacNeil (from Barra), and John Burgess.[9] He recorded all three on the first day of his Scottish tour in Sorley MacLean's flat in Queen St (Calum he met a little later). Then we took off for the north-east, and I had the privilege of watching him at work. The tapes he recorded in Scotland are the first twenty-six tapes in our archive.

(Incidentally, if he's still with you, I'm sure he'd be interested in the Masks and Movement workshop in Glasgow – leaflet enclosed.)

Whew! – that's enough for now. The rest – if not exactly silence – is well known to you. *Scotland Sings*,[10] with several contributions from me, came out in '53; they reappeared in *Personal Choice*.

Cheers, Hamish

PS Incidentally, for the record, it was when I paid the Behans a visit in Dec '52 that Brendan showed me the typescript of *The Quare Fellow*, and asked me for advice as to where to send it. I naturally told him 'send it to Joan'. This is one fact which doesn't appear in Howard's book about the theatre![11]

---

1 MacColl was researching his autobiography *Journeyman* (Sidgwick & Jackson: London, 1990).
2 Brendan Behan's *The Quare Fellow* was performed by Theatre Workshop in the mid-1950s.
3 'Camel', John Bury, a member of Theatre Workshop; the 'girl' was Margaret Greenwood.
4 Italian Communist Party.
5 Alan Lomax.
6 Joan Littlewood, Director of Theatre Workshop.
7 Christian Democrat Party.
8 Partisans of Peace.
9 John Burgess, champion piper.
10 *Scotland Sings*, songbook edited by MacColl and published by the Workers Music Association.
11 *The Theatre Workshop Story* by Howard Goorney (Eyre Methuen: London, 1981).

219 To the *Scotsman*

[Edinburgh, 31 March 1986]

Sir,

Ian Bell's fascinating article about the great Edinburgh Socialist James Connolly[1] (29 March) awoke many contradictory memories in my mind.

When I visited Ireland as a schoolboy in the 1930s, I found to my surprise that young Irish left-wingers who, like myself, sympathized with the cause of the Spanish Republic and bitterly opposed Chamberlain's craven abandonment of the

Czechs to Hitler at Munich, were almost all very cynical about Connolly's role in
the Easter Rising of 1916; far from helping to 'build Socialism', they thought of the
Rising as 'having made Ireland safe for the Martin Murphys and the Bishops, and
hardened the line of partition between North and South'.

(Wm Martin Murphy had been the leader of the bosses during the Dublin
lockout of 1913; the wholesale brutality manifested by the Dublin Metropolitan
Police at that time led directly to the formation of the Irish Citizen Army under
Larkin's leadership.)

When I quoted Lenin's famous defence of the Rising against those who had
dubbed it a *putsch*, the response was to quote another remark of Lenin: 'the
misfortune of the Irish is that they have risen prematurely.' One of my friends, a
student at TCD,[2] declared that 'it was more than a misfortune – it was a ghastly
mistake.'

Another friend gave me a copy of a short book, published in 1919, entitled *The
Story of the Irish Citizen Army*; the author of this was 'S.O Cathasaigh' (shortly
afterwards to be better known as Sean O'Casey). O'Casey had been the first
secretary of the Army Council of the ICA,[3] and his portrait of the Connolly of the
war years turned out to be quite sharply at variance with my own preconceptions,
largely nurtured on Yeats's incantatory poems about the Rising.[4]

The following quotation is from Chapter X, and relates to the period after
Connolly took over command from Jim Larkin in October 1914:

> Jim Connolly had never associated himself with any of the attacks made upon the
> National Volunteers during their earlier history – indeed, whenever he had
> previously interested himself in the affairs of the Citizen Army, which was
> seldom, his influence had been invariably exerted to moderate the mutual
> hostility that smouldered, and occasionally flared, into passionate recriminations
> – and, consequently, the relations between him and the more militant members
> of the Volunteer Council soon became cordial.
>
> . It is difficult to understand the almost revolutionary change that was
> manifesting itself in Connolly's nature. The Labour movement seemed to be
> regarded by him as a decrescent force, while the essence of Nationalism began to
> assume the finest elements of his nature. His articles that now appeared in the
> *Workers' Republic* with consistent regularity, the speeches that he delivered at
> various demonstrations and assemblies, all proclaimed that Jim Connolly had
> stepped from the narrow byway of Irish Socialism on to the broad and crowded
> highway of Irish Nationalism.
>
> The vision of the suffering world's humanity was shadowed by the nearer
> oppression of his own people, and in a few brief months pressed into a hidden
> corner of his soul the accumulated thoughts of a lifetime, and opened his broad
> heart to ideas that altered the entire trend of his being. The high creed of Irish

Nationalism became his daily rosary, while the higher creed of international humanity that had so long bubbled from his eloquent lips was silent for ever, and Irish Labour lost a leader.

One can see now that O'Casey, for reasons of his own, was overstating his case, for there can be no doubt that both Larkin and Connolly saw the outbreak of war in 1914 as an opportunity to 'realize the aspirations of Wolfe Tone' (Larkin's words) – i.e., strike a blow for Ireland's independence.

Connolly, in the *Irish Worker* of 8 August 1914, wrote: 'Ireland may yet set the torch to a European conflagration that will not burn out until the last throne and the last capitalist bond and debenture will be shrivelled on the funeral pyre of the last warlord.'

He maintained this position with heroic fortitude, and gave his life for it on 12 May 1916. The wisdom of his decision, from a Socialist point of view, is still, alas, a debatable issue.

Hamish Henderson

---

1 James Connolly (1868–1916), Edinburgh-born Irish Labour leader; one of the leaders of the Easter Rising of 1916, the last to be executed.
2 Trinity College, Dublin.
3 Irish Citizen Army.
4 'Easter 1916':

> I write it out in a verse –
> MacDonagh and MacBride
> And Connolly and Pearse
> Now and in time to be,
> Wherever green is worn,
> are changed, changed utterly:
> A terrible beauty is born.

220 To the *Scotsman* (unpublished)

[Edinburgh, 12 April 1986]

Sir,

Mr R. Mulholland, referring to Sean O'Casey's *Story of the Irish Citizen Army*, claims that it is 'full of contradictions'. What contradictions? O'Casey himself put on record his tragi-comic war with censorship – cf. the chapter 'Mrs Casside takes a holiday' in *Inishfallen, Fare Thee Well*[1] – but the booklet remains a vital source-document for the history of the period: all the more valuable because of the participation of the writer in most of the events he describes. His portrait of Connolly in *Drums Under the Windows*[2] (1945) amplifies but does not substantially alter the character-sketch written in 1919.

The chief service of Ian Bell's admirable article about Connolly was to place this great working-class hero firmly and convincingly against his Edinburgh background. There was a very widespread idea in Ireland before World War II that Connolly had been born in Co. Monaghan (one of the three Ulster counties that came to the Free State on partition), and the news that he was born in Scotland was greeted with scepticism, even among old-guard Connollyites like Kathleen and Stephen Behan.[3] As late as 1949 – that is, after the first publication of C. Desmond Greaves's researches into Connolly's early life – the gifted Monaghan-born Glasgow poet Freddy Anderson published a poem in the Clyde Group collection *Fowrsom Reel* which included the line 'in Ballybay of Connolly's birth'.

It seems likely that Connolly himself was at one time 'cagey' about his own origins – partly, maybe, because he feared that the Army might catch up with him after his 'precipitate parting from Her Majesty' in 1889. But also (as O'Casey hinted) he had later felt something of a foreigner in Ireland – shouts of 'You're not an Irishman' had greeted him at an open-air meeting in Dublin in 1896, which was broken up by cabbage-stalks – and this could not help being deeply wounding.

Nothing of all this detracts one iota, of course, from his tremendous achievements as a Socialist organizer and energizer in Britain and America, as well as in Ireland. He was without doubt one of the most formidable intellects to emerge from the Labour movement since Marx and Engels, and his whole life (and death) testifies to his matchless courage and integrity. . . . I'm sure, nevertheless, that the young O'Casey – a great writer in the making – did catch a glimpse of the complex human reality which lay behind Connolly's public career.

Unlike Lenin, Liebknecht and Gramsci, James Connolly was a genuinely proletarian Socialist, with all that that implies in the way of advantages and disadvantages; furthermore, unlike John Maclean MA,[4] he was – as Greaves's and Ian Bell's researches have shown – to all intents and purposes an auto-didact. One result of this was that his omnivorous reading led him to welcome certain ideas – for example, about the alleged 'egalitarianism' of early Gaelic society, the heated brain-children of romantically disposed German academics, and the writer Alice Stopford Green, which modern Marxist historians would tend to steer clear of. By the same token, it must be admitted Connolly's 1914 vision of a rising in Ireland, igniting world revolution has in the long run more in common with the millenarian visions of earlier centuries than with the steely route that led Lenin to the Finland Station.

I write these possibly provocative words because it is essential not to topple over on the other side of neglect, and indulge in mere hero-worship of Connolly, and we must look and see him whole – he would not have it otherwise.

Hamish Henderson

1, 2 Volumes of Sean O'Casey's autobiography.

3 Kathleen and Stephen Behan, parents of the Behan brothers.
4 John Maclean gained a Master of Arts at Glasgow University.

221 **To the** *Scotsman*

[Edinburgh, 19 June 1986]

Sir,

As I missed the correspondence about the 1820 Rising,[1] being out of Scotland when it appeared, I hope you will allow me a few reflections on the subject.

The importance of the Rising seems to me to reside not so much in what it was as in what the ruling class thought it was. The evidence shows that the Scottish — and particularly the Edinburgh — bourgeoisie got such an almighty scare from the events of April 1820 that the long-range results of this most singular of conspiracies were still to be felt many years later.

Thomas Carlyle has left a vivid description of the scene on the bourgeois side of the barricades:

A time of great rages and absurd terrors and expectations: a very fierce Radical and Anti-Radical time. Edinburgh agitated all around me by it (not to mention Glasgow in the distance); gentry people full of zeal and foolish terror and fury, and looking disgustingly busy and important; courier hussars would come in from the Glasgow region, covered with mud, breathless for head-quarters as you took your walk in Princes St; and you would hear old powdered gentlemen in silver spectacles talking with low-toned exultant voices about 'cordon of troops, Sir,' as you went along.
(*Reminiscences*, II, 68)

Among the well-fed Yeomen who rode west to do or die against the 'Radical rabble' was J.G. Lockhart, who described his experiences in a letter to his fiancée (Scott's daughter Sophia):

There seems now to be no doubt that there had been a serious and well-arranged plan on Monday last. On Wednesday evening, the greater part of the roads leading from Glasgow were in the hands of the Radicals, and various places of encampment in the neighbourhood were resorted to by the weavers from villages.

The drum was beat, such was their audacity, within a mile of the Barracks. . . . The numerous executions which must occur in a very few weeks may be expected to produce a salutory effect, but meantime, till they are over, there is no prospect of entire tranquillity.
(Marion Lochhead: *John Gibson Lockhart*. Chap. 6)

Many such passages could be cited to show with what vindictive energy the class war was fought by the haves against the have-nots in the years following Waterloo.

Prodded forward by *agents provocateurs*, our West Country weavers went to their doomed rising as an ox to the shambles. There was no planning and no co-ordination – except, of course, such co-ordination as was provided by their enemies. No wonder those who came out did so with wary diffidence, like Covenanters uncertain of Divine approbations.

Nothing could have been less like the mood of the pike-toting 'croppies' who had risen in an heroic savage jacquerie in Ireland twenty-two years earlier. Nevertheless, when it came to the bit, they stood their ground at Bonnymuir, and their leaders – or rather the scapegoats selected as their leaders – died bravely enough on the scaffold.

In discussions of the Rising one seldom meets with references to Orangeism, although the Order was already a power to be reckoned with on our side of the water. It is a curious fact that the infantry battalion stationed at Glasgow at the start of the Rising – the 1st Battalion of the Rifle Brigade, earlier known as the 95th Regiment of Foot – was one of the units in which an Orange Lodge 'cell' had existed as early as 1811. (It still had one, complete with secret oaths, ritual and passwords in 1830: see H. Senior, *Orangeism in Ireland and Britain 1795–1836*, Appendix B.)

Ironically, it was in the '95th' that John Baird – one of the leaders of the Rising, executed along with Andrew Hardie, at Stirling on 8 September 1820 – had himself served for a number of years as a 'lichtbob'.

The counter-revolutionary role of Orangeism is part of the submerged history of those years. The Lodge were willing and eager to serve the repressive policies of successive Tory Governments, quite irrespective of the religious persuasion of their adversaries. The Irish Grand Lodge even made the magniloquent claim (in a declaration dated 12 July 1813) that the Order had saved Britain from Luddism:

> The seditious agitators are stung to madness by the knowledge of the Union between the British and Irish Orangemen, which every day acquires new power and more wide extension. Following your loyal example, the British Orangemen have saved their country by suppressing the treasonable bands calling themselves Luddites.
>
> (Senior, *op. cit.*, p. 157)

It is also on record that Orange bravos, willing hatchetmen for Sidmouth and Castlereagh, served as special constables at the Peterloo Massacre of 1819 – they made 'Orator' Hunt run the gauntlet between their staves – while the ultra-reactionary Col. Fletcher of Bolton, who (according to E.P. Thompson, *The Making of the English Working Class*, p. 536) 'often had fuller sources of information on the Manchester reformers than the local bench', was actually Deputy Grand Master of the British Grand Lodge based at Manchester.

Despite the significance of this 'underground history', references to Orangeism in works like Professor Smout's classic *History of the Scottish People 1560–1830* – and even in his recent *A Century of the Scottish People 1830–1950* – are conspicuous by their comparative paucity.

Hamish Henderson

1 The first five paragraphs of this letter comprise the text originally cut from letter 165, 13th April 1970.

222 **To the** *Scotsman*

[Edinburgh, 5 July 1986]

Sir,

To get the ideological demands of the 1820 Radicals into focus, it is necessary to go back twenty-five years – to the time when (in Cockburn's words) 'everything was connected with the Revolution in France . . . everything, not this or that thing, but literally everything, was soaked in this one event.' The world of Wilson, Baird and Hardie was still the world Burns had described when he wrote (referring to the hazards attendant on membership of a 'seditious' organization):

> The shrinking Bard adown the alley skulks,
> And dreads a meeting worse than Woolwich hulks,
> Though there his heresies in Church and State
> Might well award him Muir and Palmer's fate . . .[1]

The two martyrs Burns singles out for mention in this passage are Thomas Muir, Scottish advocate, sentenced to transportation to Botany Bay for fourteen years, and the Rev. Thomas Palmer, English Methodist, sentenced to transportation for seven.

No book – apart from the Bible and *The Pilgrim's Progress* – ever had such an effect on broad masses of the Scottish people as Tom Paine's *The Rights of Man*. The English reformer Maurice Margarot (Braxfield's 'waspish' antagonist, also sentenced to transportation) was a popular hero in Edinburgh at the time of his trial – as was his colleague from the London Corresponding Society, Joseph Gerrald.

The contacts between the reformers of both countries were of the most intimate and cordial; and yet Scottish democrats like Lord Daer (one of Burns's heroes), who were active members of the Friends of the People, were also unequivocally in favour of the recovery of Scottish national sovereignty.

In January 1798 the British Government received secret intelligence that the French Directory had decided, if their invasion plans were successful, to set up separate republics in England, Scotland and Ireland. The 'Scottish Directory' was to include Muir (then in France, after his escape from Botany Bay), Col. Norman MacLeod (MP for Inverness, a member of the Friends of the People, and another of Burns's heroes) and Angus Cameron (the 'inspired orator' who had tried to raise the Perthshire Highlands against the Militia Act, and was also at that time a refugee). However, General Bonaparte reported adversely a month later on the whole plan of invasion: a decision he was later to regret, on St Helena.

This was the background to the ideas and aims of the Scottish Radicals of 1820. The Strathaven weaver James ('Pearly') Wilson — executed on Glasgow Green on 30 August 1820 — had been a delegate, back in 1793, to the conventions of the Friends of the People; he probably met the English delegates, and certainly would have shared the popular admiration for them and their ideas. At the same time he would have found no incongruity in applauding the sentiments expressed by Burns in his Nationalist song 'Such a Parcel of Rogues in a Nation'.

The real conundrum of 1820 is a question not so far addressed by either side in the present correspondence: namely, what on earth happened to the members of the Committee for Organizing a Provisional Government, who were arrested in Glasgow on 21 March 1820? These individuals have disappeared, as it were, into a black hole of history; even their identity is uncertain.

This is astounding. Prisoners invariably have relatives and friends who try to keep their plight before the public eye. Every last detail relating to the 'Bonnymuir rebels' transported to New South Wales has been ferreted out and put on record by Margaret and Alastair Macfarlane in their book *The Scottish Radicals*. But of the fate of the 'Provisional' Committee nothing, but nothing, is known.

May I venture a guess? Ever since the time of Sir Francis Walsingham, successive English Governments have paid well-funded attention to the securing of under-ground political intelligence. When the authorities began to interrogate the arrested Committee members, they may well have discovered a 'Man Who Was Thursday' situation. Did the Committee consist, more or less in its entirety, of members of two or more rival intelligence organizations who were mutually unknown to each other, and had been 'jollying each other along'? If so, the Government would have had no alternative but to allow them to drift away discreetly into obscurity.

Nobody reading the account of the antics of the Government spies King, Turner, Craig and Lees, as described by Messrs Berresford Ellis and Mac a'Ghobhainn in their book on the Rising,[2] will be disposed to dismiss this speculation as totally fantastic or incredible.

As for the Radical proclamation posted up all over Glasgow by the spies and their dupes, it is dated 1 April 1820, and can certainly be accounted the most spectacularly successful All Fools' Day spoof in history.

Hamish Henderson

1 From Robert Burns's 'From Esopus to Maria'.

2 *The Scottish Insurrection of 1820*, with a Foreword by Hugh MacDiarmid (Gollancz: London, 1960).

223 To Edinburgh *Evening News*

[Edinburgh, 1 October 1986]

Sir,

Reviewing the Gaelic version of the famous award-winning film *Hallaig* – is your televiewer such a recluse that he had not heard of it? – John Gibson refers to Sorley[1] as 'evidently a revered Gaelic poet'. 'Evidently'! There speaks the inimitable voice of crass Scots Philistinism. Surely news had reached the *News* that Sorley is a world-famous poet, whose work has received numberless accolades from the foremost critics, and who has demonstrated that Scotland's oldest literary language is still capable of sustaining work of the highest order.

In suggesting that Gaelic is of no interest to many Scots, Gibson is simply wrong. One could provide ample evidence that there is a great and growing interest in both the language and the culture associated with it. If Gibson wants proof of this, he might like to attend some events of the National Mod, which starts in Edinburgh on 11 October.

Yours etc., Hamish Henderson

1 Sorley MacLean.

224 To Ewan MacColl

[Edinburgh, 7 October 1986]

Dear Ewan,

Another of your letters enclosed. The date in it surprised me: I thought I'd already met Alan[1] – and indeed recorded for him – before then. Could Bert Lloyd[2] have been a previous link? Maybe we were all putting the finger on each other at that time.

However, your wish was certainly fulfilled when he came north a few months later (June '51 – I'm certain of that): the 'big Gaelic stuff' (in the persons of Flora MacNeil, Calum Johnston and Sorley MacLean) was laid on, on the first day of his Scottish trip, and he was introduced to Calum a few days later. In the north-east I introduced him to John Strachan,[3] and put him on the trail which led to Willie Mathieson, Jessie Murray and Jimmy MacBeath[4] – and in Glasgow he met Morris Blythman, Johnny MacEvoy,[5] etc. This certainly enabled him to record at speed – as he himself noted in the letter of 20 Sep. '51 (copy enclosed).

His second letter (22 Oct.) documents the hellish time I had in the fifties, beating my wings against Lord Reith's establishment. (He (Reith) had left the BBC, by then, of course, but was still powerful in Scotland, because of his friendship with the Rev. Melville Dinwiddie,[6] and others of the unco guid). (See PS.)

Incidentally, could you please send me a *firm* address for Alan? A packet I sent him, several weeks before the Symposium, was returned to me recently, having been redirected *twice* in the States, and then 'returned to sender'. I'm particularly anxious to send the stuff back to him, for I got the impression, when I saw him in London, that he thought I hadn't answered his recent letters.

Cheers, Hamish

PS I should add that although Alan's appearance did me no good with the Scottish BBC – he was altogether too big and incalculable a phenomenon for them – the tour I did with him in the Summer of 1951 was of major value to me in my efforts to gain a foothold inside the newly founded School of Scottish Studies. My chief ally was Calum MacLean, who was the first full-time appointee on the School's staff (as from Jan. '51).

I'd first met him on the island of Canna in '46, when we were both guests of John Lorne Campbell – as was Seámus Ennis. (Calum was still working for the Irish Folklore Commission at that time; Seámus Delargy and Seán O Suilleabháin[7] – my first folklore mentors, outside Italy[8] – had decided to 'colonize' the Scottish Gaidhealtachd.) I got in touch with Calum by phone, when Alan arrived, and he gave him an immense amount of help . . . when Alan got back from the Hebrides, and deposited copies of his tapes with Sidney Newman (the Professor of Music) we – Calum and I – both made sure that the best items on these twenty-five tapes were listened to by Newman himself, and by David Abercrombie of the Phonetics dept, and by Angus McIntosh (English). (All these gents were on the advisory committee of the School.) The result was the first approach to me (Dec. '51) to do an extended tour of the north-east for the University.

1 Alan Lomax.
2 A.L. Lloyd, collector, broadcaster, and folk-singer.
3 John Strachan, Aberdeenshire farmer and folk-singer.
4 Willie Mathieson, Jessie Murray and Jimmy MacBeath, Aberdeenshire folk-singers.
5 Morris Blythman, pseudonym 'Thurso Berwick', poet, song-writer and folk-singer; taught at Alan Glen's High School in Glasgow. Johnny MacEvoy, folk-singer and song-writer.
6 Reverend Melville Dinwiddie, Director of BBC Scotland.
7 Seámus Delargy, first Director of the Irish Folklore Commission; Seán O'Suilleabháin, archivist of the Irish Folklore Commission.
8 Henderson's Italian 'mentors' included Roberto Leydi, a journalist with a strong interest in Italian folksong, who encouraged him to visit the Piedmontese rice fields where he heard the songs of the Mondine (women's songs of the rice harvest); and the writings of the distinguished folklorist Diego Carpitella.

1987

225 **To Bobby Carroll**[1]

[Edinburgh, 18 June 1987]

Dear Bobby,

The photo of John Maclean I sent you was presented to the School in 1952 by Louis Gradman, of 7 Royal Terrace, Glasgow. (He also gave his address as c/o Workers Circle, Gorbals.)

Louis told me the following anecdotes about Maclean:

John Maclean was loved by the Jewish population of the Gorbals. He stood out against anti-Semitism.

One Jewish tailor wanted to make a suit for him, and give it him, but Maclean was 'proud and unapproachable'. So how to get the measurements? The lads invited Maclean to talk to them after a meeting, and the tailor danced around behind him, while Maclean was holding forth and gesticulating, taking the measurements. He was totally astounded when the suit turned up, with all the measurements exact.

Maclean couldn't pay the rates — [he] decided to take in lodgers — but they were all unemployed men.

On one occasion, knowing that there were plainclothes police spies in the audience at one of his meetings, he said: 'All of you in the pay of capitalism — the man to destroy capitalism is HERE — and his name is . . . [long pause] Charlie Chaplin.'

Louis Gradman did not think Maclean suffered (as had been alleged) from hallucinations — he was 'normal to talk to right up to the end'.

Maclean when heckled on religion would never allow himself to be drawn in. Brushed such questions aside with 'What we are concerned with here . . .' etc.

A film of Maclean's funeral was made by Mr Anderson of Anderson's Drapery Stores, Old Graveyard, Rutherglen Rd.

There was a big Jewish community in the Gorbals in Maclean's time. The Ukrainian Relief Fund produced a button-hole badge with Maclean's picture on it.

At one meeting a litle Jewish lad ended a tribute by comparing Maclean to Jesus Christ!

Cheers, Hamish

Copy to Andrew Maclean.

---

1 Bobby Carroll, Dundee artist.

1988

226 **To the** *Scotsman*

[Edinburgh, 26 April 1988]

Sir,

As the name and reputation of Louis de Saint-Just,[1] chief ideologue of Robespierrism, and martyr for the cause, are currently being tugged to and fro in your correspondence columns, it may interest your readers to know that there is in existence a document which directly links the name of this illustrious revolutionary with that of the Scottish reformer Thomas Muir of Huntershill, who in 1793 was sentenced to transportation to Botany Bay for fourteen years, after an outrageously unfair trial, presided over by the notorious Lord Braxfield.

His trial naturally awakened keen interest in France, and Saint-Just's name is to be found at the head of a list of signatories to a resolution of the Committee of Public Safety, ordering the French Admiralty to attempt a rescue of the banished reformers. Here is a translation of the text of this resolution, which is preserved in the archives of the French Foreign Office:

> Order of the Committee of Public Safety of 30th pluvióse of the Republic, one and indivisible. [This date, in old 'slave-style', as Carlyle ironically dubbed it, equals 18 February 1794.] The Committee of Public Safety, in conformity with the principles of the Constitution which offers refuge in France to men persecuted in the cause of freedom, instructs the Minister of the Navy to take all measures necessary to deliver Muir, Palmer and Margarot, and intercept the vessel which is carrying them into exile.

> Signed: Saint-Just, Barère, Jeanbon St André [and five others, including Carnot, the 'organizer of victory'].

The present-day Vigilantes[2] of Saint-Just have sprung into action in defence of Ian Hamilton Finlay, because he has been accused – incredibly – of being a sympathizer with Fascism. As 'evidence', Finlay's traducers have pointed to his use of the SS symbol in his work *Osso* (Italian for bone). This is as if one were to accuse Brecht of sympathy with the Nazis because he made use of the paraphernalia and rhetoric of Hitlerism in *Arturo Ui*.

I know that M. Mitterrand has plenty of other things on his mind at the moment, but I would earnestly request the French embassy to let him know, in due time, that if he does not want the final weeks of his present term of office to be disfigured by a ridiculous and ignoble stain, he should consider taking early steps to intervene, as he is surely entitled to do, and urge the Minister of Culture to reinstate Mr Finlay's unjustifiably cancelled commission.[3]

Hamish Henderson

1 Louis de Saint-Just (1767–94), French revolutionary, a Jacobin; he is used in Ian Hamilton Finlay's work as an example of commitment.
2 The Saint-Just Vigilantes are a part-imaginary, part-real organization recruited from Finlay's supporters.
3 Finlay was awarded a major artistic project to commemorate the bicentennial of the French Revolution. His proposal – a garden at Versailles, on the site of the first meeting of the National Assembly in 1789 – was cancelled by the French Government after a defamatory campaign against his work.

227 **To the** *Scotsman*

[Edinburgh, 5 May 1988]

Sir,

Joanna Zeigler thinks that Saint-Just was a 'juvenile delinquent', and Robert Crozier accuses me of 'Scottish chauvinism' because I quoted a document linking the names of Saint-Just and Thomas Muir. How weird can this correspondence get?

I called Saint-Just an 'illustrious revolutionary hero' because that is exactly what he was. I was referring not only to his noble intransigence and his 'assurance tranquille' in the face of all the perils, internal and external, which faced the young Republic in the Summer of 1793 – and for a few weeks it really seemed touch and go whether it would survive at all – but also to the dauntless bravery he exhibited when sent as a *représentant en mission* to the Armies of the Rhine.

Sorley MacLean started his poem *Curaidhean* (Heroes) with the words *Chan fhaca mi Lannes aig Ratisbon* (I did not see Lannes at Ratisbon). He might with equal justice – if the poetry had permitted – have written *Chan fhaca mi Saint-Just aig Weissembourg*.

Carlyle, writing when it was still possible to collect eyewitness accounts of these tremendous battles, describes the scene in vivid painter-like prose:

See Saint-Just, in the Lines of Weissembourg, though physically of a timid apprehensive nature, how he charges with his 'Alsation Peasants armed hastily' for the nonce; the solemn face of him blazing into flame; his black hair and tricolor hat-taffeta flowing in the breeze! These our Lines of Weissembourg were indeed forced, and Prussia and the emigrants rolled through: but we *re-*force the Lines of Weissembourg; and Prussia and the emigrants roll back again still faster – hurled with bayonet-charges and fiery *ç'a-ira*-ing.

Gaelic impetuosity mounts ever higher with victory; spirit of Jacobinism weds itself to national vanity: the Soldiers of the Republic are becoming, as we prophesied, very sons of Fire.'

Crozier refers to 3000 dead in Paris in nine months of the Terror. Is he aware that upwards of 700,000 French soldiers are estimated to have died in the Revolutionary Wars of the 1790s against the massed despotisms of Europe? Pitt, in the House of Commons, had called for 'a war of extermination'. In the words of Albert Sorel:[1] 'Before the Revolutionary Tribunal was organized in Paris, terror was the order of the day in the secret calculations of the émigrés, and in the counsels of the coalition.' In the Summer of 1793 counter-revolutionary terror reigned in no less than *sixty* departments of France. The situation seemed utterly desperate.

However, by the Spring of 1794 an incredible transformation had taken place, and to this reversal of fortunes the heroism of Louis de Saint-Just had contributed in no small measure.

Hamish Henderson

1 Albert Sorel (1842–1906), renowned French Marxist historian of the French Revolution.

228 **To the** *Scotsman*

[Edinburgh, 28 May 1988]

Sir,

The silly season has come early this year. The Right Reverend Thatcher thinks Adam Smith[1] is her spiritual ancestor, and her local satrap Malcolm Rifkind wants us to believe that Scottish culture began with the Act of Union! (And for good measure, he seems to think that the corrupt eighteenth-century Gauleiter-godfather Henry Dundas[2] was a model for moral rectitude.)

One could afford to laugh at this scene, half ludicrous and half dolorous, were it not so sickeningly obvious that this bonny couple – who, as far as I am concerned, are at present running neck and neck as pains in the neck – actually have it in their power to wreak terminal havoc with many of our most valuable native Scottish traditions.

This very real threat is epitomized, for me, by the infamous decision to close down Newbattle Abbey College.

It will not have escaped Rifkind, Forsyth and their underlings in the Scottish Education Department that of the score or so letters about the fate of the college which have appeared in your columns in the last six months, only one has supported the idea of closure. This was from the egregious Nicholas Fairbairn, whose ill-informed burblings were seen off gently – all too gently, in my opinion, in view of the gravity of the situation – by Professor Innis MacBeath and others.

Gavin Muir, son of Edwin, has been kind enough to show me the reply he received from the SED to a letter he wrote protesting against the decision to close the college. The arguments and figures quoted in the reply are transparently, indeed outrageously, phoney. These folk obviously think they can get away with murder.

I challenge Rifkind and Forsyth, either singly or with their two intellects in combination, to name one single Oxbridge college which can equal, since World War II, the extraordinary drum-roll of talent, achievements and (in two or three cases, real genius) which Newbattle has to its credit, and which it has brought to flowering.

In the words of Ron Curran – spoken during the Newbattle campaign concert in January, when over thirty poets, novelists and musicians came together to support the college – 'You cannot close a place so unique. Newbattle is not just a track to the university; it enriches the quality of life of the individual.'

The closing-down of Newbattle would be an act of wanton educational and cultural vandalism. We must not let the rump of the Tory Party in Scotland get away with it.

Hamish Henderson

1 Adam Smith (1723–90), Scottish philosopher and economist.
2 Henry Dundas (1742–1811), lawyer and statesman.

229 To the *Scotsman*

[Edinburgh, 9 July 1988]

Sir,

In extolling the legacy of the 'Glorious Revolution' of 1688, the Right Reverend Thatcher is rather less at sea than in some of her other historical excursions. Indeed, there is a peculiar paradoxical aptness in the accident that it should fall to the leader of the present Tory Government to acclaim the achievements of that particular 'revolution'.

In the book *Albion's Fatal Tree*, which Douglas Hay co-authored with E.P. Thompson and others, Hay has this to say on the subject:

The Glorious Revolution of 1688 established the freedom not of men but of men of property. Its apologist, John Locke, distorted the oldest arguments of natural law to justify the liberation of wealth from all political or moral controls; he concluded that the unfettered accumulation of money, goods and land was sanctioned by Nature and, implicitly, by God. Henceforth, among all men on the right side of the great gulf between rich and poor, there was little pretence

that civil society was concerned with peace or justice or charity . . .
'Government,' declared Locke, 'has no other end but the preservation of
property'.

In the same poem which provided the title for Hay's and Thompson's book, the
poet-prophet William Blake, writing at a time when the fatal tree was bearing its
most bountiful harvest of 'strange fruit' (the ragged malefactor-victims of the men
of property), asked a pointed question:

> What are those golden builders doing
> Near mournful ever-weeping Paddington?[1]

What indeed! One has the strong feeling that it is in the neighbourhood of
Blake's sinister tree, rather than in the studies of the Scottish Enlightenment, that
one has to look for the spiritual roots of Thatcherism.

    Hamish Henderson

---

1 From *Jerusalem* 27:25.

230 To the *Scotsman*

                                  [Edinburgh, 28 July 1988]

Sir,

A cogent comment on the problems of bilingualism, currently preoccupying
some of your correspondents, is provided by the great Italian Marxist philosopher
Antonio Gramsci, writing in 1927 from one of Mussolini's jails to his sister
Teresina in Sardinia. Referring to her son Franco, he says:

> I hope you will let him speak Sardinian and not go on at him to speak 'properly'.
> I thought it was a big mistake not to let Edmea [his brother Gennaro's daughter]
> speak Sardinian freely when she was a little girl. It damaged her intellectual
> development, and put a strait-jacket on her imagination.
>
>   Remember Sardinian isn't a dialect, but a real language, although it can't
> boast much of a literature. It's good that a child should learn more than one
> language, if that's possible. After all, the Italian you would teach him would be a
> poor crippled speech – a mere childish mixter-maxter. He wouldn't make
> contact with the world around him, and would finish up not with a language but
> with just a couple of jargons. An Italian jargon when he's 'talking proper' with
> you, and a Sardinian jargon, picked up in dribs and drabs . . .
>
>   I really do entreat you, from my heart, not to make the same mistake; allow
> your children to suck up all the 'Sardism' they want, and let them develop
> spontaneously in the natural environment they were born into. I assure you this
> won't be a stumbling-block for their future development – quite the reverse.

Of course, these wise words of Gramsci's apply with equal force to both Gaelic and Scots. It must never be forgotten that both Gaelic and Scots, unlike Sardinian, are proud possessors of a glorious literary tradition. In the recent past, Scots has had MacDiarmid, and Gaelic has a towering poet – no need to name him![1] – who is reckoned by informed critics to be one of the finest poets writing in Europe today.

Indeed, it is the excellence of much modern Gaelic poetry – and not least, it should be added, that of your contributor Aonghas MacNeacail[2] – which should entice anyone seriously interested in literature to learn something of the language.

What is culture if not our human consciousness of the natural historic ambience into which we were born, and whose colours and sounds we have inherited? For many if not all Scots this must surely include the eloquent and ingenious Gaelic patrimony.

Recognition of that simple fact will certainly not preclude the acquisition of other languages, and the exploration of other cultures – as Gramsci says, quite the reverse!

Hamish Henderson

---

1 Sorley MacLean.
2 Aonghas MacNeacail (b. 1942), poet, writes predominantly in Gaelic.

231 **To the** *Scotsman*

[Edinburgh, 24 November 1988]

Sir,

Mr Michael Hirst, Vice Chairman of the Scottish Conservative Party, gives it as his opinion (23 November) that the Committee of 100[1] against the poll-tax 'contains virtually no one of any standing in Scottish life'.

As I am a member of the committee myself, it is not for me to jib at such a distinguished individual's status; nevertheless, I'd like to suggest that the committee does encompass a pretty representative cross-section of the Scottish population – the 'kindly Scots' of popular parlance. Furthermore, the fact that there are several unemployed people on the list makes it all the more a realistic and down-to-earth reflection of Scottish life under the present Government.

I suppose Mr Hirst would have considered the committee's membership more impressive if it had included a bevy of well-heeled Scottish peers, or names familiar to readers of society glossies. Others may feel that the list has greatly benefited from the total absence of the sort of characters Hugh MacDiarmid described as 'famous fatheads, and noted connoisseurs of bread and butter', as well as of the sort of people whose 'standing' rests merely on the fact that – in the words of Figaro – they 'gave themselves the trouble to be born'.

Reading the names on our list reminded me of another document – the list of delegates to the First General Convention of the Friends of the People, held in Edinburgh in December 1792, which was forwarded by a Government spy to Henry Dundas, the corrupt Gauleiter-Godfather who 'managed' Scotland for Pitt the Younger.

One can just imagine the supercilious sneer on the face of Dundas as he read names like 'John Wilson, James Smith (Gorbals, Glasgow); Smith, Tait (Penicuik); A. McVicar (Gallowgate, Glasgow)' – and some hundred others. They were clearly 'base mechanicals' – tradesmen, artisans. With what hilarity the Tory backwoodsmen must have regarded this list of a composite 'John the Common-weil'! Why, all the Lord Tomnoddys of the day were conspicuous by their absence!

And yet W.H. Meikle (in his *Scotland and the French Revolution*) gave it as his considered opinion that this Convention was 'one of the most noteworthy assemblies in the history of Scotland. Insignificant in point of numbers, and even in its personnel, it gave voice for the first time to the newly awakened aspirations of democracy.'

I have every hope that our committee will perform much the same function in the fight against prepotent and authoritarian Thatcherism.

Hamish Henderson

---

1 The Committee of 100, organized by Labour MPs Maria Fyfe and John McAllion.

1989

232 **To Timothy Neat**

[Edinburgh, 6 April 1989]

Dear Tim,

Many thanks for 'The Druid and Pupil'[1] – it certainly reads well. However, it should maybe be made clear that this is a gifted poet's re-make of a traditional piece – it bears much the same relation to variants such as 'The Vespers of the Frogs' as Lord Hailes's 'Edward' does to variants like Jeannie's 'Son David'.[2] Hailes sent 'Edward' to Bishop Percy for inclusion in the *Reliques*,[3] and it at once became an internationally famous ballad-text – but (like 'The Druid') it bears unmistakable marks of the poet's hand. And that, naturally, makes it all the more effective!

Incidentally, I think I've spotted the reason for the title [The] Vespers of the Frogs. (Text and translation of Jean-François's[4] version enclosed.) It's due to a mix-up between the Breton word for part ('part of the first part'), which is *rann*, and the Breton word for frogs, which is *raned*. So a better title would be vespers (or incantatory repetition) of the parts.

(Villemarqué's[5] title for his piece – The Druid and disciple is a subtitle – is *Les Séries* (the series, in the plural).

See you soon, I hope!

Cheers, Hamish

I'll have to hear Ishbel[6] reciting it!

The Vespers of the Frogs

(as sung by Jean-François Quérnérer)

Little Joseph, little son, Joseph, what do you want?
A song from you.
And what shall I sing you?
A part of the first part – what you know at present.

One day – squatting down to play.

Little Joseph, little son, Joseph, what do you want?
A song from you.
And what shall I sing you?

A part of the second part — what you know at present.

Two fingers of silver.

One day — squatting down to play.

[same pattern]

A part of the third part — what you know at present.

Three sailors and three sailors.

Four horses disputing four cows.

Five black cows coming out of the dark forest.

Six brothers, six sisters.

Seven days, seven moons.

Eight new carts coming from Plounevez
Laden with freshly-cut corn, at the risk of their lives.

Nine men with me every day at the threshing.
Three to bring — three to take away — three to grind,
Near the house of the great Lord.

Ten armed men coming back from Nantes,
Their swords broken, their shirts bloody.
It's sad to behold their grievous hurt.

A sow and eleven piglets, coming out of a wood grunting:
the piglets calling to one another.
. . . A nanny-goat and a billy-goat.

Twelve hounds returning from the meet,
And their master telling them: here's a hare!
Start him up, chase him back, and in my bag he'll go.

A sow and eleven piglets . . .
ten armed men . . .
nine men at the threshing . . .
eight new carts . . .
seven days . . .
six brothers . . .
five black cows . . .
four horses . . .
three sailors . . .

two fingers . . .
one day . . .

A part of the twelfth part — and now I know no more.

Les Vêpres des Grenouilles

(trans. of *Gouspereu er Raned*, sung by Jean-François Quéméner)

Petit Joseph, filleul, Joseph, que veux-tu?
Une chanson de toi.
Et que te chanterai-je?
Une partie de la première partie, que savez-vous à présent.

Un jour — accroupi à jouer.

Petit Joseph etc

Une partie de la deuxième partie.

Deux doigts d'argent.

Trois marins et trois marins.

Quatre chevaux disputant des vaches

Cinq vaches noires venant de la forêt sombre

Six frères, six soeurs

Sept jours, sept lunes.

Huit chars nouveaux venant de Plounevez
Chargés de blé nouveau, au risque de leur vie.

Neuf hommes chaque jour sont avec moi à battre.
Trois à mettre, trois à enlever, trois a broyer,
Près de la maison du grand Seigneur.

Dix hommes armés revenant de Nantes,
leurs epées brisées, leurs chemises ensanglantées,
Une pitié de voir de quelle façon ils sont abimés.

Une truie et onze pourceaux sortant d'un bois en grognant,
s'interpelant de pourceau à pourceau.
. . . une chèvre et un bouc.

Douze chiens de chasse revenant de l'assemblée
et leur maître leur disait, voici un lièvre.
Envoyez-le, renvoyez-le, dans mon sac il sera mis.

(281

> Une truie etc
> Dix hommes etc etc
> Une partie de la douzième partie
> Je ne sais plus maintenant.

The Druid and his Disciple

An ancient Breton song/dialogue collected in the early nineteenth century by Vicomte De La Villemarqué – translated into English, for the first time, by Hamish Henderson, 31 March 1989.

Druid Handsome boy, beautiful Druid's son,
Tell me, my handsome one;
What do you want me to sing to you?

Disc. Sing me the series of number one,
So that I can learn it.

Druid There is no series of number one:
There is Single Necessity;
There is Sin, father of Sorrow:
Nothing before, nothing after.

Handsome boy, beautiful Druid's son,
Tell me, my handsome one,
What do you want me to sing to you?

Disc. Sing me the series of number two,
So that I can learn it today.

Druid Two oxen harnessed to a shell:
They're pulling it; they breathe, they die.
There's a marvel for you!

There is no series of number one:
There is Single Necessity;
There is Sin, father of Sorrow:
Nothing before, nothing after.

Handsome boy etc.

Disc. Sing me the series of number three:
So that I can learn it today.

Druid   There are three parts of the world:
Three beginnings and three ends,
For man as for the oak.

Three Kingdoms of Merlin,
Full of golden fruit, brilliant flowers,
Little children laughing.

Two oxen harnessed to a shell:
They're pulling it; they breathe and die.
There's a marvel for you!

Handsome boy etc.

Disc.   Sing me the series of number four,
So that I may learn it today.

Druid   Four stones to sharpen,
Stones to be sharpened by Merlin,
Who sharpens the swords of the valiant.

There are three parts of the world etc.

Druid   Five terrestrial zones;
Five ages in the duration of Time.
Five rocks on our sister . . .

Druid   Six little children of wax,
Given life by the energy of the Moon.
If you don't know, I do!

Six medicinal plants in the little cauldron;
The little dwarf mixes the brew,
His little finger in his mouth . . .

Druid   Seven Suns and seven Moons,
Seven planets, the Hen included.
Seven elements in the stour of the Air . . .

Druid   Eight winds which blow;
Eight fires with the Great Fire,
Lit in the month of May, on the mountain of the Earth.

Eight young calves white as foam,
Eating the grass of the Deep Isle:
The eight white calves of the Lady . . .

Druid   Nine little white hands on the threshing floor,
            Near the tower of Lezarmeur,
            And nine mothers grieving bitterly.

            Nine sacred virgins who dance
            With flowers in their hair,
            And in robes of white linen,
            Around the fountain,
            In the light of the full Moon.

            The great sow and her nine piglets,
            At the door of their sty,
            Snorting and snuffling.

            Little one, little one, little one,
            Run to the apple tree.
            The old boar will teach you a lesson . . .

Druid   Ten enemy vessels seen coming from Nantes.
            Bad luck to you! Bad luck to you!!
            Men of Vannes! . . .

Druid   Eleven armed priests coming from Vannes,
            With broken swords;
            And their robes all bloody;
            And on crutches;
            And three hundred more than these eleven . . .

Druid   Twelve months and twelve signs;
            The penultimate, the Sagittarius,
            Lifts his bow with an arrow ready.

            The twelve signs are at war.
            The beautiful Cow, the Black Cow with a white star
            on her forehead, comes out of the forest.

            In her breast is the head of the arrow;
            Her blood flows in floods;
            She slumps forward, her head lifted.

            The trumpet sounds; fire and thunder;
            Rain and wind; thunder and fire.
            Nothing! Nothing more! No more of a series of numbers.

            Eleven armed priests etc.

Ten enemy vessels etc.

Nine little white hands etc.

Eight winds which blow etc.

Seven suns and seven moons etc.

Six little children of wax etc.

Five terrestrial zones etc.

Four stones to sharpen etc.

There are three parts of the world etc.

Two oxen harnessed to a shell etc.

There is no series of number one:
There is Single Necessity;
There is Sin, father of Sorrow:
Nothing before, nothing after.

This poem is to provide the centre-piece of the film *Deep Song of Armor* currently being developed by Timothy Neat in association with Hamish Henderson and Claudine Mazeas.

---

1 'The Druid and the Pupil', Breton folksong translated by Henderson (from a French translation).
2 Jeannie Robertson: 'Son David', Child Ballad no. 13.
3 *Percy's Reliques*, a classic eighteenth-century ballad collection.
4 Jean-François Quéméner, Breton folk-singer.
5 Marquis de Villemarqué, Breton folklorist; 'The authenticity of his versions have led him to be dubbed (by some) the "Ossian" MacPherson of Brittany, however, subsequent collecting in the twentieth century has tended in many cases to authenticate his texts' (H.H.).
6 Ishbel Neat (b.1981), daughter of Timothy Neat.

233 To the *Scotsman*

[Edinburgh, 12 June 1989]

Sir,

In his article today ('The importance of keeping the family name alive') about the Scottish surnames which are to be found, in various shapes and disguises, in Germany and other Central and Eastern European countries, James Gilhooley mentions a 'Herr Maclean', a descendant of Jacobite refugees, who served with the Wehrmacht in World War II.

In all probability this was the Major Maclean of Coll – that was how he always wrote his name – who was OC 5th Panzer Regiment workshops in the Western Desert in 1942.

His name became well known to officers working for 'Y' (wireless interception), because his reports on the number of tanks in the workshops under his command provided us with invaluable information as to the number of Mark IIIs or Mark IV Specials at Rommel's disposal at any given time.

Incidentally, he invariably signed off as 'Maclean of Coll', not using 'Von' in place of 'of', as might have been expected.

Hamish Henderson

234 To Naomi Mitchison

[Edinburgh, 29 August 1989]

Dear Naomi,

Very many thanks for this most welcome and useful budget of Kintyre songs. By an odd coincidence – or maybe by a stroke of benign synchronicity – I had been searching among some old correspondence the day before it arrived, and a card from the late Willie Mitchell (butcher and song-collector) had tumbled out among the other stuff, and was still lying on my desk. So, if I'd failed to recognize his handwriting on the pages of songs you sent me, I would have had the card there, to clinch the collector's identity! (I've made a photocopy of the card, and enclose it herewith.)

We have in the archive a photocopy of Willie's MS songbook, which he let me borrow in the mid-fifties, and most – if not all – of the songs you sent *do* naturally appear in it. However, there may well be variants, omissions or added stanzas, and I'll examine your texts with care. Also, the notes appended to the various songs you've sent are mostly much fuller and longer than in his notebook – very understandable seeing he was setting them all down for somebody else! There's probably valuable additional information tucked away in these notes, and if so, I'll insert the necessary cross-references.

I've noticed, since writing the above, that we *don't* have 'The Follinash',[1] which now joins the archive as a debuttant [sic]. Willie is no doubt right when he suggests that it's by the same antiquarian rhymester who penned the inimitable 'Flory Loynachan'.[2] Funny – I can't think of any other tradition which flaunts such a bizarre use of already semi-archaic linguistic verbiage to make a product which almost gets away with it as poetry.

It was lovely to hear from you, dear Naomi – and, once again, thanks a million.

Slàinte! Hamish

PS I've just been in London – foul air-polluting throat-thickening city – for the launch of another book of war poems – *More Poems of World War II*.[3] This is the latest (and – I rather hope – the last) in a series of books which are the distant progeny of a magazine called *Oasis*, which appeared in Cairo during the war. (I had a poem in it, sent from the desert, but I didn't see the mag till after the war – Tambi[4] had somehow got hold of a copy of it.) Victor Selwyn, one of the original editors, has been indefatigable in soliciting songs written in the various theatres of war, and – although the bulk of these are not really very good – there are occasional gems, which would never have seen the light of day, but for Victor.

A year or two ago, Victor organized an *Oasis* cassette tape, which was got together by the late Michael Croft, of the National Youth Theatre. They used a recording of Monty's speech to HQ Eighth Army on 13 August 1942, which ends with the practical words: 'If we cannot stay here alive, then let us stay here dead.'

1, 2 Two songs in an unusual local dialect.

3 The anthologies edited by Victor Selwyn included *Return to Oasis*; *From Oasis into Italy*; *Poems of World War II*, and finally *More Poems of World War II*.

4 Tambimuttu.

235 To Andrew Sinclair[1]

[Edinburgh, 6 September 1989]

Dear Andrew Sinclair,

Thanks for your letter, and for your kind remarks about my poetry. As a matter of fact I was in London a fortnight ago, for the launch of *More Poems of World War II*, the last in the series of books stemming from the Middle East poetry anthology *Oasis*, which was published in Cairo in 1943. As an original contributor to *Oasis* (which I didn't see, incidentally, until I paid a visit to Tambi with George Fraser[2] after the war), I got roped in eventually as a sort of editorial adviser, but most of the hard work of selection was done by the late Ian Fletcher[3] in Reading. His job was difficult, because – needless to say – the standard was not always all that high, but he and Victor Selwyn unearthed some real gems, like John Brookes's 'Thermopylae 1941'.[4]

Also, the books have included poems in Gaelic: not only by major poets like Sorley MacLean and George Campbell Hay, but also by 'unknowns'. It would have been sad if there hadn't been a Gaelic poem about Alamein in any of the war poetry anthologies, seeing that the 51st Highland Division was one of the assault divisions of 30 Corps.

I saw some old friends at the launch, including Paddy Fraser (George's widow), and Gavin Ewart – but Spike Milligan[5] (who was expected) didn't turn up, which naturally disappointed everyone.

Thanks for the invitation to the get-together on 26 Oct. I'd dearly like to come, but I don't think I'll be able to; I'll almost certainly be abroad then, having a much delayed holiday. (Some friends have invited me to visit them in Seville.) But please give my greetings to the gathering.

A thought – why not invite Victor Selwyn? He's carried the torch for war poetry so long that he's almost entitled to an invite!

Best wishes, Hamish Henderson

[PS] You'll be sorry to hear that I returned to Edinburgh with a very bad throat, which is still bothering me. I don't know how Londoners survive in their polyfumous polluted city! I felt like a thirties evacuee from St Kilda or the Blasket who has reached the 'mainland', and encountered maladies against which he has no built-up immunity.

1 Andrew Sinclair, novelist; author of *War Like a Wasp: The Lost Decade of the 1940s* (Hamish Hamilton: London, 1989).
2 G.S. Fraser.
3 Ian Fletcher, Professor of English at Reading University.
4 Henderson praises this poem in his essay 'The Poetry of War in the Middle East, 1939–1945', *Aquarius* 17–18, 1986/7, reprinted in *Alias MacAlias*.
5 Spike Milligan (b. 1918), comedian and author.

236 To the *Scotsman*

[Edinburgh, 8 September 1989]

Sir,

Last week, like some thousands of my fellow-citizens, I received through the post a seven-day warning regarding non-payment of the poll tax. I need hardly say I am ignoring it. I regard this tax not only as utterly immoral but also as utterly stupid, a view increasingly shared, I am led to believe, by many of those on the right who initially supported it. I am resolved to fight this one out to the bitter end.

The thought does not dispirit me in the least. What has dispirited me, and left me sick at heart, is the news that after all the valiant efforts of students, staff and well-wishers to save Newbattle Abbey College, and to muster funds to keep it open, the governors have decided to dismiss staff and use the money so painstakingly collected to 'restructure' the college. I am informed that the redundancy payments for staff are derisory.

Why are we faced with this wretched situation? Because Scotland is ruled, against its wishes, by the rump of the native Tory Party (a philistine junta, if ever there was one).

The humane and civilized values that Newbattle stood (and stands) for, which are increasingly threatened by the depths-dredging operations of the commercialized mass media and the tabloid press, are allowed to go by the board.

Hamish Henderson

1990

237 **To the** *Scotsman*

[Edinburgh, 3 October 1990]

Sir,

Reading Allan Massie's[1] piece today on German reunification, my memory was drawn back irresistibly to Heine's haunting lines (*Denk' ich an Deutschland in der Nacht*[2]):

> Thinking of Germany in the night,
> Sleep leaves me till the clear daylight.

Hamish Henderson

---

1 Allan Massie, novelist and columnist for the *Scotsman*.

2 From Heinrich Heine's *Nachtgedanken* ('Night Thoughts'); the translation is by Henderson.

1991

238 **To Amleto and Luciana Micozzi**[1]

[Edinburgh, 21 March 1991]

My dear Amleto, and Luciana,

Many thanks for your postcard from Ovindoli – it reminded me of the Apennine Winter of 1944, and Alpini songs in gaunt deserted farmhouses. Since it came, the Gulf War has also come but not really gone: in Kuwait there's work for Red Adair and his fire-fighting mates for the next decade! As you know, there were quite a few Scottish regiments out there too, but luckily few casualties – and those mostly from so-called 'friendly fire'. It reminded me of similar 'mishaps' in Africa – *and* Italy – during World War II. (Apparently it was a feature of World War I too!)

Going through some old correspondence the other day, I came across Ishbel's[2] first letter to me after she'd met you, and I thought you might like to have a copy of this (enclosed). And while I'm about it, I'm also enclosing a press cutting about Sorley's most recent award (the Queen's Gold Medal for Poetry!), and the *Glasgow Herald* review (the best one yet!) of the re-published *Elegies*. And – seeing I put it aside for you! – a cutting about an award of my own.

I greatly enjoyed our Sunday outing to the Lago di Nemi – and so made a point of listening to a radio programme called *The Priest of Nemi*, which subjected the Ramo di Oro[3] to a fascinating critical reassessment . . . And then, the following day, there was a showing on TV of Coppola's amazing film *Apocalypse Now* (an appropriate prelude to the Gulf War!). As you probably know, the film is loosely based on Joseph Conrad's novella *Heart of Darkness*, which itself makes imaginative use of the Golden Bough. (Coppola makes the link quite explicit – a copy of the Golden Bough is clearly visible on Colonel Kurtz's table. And he even keeps the name Kurtz.)

Well – that's enough cuttings for one letter! I was glad to hear the news of Susanna's *piccolo Cesare*, and look forward to seeing him on my next visit to Italy (which I hope will be soon).

Love to you all,

Cheers, Hamish

I found 'L'Anima della Valadier'[4] in a notebook of 1945, and enclose it too.

---

1 Amleto Micozzi (b.1928), poet; Henderson first met him in Rome in 1944.

2 Ishbel MacLean; daughter of Sorley MacLean. Sorley MacLean and his family went to visit Micozzi when they were on holiday in Italy.

3 The Golden Bough

4 'L'Anima della Valadier', a poem by Amleto Micozzi dating from World War II. The poem describes the British officers' club set up in the Roman hillside restaurant, La Valadier.

239 To the *Scotsman*

24 April 1991

Sir,

— St Andrew is now universally accepted as the patron saint of Scotland, but in earlier days he seems to have had at least one serious competitor. One intriguing hint as to the latter's identity is to be found in Rabelais.

Chapter IX of *Pantagruel* (1532) describes the first appearance on the scene of Panurge, who addresses Pantagruel in no less than thirteen languages or jargons before he deigns to speak French. One of these languages is Scots — a quite readily decipherable Scots — and after Panurge has made another speech (this time in Basque), Pantagruel's servant, Carpalim, asks him: 'By St Treignan, are you from Scotland, or did I mishear you?' In his commentary Pierre Michel states confidently: 'St Treignan or St Ringan is the national saint of Scotland.'

And who might this gentleman be? Actually his identity is no secret: he is without doubt none other than St Ninian — or Nynia — who founded the famous monastic settlement of Candida Casa at Whithorn in Wigtownshire in the first quarter of the fifth century ad, who made a pilgrimage to Rome, and who evangelized the southern Picts.

It is easy to see why Ninian might well be a more acceptable patron saint than Andrew — or even Columba — particularly, though not exclusively, among the Gallovidians.

He had at least one vital thing in his favour: he was a native Brython, quite possibly from the same area, and the accounts of him in history and folklore combine to delineate a recognisable human individual. (In this he resembles St Patrick, also a Brython, whose historical identity and personality is quite clear-cut.)

Whatever the truth of this, the passage from Rabelais suggests that for the King of France's Scots Guards, at any rate, Ninian/Ringan/Treignan was the saint to swear by. It would be interesting to know of other historical evidence that he was regarded as *le saint national de l'Ecosse*.

Hamish Henderson

240 To Carla Sassi[1]

[Edinburgh, 25 April 1991]

My dear Carla,

I owe you many apologies for not writing sooner. Of course, I'd be delighted — and honoured — if you included poems of mine in your Scottish anthology: I'll leave the choice to you. (Or would you like me to make some suggestions?) Don't worry about copyright: I make you a free gift of anything you want to include!

When I visited Italy in 1950, to work on the translation of *Lettere dal Carcere*,[2] I carried with me the complete text (typescript) of the Cuillin, as well as Sorley's own English translation, and when Amleto Micozzi (whom I'd first met in Rome after the 'liberation' in 1944) came to visit me in Milan, I showed him the poem, and spent some time going over both the Gaelic and English text with him. Within a month or two he had produced Italian translations of quite long tracts of the Cuillin, and I was naturally keen to make the existence of the poem known to a number of the writers I met – through Einaudi,[3] and also through 'Al' Aldovrandi, whose bookshop in Milan was quite a rendezvous for left-wing intellectuals. Pasolini was still in Friuli at the time (I think), for this was April/May/June 1950, but among the poets and writers I spoke to about Sorley were: Alberto Moravia, Elsa Morante, Montale, Quasimodo, Franco Fortini, Vittorini and Pavese. I remember receiving an invitation to a party at Einaudi's apartment, and I read sections of Amleto's translation of the Cuillin to a gathering which included Pavese, Vittorini, Aldovrandi and Carlo Levi. (Also present, if I remember rightly, was Alfonso Vinci, who as 'Bill' had commanded the 2nd Partisan division of the Valtellina.) I also showed the translation to Carlo Gramsci, Antonio's younger brother, who gave me a lot of help with the Sardinian expressions in *Lettere dal Carcere*. So you see I really was trying to make Sorley's name known in Italy, at a time when it was not well known in England! Much later, when I read 'L'Appennino'[4] – the opening of which *does* somewhat resemble the opening of the Cuillin – I wondered if somehow news of the Cuillin (and maybe even excerpts from Amleto's translation) had reached Pasolini.

Amleto may remember more about this: his address is Via Canzone del Piave 13, Roma.

All best wishes,

Love, Hamish

[PS] I enclose an offprint of a review of Packy Byrne's tape-recorded autobiography.

---

1 Carla Sassi, Lecturer in English at the University of Trento; co-editor with Marco Fazzini of *Poeti della Scozia Contemporanea*, (Supernova: Venice, 1992). The Anthology includes Sassi's translations of Henderson's 'The Flyting O' Life and Daith' and 'Freedom Come-All-Ye'.

2 Gramsci's *Prison Letters*.

3 Publishers of Gramsci's Collected Works.

4 Pier Paolo Pasolini (1922–75); poet, novelist and film-maker. The opening passages of 'L'Appennino' (1953) and MacLean's 'The Cuillin' (composed 1939, first published in its entirety in *Chapman* magazine nos. 51–57, 1987–88) are not in fact very similar. The connection Henderson makes is an interesting one: both poets wrote in a minority language, Gaelic and Friulano, which they had dedicated themselves to renewing; both were Communists at the time they wrote the work in question; and both chose a

mountain range as their theme. Henderson narrowly missed meeting Pasolini when he was in Italy in 1950. It was on this visit that Henderson read passages from 'The Cuillin' to a group of leading poets and intellectuals, including Moravia and Elsa Morante, who later became close friends of Pasolini; so, unlikely as a direct connection between the two poems seems, there are some grounds for the comments Henderson makes here.

241 To *ZED$_2$O*[1]

[n.d.; issue no. 2, August 1991]

Dear *ZED$_2$O*,

I have been reading your Water/Solidarity issue with pleasure – especially the article about Blok, Futurism etc. The mention of Gramsci is quite appropriate – he was one of the first critics to deal perceptively with the Futurists, just as he was the very first to acclaim the genius of Pirandello. I also liked very much Janet MacKenzie's story about 'recarnation'. The weirdo in a berryfield dreel: I think I saw him there once myself! The one thing I really didn't like was the use of Prince Smirsky as a pseudonym. Of all the countless victims of Stalin, Mirsky[2] has a tragic place all to himself. By an odd synchronic coincidence, I got a letter from Prof. Gerald Smith about his work on a biography of Mirsky on the same day I got my copy of *ZED$_2$O*. I'd reminded him about Gramsci's mention of Mirsky in Letter 86 of my translation of the *Lettere*, and my note about Mirsky's fate when he returned to the Soviet Union. (I've made a copy of this for you . . .)

Prince Dmitri Mirsky (1890–1939) was a son of Prince Sviatopolski-Mirsky, Russian Minister of Home Affairs, 1904–5. He welcomed the revolution of February 1917, but opposed the October revolution, and fought with the 'Whites' in the Civil War as a staff officer in Denikin's army. He then emigrated to England, where he taught Russian Literature at King's College, London. He became a close friend of Jane Ellen Harrison, the 'Grecian anthropologist' of Newnham College, Cambridge, who wrote Prolegomena to the Study of Greek Religion and Themis, and was a member of the circle which included Gilbert Murray and the Cornfords (Francis and Frances). He did a great deal for Russian studies in England, and (as Gramsci hints) became converted to Marxism, joining the Communist Party of Great Britain in 1931. In 1932 he decided to return to the Soviet Union, and for some years was one of the most eminent Soviet literary critics. In 1937 he was arrested when the Writers' Union was 'purged', and given a summary sentence by an NKVD troika; the rest of his life was spent in the camps of the Gulag. According to eye-witnesses, he succumbed to extreme anguish and despair, and is said to have died insane in a camp near Vladivostock in January 1939.

Ironically, it was to him that Hugh MacDiarmid dedicated the title poem of *First Hymn to Lenin* (1931); this contains the following stanza:

As necessary, and insignificant, as death
Wi' a' its agonies in the cosmos still
The Cheka's horrors are in their degree;
And'll end suner! What maitters 't wha we kill
To lessen that foulest murder that deprives
    Maist men o' real lives!

(I am indebted for much of this information to Professor G. Smith, New College, Oxford.)

    Yours, Hamish Henderson

---

1 *ZED₂O*, literary magazine edited by the poet Duncan Glen (b. 1933); Lecturer in Typography and Graphic Design, Professor of Visual Communication, editor of *Akros* magazine and publications, one of the most important publishers of Scottish poetry in the period 1965–75. Glen was also one of the most dedicated supporters of MacDiarmid during his later life.

2 Henderson's poem 'The Cell, part 2' was dedicated to the memory of Mirsky, published in *Chapman* 42, VIII.5, Winter 1985.

1993

To the *Scotsman*

[Edinburgh, 1 March 1993]

Sir,

Watching on television the close-up shot of Gary Armstrong at the Scotland–Wales rugby match, I was reminded of a poem shown to me some years ago by a lad from the other side of the Border – from Blaydon, if I remember rightly.

The poem was entitled 'The Armstrong Nose', and went as follows:

> Thor's a family famous,
>   so it goes.
> Ye can pick them oot
>   B'thor Armstrong nose.
>
> It's kindae big
>   And on the front.
> Thor still around –
>   Ye just need hunt.
>
> Since Kinmont Willie
>   Rade aboot
> They've aal been noted
>   For their snoot.

Seeing that the Armstrong clan has also been long noted for the prowess of its members in Borders rugby, it is reassuring to know that this outstanding double mark of distinction will again be to the fore at the sporting epic at Twickenham on 6 March.

Yours, etc., Hamish Henderson

243 To the *Scotsman*

[Edinburgh, 8 September 1993]

Sir,

In his entertaining account (Agenda, today) of the famous 'naked lady in the McEwan hall' episode at Edinburgh's 1963 drama conference, John Calder[1] refers to the 'lone piper' who began playing a march at the same moment as the nude Anna Kesselaar began her Lady Godiva act along the platform of the organ gallery. This piper was the late Hamish MacLeod, a colourful character from Lewis and an ex-Seaforth, who had been enlisted for the occasion by me.

Although he was undoubtedly game for any sort of spree, the organizers of the 'happening' decided not to let him in on the secret beforehand, and it was plain, later on, that he had not fully understood the nature of the rival attraction which had diverted attention from his playing.

Indeed, his comment later that day (in Sandy Bell's bar) deserves to be put on record: 'The pipes were going really well.'

       Hamish Henderson

---

1 John Calder, publisher.

H.H. playing snowballs with Violet Armstrong, Dry Drayton, Cambridge, winter 1940.

Left: H.H. with Italian partisans, 1944. *Right*: H.H. addressing a partisan reunion in Dongo, 1950.

H.H., ?, E.P. Thompson, Morris Sugden, ?, Marian Sugden.

Piero Sraffa (courtesy of Cambridge University Libray)

H.H. with Jeannie Robertson and her husband Donald Higgins.

The Linburn Ceilidh (back row: second from left, Stuart McGregor; centre grouping Jeannie Robertson, H.H., Jimmy MacBeath, Tom Scott)

Right: H.H. and Kätzel in Dublin, 1961

Below: Ewan McColl and Peggy Seeger
(courtesy of the School of Scottish Studies)

H.H. with his family, Christmas 1975

H.H. with Paul Fernie; Mandela Day Rally, Glasgow, 1993.

H.H. in his room in the School of Scottish Studies, Edinburgh.

Afterword
by
Alec Finlay

A River That Flows On:
A critical overview of Hamish
Henderson's life and work[1]

I The Confluence of the Folksong Revival and the Scottish Renaissance

How is he [Burns] great, except through the circumstances that the whole songs of his predecessors lived in the mouth of his people, that they were, so to speak, sung at his cradle; that as a boy he grew up amongst them, and the high excellence of these models so prevailed him that he had therein a living basis on which he could proceed further.
Eckermann, *Conversations of Goethe*[2]

. . . You more than any other poet I know, are an instrument through which thousands of others can become articulate . . .
E.P. Thompson, Letter to Hamish Henderson, 10 February 1949 [25]

The letters gathered together here touch on every aspect of Hamish Henderson's life and work; from his wartime experiences in the desert to his political commitments, poetry, songs, translations, and his contribution to the renewal of Scottish folk culture over the past fifty years. Like Robert Burns, his life work bridges the false gap between 'heich' and 'laich'[3] arts, renewing the carrying stream of traditional culture through a popular Folk Revival. His guiding influence over this revival has taken the form of a kind of personal folk-pedagogy: a deep intellectual and instinctive understanding of our national literature and folk art, which he treats as a natural birthright, and a spontaneous and infectious joy in the living oral tradition.

These letters are a commentary on Henderson's poetry and songs, and on the origins and development of the Folksong Revival. His creativity cannot be measured simply in terms of the works he has authored; his contribution as friend, confidant and supporter of many traditional singers, and as the architect of a popular movement, must also be taken into account.

The Folk Revival forms a bridge between the Scottish Renaissance of the 1920s and 1930s, conceived and inspired by MacDiarmid, and contemporary Scottish culture. With the benefit of hindsight this second flowering of Scottish culture can be seen to widen the scope of its predecessor. Seen from Henderson's point of view, the renewal of the oral tradition provided a necessary counter-balance to the predominance of literature in the Renaissance; while, for MacDiarmid, such a broad-based, and, as he saw it, indiscriminate popular renewal of the folk tradition represented an inherently anti-intellectual influence. I will return to these battlefields. What can now be asserted without dispute is that contemporary Scottish culture is undeniably richer for the confluence of the Revival and the Renaissance, as together they have given succour to one of the periodic upswells in the confidence of Scotland's national consciousness.

II Hugh MacDiarmid: The Langholm Byspale[1]

Rescuing the Scots tongue from the slough of havering provincialism . . . MacDiarmid demonstrated incontrovertibly by his own example that it was still capable of becoming art poetry . . . [his] stand in defence of these ideas against every kind of defamation and calumny has been little short of heroic. Now, having won through, he towers in rugged monolithic eminence above the contemporary Scottish scene.
Hamish Henderson (1948)[2]

> I try to make sense of your tortured logomachy . . .
> Amidst all the posturings tantrums and rages . . .
> Just what do you stand for MacDiarmid?
>   I'm still not certain . . .

Hamish Henderson, 'To Hugh MacDiarmid on reading Lucky Poet' (1945/ 1967)[3]

The correspondence with Hugh MacDiarmid, which spans three decades, is the most fascinating single thread, or loosed arrow, which runs through these letters. All the surviving letters that are of lasting interest are included, from the first [7], written in 1946, when Henderson was twenty-seven and MacDiarmid fifty-four, to the last [191], written three years before MacDiarmid's death. Clearly their shared lives and battles were amongst the most important defining experiences in Henderson's life.

MacDiarmid's influence, in all its snake-like contortions and contradictions – the fiery example of his vision, his vituperations, the dark shadow of his occasional malignance, and, of course, towering above all these, the lasting monument of his poetry – stands forth to this day in 'rugged monolithic eminence'. As his recent reminiscences have shown, Henderson is still working over their relationship. What stands revealed in these letters is the unfolding commentary on their life and work. It is a fascinating document of two forceful creative personalities, as well as being a record of modern Scottish and European affairs. The gradual erosion of their common political ground over the post-war years, in which they explore all the nooks and crannies of nationalism and socialism, typifies the pendulum attraction and repulsion which came to dominate their relationship. Although Henderson never lost his willingness to champion MacDiarmid's poetic achievement, his support was, and is still, matched by forceful criticisms on many cultural and political questions over which they differed.

Of their flytings, Henderson has suggested that they were inevitable, that MacDiarmid '*had* to have them';[4] and so, over the course of a decade (1959–69), they matched each other blow-for-blow. The flyting is a mode of rhetoric, part public performance, part personal compulsion; it is not, however, an art-form which best serves objective fact. In these disputes we witness a shadow-play, with all the exaggerations and distortions that follow. At times there is something ridiculous in their quirkiness, when, for example, public rancour co-exists with amiable personal correspondence. They each had an uncanny ability to touch the other's strengths and weaknesses. For instance, in the 1964 'Folksong Flyting' Henderson's counter-attacks are amongst the most eloquent and hard-hitting critical judgement MacDiarmid ever had to face. Beyond this, there is always a search for deeper meaning in their struggles. There are many instances when Henderson weighs up the relationship between MacDiarmid and Scotland, finding some fault with both. As their disputes grew in intensity they came to project onto each other a sense of the riven national consciousness, over the soul of which they did battle.

> But it's Scotland that's driven you to ruination . . .
> The meanness, the rancour, the philistine baseness, the divisive canker . . .[5]

Hamish Henderson, 'To Hugh MacDiarmid on reading 'Lucky Poet' (1945/1967).

The portrait of MacDiarmid that emerges here reveals the worst of his faults, a sometimes life-denying isolationism. However, Henderson's public and private remarks move beyond these personal dimensions to encompass a commentary on poetry and authorship. This, unconsciously perhaps, contains some penetrating reflections on his own creativity, and, in psychological terms, an Oedipal interpretation of their relationship and the complex struggles which dominated it becomes unavoidable. As with so many great artists before him, MacDiarmid seems to have inevitably drawn such complex psychological responses from his disciples, a mixture of devotion and rebellion; just as Henderson has for his part understood the need to rebel against the stern father-figures he chose.[6]

Before considering their struggles, we must first consider the early alliance: the immediate post-war years in which MacDiarmid was mentor and Henderson disciple. The point of closest contact between them coincides, not surprisingly, with Henderson's most direct political statements, both in terms of Marxism and

Nationalism, and with his greatest success as a poet. Indeed there was clearly a sense that this young man, still in his twenties, was a possible successor to MacDiarmid.

III 'A True and Valued Testament': The *Elegies for the Dead in Cyrenaica*[1]

> So I turn aside in the benighted deadland
> to perform a duty, noting an outlying
> grave, or restoring a fallen cross-piece.
> Remembrancer . . .
> 'Tenth Elegy'[2]

The *Elegies* were begun in the desert in 1942, worked over in the Lochboisdale Hotel, South Uist, in 1946 (thanks to friendly patronage of the proprietor Finlay McKenzie), and finally completed during a visit to Naomi Mitchison at Carradale in Kintyre, in 1947. They received the Somerset Maugham Award in 1949, and still stand as one of the greatest poetic memorials to World War II written in English. What separates them from most of the modern poetry of war is the attempt to write a philosophical poem, to discern a wider significance in the conflict: 'a symbol of our human civil war, in which the roles seem constantly to shift and vary'.[3]

Henderson has recorded that the only books of poetry that he carried through the desert campaign were *A Drunk Man Looks at the Thistle*, and Sorley MacLean and Robert Garioch's *17 Poems for 6d.*[4] MacDiarmid's influence on the *Elegies* in terms of style and form is not predominant; however, in at least two ways they do bear comparison with his work and ideas. Firstly, Henderson shares MacDiarmid's concern with the enduring political, cultural and historical problems of Scotland. He finds a meaningful echo of the 'universal predicament'[5] of war in the experiences of the Highland soldier, who faces the familiar historical dilemma of serving in an army of the Crown: 'conscripts of a fast vanishing race, on whom the dreadful memory of the clearances rests and for whom there is little left to sustain them in the high places of the field but the heroic tradition of *gaisge* (valour).'[6] The poet's role is that of a bardic historian, recording another of his clan's wars. There are many levels of allusion in the *Elegies*. There is the imaginative fusion of Cyrenaica and Scotland is suggested in landscapes which merge: 'the wilderness of your white corries, Kythairon . . .'[7] (a similar parallel occurs between the native land and Sicily in his song 'The 51st Highland Division's Farewell to Sicily'). Memories of the 'treeless machair'[8] and 'circled kirkyard',[9] symbolic echoes of the spiritual and artistic desolation wreaked by Calvinism which would later become a focus of his anger, find their counterpart here in the physical waste of the desert, an implacable foe.

On a personal level the *Elegies* represent a spiritual quest, and this culminates in the day the poet spends wandering amongst the remnants of the Pharaohs' once glorious empire, searching the Valley of the Kings for Rilke's 'single column'.[10] These real and imaginary fragments of history and culture give a sense of the desert's consuming power. In this desolate, shifting landscape the quest for meaning, the confrontation of an inner spiritual desert of doubt, intensifies his yearning for the shared human values of love and solidarity. The interior emotional struggle begins as a parallel to the exterior political drama, and then merges with it, and finally emerges as the dominant theme. If the war is a forceful historical imperative drawing the speculative imagination back to the realization that any resurrection must, can only be, achieved in the specific and precarious terms of this world, so love and imagination are the beacons that lead beyond the field of war, towards renewal and reconciliation:

> Run, stumble and fall in our desert of failure
> impaled and unappeased. And inhabit that desert
> of canyon and dream – till we carry to the living
> blood, fire and the red flambeaux of death's proletariat.
> Take iron in your arms! At last, spanning this history's
> apollyon chasm, proclaim them reconciled.[11]

'How are we going to reconcile the survivors with the dead except by facing up to the problems they would have faced had they been alive?'[12] From the crucible of war Henderson brought home a new understanding of the Scottish psyche and Scottish history. Setting aside his philosophical theme, he expresses his political concerns with a new directness in his essay 'Scotland's Alamein' (1947).

> Rightly or wrongly [the 51st Division] became a kind of symbol of Scotland. All the repressed nationhood of this luckless land broke out . . . Here, at any rate was something distinctively Scottish, asserting its identity in the field with a bit of panache . . . It is all the more bitter, therefore, to contrast this picture of Scotland at war with the spectacle of our countrymen in peacetime . . . They had better wake up to the fact that Scotland's national situation today is fully as perilous as the Eighth Army's [at El Alamein].[13]

There is an interesting parallel here with MacDiarmid's own experiences in World War I, which likewise galvanized his sense of Scotland's political and cultural plight. Henderson describes the nature of his and Scotland's political struggle in his 'Interlude':

> We'll mak siccar!
> . . . mak siccar against the monkish adepts
> of total war against the oppressed oppressors
> . . . against the worked out systems of sick perversion
> mak siccar
>   against the executioner
> against the tyrannous myth and the real terror.
> *mak siccar*[14]

Fascism is identified here as a tyranny of political, emotional and spiritual dimensions – what a few years later he would call a 'pluralism of superstructures' – and his search was for a politics, and equally an art, drawn from wartime experiences of solidarity and struggle, which could surmount this tyranny.

The second point of comparison with MacDiarmid is the scope of the poetic task Henderson sets himself; the breadth of his concerns. When MacDiarmid reviewed the *Elegies*[15] it was primarily as war poems that he praised them: 'they compare with most of the war poetry of Rupert Brooke, Siegfried Sassoon and Wilfred Owen'. Generous though the comparison is, it obscures their range of reference. The influences which make this range possible include these distinguished predecessor war poets, but also pre-war Cambridge, the generation who came under the spell of Auden and Eliot, and fellow poets such as Stephen Spender, Nicholas Moore, and John Cornford (the martyr of an earlier episode in the ongoing struggle against Fascism). Aside from these, perhaps the most important poetic influences of all were the great German poets, Heine, Goethe, Hölderlin, and Rilke (in particular the Rilke of the *Duino Elegies*).[16]

Henderson's search for a reconciliation between 'our own and the others' is realized in the fusion of the poetic influences of Cambridge with the poetry of the enemy, bearing out his urge to redeem the 'oppressed oppressors', consolidating the uneasy alliance forged between opposing armies confronting a common enemy in the desert. There is a similar sympathy for the lot of the soldiers of both armies in Sorley MacLean's poem 'Death Valley',[17] in which the poet asks whether the corpse of a young German is that of an 'oppressor' or one 'oppressed':

> Was the boy of the band
> who abused the Jews
> and the communists, or the greater
> band of those
>
> led, from the beginning of generations,
> unwilling to the trial
> and mad delirium of every war
> for the sake of rulers?

The tyranny that Henderson and MacLean oppose here can no longer be identified solely with one nation or people. The lines of patriotism are concealed beneath shifting desert sands. Henderson's message caused some controversy at the time, the *TLS*'s reviewer described it as a 'Teutonic oversimplification'.[18] It is of course typical of his internationalism, which was fostered by his study of Modern Languages at Cambridge, and his youthful translations of European poetry. His achievements as a translator of prose and poetry place him in that great tradition of modern Scottish translation; a tradition beginning with MacDiarmid,[19] and following his example, Edwin and Willa Muir, Robert Garioch, Edwin Morgan, Sydney Goodsir Smith and George Campbell Hay.

MacDiarmid's vision of poetry was heavily influenced by the supreme example of Rilke. Choosing to echo the structure and epic scope of the *Duino Elegies*, Henderson was also implicitly signalling his attempt to fashion a work with an equivalent reach to that of both of these masters. In his essay, 'The Elegies of Rilke and Henderson',[20] Richard E. Ziegfeld compares their works, noting the impact of immediate pressing historical and political concerns on Henderson's work: '[He] seeks to confront death and achieve Rilke's vaunted reconciliation, not in an invisible world within man's mind, but by means of his visible art, which is manifested ''here'', within history.'[21] Such demands are made of the war poet, on *Elegies* which stand testament to the fallen. Henderson's battlefield stands some distance from the lonely Castle of Rilke's solitary inspiration. A 'passionate concern for the individual's . . . consciousness',[22] the highest achievement of Rilke's art, is veiled in the *Elegies* by the task of documenting the very real drama of war.

In comparison, MacDiarmid placed himself closer to the solitary figure of Rilke, and in his 'In Memoriam' for Rilke, 'Vestigia Nulla Retrorsum', composed in the 'stone world' of Shetland, he writes how:

> A naked stone from the castle wall
> Of Duino itself riven might be brought here to serve!
> And yet no different from many another stone
> Of this small island incredibly grey and lone.
> Valery did not know how you could bear to live
> In that old stronghold of silence visible.[23]

In a poem of the same period, also written on Whalsay, 'The War with England', MacDiarmid anticipates Henderson's imaginative connection of Scotland and the desert (known to MacDiarmid only through his reading of Doughty's monumental study *Arabia Deserta*):[24]

> I was better with the voices of the sea
>   Than with the voices of men
> And in desolate and desert places
>   I found myself again.[25]

Their different representations of the deserts, which nevertheless express something of the real, something of the symbolical, underline their respective tendencies to isolation and communality — MacDiarmid's rediscovery of his isolated self during his stony exile, and Henderson's sense of the solidarity its brutishness brought out in the opposing armies. For MacDiarmid, his lonely sojourn was a psychological and metaphysical test. In 'On a Raised Beach' he writes of going apart: 'Into a simple and sterner, more beautiful and more oppressive world,/Austerely intoxicating; the first draught is overpowering;/Few survive it. It fills me with a sense of perfect form',[26] and 'an emotion chilled is an emotion controlled'.[27] Henderson was not unaware of the personal cost of MacDiarmid's genius. Worn down by poverty, suffering a continuing sense of loss as a result of his separation from his first wife Peggy, his poetry became the focus of a psychological struggle of will to overcome his own sensitivity. The magnificent achievement of the poetry he wrote on Whalsay exhausted him, contributing to his psychological breakdown in 1935. The poetics born of this 'desert' was shorn of lyricism, and, from Henderson's point of view, the triumph of the epic over the earlier lyrical voice could not necessarily be considered a victory.

Henderson's own single epic poem was born of very different experiences: wartime brought with it a particular bond of closeness, especially in the great battles, such as Alamein or Anzio, or in the comradeship of his time with the Resistenza, all of which remain vivid in his memory to this day. The telling examples of heroism, humanity and solidarity which he was witness to helped to heal the horror of war. The defeat of Fascism influenced his idealistic post-war political commitments, and inspired his search for a popular art, one which would carry him away from the 'discipline'[28] of art-poetry towards song.

IV The Years of Transition

> Thus ev'ry kind their pleasure find,
>   The savage and the tender;
> Some social join, and leagues combine;
>   Some solitary wander . . .
> Robert Burns, from 'Now Westlin Winds'

MacDiarmid was the first and foremost influence on Henderson's ideas during the immediate post-war years. His influence polarized Scottish culture, forcing poets and others to choose sides: Henderson was never in any doubt where his allegiance lay.

In a letter [161] written to MacDiarmid in 1970 Henderson talks of his first encounter with MacDiarmid's poetry, which took place before the war, during his school days at Dulwich College, where, aged seventeen, he gave a talk to the Literary Society on 'On a Raised Beach' and other poems.[1] In the aftermath of the war, until the early 1950s when he began his fieldwork for the School of Scottish Studies, Henderson was a loyal supporter of MacDiarmid's — a role many young allies filled over the years — during a time when he had neither recognition, position, nor income commensurate with his achievement. Henderson was a tireless supporter of his poetry, as well as making every effort to get him paid work, journalism or reviewing, and providing whatever small financial support he could afford.

The clearest evidence for the importance of his role at this time is his undertaking the editorship of a proposed *Selected Poems*, to be published by the Scottish Committee of the Communist Party. While he was in Belfast, working with the W.E.A. (1948–49), he was also entrusted with guest-editing an Irish number of MacDiarmid's *Voice of Scotland* (like MacDiarmid before him, he has maintained a lifelong interest in the culture and politics of Ireland). Neither the *Selected Poems* nor the issue of *Voice of Scotland* appeared – both falling foul of the ups and downs in the relationship between MacDiarmid and his printer patrons – nevertheless, Henderson continued to try and persuade other Scottish and English publishers to publish MacDiarmid's work.

Another important marker in their relationship is Henderson's brief association with 'The Makars Club',[2] the grouping of younger poets committed to the use of Lallans as a literary language. Henderson appears as a signatory to an important group letter, [20] and, in a number of his own public letters [21, 56, 57] in the late 1940s and early 1950s, he argues in favour of Lallans (despite the fact that most of his own poetry was written in English). Later, as we shall see, he developed his own political ideas about the Scottish voice and became a strong critic of some of the Lallans Makars.

Evidence that Henderson was also willing to question and criticize MacDiarmid from an early date can be found in his review of *A Kist of Whistles* published in the left-wing weekly *Our Time* (November 1947), in which he praises MacDiarmid's past achievements, but makes his view clear that his new 'experimental work' in English 'seldom reaches the level' of his earlier poetry written in 'his mother tongue'; turning the Lallans argument against its author he was anticipating a trick he would use more than once in the battles to come.

During Henderson's journey to Germany in 1947 he encouraged his friend Heinz Vogt, who was living with the surviving members of his family in a coal cellar in the ruins of post-war Meiderich, to translate poems from *Pennywheep*, as well as attempting some of Sorley MacLean's Gaelic poems.

In Italy in the summer of 1950 Henderson saw to it that MacLean's work was translated into Italian, and he read extracts from 'The Cuillin' (having borrowed the only copy of the English translation from MacLean), to an audience which included Moravia, Montale, Pavese and Quasimodo.[3] There are many other examples of his proselytizing on behalf of MacDiarmid's work and that of other Scottish poet friends, up until the time when his work for the School of Scottish Studies demanded his full attention.

In his most important article of the immediate post-war period Henderson commits himself to 'MacDiarmidism', presenting MacDiarmid and John Maclean as the two central figures in the post-war renewal of Scottish culture. Although he is now firmly associated with Edinburgh and the Meadows, it is interesting that at the time Henderson allied himself with Glasgow, which was in these years politically, and arguably artistically, the more progressive city, largely through the presiding influence of MacDiarmid. The article, titled 'Flower and Iron of the Truth'[4] (published in *Our Time*, 1948) presents an overview of contemporary Scottish literature. The poems Henderson chose to illustrate this speak much for his concern to gather together the four points of the saltire: they include poems celebrating John Maclean by Sorley MacLean and Sydney Goodsir Smith, MacDiarmid's 'Common Riding', and a poem about the Highland clearances by George Campbell Hay, 'Lomsgrios na Tire' ('Destruction of the Land'). The issue concluded with a discussion of Lewis Grassic Gibbon's work from a Marxist perspective, by MacDiarmid.

In his discussion of contemporary Scottish poetry, Henderson distinguishes between two 'schools' deriving from different aspects of MacDiarmid's work:

> The first includes those poets known as the 'Lallans Makars', Albert Mackie, Sydney Goodsir Smith, Maurice Lindsay and Douglas Young . . . [They] desire to extend and enrich the capacities of the revitalised Scots tongue as a vehicle for literature. Hence, constituting themselves a kind of unofficial Academy . . . The second of the two schools I referred to is gradually emerging. The poets belonging to it are not primarily interested in the language question . . . They are resolved . . . to produce work which will interpret more immediately the reality of the Scottish people – of the commons of Alba, the industrial proletariat . . . [and the] Highland remnant. In a word they have comprehended the need for a literature of presentification. Reacting strongly against the seeming archaism of the Makars – an archaism more of subject matter than language . . . The poets of the second school (sometimes called the 'Clyde Group') . . . fear that [Lallans] may turn into a mere academic exercise, a field of Alexandrian virtuosity – a 'pluralism of superstructures' above a life with which it has lost all contact.[5]

The 'Clyde Group' included the poets John Kincaid, 'Thurso Berwick' (Maurice Blythman), George Todd and Freddie Anderson,[6] all friends of Henderson's (his letter [166] to Tom Scott of 1970 shows that he continued to champion their work long after they had slipped from popular and critical attention).

In another article, 'Lallans and all that', published in *Conflict* in March 1949,[7] he is even more blunt in his criticisms of the 'so-called "Lallans Makars"' – Maurice Lindsay and his maudlin mates . . . These bourgeois nationalists, hopelessly hobbled from the start by their political gormlessness . . . are now . . . being assailed and worsted by the younger Scottish Marxists of the Clyde Group . . .'[8] Henderson goes on to outline the task of this new vanguard as 'preeminently that of gaining direct contact with the people'. He continues:

> At the John Maclean Memorial Meeting there was a thrilling example of this, when Thurso Berwick's poem was interrupted at one point (*A MacLean is ai yuir*

banquet!) by loud spontaneous applause from the huge audience. This is the only time in my life I can remember this happening.[9]

In retrospect the 'Clyde Group' can be seen as part of a modern tradition that includes Unity Theatre, the Glasgow Folk Club, and folk-singers such as Matt McGinn; the protest songs and poetry of the 'Ding Dong Dollar'[10] anti-Polaris demonstrations at the Holy Loch in the early 1960s; Workers City, contemporary writers, such as the poet Tom Leonard and the novelist James Kelman and artists such as Ken Currie. Leonard's anthology *Radical Renfrew*[11] gives the movement an even richer historical sense of tradition.

Henderson's celebration of 'direct contact' between poetry and the people, and his disapproving references to the Makars as an 'Academy', foreshadow his arguments against the 'bookish' arts in the mid-1950s, and the Flytings that were to follow. 'Flower of Iron of the Truth' and 'Lallans and all that' are important markers of his early thinking, and, although he would develop away from this rather narrowly sociopolitical position – in what is after all a relatively youthful article, typical of the times – 'presentification', a key term, and the other ideas he introduces here, are a crucial stage in the development of his aesthetic. This article marks both the high point of his alliance with MacDiarmid, in his trumpet call for a Scottish Workers Republic, but also, implicitly, the transition which was to follow, away from the dominant influence of MacDiarmid's politics and poetics, towards the new perspective of the Folk Revival. His aspiration for a 'committed' poetry, one which would speak directly to 'the reality of life in Govan or Hamilton – or for that matter . . . Comrie or Lochboisdale . . .',[12] signals the real and symbolic journey he was to make in the following decade; and his break with the orthodoxy of Lallans declares his determination to develop his own ideas about the Scottish voice.

These early critical writings declare the close relationship between politics and culture which held true for the rest of his life. The essence of his political outlook is defined in this complex tension between a 'pluralism of superstructure' and, in opposition to this, a life of 'contact with the people'.[13] In a matter of two or three years this life of 'contact' would become a reality in his collecting tours. As we have already seen in the *Elegies*, this 'superstructure', which assumed its apotheosis in Fascism, was not simply a political entity; it includes the imposition of any barriers of race and creed, any attempt to curb or confine love. There is an inevitable tension between such personal and political issues, and this has remained the primary influence on the development of his creative voice. In the *Elegies* this took the form of tensions between the individual voice, the poet's idealistic convictions, fears and desires, and the 'remembrancer's' public task of witness, recording the shared experience of battle.

The conclusion of the post-war, post-*Elegies* period is the transition of the 'remembrancer's' art into a new renewed commitment to the oral tradition and folksongs. In the Winter of 1947 Henderson's *Ballads of World War 2*[14] appeared. This was the first published example of his collecting. Henceforth the 'direct contact' with the people that he now sought would be achieved in the popular art of folksong, rather than in a work of 'art-poetry' with the intellectual aspirations of the *Elegies*. The choice that he made when he did commit himself to folksong went against literary fashion, against the Modernist sensibility which had been such a strong influence on him at Cambridge, and, in time, it also brought him into conflict with MacDiarmid, who condemned it as politically and culturally disastrous.

MacDiarmid had every right to these suspicions – his attacks (supported by Henderson [13]) on Hugh Roberton, the Glasgow Orpheus Choir, the Burns cult, and the popularity of Kennedy-Fraser's settings of Gaelic songs, make it very clear what he thought of the worst of so-called folksong.

In his early essays Henderson had constructed an argument of self-justification for his new commitment from a political point of view. In the Folk Revival he discovered an art which could offer genuine opposition to the political tyranny outlined in the *Elegies*. The emotional tenor of the Revival came as close as it was possible (in peacetime) to the solidarity and idealism which inspired his wartime experiences.[15] Some recent remarks bear this out: '[my songs are] a sort of fusion of my two greatest loves: the anonymous song poetry of Scotland . . . and the comradely solidarity of the anti-fascist struggle which dominated my early manhood.'[16] Poetry and the oral tradition coexist from the earliest stages in his career, and, in understanding his attitude to both it is important to remember that he had been close to song as a child – it was the art he was born to and which remained closest to his heart. The political interpretations he placed on this transition never entirely supersede this personal sense of belonging.

V The Words I Must Go On Looking For

In order to unravel this transition from poetry to song it is necessary to go back and look once again at the *Elegies*. One of the most perceptive reviews to appear at the time of their publication was by the Marxist historian E.P. Thompson[1] – a friend of Henderson's since they first met at Cambridge in 1946. Thompson's praise for the *Elegies* does not preclude some critical questioning: 'How far Mr Henderson will be able to consolidate and extend his achievement is less certain. There are in the *Elegies* occasional indications of lack of confidence.'[2] In Thompson's view the influence of modernism, and in particular of Eliot, is to blame:

> He desires to speak directly, out of his experiences, to his fellow men. But he is all the time aware that the audience he is most likely to reach is circumscribed by the coteries and sophisticated reviews. If he can only cast off this censor and

assert his confidence, not in an impersonal dialectic but in the people who make their own history, he will find in himself an unusual ability to speak their most mature thoughts and sing them on the way to victory.[3]

There is much of Thompson's own political idealism in this. However, his criticisms go to the heart of the issue of voice. His remarks are prescient, because the resolution Henderson sought was achieved in *song* – in a fusion of personal and communal expression, bridging the rift between the intellectual forms of Modernism, which Henderson came increasingly to identify with MacDiarmid's later work, and the voice of the people. In a letter written in response to the *Elegies*, Thompson considers the full import of Henderson's chosen task:

> I greet you with humility campagno, for you are that rare man, a poet. You have achieved poems out of our dead century . . . and you must never let yourself, by the possible insensitivity or even hostility of those who should be your greatest allies, be driven into the arms of the 'culture boys' who 'appreciate' pretentiousness and posturing. They would kill your writing, because you, more than any other poet I know, are an instrument through which thousands of others can become articulate. And you must not forget that your songs and ballads are not trivialities – they are quite as important as the *Elegies*. (10 February 1949) [25]

Henderson was never in danger of forgetting his songs: they become central to his creativity; and as an 'instrument' of change in the Folk Revival, he set about healing this rift in contemporary Scottish culture.

In his poetry Henderson made his own experiments with 'presentification'. He attempted to fuse the speech of the common people with the voice of the art-poet; for example, in the speech of the swaddy in the *Elegies*. In his poem 'So Long: 22 May 1943' he bids a soldier's farewell to the desert:

> Halfaya and Sollum: I think that at long last
>   we can promise you a little quiet.
> So long. I hope I won't be seeing you.
> To the sodding desert – you know what you can do with yourself.
>
> To the African deadland – god help you –
>   and good night.[4]

The different experiments with voice in the *Elegies*, where Henderson mixed this kind of informality with philosophical speculation, were only partially successful. They revealed a tension which Thompson felt was inevitable, given the gulf between the ordinary swaddy and the 'coteries' of literature. Thompson refers us to some of Henderson's best known and most often quoted lines, from the conclusion to the Sixth Elegy 'Acroma':

So the words that I have looked for, and must go on looking for,
are words of whole love which can slowly gain the power
to reconcile and heal. Other words would be pointless.[5]

This passage is the emotional high point of the whole work; but Thompson finds the abstract quality of its expression a weakness:

In these lines one of his finest Elegies is sabotaged. The impersonal 'I' of the earlier verses becomes self-conscious; the focus of attention is shifted from the men and their actions to the poet and his words. Eliot pays an unwarranted visit into the rhythm. With 'whole love' (whatever was in Mr Henderson's mind) all our paths of reference are blurred — we are groping around among Auden's 'interest itself in thoughtless heaven' and 'changes of heart' accomplished in padded armchairs.[6]

One of the most distinctive characteristics of the *Elegies* — one which originates in their long period of composition during and after the war — is the juxtaposition of the dramatic voices which speak to us from the battlefield, telling of 'the men and their actions', and the retrospective act of remembrance with which the poet gives the work as a whole its shape and meaning. The personal resonance of 'whole love' is, in Thompson's terms, an afterthought projected onto the political struggle, yet for the poet it is essential to the cause he fought for. The effort required to harness his voice to the creation of an 'art-poem', balancing emotion with intellectual argument, is acknowledged in the Prologue: '. . . a bit/That sets on song a discipline,/A sensuous austerity.'[7] It was this mask of austerity that the Folk Revival would free him from. In the *Elegies*, the poet tells us: 'synthesis is implicit', but in song, in the immediacy and empathy of performance, which has been so essential for Henderson, it becomes explicit, as he addresses his audience directly, face-to-face.

Following the publication of the *Elegies*, and despite their success, Henderson published few poems of substance.[8] It appeared that the great expectations of him as a poet were not to be realized — if we go forward for a moment to the end of the 1950s, when the first of the Flytings brought folksong and art-poetry into confrontation, in the 'The Honor'd Shade Flyting', MacDiarmid implied that Henderson had indeed failed to live up to these expectations. Replying in his own defence, Henderson describes the attitude he now held towards his art: 'The final shape of a new long poem I have been working on eludes me . . . in any case I have come to set greater store by my songs "in the idiom of the people" than by other kinds of poetry that I have tried to write.' [87] The quotation is from Burns, and the implied parallel is a revealing one, as our national poet also set aside poetry in favour of song in his last years. Here is a new and meaningful prototype — one to rival MacDiarmid's influence — with which Henderson can readily defend and explain his allegiance to folksong. Thus Burns becomes one of the first battle-grounds in the Flytings, as I will examine in more detail later.

When MacDiarmid accuses Henderson of underachieving – and he does have evidence to justify the accusation – he is indicting the same hesitancy Thompson drew our attention to in his review of the *Elegies* (and, in the letter quoted above, Henderson had in effect admitted to this). But what was the nature of this hesitancy, and was it responsible for his abandonment of poetry? As I have already suggested, there were tensions in his work which suggest that the poetic forms and tenor of Cambridge were an uneasy vehicle for the ideas and emotions he wished to express. Not only were these idioms distant from the communal arts he grew up with, and the Nationalist issues which now concerned him; but, even more importantly, 'art-poetry' itself was no longer the only, the most natural outlet for his creative voice. In other words, his quarrel was as much with the vehicle as the message, and this was the primary reason why he also rejected the obvious alternative to Cambridge, the new Scots poetic vanguard formed by the Makars, who followed MacDiarmid's example.

VI The Journey of Transition

What is culture if not our human consciousness of the natural historic ambience into which we were born, and whose colours and sounds we have inherited . . .
Hamish Henderson (Letter to the *Scotsman*, 28 July 1988) [230]

A period of transition followed the literary success of the *Elegies*. A key event, and one which had a great influence on Henderson's outlook, was the memorial meeting honouring the 25th Anniversary of John Maclean's death in Glasgow, November 1948, which Henderson helped to organize and chaired. He addressed the rally and his song, 'The John Maclean March', composed for the occasion, was sung by William Noble.[1] The important influence of his political beliefs, his 'revolutionary humanism',[2] on his art is borne out by the way so many of his folksongs have been composed with specific political events in mind.

Then, in the Spring of 1950, travelling on the prize-money he received from the Somerset Maugham Award, he set off for Italy. His reason for returning there is described in a letter to MacDiarmid [37]: 'I am working hard [translating] Antonio Gramsci's *Letters from Prison*, a book of the first importance. G. was certainly the most important Marxist thinker outside Russia in the period 1920–35.' Henderson had first heard of Gramsci from his comrades in the Resistenza; and later, in 1950, he met Gramsci's friend, the political economist Piero Sraffa, at Cambridge. Henderson was therefore one of the first people outside Italy to be in a position to recognize his political and philosophical importance. Receiving Gramsci's writings as they were published in Italy, their influence on his own thinking was immediate. Gramsci makes a crucial though unacknowledged appearance in the phrases, 'a literature of presentification' and 'pluralism of superstructures' in 'Flower and Iron of the Truth'. His theoretical writings shaped Henderson's campaign to revive the Scottish traditional arts over the course of the following decade. He was the justification for a political utilization of folksong, as Henderson writes in his Introduction to the *Prison Letters*, 'fostering an alternative to official bourgeois culture, seeking out the positive and 'progressive' aspects of folk culture.'[3]

Alongside the crucial political and cultural influences of MacDiarmid and Gramsci was a third important influence, that of the progressive Marxist thought he encountered at Cambridge in the 1940s and early 1950s. Henderson's circle during his second period of study at Cambridge included E.P. Thompson and Sraffa, and also the influential social thinker and critic Raymond Williams. Such friends and mentors were in contrast to the idealism of the poets he knew in the 1930s: radicalism was now allied with pragmatism, as they all had direct experience of exerting power and influence during the war, Henderson included. They were prepared to temper their idealism in pursuit of real cultural and social renewal. This pragmatic outlook is a key difference between the political paths followed by MacDiarmid and Henderson: although they frequently found themselves standing beneath the same banners as Communists and Nationalists, Henderson always tended towards the achievable, whereas MacDiarmid frequently forced issues to the fore by dint of the very isolation or extremism of his position.

Henderson's journey to Italy was an overtly political project, a turning aside from his literary career. If the Folk Revival was also consciously planned, its beginnings can still best be traced to a chance encounter – one signalled in a letter Henderson received from his friend Ewan MacColl in February 1951 [42], warning him of an imminent arrival:

> There is a character wandering about this sceptred isle at the moment . . . Alan Lomax. He is a Texan and the none the worse for that, he is also about the most important name in American folksong circles. He is over here with a super recording unit . . . Columbia Gramophone Company are financing his trip. The idea is that he will record the folk-singers of a group of countries . . . He is not interested in trained singers or refined versions of the folksongs . . . This is important, Hamish. It is vital that Scotland is well represented in this collection.

With the synchronicity of this meeting all of the elements that would gel into the modern Folk Revival fell into place.

VII The First Years of the Folk Revival

> My mother used to go to a little house belonging to a travelling family. She enjoyed singing and these were native Perthshire Gaelic speakers so this must have been the very edge of Gaeldom at the time, just outside Blairgowrie. In that house you would either hear Gaelic or Scots.[1]

Both my grandmother and my mother were singers and my grandmother had a great store not only of songs but of stories and poems. She could recite the whole of Walter Scott's 'Glenfinlas' from end to end . . .[2]

Hamish Henderson was a born collector. It was a natural birthright of the oral culture to which he belonged. From his first collecting forays as a teenager, to his time as a soldier and Intelligence officer, when he was always ready, notebook in hand, filling pages with his own poems, songs and translations, and the songs, stories and bawdy verses of British soldiers, German and Italian P.O.W.s, and Resistenza partisans, as well of course as the troop movements, and the disposition and morale of the enemy. On his trips to Germany and Italy in the late 1940s and early fifties he sent home letters peppered with folksongs and poetry. In 1946 he was invited to Canna by the island's owner, the distinguished folksong scholar John Lorne Campbell, and there he met Seamus Ennis and Calum MacLean (brother of the poet Sorley who Henderson did not meet until later that year). They were in Scotland collecting under the auspices of the Irish Folklore Commission, there being no equivalent Scottish institution. Calum later became the first full-time appointee to the School of Scottish Studies, and remained a friend and staunch ally of Henderson's until his tragically early death in 1960.

When McCarthyism forced Alan Lomax to temporarily quit America, he brought with him a piece of machinery already in common usage amongst collectors in the States, which became the chief weapon in the armoury of the Revival, a tape-recorder.[3] This made possible a fidelity to the oral tradition, a 'presentification' of the spoken and sung voice, creating a new kind of Revival in which the oral arts remained predominant, rather than print, which had always come to dominate in the past. Thanks to the new recording technology, the ballads no longer suffered from the old problems of texts being separated from their tunes. As for Henderson's collecting, Ewan MacColl described it as 'one of the great Scots collections, worthy of being ranked with those of Gavin Greig and David Herd'.[4]

After the success of his first trip to the north-east apprenticed to Lomax, the newly formed School of Scottish Studies financed a number of further collecting trips – 'God's own job', as he describes it in a letter to Marian Sugden [54] written in 1951. It was on these tours that Henderson first met Willie Mathieson, John McDonald, John Strachan, and then, in 1953, Jeannie Robertson. The importance of this meeting was immediately clear to Hamish, and it was one he had predicted – that there would be someone with such a rich repertoire, probably a woman, possibly a traveller, the only surprise being that he had expected to find her in the country. The short walk between the University Library in King's College, Old Aberdeen, where he would study Gavin Greig's great folksong collection, to Jeannie's house in nearby Causewayend, where he would often enough walk into an impromptu ceilidh or story-telling session, became symbolic of the gulf between academicism and the living tradition. It was this cultural apartheid that he set about to remove once and for all:

> As far as the theory – the whole 'idea' – of a Folk Revival was concerned, I was very much preoccupied with just this at the beginning of the fifties, partly because I had been working on a translation of the 'Prison Letters' and other writings of the great Italian Marxist philosopher Antonio Gramsci . . . Gramsci's insights, combined with the experience I had gained during field-work with Alan Lomax and his tape-recorder, suggested one urgent need: that of placing examples of authentic native singing-styles, and – wherever possible – actual performances of good traditional artists within the reach of the young apprentice singers of the Revival . . . [Calum Maclean and I] rapidly came to realize that by embarking on the study and collection of folk material we were engaged willy-nilly in a political act.[5]

In 1954 he was finally appointed as a full-time research fellow at the School, and, in the Summer of 1955, he returned on a collecting trip to his home town, Blairgowrie, where, as Maurice Fleming had informed him, there was a wealth of traditional material to be harvested amongst the travellers. Here he was:

> overwhelmed by the wealth of song, story and lore which flowed from the travelling people who had gathered for the berry-picking. Never had it been so clear to him that this was not a question of isolated survivors preserving old fragments of balladry; this was an alternative culture shared by the whole gathering, old and young . . .[6]

This alternative culture was to become his new spiritual home.

In these field trips he discovered a world that was both new and known to him; known from childhood memories, but only now discovered in its full richness. From the moment that he committed himself to the Folk Revival, we can see Henderson moving gradually closer to his childhood home; away from the Glasgow of John Maclean and the urban proletarian sympathies of the 'Clyde Group'; back towards the north-east, the land and its songs. Although he has never reneged on his political allegiance to Marxism and working-class culture, it was inevitable that he now moved away from an urban poetry of commitment – another accusation of MacDiarmid's – as, under the new presiding influence of Gramsci, his political vision and artistic aesthetic was transformed. It is as if he had been given permission to remain true to his rural origins – whereas MacDiarmid was persuaded that the urban proletariat was the only legitimate vehicle for progress. The reconciliation he achieved is celebrated in his song 'The John Maclean March', in which Neil, the Highland teuchter, joins hands with Jock and Jimmy, and the red and the green are worn side by side.[7]

Henderson's interest in the songs of the rural labouring classes was a far cry from the 'lanely wishan wells'[8] of pastoral sentimentality that he had criticized so strongly in the past. Devoting his creative energies to the world of farm workers and, more remote yet in social terms, to the travellers, he found himself moving away from limited contemporary political and literary perspectives. He grasped the possibility of challenging the cultural hegemony that shaped the national voice, just as MacDiarmid had in the 1920s. As he travelled round the Highlands in the service of this new cultural project, he was interacting with the carriers of a traditional culture which had its roots in the distant past. The role of field-collector drew out the warm sympathy that is so characteristic of him, and, as well as recording others, he soon became a carrier and performer himself, appearing on Lomax's Scottish album, and carrying a steady flow of songs and stories back to the archives of the School in Edinburgh, which were then passed on through ceilidhs, folk clubs, records and radio programmes to the young apprentice singers in the cities. This was all part of the work of creating the modern Folksong Revival.

VIII The Progress of the Folk Revival

> The Epworth Haa wi wunner did
> behold a piper's bicker;
> wi *hadarid* and *hindarid*
> the air gat thick and thicker.
> Cumha na Cloinne pleyed on strings
> torments a piper quicker
> to get his dander up, by jings,
> than thirty u.p. liquor,
>   hooch aye!
> in Embro to the ploy.
> Robert Garioch, from 'Embro to the Ploy'

> Hamish's extempore performances were as far as I am concerned one of the most memorable aspects of the early People's Festivals . . . By day one encountered him on the streets and squares of Edinburgh, generally accompanied by one or two of his discoveries, Jimmy MacBeath, Frank Steele or Jeannie Robertson . . . At night he would be found presiding over the ceilidh which began at 11 p.m. and finished at two or three in the morning. There must have been hundreds of Edinburgh folk who heard their first traditional song at those splendid affairs.
> Ewan MacColl, September 1989[1]

Henderson was now the prime mover in a new popular movement. Central to his strategy was an understanding of how the oral tradition is passed on from one generation to the next — something he had plenty experience of. By far the most important of its methods is that of example. He made contact with singers and storytellers, and with travellers of the north-east and Sutherland, who for social — which is also to say political — reasons had been ignored by academe. It is impossible to imagine a social group more isolated from contemporary society, nor one with closer ties amongst themselves, than the travellers, and it was amongst them that he found many of the finest examples of the traditional arts upon which the new Revival was founded.

They were the most respected of the tradition carriers, Jeannie Robertson being a prime example. Ailie Munro records Henderson's role in bringing to light this wealth of material preserved amongst the travelling community.

> There is wide recognition among travellers of the pioneering art which Dr Hamish Henderson played in collecting their songs and stories. Bryce and Betsy Whyte: 'Hamish started things . . . it took courage on his part.' Courage indeed, for he took time to fraternize, to win confidence and trust, to sleep in rough tents. In the early fifties, to be on such friendly equal terms with social outcasts was hardly the way to win friends and influence people of the Establishment, academic or otherwise.[2]

Norman Buchan has summed up the importance of the vision Henderson brought to the Revival movement:

> I can't see, it's difficult for me to imagine how the Folk Revival could have taken off without Hamish and Hamish's work. First, there was the keel of the School of Scottish Studies, which said: This is important; this matters; this must be collected! Then, curiously enough, you had a collector who was interested in the living thing, that also songs had to be made, who wrote songs himself. This is a great distinction, that he recognized it wasn't an archaic, an antiquarian ploy that he was on. It was something that was living. Curiously enough for someone who was a poet, and a very good poet, he fortunately did not wish to discriminate in his folk collecting, that he knew the task of collecting was to dredge, was to trawl, and you took everything up . . . whether they mattered a good deal or not, the body was incomplete without them . . . He had both the quality approach, as it were, understanding the importance of a big ballad, under-standing the importance of a living tradition, but also knowing that the squibs were part of the process. He understood the process as well. And this, I think, was quite remarkable.[3]

Henderson's understanding of the process fused together the oral tradition and modern collecting techniques. Above all, he accorded the singers respect. His faith in the value of live performance shines through in the sleeve notes he wrote for 'The Muckle Sangs':

In the long run it seemed to us that it was the singers themselves who could elucidate best some of the still resistant problems of ballad-scholarship . . . The language, the music, the atmosphere, the personality of Scots folksong can best be got straight from them . . . this wonderful fluid thing, representing the actual world of the ballad singers, a shared sensibility still artistically vital and fertile . . . It is no exaggeration to say that, the better the singer, the more likely was he or she to adopt a stance of dignified humility when talking about the tradition . . .[4]

Refer to the sleeve notes in a record by any singer who was apprenticed to the Revival and you can find references to the sources of each song, and, along with printed sources such as the old song-books and chapbooks, these will often also include the names of particular singers whose version the singer learnt from. During the first two decades of the Revival great emphasis was placed on these 'source-singers'.

The Revival needed an urban platform for the material that was arriving from the regions. The People's Festival Ceilidhs of the early 1950s provided the ideal opportunity. Norman Buchan recalls one such evening:

As I went into the Oddfellows Hall the bloody place was packed, feet were going, and it was Jimmy MacBeath singing 'The Gallant Forty-Twa'. Hamish had assembled these people. Jessie Murray sang 'Skippin' Barfit through the Heather' . . . Flora MacNeil was singing 'Silver Whistle' . . . beautiful! I'd never heard anything like this. John Strachan was singing about forty verses of a ballad; John McDonald, the mole catcher, singing one or two of his own songs and bothy ballads. An amazing night for people who'd never heard them before! It swept me off my feet completely.[5]

In his programme notes for the 1952 People's Festival, Henderson made his aims clear:

If the Ceilidh succeeds in its purpose, it will perform something of tremendous cultural significance for Scotland. In our cities the folk tradition has never completely disappeared, in spite of all the inroads made upon it, and it is still possible to graft these flowering branches from the North and West upon a living tree. We are convinced that it is possible to restore Scottish folksong to the ordinary people in Scotland, not merely as a bobbysoxer vogue, but deeply and integrally.[6]

This was as radical and far-reaching a project as that proposed by MacDiarmid in the 1920s.

And what of the relationship with MacDiarmid? Throughout the 1950s they remained ostensibly on good terms, as can be seen from their correspondence –

although Henderson's work for the School prevented him being as much of a help as previously. Henderson took a significant early opportunity to pay homage to MacDiarmid, dedicating the 1952 Ceilidh in honour of his sixtieth birthday. As he recalls: 'MacDiarmid was invited to sit on the platform, and at the beginning the entire audience stood while Calum Johnstone played "Blue Bonnets over the Border" as a tribute to Scotland's greatest living poet.'[7] When the Ceilidh had finished, MacDiarmid rose to propose a vote of thanks to the performers;

> Our tremendous treasury of folksong in Scotland, whether in Lallans or Gaelic . . . has been occluded, very largely for political reasons, from the majority of our people. The Edinburgh People's Festival, and the movements in which my friends on the platform and others in the audience are concerned, is a reassertion of that tradition . . .[8]

In 1953 he discussed the evening again:

> These Scottish folk-singers were real artists. Every one of them was culturally worth all the famous artists, conductors, actors and actresses of the official Festival a thousand times over . . . whenever you hear one of them singing you have before you the aesthetic impulses of all times (genuine even if often on a merely elemental level) – and another exemplification of the way in which we in Scotland have bartered our birthright for a mess of commercial pottage.[9]

By allying the Folk Revival with the best of Scottish poetry, Henderson felt he had immeasurably strengthened both. It was a strategic move; one which reflects his desire to reunite the 'heich' and 'laich' arts and to give a new and necessary breadth to the ongoing Scottish Renaissance. However, by the end of the 1950s this much sought alliance lay broken in pieces. The Flytings of 1959 and 1964 destroyed the closeness of the friendship. As we shall see, their closeness in terms of shared political and cultural ground had begun to diminish some years before.

IX The Flytings and Their Origins

> Another set with ballads waste
> Our paper, and debauch our taste
> With endless 'larums on the street,
> Where clouds of circling rabble meet.
> The vulgar judge of poetry . . .
> Alan Ramsay, from 'The Scribblers Lashed'

Mr Henderson seems to find his ideal man in the 'muckle sumph', and to wish to scrap all learning and all literature as hitherto defined in favour of the boring doggerel of analphabetic and ineducable farm-labourers, tinkers and the like. He is presumably at home amongst beatniks and beatchiks . . . He evidently wants to stabilize people at a low level corresponding to a state in which society has virtually ceased to exist.

Hugh MacDiarmid, Letter to the *Scotsman*, 19 January 1960 [88]

What are we to make of such comments? When MacDiarmid made this repudiation, the achievements of the Folk Revival were already clear to see — in the new folksong clubs, ceilidhs and records, as well as in Henderson's own writings on the subject. The Revival had kept its strong commitment to art-poetry. It was also an invaluable source of 'propaganda' for various nationalist and left-wing political views which MacDiarmid was in favour of, from songs celebrating the reiving of the 'wee magic stane' to the 'Ding-Dong-Dollar' anti-Polaris L.P.s and poetry anthologies of the early 1960s.

Following the example of MacDiarmid's campaign in the 1920s, the proponents of the Revival knew that it was essential to popularize; and where MacDiarmid had concentrated on publishing magazines, criticism and anthologies, as well as promoting his own work, Henderson wanted above all to get the new songs and singers heard as widely as possible. One of the Revival's central aims was that of making direct contact between the best of the traditional or 'source singers' and the younger apprentices in the cities. He and his allies were vociferous champions of the 'natural' folk-singer, against the 'art' or trained singer.[1] This brought him into conflict with the BBC, who remained stiflingly conservative in their attitudes on the issue of voice.

In 1955 he went on the offensive in an essay titled 'Enemies of Folksong', published in the *Saltire Review*.[2] Attacking the historical prejudice against folk culture, he clearly had some contemporary foes in view, including the Labour Party, who had banned the People's Festival Ceilidhs in 1952. Here, for the first time, Henderson also allowed himself to discuss the antagonisms between folksong and art-poetry: 'Folksong is a challenge to the culture of the elite, [because] it expressed with power and elan the communal creativeness of the people against a book-song and art-poetry increasingly contracted and withdrawn from the life of the common people.'[3] These comments appeared some four years before the 'Honor'd Shade Flyting'. They coincided with the publication of MacDiarmid's *In Memoriam James Joyce*, the most substantial example of his late epic poetry, and a work which saw him move further away from the folk influences that inspire his earlier work. Bearing this in mind, Henderson's essay is evidence of the inevitable conflict of aesthetic still to come. In the essay he does not accuse MacDiarmid or his poetry directly, but keeps his criticisms concealed, or, at the very least coded. However, it is clear that the early alliance he sought with art-poetry was gradually being replaced by a portrayal of the oral tradition unfairly trodden upon by its elder brother in the Muses.

In their Flytings MacDiarmid remained true to the anti-nomianism which led to so many of his battles: focusing on any point of difference between his own position and that of an opponent, and applying unyielding pressure until these divergences of opinion yielded their full quota of meaning. From Henderson's point of view, despite his implicit censure of the direction MacDiarmid's poetry was taking, up until their first Flyting MacDiarmid remained a natural ally – out of respect for his achievements, but also for reasons quite specific to the Revival, which I will explore shortly. Once the split between them was irrevocable, which it was as soon as MacDiarmid attacked the Revival, Henderson hit back forcefully, applying a wedge of his own to drive open their mutual differences.

X The Relationship Between the Folk and Literary Traditions: Models of Authorship

For any Scottish writer who wishes to reconcile individual expression with a wider sense of national consciousness, questions of national identity and voice are raised: questions MacDiarmid so consistently brought to the fore. In his essay, 'Dialectics of "Voice" and "Place": Literature in Scots and English from 1700',[1] Roderick Watson draws attention to the important role of the oral tradition, communal festivals, the poetry and song of public occasions, the popular idioms of ballad, and flyting, and the disputations of Court, Kirk and Law Court, in this search for such a national identity in Scotland. Henderson championed this energizing force: he epitomizes the tendency Watson refers to as privileging 'speaking' over 'writing'.[2] As I have already discussed, these aspects were present in the tension between the 'speaking' voice of the swaddy and the 'writing' voice of the art-poet in the *Elegies*. In the Folk Revival, 'writing' did indeed give way to 'speaking', to song. Responding to these peculiar and distinctive characteristics, Henderson frequently returns to the interwoven relationship between the literary and oral traditions.[3]

There is a tendency amongst many of Scotland's greatest authors to carry this interplay to a natural conclusion, by setting aside or undercutting authorial identity in favour of the communal identity of the folk idiom – the songs of Robert Burns being the most famous example of this. A kind of bastard child of this tendency is the frequency of the alias in modern Scottish literature, and MacDiarmid is, as Henderson says in his essay 'Alias MacAlias',[4] the most fascinating example of this.

The desire for anonymity, or the communality which would eventually lead there, is at the root of Henderson's commitment to the Folk Revival – a movement in which, contradictorily, he has been a larger than life presence. This explains his reluctance to publish his own songs, preferring to see them transmitted, and gradually altered, within the carrying stream. The attempt to replace a literary model of authorship with one drawn from the very different models of the Folk tradition contributed to the break with MacDiarmid, who – despite the challenging inconsistencies in his own creative methods which I will come to shortly – held resolutely to the sovereign power of the creative consciousness, embodied in the supreme figure of the poet. An example of the Revival's challenge to conventional models of authorship is a letter [120] Henderson sent to the *Scotsman* (a reply to Douglas Young's coda to the 'Folksong Flyting' of 1964 [119], it has remained unpublished until now), in which he states: 'The "folk process" is a useful shorthand phrase for what happens to songs when they begin to take on a life of their own, start shedding some things and acquiring others, and generally assuming a new form, or forms. It's not the origin of the song which really matters, but what becomes of it . . .' Henderson elaborates on this alternative communal model of the creative process in an essay on Hebridean Waulking Songs (1970), songs in which: 'Elements have become locked together, and have disengaged, some changes probably occurring in the free-flow of improvisation – the result perhaps of the momentary whim of some long-dead soloist – and others (one senses) corresponding to a deep underlying aesthetic pattern . . .'[5] This deeper pattern is at the heart of his credo.

It is worth recounting an amusing episode from one of his own collecting tours. Maurice Fleming tells the story of how one day in 1964, sitting in the kitchen of a Mrs Mona Stewart in Galloway, she turned to Henderson and said:

'Put on your tape-recorder again. I'll sing you a song you'll really like.' Hamish switched it on and she began to sing. To his amazement it was his own 'Freedom-Come-All-Ye'! The tune had 'developed' considerably, and so had the words, but it was his song all right. When she had finished Hamish didn't know what to say . . . Should he tell her he had written it? . . . In the end he took his courage in his hands and told her. Mrs Stewart had learned the song two years before from a Glasgow singer now in the U.S.A. Where he had learned it from is anyone's guess.[6]

Such events – not uncommon during his collecting tours – were proof, if any were needed, of the validity of his faith in the folk process.

This attitude to authorship helps to explain Henderson's open-minded response to the controversy over MacDiarmid's poem 'Perfect', and the other examples of unattributed quotations appearing in his poetry. The interesting correspondence with Erich Heller (published here for the first time), in which Henderson tracks down, and attempts to diplomatically attribute another such 'borrowing', develops this point. For Henderson this was a useful example of the common currency between the folk and literary traditions, and evidence of the influence of the folk tradition on MacDiarmid: 'This acquisitive attitude to material from all sorts of sources is strongly reminiscent of the folk poet, who frequently appropriates lines or even whole stanzas from other poems or songs.'[7] As Edwin Morgan notes in a recent essay on contemporary literary models of authorship: 'Ballads and folk poetry are collage texts; there is no finished or ideal text that can escape from the continual state of flux and growth and transformation, and more than one author is involved.'[8] Henderson was similarly always willing to ally the renewal of the traditional arts with modern or avant-garde concepts of authorship, nourishing the sources that writers like Joyce, Yeats and Pound had trawled. Despite the apparently divergent attitudes to authorship which seem to separate folksong from art-poetry, parallels such as these emerge.

The importance of translation in the modern Scottish poetry Renaissance has much in common with this spirit of experimentation with models of authorship. MacDiarmid's translations foreshadow his use ˙of unacknowledged quotations, 'translating' other people's work into his own. The translations themselves were often based closely on prose versions supplied by friends.[9] In his essay on 'Ossian' MacPherson, published in *Scottish Eccentrics*,[10] MacDiarmid explores his attitude to translation, and, given the subject at hand, his comments have some bearing on the folk tradition. 'Ossian' MacPherson represents an admixture of author, fraud, translator and folk-poet. The fraud that he perpetrated is held up for ridicule, but there is also a sneaking sympathy on MacDiarmid's part – and not only for MacPherson's audacity. In terms of Gaelic culture the 'translations' are a travesty, yet, MacDiarmid argues, had they been genuine they would hardly have been read and could not have had the enormous influence that 'Ossian' did. MacPherson himself 'entirely misconceived'[11] the nature of his own achievement. It was beyond his ken that these poems would provide a new mythology, embodying the 'emotional ferment and idealistic revolt initiated by Rousseau',[12] and anticipating the cataclysmic European revolutions that followed. From MacDiarmid's point of view 'Ossian', MacPherson's fraud, was justified by this synchronicity, and by the fact that Europe had at this time neither the ability, the willingness, nor the need, to recognize the reality of Gaelic culture.

MacDiarmid extended his argument, suggesting that the art of translating is itself a 'fraud', if by translation we imagine that a work of art passes intact from one culture and language into another. MacPherson's poems are poems in English, and any translation of worth must be considered as such. Whatever folk influence lies submerged within these poems/translations they constitute a new work. The model of authorship MacDiarmid describes here claims to originate in the 'true nature' of the 'Scottish genius', which he explains lies is in his 'continual propensity for a genuine "transition" into another field'.[13] The reasoned and objective art, which translating is commonly considered to be, depends upon norms the Scotsman rejects, and skills that he does not have – as ever, for 'Scotsman' we may do better to read 'MacDiarmid' – depends furthermore upon the 'selecting, organizing, and ordering of experience which is alien' to a Scotsman. Rather the Scotsman's genius is to be found in 'the play of personality, the indulgence of impulses'.[14] It is 'transition' rather than 'translation' that excites MacDiarmid – an echo of Henderson's 'not the origin' but 'what becomes of it'.

The act of absorbing the mask of another personality into our own[15] (a technique Henderson also uses, to make personal revelations, as I will discuss shortly in relation to his translations), of remaking ourselves, takes on a metaphysical dimension. Appealing to a Shestovian rejection of relativist 'norms' and 'general ideas',[16] [MacDiarmid] portrays the daring of the poet as a metaphysical flight from 'empiria'. Such 'frauds' as he and MacPherson dare to perpetrate are a diabelerie justified by the ruling daemon of poetry, which stands always outwith the bounds of society and convention.

MacDiarmid would never approach a figure like MacPherson from the point of view of communal folk influence. The different models of authorship that he and Henderson are concerned with share a blurring of the borders of the individual creative intelligence, yet they remain distinctively different in their origins and conclusions. By comparing these models it is possible to see that Henderson's bear out his determination to avoid the twin tyrannies of the 'superstructure' of power and the isolated eyrie of solipsistic genius.[17] In his strongest attacks MacDiarmid – or at least the author-figure he has come to personify – becomes a symbol of 'craggy' remoteness, of an over-bearing intellectual ambition divorced from social responsibility. Henderson concentrates his later criticism on the mask of diabelerie MacDiarmid adopted: the poet as 'superman'. W.N. Herbert discusses this aspect of MacDiarmid's creative persona in his book-length study *To Circumjack MacDiarmid*:

> [MacDiarmid's] idea of the poet as unashamed genius, as announced in a letter to (Neil) Gunn, embodies a pathological need for significance . . . : '. . . behind all the complex network of my activities there is a definite irrationalism, which will not be pinned down and which proceeds from the belief that I personally embody certain forces – . . .'[18]

For Henderson this mask of the poet represented the 'tyranny' of Modernism, of a retreat into elitism and political extremism, the historical consequences of which his generation had to bear. Wrestling with this shadowy authorial figure he came increasingly to idealize the communal values of song. In his later critical writings he frequently had occasion to draw attention to the influence of the folk tradition on MacDiarmid's work, presenting such contact with the arts of the common people as a necessary antidote, as here in a text written in 1968, but not published until after MacDiarmid's death:

> Hugh MacDiarmid, for all his great services, is totally at sea on this approach which throws into sharpest relief the reasons for the murderous alienation of the poet in contemporary society. We must abjure self-gratificatory elitism – and particularly the quasi-solipsistic elitism which one senses in much of MacDiarmid's work . . .[19]

However, it is equally important to recognize that the communal arts have their own problematical characteristics as a model for authorship, most obviously because they encourage a tendency to self-censorship. Henderson's idealistic commitment to folksong can be seen as an avoidance of a kind, born of his inability to commit his emotional self in the absolute personal sense that the greatest poetry demands – here we return to his hesitancy as an author. He has never denied his sense of art-poetry as the greatest of the arts, and never lost his sense of poetry as a calling within his own life, even after he chose to make it secondary to his own work establishing and promoting the Folk Revival. His choice was true to his own creative and emotional voice, as well as being – in just the same way as MacDiarmid's – a response to national and political ideals and precedents; and it is in this sense that their battles, their creative personae, and their differing models of authorship, clearly fall into established patterns in Scottish culture.

XI 'A Wild and Perfect Garden'

> The best of our literature is impregnated through and through with the despised folk tradition.
> Hamish Henderson[1]

> [The] disaffected and the powerless . . . know that out in the public world a polished speech issues orders and receives deferences. It seeks to flatten out and obliterate all the varieties of spoken English and to substitute one accent for all the others . . . the vernacular imagination . . . expresses itself in speech and feels trammelled by the monolithic simplicities of print, by those formulaic monotonies which distort the spirit of the living language.'
> Tom Paulin[2]

Outcast and virtuous, belonging to a simpler, better life; these characteristics of the oral tradition lead Tom Paulin to describe it as 'a wild and perfect garden', echoing Henderson's idealistic vision. Paulin is keen to acknowledge the stimulus of the art-poet's sojourn in this happy valley: 'speaking', revivifying and re-energizing 'writing'. Henderson only differs in his marked preference for song, the landscape of his own youth; the undisputed and preeminent art of the common people. In his essays he portrays the art-poet as someone who *may* be redeemed by a renewed contact with the arts of the common people. This prejudice against print, which is quite marked in some of his later essays,[3] reflects his desire to redress the balance in contemporary Scottish culture. Reviving the oral tradition will be of common benefit to literature and song. Henderson bases this argument on firm historical precedent, as every previous Scottish Renaissance in poetry had gone hand-in-hand with a popular folksong movement similar in character to the modern Revival:

Throughout Scottish history there has been a constant interplay between the folk-tradition and the learned literary tradition – an interplay more constant and fruitful with us than in the literatures of most other European countries. Burns is the preeminent example of a poet who understood and recreated his own work in the folk tradition of his people. If the Renaissance in Scottish arts and letters is to be carried a stage further, our poets and writers could maybe do no worse than go to school once again with the folk-singers.[4]

In the latter part of the 1950s, as they manoeuvred for position, Henderson and MacDiarmid returned to their different interpretations of Burns' legacy. Burns was a crucial precedent for Henderson. As the most important creative influence on an earlier Folksong Revival he 'set up a folk song-workshop of his own, and transformed, without seeming effort, our whole conception of the meaning of traditional art for society . . .';[5] yet, as Francis Collinson describes, he 'quixotically chose to do his song-writing anonymously and without financial reward.'[6] Henderson stresses the influence of the folk tradition on Burns's creative methods in terms that are already familiar: 'appropriating opening lines or even whole stanzas from earlier or contemporary authors – or from popular tradition – and using them as a basis for his own productions . . .'[7]

MacDiarmid's criticisms of the Burns cult are well known: of particular relevance here is his essay 'Robert Fergusson: Direct Poetry and the Scottish Genius'[8] (published in 1952, the very same year that he made his speech of praise at the People's Festival Ceilidh; and preceding the 'Honor'd Shade Flyting' by some seven years). This is primarily an attack – his first public attack – on the fledgling Folksong Revival, a prospect which prompted his comparison between Burns and Fergusson: 'Burns betrayed the movement Ramsay and Fergusson began'.[9] The language question is 'the crux of the whole matter'.[10] Fergusson represents the possibilities of a direct use of Scots speech as a literary language, allied to a firm political resolve resistant to 'all Anglification',[11] and a commitment to the poetry of city life, and hence to the urban proletariat. Burns, at his worst, represents Scottish sentimentality, anti-intellectualism, political wavering, and implicitly a romanticized attachment to the rural poor. He would later summarize this argument in a short piece written for the *Guardian*: 'I think he [Burns] sacrificed the possibilities he had of becoming a great poet very largely to his work of renovating and redefining Scottish folk-songs. That wasn't his proper business at all, and I deplore that he spent so much time on it.'[12]

MacDiarmid's attacks on the Folksong Revival derive from his political and historical analysis. He castigates the 'dangerous' popularity of folksong, which encourages 'maudlin sentiment'[13] and 'permanent juvenility',[14] and is opposed to 'modern development', 'scientific progress',[15] thus betraying the intellectual concerns of his own poetry. In his analysis folksong is intricately connected with the social conditions of the Scottish peasantry and rural labourers of the eighteenth and nineteenth centuries. In a letter written towards the end of the 'Honor'd Shade Flyting' (1960) he claims that: 'Mr Henderson evidently wants to stabilize people at a low level corresponding to a state of society that has virtually ceased to exist . . .'; and, in *Aesthetics in Scotland*: 'the folksong movement is hopelessly bogged down in senseless repetition and a hopelessly sentimental attitude to an irrecoverable past.'[16]

Need the oral tradition be any more tied to particular social and historical conditions than literature, than the Scottish Renaissance MacDiarmid had forged? This appears to be an argument between the two arbiters of the Scottish voice, 'writing' and 'speaking': poetry, which had up until now been the defining medium for the new cultural movement, and folksong, which, from MacDiarmid's point of view, was incapable of forming an avant-garde culturally or politically, because its popularity involved an inevitable compromise. Folk Culture was a fit subject for anthropologists and sociologists, but could never project itself beyond these circumscribed social conditions, as great art could.

For Henderson art-poetry and folk song were not competing but complementary aspects of an interwoven tradition. The achievements of any avant-garde depended on its respecting the integral balance in Scottish culture. If the Revival could graft the best of the traditional arts onto the urban population, reintegrating the culture of the rural regions with that of the proletariat, it would reconcile the antagonisms MacDiarmid's political analysis perpetuated.[17]

Despite MacDiarmid's pointed avoidance of the parallels between the synthetic manipulation of literary tradition he engineered some three decades before, and the methods of the Folk Revival, there are clear similarities, as, for instance, in Henderson's defence:

> And if it is objected that this is a 'forced' development due mainly to the efforts of those concerned with the current Folksong Revival, I would counter by claiming that the tradition as it exists today is in large part the heritage of many similar revivals in the past: for example, those which we associate with the names of Gavin Greig, Robert Burns and Allan Ramsay. It is an honourable list, and one that Scotland can be proud of.[18]

Henderson and MacDiarmid can be seen to share remarkably similar overall cultural strategies: both dedicated to the reassertion of Scottish traditions, both focusing on the relationship between voice, psychology and national consciousness. It is worth considering these parallels further. In his consideration of MacDiarmid in *The Crisis of the Democratic Intellect*, his friend George Davie asks how it was that the Renaissance movement surpassed the 'desiccated, impoverished and localised form of lowland Scots':[19]

How did it come about that the 'Back to Dunbar' movement resulted in a renovation of the provincial and limited Scottish canon of Scots as used by the versifiers of the time, which raised its intellectual level to a sufficient extent to constitute it a vehicle for philosophical poetry of a modern kind.[20]

His answer is succinct: the 'crust of custom'[21] was broken. MacDiarmid studied the literary revivals of Norway, Catalonia, and Ireland, and following these examples he revived a modern literature, one based on 'the literary achievements of the classic periods in the own country's past, when the language . . . had been in full flower.'[22] In a similar way, Henderson was inspired to break the 'crust of custom', renewing a folk tradition then every bit as moribund and stereotyped as poetry had been in the 1920s, by bringing the new source-singers to the fore, and creating a new canon based on the flower of traditional song. As in past Folk Revivals, a few influential figures were responsible for laying down this new canon of songs and new models of interpretation. To the names of the great literary figures who had dominated previous revivals, Scott, Hogg, Burns and Ramsay, and collectors, composers and singers, Ord, Greig, Duncan, and Mrs Brown of Falkland, was now added Jeannie Robertson (the greatest influence on the canon of the modern Revival), Ewan MacColl and Henderson himself.

In letters to the Scottish press in 1948 [21] Henderson defended the Renaissance, not on the grounds of the inherent 'Scottishness' of their work, but because they represented an *avant-garde*. Alan Riach has pointed out, with regard to MacDiarmid's interventions in tradition, that within these there often lies the familiar subversive aims of an avant-garde.

> [MacDiarmid was] actively subverting the notions of stability, continuity, centrality and authority which the word 'tradition' implies. Both activities — the reassertion of tradition and the subversion of cultural hegemony — were idiosyncratic, but they point towards a distinguishing characteristic of Scottish literature as a whole: its profound sense of local value stretching back through a distinctly national history, its traditionalism and, simultaneously, its radicalism.[23]

Can the same be said of Henderson? Popularity was essential to the success of the folksong movement. As its success grew, the direct influence of Henderson and the other figures who had shaped it naturally lessened; yet it is also true that, in their cultural projects he and MacDiarmid both simultaneously challenged the centrality of their own public roles by, for example, championing socially isolated groups, such as the travellers, or radical political ideas, as with MacDiarmid and his enduring Stalinism. Henderson's writings on gender, sexuality and Nationalism can also be considered in this light.[24]

Returning now to the reticence Henderson showed in his attacks on MacDiarmid. In the Flytings he seems to avoid attacking MacDiarmid's poetry; rather he concentrates on the extremism of the political and social ideas which orbit around the work. This can perhaps be explained by the particular importance MacDiarmid's poetry held with respect to the Revival. While Henderson could happily cite the achievements of his poet, song-composing and folksong collecting predecessors, Burns, Scott and Hogg, as evidence of the interwoven relationship between art-poetry and the folk tradition, he could not present a figure of equivalent literary stature in the modern Revival. His insistence that MacDiarmid's poetry had always one foot in the Folk tradition was an attempt to do just this; and, when he praises MacDiarmid, describing him as 'the greatest poet since Burns, who has devoted his life to the cultural resurgence of his country' and someone whose 'work exemplifies many of the best features of the marriage between folk-song and art song . . .', he is tying him firmly to this role within the carrying stream – as the comparison with Burns confirms – as well as demonstrating his belief that an avant-garde can, or must even, be integrated within popular culture in Scotland.

His later criticisms of MacDiarmid centre on what was really an issue of faith; knowing that MacDiarmid was the only poet capable of sustaining the new popular project in terms of art-poetry, he could not forgive his distrust of anything tinged with populism, a distrust which eventually broke their alliance apart. As it was, the success of the Revival only seemed to confirm MacDiarmid in his view that great art must of necessity be unpopular:

> Better a'e golden lyric
> The mob'll never ken
> For this in the last resort
> Mak's them less apes, mair men . . .[25]

The essential difference in their projects was inevitable because, as George Davie points out, MacDiarmid's poetry was determinedly antinomian:

> The starting point of the argument [MacDiarmid's] . . . is the historic rivalry between national groups as well as within national groups, over the question of excellence in culture, knowledge, thought, etc . . . some groups will always be superior to others . . . [and] there is within each group a corresponding struggle between the elite, the intellectual few who do the discovering, and make possible the progress, and the anti-elitist many, who are not equal to participating in the general argument, and who seek, often successfully, to bring to an end 'The insatiable thocht, the beautiful violent will,/The restless spirit of man' by imposing egalitarianism, of which the Burns International is for [MacDiarmid] the great example.[26]

Taken on almost any level, these notions of 'violent will', national rivalry, and metaphysical strife, represent the crux of their dispute. They represented a tyranny Henderson had rejected, given his formative experiences in Nazi Germany, fighting fascism in the desert war and Italian campaigns, and then witnessing the ruins of post-war Germany. The poetry he sought to nurture was a poetry of the excluded. He held up a poem such as MacDiarmid's 'The Seamless Garment'[27] as the antithesis to the poet's own elitism and pessimism. In a letter [177] written to MacDiarmid in the early 1970s he describes an incident which seems to bring this poem to life, illuminating the differences in their creative temperaments:

> Last weekend I was down in Newcastleton for the village's annual folk festival. It was a very enjoyable occasion – almost as good as the Langholm Common Riding – though hardly as old of course – while I was there, I met two young blokes, one of whom comes from Langholm and the other from Longtown. They both apparently work in the mills in your home town. As there had been quite a bit of poetry, as well as song, at the folk festival, I asked them if they had read 'The Seamless Garment', and as of course they hadn't, I recited it to them in the street, then and there. The upshot was that they wanted copies of it, so today I photocopied it (from my own copy of *The First Hymn to Lenin*), and dispatched the copies. I tell you this little story to show you that – by courtesy of the folk festival – 'the guid wark gangs bonnilie on' . . .

For Henderson the flower of folksong was capable of expressing what Lorca calls, 'all the rare complexity of the highest sentimental moments in the life of man.'[28] Given a choice between the tyranny that genius so often seemed to carry in its wake – Hölderlin's madness, Rilke's loneliness, MacDiarmid's 'insatiable thocht' – and the warm conviviality of folk culture Henderson set this zenith aside. In contrast, in his later work MacDiarmid expressed the belief that great poetry served 'the engagement between man and being', heights to which only the greatest intellect or spirit could aspire and which could never be expressed adequately in folksong, rooted as it was in the physical world of the soil and the senses. Such tensions, for instance, those between the forces of progress, poetic, political, technological or scientific, led by an elite – the MacDiarmidian approach – and the popular will, the common good – which Henderson appeals to – are constants in any culture. In his writings on the Scottish philosophical tradition George Davie traces these tensions in the disputes of the Enlightenment, and describes them in terms that can easily be applied to the later Flytings between poetry and folksong:

> The stultification of the majority, due to cultural apartheid, is likely be a species of sympathetic contagion to affect the mental balance of the society as a whole . . .';[29]
> '. . . The . . . real danger of an intellectual atomization in which the learned and conversable, as Hume calls them . . . get out of contact with one another, losing in

the process the sobering sense of the common origin of their respective modes of culture in what Hume refers to as the animality of the vulgar . . .'[30]

In many ways it was as a reaction against MacDiarmid's over-intellectual approach that Henderson, like Burns before him, came to celebrate the 'animality of the vulgar'. He has always delighted in celebrating the sexual comedy, as in his poem 'Auld Reekie's Roses',[31] the bawdy songs he collected, and in his writings on folk culture. Bearing in mind the Rabelaisian example of MacDiarmid's earlier poems, 'Harry Semen' and the well-known passages in *A Drunk Man*, it seems as if over the course of his life Henderson has made a series of strategic interventions in MacDiarmid's work and the movement he created.

If we are to draw conclusions about their battles it will not be by holding fast to the positions of thirty years ago. In a letter sent to me shortly before he died, Michael Grieve wrote that while he agreed that the differences between his father and Hamish had been overemphasized, his father most certainly insisted on those differences at the time, as a way of focusing attention on the implications they held for Scottish culture. There was every reason that MacDiarmid should distrust a Folk Revival, as such, given his experiences in the 1920s and 1930s; yet it is still true to say, with the benefit of hindsight, that his attacks on folksong betray a lack of faith, given what Henderson and the Revival actually achieved. I am sure Henderson would be the first to agree that the Revival he fought for and defended can now be seen to belong in the cultural period of 'MacDiarmidism', as Angus Calder has named it; and there is not necessarily a contradiction inherent in his having had to vigorously oppose the man within that '-ism', especially when that man is the janus-figure we know him to be.

XII The Folk Revival and the Scottish Voice: 'Deviations to Highland and Lowland'

'I stand at a moment in history when instinct, its traditional songs and dances, its general agreement, is of the past. I have been cast up out of the whale's belly though I still remember the sound and sway that came from beyond its ribs . . . The folk song is still there, but a ghostly voice, an unvariable possibility, an unconscious norm. What moves me and my hearer is a vivid speech that has no laws except that it must not exorcise the ghostly voice. I am awake and asleep, at my moment of revelation, self-possessed in self-surrender; there is no rhyme, no echo of the beaten drum, the dancing feet, that would overset my balance.' W.B. Yeats[1]

Yeats, himself a collector, stands at the edge of a precipice which marks the imminent and seemingly irrevocable death of the folk tradition. Henderson's view is more hopeful: he asserts with characteristic political good faith that the arts of the common people are capable of renewing themselves, even when they seem on the verge of extinction. This faith is based on his cyclical interpretation of Scottish culture. However, despite this optimism he does not deny that the disabling effects of modern industrial society have destroyed this 'general agreement'. He set out to remedy this disastrous cultural alienation.

The songs and stories that he and others collected, particularly the examples discovered in the isolated world of the travellers, were tangible evidence that the 'ghostly voice' Yeats had listened to fifty years before was still alive, still renewing itself in the carrying stream. The primary aim of the Revival was, firstly, to record these songs and stories; and secondly, and in a way even more importantly, to create a renewal of these traditions, especially among the young, so that the material could be preserved in its only true form, in living interpretation. The Revival was, as Henderson admitted, an intervention, a synthetic means to reassert a traditional process. Once it was initiated, and modulated by the influence of the living tradition, he believed that it would become self-perpetuating, as indeed it did. The diverse sources that came together to shape the Revival resemble those that shaped the poetic Renaissance MacDiarmid had masterminded in the 1920s: both movements were catholic, and, for all MacDiarmid's disapproval, the Revival's heterogeneous mixture of traditional ballads and contemporary protest songs, skiffle and Music Hall, Dylan and MacBeath, was a creative stimulus every bit as rich as the heady mixture of *Jamieson's Dictionary* and racy Scots speech that had captured his imagination thirty years before.

MacDiarmid had instilled a sense of mission in a generation of Scottish poets to revive the nation's languages, including the Makars who revitalized Lallans, and Sorley MacLean who dedicated his life to Gaelic poetry and the Gaelic language.[2] Taking inspiration from these examples, Henderson applied himself to his own native Perthshire, and to the great hinterland of the Mearns and Fyvie. He is as proud a native of the lands between the Shee water and the Buchan coast, as MacLean of Skye, or MacDiarmid of the Borders.

The Revival became a new arena to explore the possibilities of an art of 'presentification', which would now highlight the material realities of the Scottish voice in all its distinctive variations and languages.[3] Although the Folk Revival was a popular movement, and a profoundly democratic one, it would be wrong to think that it did not present a certain hierarchy of artistic achievement. From the outset Henderson gave priority to the 'muckle sangs'; in this lay Jeannie Robertson's seminal importance and influence. His veneration of her ballad interpretations asserts a 'classic' standard for the whole Revival movement; they are models of the traditional singer's art, and form a living connection with the voices of the past.

This popular campaign extends the cultural project MacDiarmid had begun in the 1920s. As MacDiarmid's ideas about the Scottish voice evolved, his interest moved backwards through time, from his own memories of the Scots spoken in his

Langholm childhood, to literary precedents, Ramsay, Fergusson and Burns, the Border Ballads, and then back further to the more ancient forms of Scotland's languages, the Makars, the great Gaelic poets, and thence finally, through his readings in linguistics and anthropology, to the Celtic and pre-Celtic roots traced in his own idiosyncratic manner in *In Memoriam James Joyce*. If we take the *Golden Treasury of Scottish Poetry*[4] (which MacDiarmid edited while living on Whalsay) as a high-point in the development of these ideas – and the primary statement Henderson encountered while he was formulating his own ideas – this anthology includes many examples of folksong and anonymous folk-poetry. In his introduction MacDiarmid argues in favour of a radical and more broadly-based understanding of the Scottish voice. Scotland's Latin and Gaelic poets, and the anonymous Ballads, are placed alongside the greatest works of the Makars and the modern Renaissance, in an alliance against the insidious influence of Anglification.

Although he rejects MacDiarmid's separatism and anglophobia, Henderson does not take up this concern with linguistic diversity. The Folksong Revival broadened the exploration of the old tongues. The vocabulary of Henderson's songs, especially a song such as the 'Freedom-Come-All-Ye', is every bit as complex and wide-ranging as the Scots MacDiarmid used, and, like MacDiarmid's early Scots lyrics, it has the virtue of being widely recognized and still frequently heard.

The primary difference between his position and MacDiarmid's lies in their very different interpretations of the implications of this linguistic project: MacDiarmid imagined a campaign the eventual conclusion of which would be the renewal of Gaelic as the dominant national language – an argument paralleled by some of his most controversial comments about the 'true racial life'[5] – while Henderson committed himself to an ongoing diversity, precisely because this was the best guarantee against such overbearing nationalist sentiments – a necessary challenge to the ascendancy of any single tongue, something Scotland has never had.

Such debates in Scotland have always gone hand in hand with the debate over political identity. In the first half of the century the sustainability of Lallans, or literary Scots, as a popular creative medium became a metaphor for the political and cultural viability of the nation as a distinct and separate entity. Detractors attacked Lallans as a purely literary language with no relation to the speech of the common people, and in doing so, indicted any companion nationalist aspirations. Roderick Watson summarizes MacDiarmid's counter-argument: 'In the early days of the modern Scottish literary Renaissance it seemed particularly necessary to insist on Scots as both a language and a literary tradition entirely separate from English.'[6] However, as cultural confidence has grown it has become possible, necessary even, to acknowledge Scotland's linguistic and cultural diversity, and champion this as a strength rather than a weakness. By stressing 'speaking' over 'writing' the Revival was an insistent reminder that 'all languages are [in Gavin

Douglas's words] "bastard" affairs . . . there are real problems of definition whenever the chimera of a "standard" language is erected . . . Orthography and lexis'[7] can all too easily become questions of race and blood, once again, folk culture is envisaged as a counter-balance to any such extremism.

In his early writings Henderson concentrated on the contemporary political dimensions of the issue of voice, down-playing the historical dimensions, and expressing his distrust of the 'literary–historical cross-talk'[8] so beloved of poet-scholars, whose arguments he portrays as bourgeois mystification. In 'Lallans and all that' 'presentification' is defined in a straightforward assertion: 'the speech of the people is still a helluva lot nearer to the language of Burns than to the stringy argot of a B.B.C. announcer';[9] proof in itself that a 'contemporary and popular literature' could be achieved in the Scottish tongue. The limited scope of reference of these early articles is their greatest weakness, but the origins of his own popular project can still be discerned in them, particularly in his insistent focus on the spoken voice. As Gramsci illuminates his political thinking, he extends his criticism towards the new aim of reuniting 'Govan or Hamilton . . . with Comrie or Lochboisdale'; not with the intention of creating a single homogeneous nation, rather he approves of the philosopher's vision of a folk culture which can never be entirely subsumed within any one narrow definition of political identity: 'That which distinguishes folk song in the framework of a nation and its culture is neither the artistic fact nor the historic origin; it is a separate and distinct way of perceiving life and the world, as opposed to that of official society.'[10]

This evolution of his ideas about voice can also be traced in the letters; for example, in 1953 he writes to the *Scotsman*, arguing for a '*lingua Inglese in bocca scozzese*: What is needed is an accepted standard of Scots–English pronunciation – not a hard and fast standard but a flexible line which would permit and indeed encourage, deviations to Highland and Lowland.'[57] The Folk Revival extended the Scottish voice in a way the printed word could not. It added to the literary model of Lallans, Synthetic, Plastic or Aggrandized Scots, Henderson's favoured communal creative voice, Ballad Scots, and his own creative voice, Perthshire Scots,[11] as well as the 'wee cock sparra' Glaswegian of Matt McGinn, the gallus brogue of Jimmy MacBeath, and the classic ballad style of Jeannie Robertson – a whole melting-pot of singers' voices, 'deviations to Highland and Lowland':[12]

Just as the traditional manner of singing the older modal tunes often defies orthodox musical notation, so numerous linguistic and phonetic points . . . leap out at one from the [School's] tape-recordings with a freshness and immediacy which amount in some cases to a positive revelation . . . The Buchan folk-singer does not sing in the same way that he speaks . . . the language of the older folk-song is never purely 'colloquial'; it is formal, even stylized . . . It is in the great songs, licked into shape like pebbles by the waves of countless tongues, that this sense of formality is most marked.[13]

Folksong is 'a collective art displayed by individuals':[14] thus the unrivalled sung interpretations of the best of the traditional singers bear the modulations of past singers and past ages, what Lorca called 'the fountain and the stream of the antique song',[15] the imprint of an ancient artistic lineage, a communal timbre and historical richness – characteristics which reach a peak in the singing of some of the travellers. As MacDiarmid had before him, Henderson was journeying through deep subconscious undercurrents of the Scottish voice. This psychological exploration of the emotional intensity embedded in the words and rhythms of an ancient song, calls us back to the 'wild and perfect garden' in a way that the written word cannot. As he writes in a recent essay: '. . . one must expect a partisan song to go under unless it contrives to give voice to an emotion which transcends the actual political moment . . .'[16]

Folksong has consistently been identified with a golden age in Scottish culture. It is often presented as belonging to a time before the divisions in our national voice – the linguistic dichotomy imposed in the seventeenth and eighteenth centuries which debilitated the national consciousness, forcing literate Scots to 'carry two languages in their heads: English for writing, Scots for speaking, English for "proper" occasions, Scots for real life . . . [Creating] the peculiarly Scottish dissociation of sensibility whereby, as Edwin Muir put it, Scotsmen *felt* in Scots and *thought* in English . . .'[17] This schizophrenia is an event from which Scotland's national consciousness is supposed never to have recovered. The pessimism of this modern analysis is challenged by Henderson. MacDiarmid's argument confronted the psychological stunting effect that Edwin Muir described, but it also depended on emphasizing this same aspect, in order to press home contemporary political concerns. Henderson, on the other hand, celebrates the vitality of the living oral tradition, the life-blood of fusion coursing through Scottish culture.

The ballads remain at the heart of Henderson's aesthetic. His ideas on the question of voice are drawn together in a retrospective essay, 'At the Foot o' yon Excellin' Brae' (1983), which favourably compares the folksong tradition with Scots art-poetry, and seeks to break open the bastion of MacDiarmid's cultural separatism: 'The purpose of this present essay is to demonstrate that a curious "bilingualism in one language" has always been a characteristic of Scots folksong at least since the beginning of the seventeenth century.'[18] The criticism of Lallans becomes direct: it is described as a 'self-conscious literary Scots', which 'came increasingly to seem documentations of a sad case of arrested development'.[19] The underlying political currents rise to the surface, in a passage which repudiates MacDiarmid's absolutism: 'The anonymous ballad-makers . . . were operating in a zone which ignored national and political boundaries. The themes of the great tragic ballads . . . cross national boundaries.'[20] Then, making close reference to the distinctive qualities of the oral tradition, Henderson reasserts the uniqueness of the Scottish voice within a new internationalist perspective:

> 'the unchallenged excellence of our ballad versions', is an achievement residing in, 'the actual nature of the language in which they are couched – in what we may term "ballad-Scots". This, the idiom in which the virtuoso song-makers were operating, is a flexible formulaic language which grazes ballad-English along the whole of its length, and yet remains clearly identifiable as a distinct folk-literary lingo . . . [Thus] in the folk field as well as in the less agile literary Lallans, Scots may be said to include English and go beyond it.'[21]

This is a bold claim, one truly in the manner of MacDiarmid. It asserts the importance of the folk tradition, and redoubles the claim for the Scottish voice, or voices, which are no longer to be defined by the standardized conventions established by print, but rather in the plethora of spoken and sung voices of the Scottish people, and, in particular, in the interpretative styles of the greatest of the Revival singers.

XIII From the Shee Water to the Cam

> . . . I know I'm attached to it, in the heat
>
> of the instincts and aesthetic passion;
> attracted to a proletarian life
> that preceded you; for me it is a religion,
>
> its joy, not its millennial
> struggle; its nature, not its
> consciousness . . .
> Pier Paolo Pasolini, from 'The Ashes of Gramsci: Part IV'[1]

> I hope you will let him speak Sardinian and not go on at him to speak 'properly' . . . Remember Sardinian isn't a dialect, but a real language . . . I really do entreat you . . . allow your children to suck up all the "Sardism" they want, and let them develop spontaneously in the natural environment they were born into.
> Antonio Gramsci, from a letter to his sister Teresina, 23 March 1927 [See 230]

Where do MacDiarmid and Henderson stand themselves in the light of their concern with the psychology of the creative voice? In MacDiarmid's poetry the rediscovery of 'the vernacular' released a new emotional range and depth, returning him to the voices of his Langholm childhood, and, in particular, his relationship with his parents. In Henderson's poetry, and much more so in his songs, there is a similar journey of rediscovery, carrying him back to the carrying stream, the maternal voice, and memories of the songs of his mother and grandmother that he grew up with – he has retained a vivid memory of his mother, although she died when he was only thirteen. This journey carried him away from the 'paternal' voices of Cambridge, Modernism and MacDiarmid. The love and the cruelty described in the great ballads are as true to contemporary Scotland as they ever were, just as in their Flytings, MacDiarmid's Stalinism becomes a new mask for Scottish Calvinism, the elect crying down judgement on the damned.

Women have always been to the fore in the Scottish folk tradition, from Mrs Brown of Falkland to 'Big Mary of the Songs', and the modern Revival was no exception to this. Many of Henderson's 'discoveries' have been women. A comparison of the representation of women in the Folk Revival and the Renaissance would certainly favour the Revival. Emotionally the respective 'masculinity' and 'femininity' of MacDiarmid and Henderson – a comparison which is illuminating, even if it does indulge in some generalities – is illustrated by the amusing or sometimes rather grotesque parodies of maleness in MacDiarmid's poetry, and the ambiguities in the emotional relationships in Henderson's work – here we are back with the ambiguous 'whole love' Thompson questioned. This theme is developed in the dedication to androgyny, the well-spring of his creative Muse, which accompanies Henderson's translations from Campana and Cavafy, heterosexual and homosexual love, published in *Chapman* magazine in 1985[2]; or, in a more general sense, in his explorations of the masculine sadomasochistic characteristics of Nazi Germany, and the feminine openness and emotional sensitivity he identifies with his beloved Italy.[3] We can also compare MacDiarmid's need to see ideas clash and collide, with Henderson's search for symbiosis and inclusivity. The origins of his deliberate undercutting of the dominant figure of the author, the unwillingness to accede to the categorizations of history and politics, these can speculatively be traced back to such deep-rooted psychological traits.[4]

Henderson describes his own song the 'Freedom-Come-All-Ye' as written in Perthshire Scots, the language of his childhood. This Perthshire speech is another example of cross-fertilization in his life, the progeny of local Scots, the encroaching accents of the Lowlands to the south and the lands of Fyvie and the Mearns to the north, along with remnants of Perthshire Gaelic and traveller cant. He is always placing himself at such crossroads. Multiplicity is one of the most recognizable aspects of his credo. I have already stressed the political weight that his attitude to voice carries, as a rejection of the excesses of nationalism, part of his endeavour to encourage a vision of national consciousness composed in terms of a diverse people rather than a homogeneous nation. His enthusiasm for Ballad Scots seems to echo MacDiarmid's campaigning slogan 'Back to Dunbar!' – sharing with it a delight in 'direct utterance'[5] – however, it cannot be understood in the particular political and historical sense MacDiarmid intended.

Henderson's nationalism is coloured by his identification with that most dispossessed group of all, the travellers, who cannot be placed within conventional national borders, and who, in terms of 'presentification', brought with them a voice which bore an ancient pattern. Their nomadic traditions carry back to a time before Scotland was a fixed entity, and their way of life is pre-Capitalist. An identification with values outside the bounds of bourgeois society recurs again and again in his letters and essays, in which the past always functions as a vibrant model for change, undercutting the mores of contemporary society and culture. For instance, to read his essay 'The Women of the Glen: Some Thoughts on Highland History',[6] is to uncover a manifesto of social and sexual liberation; a piece of undisguised autobiographical idealism, in which there are telling echoes between his descriptions (quoting from Classical authors) of the male love-bond in Celtic warrior society, and his own memories of wartime comradeship.

XIV The Travellers: Deep Song[1]

'We [tinkers] live entirely in the past.'[2]

The strongest influence on Henderson's celebration of difference was undoubtedly his experiences with the travellers, or 'tinkler-gypsies' as he prefers to call them. It is to their world that he has returned again and again, searching out some new variant of a story or song; and it is partly as a result of his championing that their culture has been recognized as the single most crucial influence on the modern Folk Revival. His relationship with this community reflects his ability to break through a barrier of prejudice and stigma. Sensitive since childhood to the 'outcast', and the petty thrawness of parish morality, it was through the close affinity he felt for their way of life that he gradually won the respect and trust of the travelling community. The underground character of this community, with its secret languages and codes of behaviour, attracted the outsider in him – despite his democratic spirit, secretive orders seem to have held a particular fascination, from Army Intelligence and the Resistenza, to his study of groups such as the Orange Order and the Horseman's Word.

The 'ancient counter-culture'[3] of the Travellers was 'profoundly alien to most industrialized Western Society'.[4] He writes penetratingly and with great sensitivity of their nobility and the hardship of their lives. They seem to embody his idealistic social vision and his hatred of materialism. Here he draws on the work of Federico García Lorca who found a spiritual home in the lives and culture of the gypsies in the 1920s and 1930s: 'The gypsy is the loftiest, the most profound and aristocratic element of my country, the most deeply representative of his mode, the very keeper of the glowing embers, blood and alphabet of Andalusian and universal truth.'[5] For a homosexual like Lorca in the Spain of the 1930s the gypsy was a potent and provocative symbol to pledge allegiance to: 'I will always be on the side of those who have nothing[6] . . . Being born in Granada has given me a sympathetic understanding of those who are persecuted – the Gypsy, the Black, the Jew, the Moor, which all Granadans have inside them.'[7]

In Lorca, Henderson finds a figure who shares his own anti-fascism and his heterogeneous sense of nationalism. Devoutly pluralist in his usage of the vocabulary of culture, of blood, and of race, Lorca's poetry and plays are untainted by the fascism or reactionary politics of some Modernist poets. Lorca and Henderson also share an 'instinct of preservation',[8] a love of the most ancient songs which have been preserved in the margins of society, 'the most moving songs of our mysterious soul . . . maligned as debauched and dirty'.[9] Lorca's essay on the Duende is used as an implicit commentary on Scottish folk culture:

> All the Arts are capable of possessing *duende*, but naturally the field is widest in music, in dance, and in spoken poetry, because they require a living body as interpreter – they are forms that arise and die ceaselessly, and are defined by an exact presence . . . Which means that it is not a matter of ability, but of real live form; of blood; of ancient culture; of creative action.[10]

Henderson notes proudly that 'the Scots travelling people have an expression "conyach" (from the Gaelic caoineach, weeping or "keening") which corresponds with the *duende*.'[11] The parallels continue as Lorca traces the 'cante jondo' or 'deep song' of the gypsies to ancient India, back to 'the mysterious colour of primordial ages . . .',[12] and Henderson compares most ancient Scottish folksongs with 'Homer's music'. He describes how, mixing amongst the travellers in the berry fields of Blair, 'you could hear a rare 'Child' ballad, or the high flamenco-like cadences of a Gaelic love lament',[13] and still encounter 'ancient Ossianic hero-tales, whose content reflects the life of primitive hunter tribesmen.'[14] In one reminiscence he describes how his journey into the territory of 'deep song' took on an extraordinary richness in the summer tour of 1955:

> The semi-nomadic Stewarts of Lairg . . . turned out to be the custodians of a folk-cultural heritage even more voluminous than their north-east counterparts. Although every single member of the group could be considered a tradition-bearer, the principal figure – and acknowledged champion – among them was blind Alec Stewart, better known as Aili Dall. This amazing old hero had a version of 'Am Bron Binn' (The Sweet Sorrow), an heroic lay now very rare, and stories of Oisean and the Feinne, as well as a vast store of wonder tales and other Marchen . . . he had learned most of his stories from [his mother] Old Susie . . . Old Susie died in 1938 aged 91; this means she was born 13 years before the publication of the first volumes of Campbell of Islay's *Popular Tales of*

the West Highlands, and must have learned many of her stories orally in the mid-nineteenth century from relations born before the end of the eighteenth century – from folk, therefore, who in all likelihood were travelling the roads while 'Ossian' MacPherson was still alive . . .[15]

XV Poets and Folkies

By the 1960s the achievements of the Revival were clear to see. Some of the new songs, including a half-dozen of Henderson's own, had caught hold of the popular imagination and would 'bear the gree', and many of these have a complexity of argument and expression which contradicts the fears MacDiarmid had expressed. In the cities and at the new Folk Festivals young apprentice singers flourished and new interpreters of the classic ballads emerged. However, against these artistic successes had to be weighed the detrimental effects of commercial success. Throughout this period we can see Henderson fighting against commercialism, the one enemy he really feared. He argued against professionals and professionalism, and all direct money stimuli:

> Folksong has, in the past, been an 'underground', against official or establishment culture. From now on, it will also (I reckon) be an 'underground' against money-minded pop folk skullduggery, now rampant in 'folk' clubs all over the country.[1]

Henderson's opinions on these matters became less strident once the artistic success of the Revival was assured. Along with friends such as Norman Buchan, he felt a genuine concern for the welfare of the 'source-singers', who often came from poorer backgrounds. The letters from Jeannie Robertson are only one example amongst many, of the practical support and advice that he gave.

The Folk Revival was a natural forerunner of the demotic vitality of the new poetry which flourished in the 1950s. In this new flowering Henderson, like MacDiarmid, became a talismanic figure. He was to be found amongst the bohemian clanjamfrie at the Traverse Theatre, mixing with folk and pop singers, theatre folk, the Mersey Beat poets, and young Scots poets such as Alan Riddell and Alan Jackson, or at one of the new folk clubs or poetry readings.

In his later years MacDiarmid held some famously controversial views. His uncanny ability to jumble together folksong, the skiffle and beat movements, Concrete Poetry, the writings of Alex Trocchi, and place them all on the same list of proscribed items, helped to solidify an alliance between the younger folkies and poets. One amusing episode in the skirmishes between this younger generation and the Renaissance 'establishment', which bears out the influence of the Folk Revival, was the use of William McGonagall as a satirical club to hit over MacDiarmid's head – a weapon drawn straight from Henderson's arsenal. Edwin Morgan, the spokesman for the new poets, and Henderson both wrote important essays which refer to the McGonagall phenomenon, 'The Beatnik in the Kailyard'[2] (Morgan, 1962), and 'McGonagall the What'[3] (Henderson, 1965). Henderson's article, a comparison of the two Macs, was calculated to infuriate MacDiarmid. It was a last riposte to the 1964 Flyting, and a typically virtuoso display of knowledge of the folk tradition. In Edwin Morgan's case, the urban modernity which has always been a hallmark of his poetry seems at first to be at odds with folk culture; however, the similarity between his argument and Henderson's is telling. Recently Morgan commented on their common ground:

> MacDiarmid, who had become distinctly reactionary by that time, went out of his way to attack both [poets and folksong]; the attacks were usually separate, but inevitably the attacked felt something of a common cause. Although I was never in any real sense a folkie, I was an old friend of the late Norman Buchan and was well aware of what was going on in the folk world. I also admired Hamish and the work he was doing as a collector . . . We also shared an interest in language and translation, and I remember him showing me a letter of Gramsci's which made a plea for Sardinian against Italian, like similar pleas for Scots against English but based on MacDiarmidesque arguments about the actual spoken language.' (From a letter to the editor, 31 January 1995.)

In the essay Morgan takes up the argument against a divisive polarization between Scots and English:

> . . . it is a real and unavoidable incubus . . . [which] makes it all the more difficult for Scottish writers to develop integrally . . . when an exclusive choice is made . . . there may be some psychological loss . . . one that brings the constant hazard of a narrowing of outlook since Scottish speech itself is still very fluid in the range from broad Scots to standard English.[4]

Like Henderson he favours 'an unanguished flexibility in this matter of language'.[5] These essays were part of a wider reaction against the increasingly paternalistic influence of the Renaissance. Morgan expressed the problem succinctly: 'The Renaissance has begun to loosen its hold on life. It has allowed life both in Scotland and elsewhere, to move on rapidly and ceaselessly in directions it chooses not to penetrate.'[6] McGonagall represents 'some deep-rooted human feelings . . . some need of the Scottish soul . . .'[7] This plea for a more honest appraisal of the Scottish character, including its sentimentality, was part of the struggle for a new openness in emotional and political terms, and involved some criticism of MacDiarmid, whose later work was described by Morgan as suffering from a lack of warmth, 'a failure or a banishing of ordinary human sympathy'.[8] There is a strong echo between this and Henderson's attack on MacDiarmid towards the end of the 1964 'Folksong Flyting':

There are unresolved contradictions in Mr MacDiarmid's whole approach to the problems of language and the folk arts . . . [He] has come to despise and reject the 'people of his country's past' with all the ardour of a seventeenth-century 'saint' outlawing the folksinging and dancing damned to outer darkness . . . [he is] the apostle of a kind of spiritual apartheid. [118]

Another example of the influence of the Folk Revival on poetry are the experiments Ian Hamilton Finlay made with voice in his poems of the early 1960s. His use of contemporary urban dialect in *Glasgow Beasts*[9] (which was attacked by the Lallans old guard, MacDiarmid and Maurice Lindsay), is a popular use of Henderson's 'presentification'; one which belongs to the period of consolidation of the Revival in the cities, by which time singers were as likely to have urban as rural accents.

Looking again at the development of the post-war Scottish voice, it is possible to trace a lineage threading its way through the work of MacDiarmid, the Clyde Group and Lallans makars, through the Folk Revival, the poets of the 1960s, Finlay and Morgan, and later Tom Leonard, and extending into the work of contemporary writers such as John Byrne, James Kelman and W.N. Herbert (not forgetting contemporary experiments in fusing folk music and drama, for example, in the work of the Cauld Blast Orchestra and Communicado Theatre Company). This prolix Scottish voice is an increasingly subtle expression of an individual as much as a national psychology, and it is openly described as such by many of these writers.

XVI The Joy of Joy

. . . What Wilde wrote in *De Profundis* has some bearing on this . . . when he says that the object of love is to love. To feel itself in the joy of its own being. To a certain extent this is poetry too, one shouldn't divide it between the moment of creation and the created thing. Its joy is the joy of itself, to feel itself in being . . . this has always with me taken the shape of direct communication . . .[1]
Hamish Henderson, (1966)

In many ways the sum of the task Henderson set himself amounted to a kind of healing process applied to Scottish culture. This was born of his own need to discover and to constantly rediscover the moment of direct and open communication between people, whether in the spontaneous applause of the crowd at the John Maclean rally, or the intensity of a young partisan reciting Dante in memory of a lost comrade — what Lorca describes as 'the delicate bridge uniting the five senses with that core made living flesh, living cloud, living sea, of Love freed from Time.'[2] For Henderson this is 'the moment of resolve, of transformation, of insurrection';[3] a shared moment which occurs whenever a song or poem is transmitted, is reborn. This moment is the proving ground for all political and emotional truths, and reaches beyond the singularity of person or place to carry us into an awareness of our common humanity. It makes possible the crucial transformation, when 'freedom becomes people'; or, as his own song fore-tells, when 'all the roses and geans will turn to bloom'.[4]

Notes

Part I

1 This Commentary concentrates on Henderson's lifetime project, the Folksong Revival, and discusses the relationship between the Folksong Revival and the modern Scottish literary tradition. There is some discussion of Henderson's poetry, concentrating on the *Elegies for the Dead in Cyrenaica*, and his songs; a more detailed discussion of these will follow in the forthcoming *Selected Poems, Translations and Songs*. I have taken my title from a letter of Pier Paolo Pasolini's: 'As a man lives beyond his temporal death in his good works so a language lives beyond its temporal death in its good poems. As for the temporal death, it is inevitable – there is nothing to be done about it: language, says Savi Lopez . . . is a river that flows on: its life is a continual act of dying.' Letter to Luigi Cerceri, 29 January 1953, from *The Letters of Pier Paolo Pasolini*, volume one, 1940–54, translated by Stuart Hood, (Quartet Books: London, 1992, 409).

2 The translation is by Henderson.

3 Duncan Glen first used this phrase in his essay 'Hamish Henderson: Poetry Becomes People', *Inter Arts*, 1.7, October 1988.

Part II

1 'Byspale', genius, prodigy. Henderson uses the word in the title of two of his articles on MacDiarmid: 'Hugh MacDiarmid: The Langholm Byspale' (*Edinburgh City Lynx*, No. 35, 21 September 1978) and 'Tangling with the Langholm Byspale', *Cencrastus* No. 48, Summer 1994.

2 Henderson, 'Flower and Iron of the Truth', *Our Time*, 10 September 1948, 305.

3 An early draft of this poem was written in 1945, a year before his first meeting with MacDiarmid. It was not published until Henderson contributed to *Poems Addressed to Hugh MacDiarmid: Poems Addressed to Hugh MacDiarmid and Presented to him on the occasion of his seventy-fifth Birthday*, edited by Duncan Glen, Akros Publications: Preston, 11 August, 1967.

4 See Henderson's speech 'At Langholm, September 13, 1992', published in *Chapman* 69–70, Autumn 1992, 182.

5 Henderson, 'To Hugh MacDiarmid on reading Lucky Poet', in Glen (ed.) *Poems Addressed to Hugh MacDiarmid*.

6 This is also true of Henderson's relationship with Gramsci. In his writings on the philosopher he emphasizes the warmth of this folk influence, softening the severer aspects of his philosophy: '. . . in the solitude of his barely furnished cell, his thoughts constantly returned to the gorgeous resilient folk-culture of his native Sardinia, and he plied his correspondents (mother and sisters) with questions about festas, folksongs, banners and ballads. Can one doubt that there was a conscious effort to add sap and savour to a life given point only by indomitable cerebral obduracy; to

counter the rigours of an existence whose staying power was based (as he put it in one letter) exclusively on the will.' Henderson, Introduction to Gramsci's *Prison Letters*, (Zwan Publications: London, 1988, 12).

Part III

1 Page references are to *Elegies for the Dead in Cyrenaica*, (John Lehmann: London, 1948). The title is a quotation from the 'Prologue', 9.

2 *Elegies*, 'Tenth Elegy', 48.

3 *Elegies*, 'Foreword', 11.

4 The number of young Scottish poets who found themselves in the desert war has often been remarked on: they include, Edwin Morgan, George Campbell Hay, Sydney Goodsir Smith, G.S. Fraser, Robert Garioch, and Sorley MacLean, whose poem 'Glac a' Bhàis' ('Death Valley'), is used as the epigraph to the second part of the *Elegies*. G.S. Fraser comments that: 'The Middle East in World War Two produced far more – and at times even finer – poetry than all the years of attrition on the Western Front in World War One. The poetry came from a more literate and aware generation. They had read more, and employed a wider range of styles and techniques.' Fraser's further remarks, that a gap appeared in poetry after the war, as many of the poets ceased writing, cast an interesting light on Henderson's career following the publication of the *Elegies*; see *Return to Oasis: War Poems and Recollections from the Middle East 1940–1946*, edited by Victor Selwyn et al., (Salamander Oasis Trust: London, 1980, xix, xxx–xxxi).

5 *Elegies*, 'Foreword', 12.

6 Ibid., 12.

7 *Elegies*, 'Fifth Elegy: Highland Jebel', 29.

8 Ibid., 27.

9 Ibid.

10 'Synthesis is implicit/in Rilke's single column, (die eine) . . .', *Elegies*, 'Eighth Elegy: Karnak', 43. 'Rilke refers in his *Sonnets to Orpheus* to "die eine in Karnak", the one in Karnak; the single pillar which survives to live beyond the near eternal temples. I walked for hours all over Karnak to see if I could find a definite pillar.' Henderson, 'For Our Own and the Others', an interview with Colin Nicholson, in *Poem, Purpose and Place: Shaping Identity in Contemporary Scottish Verse*, Edinburgh University Press, 1992, 148.

11 *Elegies*, 'Tenth Elegy', 49.

12 Henderson, 'Scotland's Alamein', *Voice of Scotland*, III.4, June 1947, 3.

13 Ibid., 3–5.

14 *Elegies*, 'Interlude', 32.

15 *National Weekly*, 9 April 1949, 1.3.

16 Henderson heard Ruth Speirs read from her translations of Rilke in Cairo in 1942; see Letter 4. He has acknowledged the influence of German poetry on the *Elegies*, noting especially the influence of Hölderlin's later poems; '. . . the poems of his madness. In a time of tremendous suffering and war,

small wonder that poems of a poet's personal suffering, horror, ecstasy, and extreme agony should influence [me].' From an interview with Peter Orr, *The Poet Speaks*, (Routledge & Kegan Paul: London, 1966, reprinted in *Alias MacAlias*, Polygon: Edinburgh, 1992, 322)).

17 MacLean, 'Glac a' Bhais', translated by the author; from Blar, *Battlefield, 1942–43*, reprinted in *O Choille Gu Bearradh, From Wood to Ridge, Collected Poems*, (Carcanet Press: Manchester, 1989, 210–11).

18 See Raymond Ross's essay 'Hamish Henderson: In the Midst of Things', *Chapman* 42, VIII.5, Winter 1985, 12.

19 MacDiarmid included a translation of Rilke's 'Requiem: for Paula Moderson-Becker' in *To Circumjack Cencrastus* (1930). Henderson praised this in his review of *A Kist of Whistles*, '[they] predate his [Rilke's] discovery by the English literary left [by over a decade] . . .', *Our Time*, November 1947, 72.

20 Richard E. Ziegfeld, *Studies in Scottish Literature*, vol. XVI, edited by Professor G. Ross Roy (University of South Carolina, Columbia).

21 Ibid., 229.

22 Ibid., 232.

23 MacDiarmid, *Complete Poems*, 417.

24 [Charles Doughty], *Travels in Arabia Deserta* (Cambridge University Press, 1888). See also Edwin Morgan's discussion of MacDiarmid and Doughty in 'Some Figures Behind MacDiarmid', *Cencrastus* no.40, Summer 1991.

25 *Complete Poems*, 454.

26 *Complete Poems*, 428.

27 *Complete Poems*, 426.

28 'A chastened wantonness, a bit/That sets on song a discipline,/A sensuous austerity'; *Elegies*, 'Prologue', 9.

Part IV

1 See Henderson's article 'Tangling with the Langholm Byspale', *Cencrastus* No. 48, Summer 1994, 3.

2 The members of the Makars Club included Albert Mackie, Sydney Goodsir Smith, Douglas Young and Maurice Lindsay.

3 In 1948 MacDiarmid was introduced to Montale, Moravia and Elsa Morante by Henderson, who acted as their guide on the British Council sponsored tour, see Letter 17.

4 The title is a quotation from MacDiarmid's *First Hymn to Lenin*; MacDiarmid was himself quoting from a speech of Stalin's, *Our Time*, 10 September 1948, 304–6. The contents of the issue are listed in Letter 23. Henderson's essay was reprinted in *Chapman* 82, 1995.

5 Ibid., 305.

6 These four poets were published in the *Fowrsom Reel* anthology, (Clyde Group: Caledonian Press, Glasgow, 1949); all except F.J. Anderson wrote in Scots.

7 *Conflict*, the magazine of Glasgow University Socialist Club, edited by Norman Buchan, March 1949, 5–9.

8 Ibid., 6.

9 Ibid., 7.

10 'Ding Dong Dollar', an album of anti-Polaris folksongs (Folkways: FD 5444), see Letter 97. See also Henderson's 'Scots Folksong: A Select Discography', part 2, *Tocher* 27, Winter 1977, reprinted in *Alias MacAlias*, 141.

11 *Radical Renfrew: Poetry from the French Revolution to the First World War*, edited by Tom Leonard, (Polygon: Edinburgh, 1990). In his Introduction Leonard focuses on 'the right to equality of dialogue'; recognizably the same right that Henderson sought for the travellers and farm-workers of the north-east in the great collecting project of the 1950s: 'Yet when one sees the historic connection between slave and proletariat embodied in the language, one sees more clearly the actual nature of derisive laughter at working-class speech and accent today: one sees what forces are behind the vehemence with which a child will be told to alter his or her language when addressing a superior . . .' (Leonard, xxvi). The anthology spans the period of great social change that shaped modern industrial Scotland, and is suggestive of a unity in the culture of the rural and urban working class.

12 Henderson, *Our Time*, 10 September 1948, 305.

13 *Conflict*, March 1949, 7.

14 Henderson, *Ballads of World War 2*, (Lili Marlene Club: Glasgow, 1947).

15 In particular the Resistenza, which inspired a post-war popular movement, and had an enormous influence on Henderson's political and cultural beliefs.

16 Henderson, Sleeve notes, *Pipes, Goatskin & Bones: the Songs and Poems of Hamish Henderson*, Grampian Television: Aberdeen, 1992 (GPN 3001).

Part V

1 Thompson, 'A New Poet', *Our Time*, June 1949, 156, 158–9.

2 Ibid., 158.

3 Ibid., 158.

4 Henderson, *Edinburgh Review*, no. 92, Summer 1994, 78–9.

5 *Elegies*, 'Sixth Elegy: Acroma', 36.

6 Thompson, 158.

7 *Elegies*, 'Prologue', 9.

8 'The Cell' parts I and II appeared in *Lines Review* in the late 1950s. The long poem 'To Hugh MacDiarmid on reading Lucky Poet' appeared in 1967. Three long poems belonging to the post-war period remain unfinished, unpublished, or have only been published in part: 'Freedom Becomes People', 'Journey to a Kingdom', and 'Auld Reekie's Roses'.

Part VI

1 The rally is described by Ailie Munro: 'The speech by Helen Crawfurd Anderson was one of the best . . . Then came the poems, two of which demand special mention: Sorley MacLean read his marvellously succinct "Clan MacLean", first in Gaelic and then in his own English translation;

and Morris Blythman read his moving "Til the Citie o John Maclean". A special issue of the magazine *Conflict*, then edited by Norman Buchan printed the poems read at the concert'; Munro, *The Folk Music Revival in Scotland*, (Kahn and Averill: London, 1984, 48–9).

2 Henderson uses this phrase with reference to Heinrich Heine in 'Freedom Becomes People', an introductory note to the poem of the same title, written in 1968, first published in *Chapman* 42, VIII.5, Winter 1985, 1.

3 Henderson, Introduction to Gramsci's *Prison Letters*, (Zwan Publications: London, 1988, 14).

Part VII

1 Jan Fairley, 'Poetry and Politics', an interview with Hamish Henderson, *Folkroots*.

2 Nicolson, 'For Our Own and the Others', *Poem, Purpose, Place: Shaping Identity in Contemporary Scottish Verse*, 134.

3 The use of modern technology in the Folk Revival is one defence against the accusations of archaism levelled against it. For example, Ewan MacColl's 'Radio Ballads', and later, the television documentaries and film collaborations between Timothy Neat and Hamish Henderson, such as *The Summer Walkers* and *Play Me Something* (with John Berger).

4 Ewan MacColl, 'Hamish Henderson', *Tocher* 43, 1991, 14.

5 Henderson, 'It Was In You That It A' Began: Some Thoughts on the Folk Conference', *The People's Past*, edited by Edward J. Cowan, (Polygon: Edinburgh, 1980, 13–14).

6 Adam MacNaughtan, 'Hamish Henderson', *Tocher* 43, 1991, 2.

7 See 'An Analysis of the Poetic Elements in Hamish Henderson's Songs', by John Mitchell, *Chapbook*, III.6, 1967, edited by Arthur Argo (Aberdeen Folk Club, 12).

8 The quotation is from Maurice Lindsay's poetry; see Henderson's criticism of the Lallans Makars in 'Flower and Iron of the Truth', *Our Time*, 10 September 1948, 305.

Part VIII

1 MacColl, *Tocher* 43, 1991, 14.

2 Munro, *The Folk Music Revival in Scotland*, 215.

3 'Norman Buchan on Hamish', *Tocher* 43, 1991, 21.

4 Henderson, Sleeve notes, *The Muckle Sangs*, 2 (TGNM 119/D).

5 Buchan, *Tocher* 43, 1991, 20.

6 Reprinted in *Chapbook*, III.6, 1967.

7 Henderson, 'Tangling with the Langholm Byspale', *Cencrastus* no.48, Summer 1994, 9.

8 Ibid., 9.

9 Ibid.

Part IX

1 Henderson, 'A Plea for the Sung Ballad', 1963 radio broadcast on the BBC Scottish Home Service; reprinted in *Alias MacAlias*, 44.

2 Henderson, *Saltire Review*, Autumn 1955.

3 Ibid., 46.

Part X

1 Watson, 'Dialectics of "Voice" and "Place": Literature in Scots and English from 1700', in, *Scotland: A Concise Cultural History*, edited by Paul H. Scott, (Mainstream: Edinburgh, 1993).

2 See also Roderick Watson's companion essay to 'Dialectics of "Voice" and "Place",' 'Alien Voices from the Street: Demotic Modernism in Modern Scots Writing', in, "Non-Standard Englishes and the New Media", *The Yearbook of English Studies*, vol. 25, (Modern Humanities Research Association: London, 1995, 147).

3 'As Alan Lomax pointed out – one of the principal distinguishing characteristics of the Scottish folksong tradition is the part played in it by bookish individuals.' Henderson, 'At the Foot o' yon Excellin' Brae': The Language of Scots Folksong', in, *Scotland and the Lowland Tongue*, edited by J. Derrick McClure, (Aberdeen University Press, 1983), reprinted in *Alias MacAlias*, 73.

4 Henderson, 'Alias MacAlias'; a review of *The Uncanny Scot: A Selection of Prose*, by Hugh MacDiarmid, edited with an Introduction by Kenneth Buthlay (MacGibbon & Kee: London, 1968), *Scottish International*, 1969, reprinted in *Alias MacAlias*.

5 Henderson, 'Scottish Songs at Work', a review of *Hebridean Folk Songs: A Collection of Waulking Songs*, Donald MacCormick (Clarendon Press: Oxford, 1970), *Times Literary Supplement*, 29 May 1970, reprinted in *Alias MacAlias*, 130.

6 Fleming, 'Seumas Mór', *Chapbook*, III.6, 1967, 6.

7 Henderson, 'Hugh MacDiarmid: The Langholm Byspale', *Edinburgh City Lynx*, No.35, 21 Sept. 1978.

8 Morgan, 'Recycling, Mosaic and Collage', *Edinburgh Review*, no. 93, Spring 1995, 165.

9 See *Hugh MacDiarmid*, by Kenneth Buthlay, Writers and Critics series, (Oliver & Boyd, Edinburgh, 1964); 'Chapter V: Verse Translations and Scots Prose', 72–7.

10 MacDiarmid, *Scottish Eccentrics*, (Routledge: London, 1936; reprinted by Carcanet Press: Manchester, 1993, with an Afterword by Alan Riach).

11 Ibid., 239.

12 Ibid., 241.

13 Ibid., 239.

14 Ibid.

15 See W.N. Herbert on this process of 'absorbing the appropriate voice' in the 'dynamics of MacDiarmid's poetry'; *To Circumjack MacDiarmid: The Poetry and Prose of Hugh MacDiarmid*, (Clarendon Press: Oxford, 1992, 91).

16 MacDiarmid, *Scottish Eccentrics*, 239.

17 In his review 'Alias MacAlias' Henderson comments that: 'Owing to the constant fruitful interaction of folksong and art literature in our tradition, we're often faced with the sort of set-up in which no one can say for sure where MacAlias ends and Anon begins . . .', 305. See also his recent article 'Zeus as Curly Snake: the Chthonian Image' which discusses the influence of the Greek anthropologist Jane Ellen Harrison on MacDiarmid's 'Depth and the Chthonian Image'. The figure of Zeus originates in primitive nature-cults, 'rites . . . belonging to the lower stratum – primitive and barbarous as they often are'. Henderson's comments, that the 'whole theme bore a certain similarity to the curious dualities in Scottish literary tradition: the "Olympians" being the established "greats" like Dunbar, Henryson and Gavin Douglas – plus Burns, Scott, Fergusson, Garioch – and the "underworld" being the vast anonymous treasure-house of balladry and folk-song', Cencrastus No. 52, Summer 1995, 9.

18 Herbert, *To Circumjack MacDiarmid*, 99.

19 Henderson, 'Freedom Becomes People', *Chapman*, 42, Winter 1985, 1.

Part XI

1 'The Underground of Song', *Scots Magazine*, 1963; reprinted in *Alias MacAlias*, 35.

2 Paulin, 'Introduction', *The Faber Book of Vernacular Poetry*, edited by Tom Paulin, (Faber and Faber, London, 1990, xxii).

3 See, for example, Henderson's remarks concerning poets and song-writers who have forsworn print in 'At the Foot o' yon Excellin' Brae': 'That this predilection for making direct oral contact with a receptive community which has been continued right up to our own day is attested by the popularity of the work of such virtuoso music-makars as Adam McNaughtan, Andy Hunter, Eric Bogle and Ewan MacColl.' *Alias MacAlias*, 73.

4 'Programme Notes for the 1952 People's Festival Ceilidh'; reprinted in *Chapbook*, III.6, 1967, 27.

5 Henderson, 'Freedom Becomes People', *Chapman* 42, Winter 1985, 1.

6 *The Traditional and National Music of Scotland*, by Frances Collinson, (Routledge & Kegan Paul: London, 1966, 129).

7 Henderson, (Sleeve notes to *The Muckle Sangs*, (TGNM 119/D), 2).

8 MacDiarmid, 'Robert Fergusson: Direct Poetry and the Scottish Genius', *Selected Essays of Hugh MacDiarmid*, edited by Duncan Glen, (Jonathan Cape: London, 1969). A contradictory point is made by MacDiarmid in another essay of the period, 'The Scottish Renaissance: The Next Step' (1950), where he recommends to younger Scottish writers, 'the acute analysis based on a thorough knowledge of popular types, local dialects, slang, and the profound love of the streets and all sorts and conditions of people'; he then goes on to state that 'the great task confronting Scottish poetry today' is to

'reachieve a body of popular Scottish song . . .', *Selected Essays of Hugh MacDiarmid*, 107.

9 Originally from *Albyn*; quoted again by MacDiarmid in 'Robert Fergusson: Direct Poetry and the Scottish Genius', ibid., 136.

10 Ibid.

11 Ibid., 147.

12 'MacDiarmid on MacDiarmid'; reprinted in *The Uncanny Scot: A Selection of Prose by Hugh MacDiarmid*, edited by Kenneth Buthlay, (MacGibbon & Kee: London, 1968, 169–70).

13 Ibid., 133.

14 Ibid., 133.

15 Ibid.

16 MacDiarmid, *Aesthetics in Scotland*, edited with an Introduction by Alan Bold, (Mainstream: Edinburgh, 1984, 98).

17 It is also interesting to note that in the mid-1950s Henderson solicited a grant specifically to collect traditional material from Govan and inner Glasgow.

18 Henderson, 'At the Foot o' yon Excellin' Brae', *Alias MacAlias*, 74. See also Henderson's remarks to Tom Scott, rebuking him for his comments in the Introduction to *The Penguin Book of Scottish Verse* about 'pseudo folksongs': ' "Banks of Sicily" has circulated as freely and anonymously as Besom Jimmy [MacBeath]'s "Tramps and Hawkers" '; Letter 166.

19 George Elder Davie, *The Crisis of the Democratic Intellect*, (Polygon: Edinburgh, 1986, 104).

20 Ibid., 105.

21 Ibid.

22 Ibid., 104.

23 *Hugh MacDiarmid: Selected Poetry*, edited by Alan Riach and Michael Grieve, with an introduction by Alan Riach, (Carcanet Press: Manchester, 1992, xiv).

24 Alan Riach's comments bear out this rejection of a bourgeois definition of authorship: 'MacDiarmid's intentions were primarily to reintroduce into the discourse of poetry the concerns of science, linguistics, and other specialisms – but this breaks up the lyric unity of the voice and reintroduces a plurality of discourses which speak for themselves in what he calls a 'stable but changing equilibrium . . .'; conversation with the editor, March 1995.

25 MacDiarmid, *To Circumjack Cencrastus*, (William Blackwood & Sons: Edinburgh, 1930, 156).

26 Davie, *The Crisis of the Democratic Intellect*, 111.

27 In his essay 'The Language of Scottish Poetry' (*Kenyon Review* XVI. 1, Winter, 1954), the American critic Stanley Hyman praises 'The Seamless Garment' as one of MacDiarmid's poems which he felt genuinely succeeded in achieving a linguistic balance, through a more pragmatic recognition of the bilingual characteristics of Scots. This article, which uses the ballads as

an exemplary model of this kind of bilingualism, is frequently cited by Henderson in his essays and letters.

28 *Penguin Poets Series: Lorca*, selected and translated by J.L. Gili, (Penguin: 1960, xx).

29 Davie, 'The Social Significance of the Scottish Philosophy of Common Sense', the Dow Lecture, delivered at the University of Dundee, 30 November 1972; reprinted in *The Scottish Enlightenment and Other Essays*, (Polygon: Edinburgh, 1991, 58).

30 Ibid., 43.

31 'Auld Reekie's Roses'; 'Floret Silva Undique', a part of this long work, was performed by Henderson on the album *Freedom Come-All-Ye*, Claddagh Records: Dublin, 1974 (CCA7). It was also used by Martyn Bennett in a composition featuring Henderson on his CD (ECL CD 9614).

Part XII

1 W.B. Yeats, 'A General Introduction to My Work', *Selected Criticism and Prose*, (Pan Books: London, 1964, 267–8).

2 Like Henderson, MacLean committed himself to a general cultural project, in his case the preservation of the Gaelic language, and he has always given this precedence over his own poetry.

3 This is reflected in the importance Henderson gives to the tape archives of the School of Scottish Studies: 'not only an incomparable treasure house of the folksong of our country, as preserved by real folk-singers, but also a linguistic "reference library" of the first importance.' See Letter 57.

4 MacDiarmid (ed.), *The Golden Treasury of Scottish Verse*, (Macmillan: London, 1940).

5 Ibid.

6 Watson, 'Alien Voices from the Street: Demotic Modernism in Modern Scots Writing', 141.

7 Ibid., 142.

8 Henderson, 'Lallans and All That', *Conflict*, March 1949, 5.

9 Ibid.

10 Antonio Gramsci, *Letteratura e Vita Nazionale*, quoted in Glen, 'Hamish Henderson: Poetry Becomes People', (Inter Arts 1.7, 1988).

11 Henderson's Perthshire Scots includes all the remembered languages of his childhood, stretching back to his grandmother's memories of Perthshire Gaelic; conversation with the author, March 1995. Another voice he heard in his childhood was that of the Somerset folk-singer, when he visited his mother who was working as a cook-housekeeper for a family in Yeovil, in 1928. Somerset was one of the richest regions for folk culture in England.

12 The fusion of regional voices discussed here is similar in effect to Robert Burns's habit of matching Gaelic airs — of which he collected many on his tour of the Highlands in 1787 — to Lowland songs (see Collinson, *The Traditional and National Music of Scotland*, 129). Henderson's own collecting

throws up many similar instances; in his reminiscence 'The Midnight Ceilidh in the Sun Lounge of the Angus', he recalls bringing together the Campbeltown butcher, singer and song collector Willie Mitchell, and the Border shepherd and renowned ballad singer Willie Scott: 'The song "Callieburn", or "Machrihanish bright and bonnie" . . . Before the night was over, and the dawn was up, I saw the two Willies in a huddle — and it was plain to see that the old alchemy was at work . . . Three months later I recorded "Callieburn" from Willie Scott . . . but it wasn't the "Callieburn" Willie Mitchell had sung. The words were more or less the same . . . but the tune had become notably transformed. And it wasn't long before the younger singers of the Revival had latched onto it — and a new and noble folk-song variant was riding high on the billows . . .' *Alias MacAlias*, 96.

13 Henderson 'At the Foot o' yon Excellin' Brae', *Alias MacAlias*, 54.

14 A.L. Lloyd, *Folk-song in England*, (Lawrence and Wishart: London, 1967, 69).

15 Lorca, 'Balada de la Placeta' ('Ballad of the Little Square'), *Penguin Poets Series: Lorca*, (Penguin: 1960,3).

16 Henderson, 'It Was In You That It A' Began', in *The People's Past*, 9.

17 See the discussion of the Scottish voice in 'The Oral Ballads of Mrs Brown', *The Ballad and the Folk*, by David Buchan, (Routledge & Kegan Paul: London, 1972, 68).

18 Henderson 'At the Foot o' yon Excellin' Brae', *Alias MacAlias*, 52.

19 Ibid., 53.

20 Ibid.

21 Ibid., 54.

Part XIII

1 Pasolini, Le Ceneridi Gramsci; 'The Ashes of Gramsci' (part IV), *Pier Paolo Pasolini: Selected Poems*, translated by Norman MacAfee with Luciano Martinengo, (Vintage Books: New York, 1982, 11).

2 The translations were first published in *Chapman* 42, VIII.5, Winter 1985, 19–20; see the footnote to Letter 173.

3 In 'Freedom Becomes People', Henderson refers to the 'vulgar Italy so hated and despised by its bourgeoisie — its bounding voracious popular culture, its secrecy, its turbulence, its victorious gaiety and above all its unbeatable lust for life'; *Chapman* 42, Winter 1985, 1. See also Carla Sassi's Afterword, 'The Italian Song Lines', *The Obscure Voice: Translations from Italian Poetry by Hamish Henderson*, (Morning Star Publications: Edinburgh, 1994).

4 Another example of this kind of reticence is Henderson's demurral at suggestions his 'Freedom Come-All-Ye' should be considered as a national anthem.

5 Duncan Glen, *Hugh MacDiarmid and The Scottish Renaissance*, (W. & R. Chambers: Edinburgh, 1964, 51).

6 Henderson, 'The Women of the Glen', first published as 'Some Thoughts on the Clearances', *Scots Magazine*, Vol.86, no.2, November 1966; 123–8; the later, much enlarged version appeared in *The Celtic Consciousness*, edited by O'Driscoll, (Canongate: Edinburgh, 1982); reprinted in *Alias MacAlias*, 250–51.

Part XIV

1 The title is taken from Lorca's writings on the Cante Jondo, the Spanish song style which predates flamenco and has much in common with the Ballads. Henderson's review 'Lorca and Canto Jondo', *Deep Song and Other Prose*, edited and translated by Christopher Maurer (Marion Boyars: London, 1986), appeared in *Cencrastus*, no. 26, Summer 1987; reprinted in *Alias MacAlias*.

2 'They [the tinkers] want nothing to do with tramps and other solitaries. A very intelligent tinker youth once put the distinction in a nutshell when, referring to an Irish tramp who used to wander around Scotland, he declared: 'That sort of lad just lives from day to day, but we (tinkers) live entirely in the past,' quoted in Henderson's essay on 'The Tinkers', from *A Companion to Scottish Culture*, edited by David Daiches, (Edward Arnold: London 1981); reprinted in *Alias MacAlias*, 229.

3 MacNaughtan, 'Hamish Henderson', *Tocher*, 43, 1991.

4 Henderson, 'Folksongs and Music from the Berry Fields of Blair', sleeve notes to the album of the same title (Prestige International 25016, 1962); reprinted in *Alias MacAlias*, 103.

5 Henderson, 'Lorca and Canto Jondo', *Alias MacAlias*, 313.

6 Ibid., 317.

7 Ibid., 313.

8 Lorca, 'Deep Song', *Deep Song and Other Prose*, (Marion Boyars: London, 1986, 25).

9 Ibid.

10 Lorca, 'Theory and Function of the Duende', *Penguin Poets Series: Lorca*, (Penguin: 1960, 132).

11 Henderson, 'Lorca and Canto Jondo', *Alias MacAlias*, 314.

12 Ibid., 315.

13 Henderson, 'Folk-songs and Music from the Berry Fields of Blair', 102.

14 Ibid.

15 Henderson, *Tocher* 28, 267–8.

Part XV

1 Henderson, 'McGonagall the What', *Chapbook*, ed. Arthur Argo, (Aberdeen Folk Club, 1965), reprinted in *Alias MacAlias*, 291.

2 Morgan, 'The Beatnik in the Kailyard', *New Saltire Review*, no. 3, Spring 1962.

3 Henderson, op. cit.

4 Morgan, 'The Beatnik in the Kailyard', 71.
5 Ibid.
6 Ibid., 73.
7 Ibid., 69.
8 Ibid., 67.
9 Ian Hamilton Finlay, *Glasgow Beasts*, (Wild Flounder Press: Edinburgh, 1961).

Part XVI

1 Orr, 'The Poet Speaks', *Alias MacAlias*, 325.
2 Lorca, 'Theory and Function of the Duende', *Penguin Poet Series: Lorca*, (Penguin: 1960, 136).
3 Henderson 'Freedom Becomes People', *Chapman* 42, 1.
4 From Henderson's song 'Freedom Come-All-Ye'.

A note on the editor

Alec Finlay is an editor, publisher and lecturer. Publisher of the Morning Star Folios (Edinburgh: 1990–95), an annual series of collaborations between artists and poets. Editor of *Wood Notes Wild*, a collection of critical essays on the poetry and art of Ian Hamilton Finlay (Polygon, 1995) and editor of Hamish Henderson's *Collected Works*. He also lectures on poetry and the visual arts internationally.

Acknowledgements

Copyright for the letters reprinted here resides with the following:

The Estate of Arthur Argo
The Estate of Dominic Behan
The Estate of Norman Buchan
David Craig
The Estate of Helen B. Cruickshank
Edinburgh University Library, Special Collection
Ian Hamilton Finlay
The Estate of G.S. Fraser
The Estate of Christopher Murray Grieve
Duncan Glen, Zed_2O magazine, Edinburgh
The Estate of Carlo Gramsci
The Estate of Erich Heller
Hamish Henderson
The Estate of John Lehmann
The Estate of Ewan MacColl
Lines Review Editions, Macdonald Publishers, Edinburgh
Joan Lingard
The Estate of William Little
Alan Lomax
The Estate of Norman MacCaig
The Estate of John McDonald
Jimmie MacGregor
Sorley MacLean
Naomi Mitchison
The Estate of Willie Mitchell
Timothy Neat
National Library of Scotland
Northwestern University Library, Evanston, U.S.A.
The Estate of Sean O'Casey
The Estate of Jeannie Robertson
Carla Sassi
The Estate of Tom Scott

Acknowledgements

Pete Seeger
The Estate of Sydney Goodsir Smith
The Estate of William Smith
The Estate of Piero Sraffa
Marian Sugden
The Estate of Robert Garioch Sutherland
The Estate of E.P. Thompson
The Estate of Douglas Young

Index

Ringsleben, Mary, 220
Robben Island, 191
Robbie, Willie, 101
Roberton, Hugh, 16n, 310
Roberts, Robin, 46
Robertson, Ewen, 218
Robertson, Jeannie, xv, xxi, 68–70,
    73, 76–8, 101, 110, 117, 134–5,
    155, 157, 172–3, 225, 282, 285n,
    315, 317, 329, 335
Robinson, Councillor Robert, 256
Rome, 290
Rosales, Luis, 151
Rosenthal, M.L., 159
Ross, Raymond, 347n
Rubenstein, David, 157, 158n
Russell, George, 35

Sachsenhausen, 246
Saint-Just, Louis de, 272, 272n
Salari, Antonio, 41n
Salton, Marie, xvii
Sandy Bell's, 206, 206n, 213, 214n,
    295
Sassi, Carla, xvi, xvii
Schick, Paul, 175
Schmidt, Kätzel, 78
Schönfeldt, Otto, 179
Scotellaro, Rocco, 41, 42n
Scott, Alexander, 31, 32n, 195, 212,
    234
Scott, Francis George, 13n
Scott, Tom, 86–7
Scott, Sir Walter, 205, 206n
Scott Moncrieff, Douglas, 223
Scott Moncrieff, Queenie, 223–4
Seeger, Peggy, 122
Seeger, Pete, 108, 109n, 112, 225
Sellar, Patrick, 218n
Selwyn, Victor, 287, 287n, 346n
Senatore, Sonia, xvii

Senior, H., 1193, 266
Service, Robert, 118, 119n
Shepherd, Nan, 98n
Shetland, 305
Sicily, 1611, 302
Sillars, Jim, 228
Sillitoe, Alan, 122
Sinclair, Andrew, 287
Singer, (James) Burns, 143, 190,
    191n
Skye, 333
Somerville, Alexander, 126
Smith, Adam, 274, 275n
Smith, Professor Gerald, 293, 294
Smith, W. Gordon, 75
Smith, William, 129–30
Sorel, Arthur, 274n
Spender, Stephen, 303
Speer, Albert, 186
Speirs, John, 5, 6n, 7
Spoleto, xvii
Sraffa, Piero, 36, 37n, 43, 233, 314
Steel, David, 255
Steele, Frank, 317
Stephen, Ian, xvii
Stewart, Alec, 340
Stewart, Andrew, 218
Stewart, Mona, 323
Storey, David, 122
Strachan, John, 315
Strachey, John, 153, 154n
Sugden, Marian, xxi, 21n, 31, 32n,
    39, 41, 45, 59, 113, 315
Sugden, Morris, 49, 50n
Suvarov, Alexander, 258

Tait, Robert, 184, 212, 212n, 214
Tambimutti, James, 5, 6n, 287
Taylor, Henry Grant, 208, 211
Taylor, Wilfred, 149, 217
Tayport, 80, 89